COMEBACK NATION

COMEBACK NATION

HOW ISRAEL ANNIHILATED ITS ADVERSARIES IN A SEVEN-FRONT WAR FOR SURVIVAL

RABBI SHMULEY BOTEACH

AND MENDY BOTEACH

Skyhorse Publishing

Skyhorse Publishing books may be purchased in bulk at special discounts for sales promotion, corporate gifts, fund-raising, or educational purposes. Special editions can also be created to specifications. For details, contact the Special Sales Department, Skyhorse Publishing, 307 Fifth Avenue, 4th Floor, New York, NY 10016 or info@skyhorsepublishing.com.

Visit our website at www.skyhorsepublishing.com.

10 9 8 7 6 5 4 3 2 1

Library of Congress Cataloging-in-Publication Data is available on file.

Cover design by Brian Peterson
Cover photo credit: Getty Images

Print ISBN: 978-1-5107-8823-7
Ebook ISBN: 978-1-5107-8824-4

Printed in the United States of America

Dedicated to our dear friend,

IDF Colonel
Roi Yosef Levi
Hero of Israel

Archetype of the Jewish warrior-scholar. A veteran of Operation Defensive Shield (2002), the Second Lebanon War (2006), Operation Cast Lead (2008–2009), Operation Protective Edge (2014), Operation Northern Shield (2018–2019), and the Swords of Iron War (2023).

Critically wounded in battle in Shuja'iyya during Operation Protective Edge in 2014, he returned to service to command Israel's most elite counterterrorism units, including Egoz. On October 7, 2023, he ran to battle as soon as the Hamas attack began. He fought to his last breath, engaging the terrorist enemy at close range in Kibbutz Re'im alongside the soldiers he led and loved. He fell protecting defenseless children, women, and men.

He remains one of Israel's highest-ranking officers to fall in battle in general, and in the war that followed October 7 in particular.

May his soul be bound in the bond of eternal life.

May God grant comfort to his wife Yael and to his five children.

"The tunnel"—this refers to the city of Jerusalem,
as it is said: *"And the city shall be captured.*
"And the houses shall be plundered"—this refers to the spoil.
"And the women shall be violated"—these are the acts of immorality.
"And half the city shall go forth into exile"—this is the captivity.
And the Holy One, blessed be He, shall go
out and fight against them.
—Midrash on Psalm 118 (c. eighth century CE)

CONTENTS

PREFACE

As we were finalizing the draft of this book, Israel and the United States were finalizing something far more consequential: a 200-plane, 500-target assault designed to rip the head off the Iranian regime in a single, decisive stroke.

In broad daylight, as Tehran's senior leadership assembled for a high-level strategy conclave, Israel executed a doctrine it had refined for years but never unleashed at this scale: the decapitation of an entire regime. The largest air operation in IDF history, Operation Roaring Lion also tore through the fiction that had protected Iran's leadership for decades: that they could wage war by proxy, from behind layers of deniability, and never themselves pay the price. Roughly forty Iranian top-tier officials were eliminated in minutes, including the IRGC commander, the armed forces chief of staff, the minister of defense, the national security adviser, and former president Mahmoud Ahmadinejad, who had built his international notoriety on vows to wipe Israel off the map.

But the principal target was the head of the snake, Ayatollah Ali Khamenei. Thirty precision-guided bombs reduced his fortified compound to rubble. While President Trump proclaimed that America would strike Iran alongside Israel—in an operation aptly named Epic Fury—it was Israel alone that delivered the blow that shattered Khamenei's reign. For the first time in the long, battered chronicle of the Jewish people, the Jews struck down a reigning head of state sworn to their destruction. A people who for millennia could only endure and outlast tyrants had, at last, brought one to account.

Khamenei knew Israel had turned leadership gatherings into killing grounds. He had watched it happen: Hezbollah's command decapitated in September 2024, the IRGC Aerospace Command eliminated in June 2025, the entire Houthi cabinet erased in Yemen in August 2025. Each time, a room. Each time, everyone in it. Yet absolute power had bred absolute delusion. Khamenei had spent decades constructing a myth of invincibility and made the fatal mistake of believing it himself. He thought he was too feared to be touched, too historically significant to simply disappear. The world's response to his death suggested otherwise: sporadic celebrations in Iranian streets, and barely a twelve-hour news cycle abroad. Like so many tyrants before him, he proved far less indispensable than he supposed, and far less mourned than his arrogance had led him to imagine.

Over the next twenty-four hours, Israel unleashed 1,200 airstrikes across twenty-four of Iran's thirty-one provinces. Together with the airmen, soldiers, and sailors of the United States military—the single greatest force for good on earth—Israel methodically destroyed the regime's vital organs: the presidential office, the IRGC headquarters, the supreme national security council, the ministry of intelligence, and the internal security forces headquarters. Nuclear facilities, naval bases, missile depots, and military installations were hammered nationwide. In Qom, the clerical Assembly of Experts was struck mid-session, as its members gathered to elect Khamenei's successor. The scope of the campaign spoke for itself: the goal was not to bruise the regime, but to break it. Addressing the Iranian people directly, President Trump declared, "The hour of your freedom is at hand. Take over your government. It will be yours to take."

Whether Iranians can bring down what remains of the regime remains to be seen. But Iran's violent thrashing across the region has the look of a mortally wounded beast—strong enough still to draw blood, yet no longer sovereign over its own survival. Whatever comes next, one lesson has been written in fire, a modern rendering of Belshazzar's writing on the wall: that chanting "Death to America" while building the machinery to achieve it was a failing strategy, and that branding Israel "a one-bomb country" while racing to test that theory was a fatal miscalculation.

But if the operation itself was historic, the timing felt ordained. Roaring Lion was launched on the Shabbat when Jews read the commandment to remember Amalek—the archetypal enemy who sought to annihilate the Jewish people in their infancy. Every year, that Shabbat falls just before Purim, the festival commemorating the salvation of the Jews from the genocidal decree of a Persian satrap named Haman—a name whose consonants bear an unsettling resemblance to Khamenei. Iran is the geographic heir to ancient Persia, so the historical echo has never been subtle. But in announcing the operation, Netanyahu made it explicit: "Twenty-five hundred years ago, in ancient Persia, a tyrant rose against us with the very same goal—to utterly destroy our people. . . . Today as well, on the eve of Purim, the lot has fallen. And the end of this evil regime will also come."

More than any other holiday, Purim was made for this moment—the festival of the impossible comeback, the miraculous reversal, the enemy undone by his own hand. The holiday's motto is *Venahafoch hu*—the tables were turned. As Knesset Speaker Amir Ohana said shortly before the operation: "Throughout Jewish history, those words were a prayer. Today, they are our policy." The operation proved him right—and vindicated something deeper still: the teaching of the Baal Shem Tov, who insisted that one may not read the Book of Esther as a story locked in the past. The drama, he taught, is always unfolding and always alive. The blessing before the Megillah praises God "who performed miracles for our fathers in those days, in this time."

This time, those words felt literal.

This book was written in the conviction that Israel has won the war, even as the war is not yet over. Israel faced enemies on seven fronts; on every front, those enemies are bloodied and retreating. A brutal massacre, decades in the making and detonated on October 7, proved to be—borrowing George Will's phrase—"one of history's most spectacular backfires." But it was only as we submitted this manuscript that our theory gave way to fact. The largest air campaign in Israeli history confirmed what the evidence suggested: the axis that sought Israel's destruction has been broken at its core. Like Haman, hanged on the very gallows he built for Mordechai, Iran set out to encircle Israel—and succeeded only in uniting against itself the many states it spent decades trying to destabilize.

Khamenei's death, alongside the apex of his senior command, removed from history's stage the single figure most responsible for the sustained, organized campaign to destroy the Jewish people. It relieved America of one of its most implacable and calculating adversaries. And it pulled humanity back from the brink of a nuclear nightmare. All of this was achieved by a microscopic Jewish state squeezed between enemies who outnumber it a hundredfold—a state not yet eighty years old, forged in the shadow of the Holocaust, built by a people the world had counted out more times than history can comfortably recall. A people expelled from their land, scattered across continents, stripped of sovereignty, herded into cattle cars and fed into furnaces—who nevertheless returned, rebuilt, and prevailed against every enemy that ever rose against them.

The words of the prophets, written in this land thousands of years ago, now find their living proof in the story of their people. They predicted that Jews would not only return to their land, but they would rise as a light unto the nations and a looking glass through which humanity would behold its Creator. A people on whose behalf God would personally intervene. A nation that God would redeem.

The prophets did not write for their time. They wrote for every generation. But above all, they wrote for this one—when their ancient dispatches would become headlines in the morning news.

INTRODUCTION

GOD AT WAR

In a single morning, the clock turned back a century. At 6:29 a.m. on October 7, 2023, Hamas surged across Israel's border, dragging with them a savagery that belonged to the darkest chapters of history. It was a revival of the pogroms, on the scale of Kristallnacht and as demonic as the Holocaust. In moments, southern Israel became a hellscape. Sacred soil became a slaughterhouse.

Adolph Hitler's Einsatzgruppen and Bohdan Khmelnytsky's Cossacks found eager heirs in the death squads of Hamas and Islamic Jihad. They hunted Jews house to house and set whole neighborhoods ablaze. They incinerated families in their safe rooms, executed Holocaust survivors, and gang-raped and mutilated young men and women. They butchered infants—and the parents who sheltered them in their arms. They wired corpses with explosives to murder the first responders who rushed in to save whoever might still be breathing. Two hundred fifty-one men, women, and children were dragged from their homes, hauled across the border, and swallowed into the tunnels of Gaza.

Israel awoke in a different universe. The stomach-churning brutality of the massacre shattered all the familiar terminology that Israelis, over decades of war, had been conditioned to accept. This was not another "round of violence." It defiled the word "escalation." To use the word *clashes* would constitute a mockery. October 7 was an attempt to slash the Jewish state at its jugular vein.

To do so, Hamas aimed to annihilate Israel's will to live—shattering the Zionist dream and casting Jews back into the unending nightmare of their history. It sought to unleash so much death that names collapsed into numbers, faces dissolved into pixels, and human lives blurred into an indistinguishable mass of tragedy. In that orgy of violence, they detonated the dam that had held back the swelling tide of genocidal hatred born in the Holocaust—a dam the world called "Never Again."

Combining primeval inhumanity with cutting-edge technology, the terrorists turned the massacre into a grotesque cinematic spectacle. Using smartphones and GoPros, they captured their atrocities in ultra-high definition and broadcast the bloodshed to a world disturbingly accustomed to consuming Jewish suffering. Scripted films and documentaries now gave way to a live feed. Rivers of Jewish blood flowed in real time.

And that was just the opening act.

The microscopic Jewish state was hurled headlong into an all-out regional war. Almost immediately, it became clear that this would be no contained, single-front struggle. Gaza was the first battlefield to erupt—but rockets, anti-tank missiles, and armed infiltrators soon tore in from Lebanon. Terror cells ignited in Judea and Samaria. Missiles and suicide drones came screaming out of Syria and Iraq. In Yemen, the Houthis struck at the Red Sea, crippling global shipping while unleashing drones and ballistic missiles of their own. These six fronts were bound—and fueled—by a seventh: the artery pumping money, training, and weapons into each of them. The unified high command of global terror: Tehran.

Through its terrorist proxies, Iran had seized command over nations whose combined populations approached two hundred million. A merciless war machine, engineered over decades, was bearing down on a country of barely seven million Jews. David stood alone, staring down a seven-armed super Goliath.

The showdown was no less than biblical. On one side, a small country, internally divided only weeks before, stunned by the most devastating single day in its history. On the other side, a crescent of hostility stretching from Beirut to Sana'a, through Damascus and Tehran—backed by the world's largest authoritarian powers and cheered on by political and cultural elites across the West.

As in all modern wars, the battle lines stretched far beyond the battleground. On the world stage, Israel was thrust into an eighth theater: a battle for its name, its legitimacy, its very right to exist. Alongside the missiles and proxy brigades, a parallel war was waged by the UN General Assembly, the International Court of Justice, the International Criminal Court, and a consortium of Israel-hating NGOs. They convened two-faced tribunals and crafted weaponized resolutions—each a shameless instrument of political and economic warfare designed to choke the Jewish state.

Their rhetoric mirrored, almost word for word, the strategy and talking points of Hamas and Iran. Their aims were identical: to isolate Israel and strip it of the means to survive. They moved quickly. Accusations of genocide. Demands for arms embargoes. Campaigns to deny Israel the very tools required to keep its citizens alive. The message was unmistakable: Jews may die in large numbers, quietly and politely. But they may not defend themselves with force—not even after a day like October 7. Eighty years after the Holocaust, Jews were again being forced to dig their own graves. Terrorists may have launched the war. But it was velvet-gloved hit squads—corrupt judges, diplomats, and lawyers—who would finish the job.

Critics expected what many enemies openly prayed for: that Israel would lose heart, lose allies, and lose the will to fight; that it would descend into a long, bitter decline. They foresaw economic collapse, social unraveling, waves of emigration, and strategic retreat. They treated October 7 as the beginning of the end. Like the bloodthirsty crowds of medieval Europe—who packed town squares to watch Jews burned at the stake—the world seemed to lean in, waiting for its chance to witness the only Jewish state on Earth consigned to the flames.

But October 7 would not bring about the ending they hoped for. Instead, it brought the end of illusions. The end of incremental deterrence. The end of the idea that you could coexist with death cults that teach toddlers to cheer when Jews are slain. The end of the fantasy that the Iranian regime could be contained by polite communiqués and rounds of well-mannered "talks." For Israel, the war would mark the end of the destructive self-deceptions—and the beginning of the single greatest comeback in the history of modern warfare.

From that day of terror, Israel did not simply hold on and stave off collapse. It did not finish on its knees. It took off, climbed, and soared. It fought its way from the edge of annihilation to a level of power, reach, and dominance unseen in its history. The indisputable devastation of its foes was utterly without precedent in the modern world for a state of its size. Before the eyes of all mankind, Israel's day of doom became the crucible of its renewal.

It was a revelation of divine power and justice on the scale of the Exodus from Egypt, the downfall of Haman, and the fiery, sulfurous overturning of Sodom and Gomorrah. The world's foremost practitioners of evil suddenly found themselves consumed by the very flames they had stoked, their designs collapsing in on them. Once more, God had intervened to rescue His people from a genocidal Persian plot. At the splitting of the sea, Moses thundered: "God will wage war for you." And as in that immortal moment at the Sea of Reeds, Jews could once again point a finger—not toward the heavens but toward the earth—with sky-is-blue certainty and proclaim: "This is my God."

In mosque sermons and Revolutionary Guard videos, in Hezbollah propaganda reels and Western campus rallies, they spoke confidently of "the end of the Zionist entity." They promised a new regional order in which Israel would be encircled, isolated, and finally erased. Israel, they assured themselves, was nothing more than a "spider's web"—fragile, hollow, destined to collapse with a casual swipe of the Islamist hand. Terrorists and tyrants spent decades writing Israel's obituary, and yet, within a single year, Israel delivered theirs.

This book tells the story of how that happened. It traces how, in less than two years, Israel rose from disaster to dominance—from the carnage of October 7 to commanding the skies above Iran; from the twilight of apocalypse to the dawn of a new era of supremacy.

On the ground, driving that shift was costly, grueling, and yet profoundly inspiring. It became a genuine whole-of-nation effort—an entire people's trial by fire. Alongside hundreds of thousands of Israel Defense Forces (IDF) regulars—young men and women who would emerge as Israel's greatest generation—the army mobilized hundreds of thousands of reservists, pulling them from their jobs, their studies, and their families for months on end.

Civilians poured their strength into sustaining this Herculean effort. An avalanche of funds, food, gear, and essential supplies flowed in from Jews across Israel and around the world. Israel's major airlines dedicated themselves to shuttling soldiers back to their units in the field. Neighbors cared for the children of those who had been drafted. Communities pooled clothing, furniture, and goods for the tens of thousands displaced from Israel's borders. And children across the country filled boxes with drawings and handwritten letters to lift the spirits of soldiers holed up in damp and dimly lit bunkers. In every way imaginable, people found ways to join the fight.

In Gaza, the IDF undertook the largest and longest hostage-rescue mission in world history—paired with a systematic dismantling of the entire architecture of Hamas rule and terror: command centers buried beneath hospitals, rocket factories tucked under residential blocks, weapons stockpiles hidden in mosques and schools. The tunnel network—two decades in the making, built under the world's nose and with the world's money—was revealed as a fortified subterranean city for terrorists, engineered so the organization could fight and survive while civilians above absorbed the fire. Israel dove into the endless endeavor of meticulously mapping and demolishing the labyrinth, rewriting the rules of urban and underground warfare in the process.

For Israel's soldiers and their families, the price was heavy. But the direction of the war was never in doubt. Hamas battalions were dismantled one after another as the IDF methodically overran whatever ground it set its sights on. Terror chiefs who once lounged in foreign villas and strutted through diplomatic corridors posing as statesmen now found themselves dead or relentlessly hunted. Those who remained alive lived in a state of perpetual dread—paranoid, sleepless, and haunted by the sound of aircraft overhead.

To the north, Hezbollah joined in, waging a steadily escalating war of attrition. For decades, the organization styled itself as "the resistance," the spearpoint of the Iranian axis, the one force that had supposedly "defeated" Israel in 2006. It buried rockets beneath living rooms, embedded elite Radwan fighters in border villages, and converted southern Lebanon into an armory—rehearsing, year after year, its envisioned invasion of the

Galilee. Through it all, Hezbollah's leadership convinced itself that sheer scale would shield it from decisive Israeli retaliation.

They were dead wrong.

In one of the most extraordinary intelligence coups of the century, the world watched in astonishment as Hezbollah's senior ranks were cut to pieces. Pagers became personalized, pocket-sized assassins. Radio handsets detonated in commanders' vests. In a matter of minutes, men who had strutted as demigods of terror were killed and maimed, each a public sacrifice to his own astounding arrogance. In the days that followed, Israel tracked down every leadership conclave and erased it, down to the final chair—that of Hassan Nasrallah himself.

As Israel's ground campaign in Lebanon cleared the border regions of every trace of terrorist infrastructure, Hezbollah's mythic reputation was smashed beyond repair. The organization that had spent years stockpiling missiles and broadcasting teaser reels of its tunnel networks suddenly had to reckon with the fact that someone, somewhere inside Israel, had mapped its every move. The pinpoint precision, the creative ingenuity, and the total penetration of Hezbollah through every opening and orifice cemented Israel's covert capabilities as perhaps the most formidable on earth.

Farther east, Iranian generals who had long moved with impunity in Damascus watched as the proxy state they had propped up for more than a decade collapsed in a matter of weeks. As Assad fled to Russia, the Iranian operatives who oversaw weapons transfers, coordinated militias, and plotted attacks across Syria were themselves forced into retreat. In Iraq, Iranian-backed militias found their rhetoric muted and their movements constrained by the mere possibility of an Israeli strike. And in Yemen, the Houthis discovered that Israel's vaunted air force could deliver flawless waves of precision attacks more than a thousand miles beyond its borders.

Iran could not avert its gaze as its so-called "Axis of Resistance"—the buttress of its regional power, welded together over forty years—began to crumble beneath its feet. The regime was left to swallow a bitter truth: Israel could reach deeper, see farther, strike harder, and endure longer than the Ayatollah had ever dared to dream.

With time, the proxy war erupted into direct, open conflict between Israel and Iran. Two massive barrages of Iranian drones and ballistic missiles eventually gave way to a twelve-day, uninterrupted Israeli bombardment of Iran itself. In a theatrical opening strike, Israel drained the lifeblood of Iran's military and scientific leadership. The heartland of the revolution—the nerve center of global terror—found itself utterly defenseless. Its air defenses were compromised at every turn, its cities teeming with Mossad spies. Even Iran's ballistic missiles, each the size of a five-story building, lost their aura of dread. Israeli interceptors met them not only beyond Israeli airspace but in the outer layers of the atmosphere, turning multi-ton symbols of Iranian power into clustered shards of metal.

In capitals around the world, generals and analysts watched in silence, recalibrating every assumption they had ever made about the value of Israeli technology—and the value of Israeli partnership. Soon enough, American B-2s entered Iran on the "red carpet" Israel had rolled wide across its skies, devastating the key nuclear sites the regime had entombed beneath mountains.

On the last day of the war with Iran, Israel destroyed the notorious "countdown clock" in Tehran, supposedly ticking its way toward Israel's destruction. The symbolism was striking. From the depths of the worst terror attack in its history, Israel rose to rule the air above the empire that charted its demise. In the end, it was the Ayatollah who learned the truth: Iran—not Israel—was the spider's web, and it tore at the first hard touch.

Most nations that fight wars of this scale watch their economies buckle. Israel poured an extraordinary share of its GDP into defense, reserve mobilization, and emergency expenditures. By every classical economic model, growth should have stalled—if not collapsed outright. Instead, the Tel Aviv Stock Exchange surged nearly 300 percent over the course of the war. Investors who wagered on Israeli bankruptcy ate dust as the country's tech, defense, cyber, and energy sectors rocketed past every conventional measure of value. It was an anomaly that even Israel's harshest critics struggled to explain—a state supposed to be caught in its death spiral refused to behave like one.

The mood of the Middle East shifted accordingly. What had been marketed as an "Axis of Resistance" against Israel began to look more like a circle of targets locked on by Israeli radar, and an arc of impotence firmly under Israel's thumb.

In 2001, the largest terrorist attack in world history taught the world a hard truth: what happens in the Middle East never stays there. Israel's war on terror had a similar—though profoundly inverse—effect: instead of exporting chaos, it exported deterrence. For the first time since 9/11, the engines of global terror seemed, unmistakably, to be reversing course.

From the moment Hamas stormed across Israel's border on October 7, the war was destined to reverberate far beyond the region. A simple glance at the map explains why. The Persian Gulf is the bloodstream carrying roughly a fifth of the world's oil and gas supplies. The Red Sea feeds into the Suez Canal, a chokepoint through which nearly a third of global container traffic must pass. The Eastern Mediterranean is a rising theater of gas production, naval deployment, and international trade. Control of these waterways ranks among the greatest strategic prizes of the modern age. Had Israel failed to fight back, Iran and its agents would have stood poised to seize all three.

If Iran and its proxies had managed to dominate these sea routes, Tehran would have acquired unprecedented leverage over the arteries of global energy and commerce. And it would have delivered to Iran's patrons in China and Russia a region where the United States had exercised uncontested naval supremacy since the end of World War II. In one of history's most unexpected plot twists, the fate of a tiny Jewish state came to determine whether free navigation, global supply chains, and the strategic credibility of the West would withstand the combined pressure of a nascent anti-American axis.

For decades, Israel had already been one of America's strongest allies in the Middle East—sharing vital intelligence, conducting joint exercises, and collaborating on cutting-edge weapons programs. Mossad operations quietly saved Western lives by disrupting terror plots before they reached airports or city centers. And for the $3.8 billion a year Israel receives in American aid, the return on investment for the United States has been estimated at roughly $48 billion in defense contracts, shared research and development, and battlefield testing that accelerates US hardware upgrades.

But after the first two years of war, Israel's status underwent an upgrade of its own. Israel emerged as something more than an ally. It became a full-spectrum strategic partner of the United States—not a drain on American power, but a multiplier of it.

In his analysis of the conflict, noted historian Walter Russell Mead added crucial context to the war: namely, the emergence of a new "axis of revisionists" in world affairs—China, Russia, North Korea, and Iran. Europe had struggled merely to hold the line against Vladimir Putin in Ukraine. Taiwan, if attacked, would almost certainly require direct American intervention. But in the Middle East, Israel had managed to reverse the tide almost entirely on its own. In that sense, Mead argued, Israeli Prime Minister Benjamin Netanyahu is "the only leader, really, to have been able to throw back the revisionist axis in a very serious way."

In 2021, Ron Dermer, who would serve as Israel's minister of strategic affairs during the war, predicted that Jerusalem could become Washington's most important ally. For a country the size of New Jersey, the claim appeared fanciful, if not absurd. Within a few years, it would seem plausible, if not prophetic.

Even European powers that had long indulged in theatrical condemnations of Israel were forced to reconsider. As Israeli jets hammered Iranian nuclear and ballistic missile infrastructure, German Chancellor Friedrich Merz—who had once backed calls for an arms embargo on Israel—quietly admitted that Israel was doing the West's "dirty work." The shift became unmistakable when, in late 2025, Germany deployed the Israeli-developed Arrow missile defense system to shield itself against nuclear threats from Russia and beyond. A nation that had once served as the epicenter of Jewish annihilation now relied on Jewish ingenuity to help stave off its own destruction.

The IDF's transformation into a prodigy of military power was sealed when it hosted more than one hundred senior military representatives from nearly twenty countries for an intensive five-day program. The subjects were concrete and technical: coordinating drones and artillery to shield advancing ground forces; pioneering combat-medicine techniques that dramatically increased the odds of bringing wounded soldiers home alive; and developing methods for fighting an urban, subterranean enemy while reducing noncombatant casualties to levels unseen in previous large-scale conflicts.

But more striking than the curriculum were the flags stitched onto the uniforms. France and Canada—both of which had embraced the latest diplomatic fashion of "recognizing" a new Arab state even as Hamas held hostages underground—sent senior officers. So did Japan, whose government had called IDF operations in Gaza "entirely unacceptable." And so did Finland, which had publicly accused Israel of violating "international law and norms." World leaders scolded Israel, but all the while, their generals were taking notes.

What drew them was not affection, but necessity. Israel's abilities—coordinating sensors and shooters, dominating the skies while fighting street to street, keeping casualty ratios as low as it did in the most complex urban environment on earth—were battle-tested and proven beyond doubt. The IDF, once dependent on importing equipment and techniques, was steadily becoming one of the world's premier exporters of defense technology and expertise. It had written the field manual for twenty-first-century warfare: multi-domain, AI-driven, drone-saturated, fought under the microscope of global media, and waged against enemies who hide behind human shields while expecting Western publics to force their governments to break.

Thousands of years ago, the prophets foretold that the people of Israel would not merely survive their tortured history but would one day stand as "a pride to the world" and "a light to the nations"—restored to their land and shielded by the hand of God. For centuries, skeptics dismissed those words as ancient poetry. Cynics waved them away as folklore. And yet, all throughout, millions still believed that eventually—*inevitably*—they would be proven true.

Today, anyone who reads the headlines clear-eyed and honestly cannot plausibly deny that something remarkable is unfolding in full view: a small Jewish state, returned to the cradle of its creation, has shattered the gravitational pull of historical pessimism. It has defied the assumptions of geopolitics, outstripped the predictions of allies and adversaries alike, and risen to a place of influence and consequence that no sober observer can ignore. The very miracles once consigned to scripture have become front-page news.

Terminology: Words as Weapons

Before we turn to the events themselves, we must be precise about the language we use. In this conflict, language is anything but neutral. Words are weapons—used to bludgeon Israel and to smuggle in assumptions long before a single argument is made. In this book, we will not allow that. There are three terms in particular that we will avoid unless no other word fits the exact historical fact: "West Bank," "refugee," and "Palestinian."

The phrase "West Bank" sounds technical and harmless. It is not. It is a bogus term for a region that already has a name: Judea and Samaria.

The geographic anchor of the term "West Bank" is the Jordan River. Narrow, shallow, and unassuming, the Jordan is at points barely wider than a two-lane road. No one, before the mid-twentieth century, ever used that slender stream to name the ancient highlands that rise to its west. Linguistically, calling Judea and Samaria the "West Bank" is the equivalent of renaming Pennsylvania the "West Bank" of the Delaware River. Pennsylvanians would be right to reject that—how much more so Jews in the land that has borne their name for more than three thousand years.

The ridgelines and towns that diplomats casually relabel as the "West Bank" sit inside the Jewish biblical heartland of Judea and Samaria. This is the terrain where 80 percent of the Jewish Biblical narrative unfolds. Hebron, with the Cave of the Patriarchs, where Adam, Abraham, Isaac, Jacob, Eve, Sarah, Rebecca, and Leah are buried. Shiloh, cradle of the Tabernacle. Rachel's Tomb near Bethlehem. These are not UNESCO World Heritage Sites perched on some foreign plateau. They are the very bedrock of Jewish identity, the cornerstones of Jewish origins. And together with the hundreds of other sanctified sites that dot this landscape, they make Judea and Samaria not merely a region on a map, but the single most authentically Jewish terrain on earth.

The term "West Bank" is deployed not to delineate land but to dispossess it—to scorch and sever its Jewish roots. It depicts Jews in Judea and Samaria as an invasive species—a sort of linguistic crowbar, wielded to pry Jews out of their own homeland. Its goal is to normalize the *Judenrein* dystopia imagined in the Oslo Accords. In truth, the erasure of three millennia of Jewish continuity with a sterile, imperial nickname is nothing less than the greatest heist in history. In this book, we will not play along. We will use the names that have anchored Jewish memory for millennia: Judea and Samaria.

The same insistence applies to the word *refugee*.

Nowhere else on earth does "refugee" operate the way it is applied in the Arab war against Israel. In normal usage, a refugee is a person fleeing a conflict or catastrophe in real time, someone driven from home by events still unfolding. The children of refugees may inherit trauma, stories, and sometimes hardship, but they do not inherit the legal and political status forever.

The war that produced the first Arab refugees in this conflict began in 1948 when five Arab armies, backed and cheered by the broader Arab world, invaded the newborn Jewish state. Those who left or were driven out in that war did so in a specific historical moment, often in the expectation that the invading armies would destroy Israel and that they would return to pick up where they left off.

That war ended long ago. The descendants of those who left are not fleeing anything today. They are not dodging artillery or escaping armies on the move. They are, in most cases, third- or fourth-generation residents of other Arab states, living under Arab governance. To call them refugees in the present tense is to sever the word from lived reality and repurpose it as a political instrument. And it grants the Arab governments that rule over them a convenient alibi for refusing to integrate them or grant them full citizenship.

The United States fought brutal wars in Korea, Vietnam, Iraq, and elsewhere. Civilians died in large numbers. Displacement was immense. Yet no one argues that the grandchildren of those civilians are refugees, endowed with a perpetual, inheritable claim linked to their grandparents' misfortune. Refugee status does not propagate indefinitely anywhere else.

Only here has the category been deliberately frozen in time and passed down to each new generation—not as a humanitarian designation, but as a demographic battering ram meant to overwhelm Israel through the arithmetic of grievance. That is why, in this book, we will use the word *refugee* in its plain, honest sense: to describe people actually fleeing a present conflict, not the great-grandchildren of those who left a war that ended decades before they were born.

Finally, there is the most contested term of all: "Palestinian." Today, it is used as if it described a clear, continuous, and ancient nation. In reality, its modern political meaning is far more complex—and far more recent.

Historically, the term Palestine was never an ethnic or national designation. The Romans introduced "Palaestina" after crushing the Bar Kochba revolt, as a deliberate attempt to sever Jewish ties to the land. Byzantine rulers kept the name. Arab empires used it simply as a regional designation. The Ottomans administered Palestine as a vilayet—a province, not a political entity. The British Mandate continued this usage after World War I. And the term "Palestinian," during that period, was a geographic label applied to Jews, Christians, and Muslims alike. It never implied an ethnic group distinct from the Arabs of Syria, Lebanon, or Jordan. Put simply: Palestine was not a national title. It was an imperial postal code.

Up until the mid-twentieth century, the Arabic-speaking inhabitants of the Jewish homeland did not see themselves as a separate national people. Identity was mainly shaped by religion, clan, local community, or by a wider sense of belonging to Greater Syria and the Arab world. This is not conjecture; early Arab leaders and intellectuals said so plainly.

At the First Congress of Muslim-Christian Associations in 1919—convened to discuss the future of the land after the fall of the Ottoman Empire—delegates declared: "We consider Palestine part of Arab Syria, as it has never been separated from it at any time." No claim to a distinct indigenous nation was made.

In 1946, the distinguished Arab American scholar Philip Hitti, a founder of modern Middle Eastern studies, testified before the Anglo-American Committee of Inquiry. When asked if a historic Palestine had ever existed as an independent entity, he replied: "Absolutely not." If anyone could have unearthed a long-suppressed "Palestinian" national history in the archives, it was Hitti.

In 1948, when five Arab armies invaded the newborn Jewish state, the Arabs of the territory did not describe themselves as a separate nation seeking sovereignty. They identified simply as Arabs, or as part of a broader Arab whole, and they supported the invading armies openly. When Jordan controlled Judea and Samaria and Egypt governed Gaza—both for nineteen years—there were no demands for a "Palestinian state."

No one spoke of "occupation." These were familiar Arab territories under familiar Arab rulers. Independence was not suppressed; it was not seriously imagined.

When the Palestine Liberation Organization was founded in 1964, its purpose was not to liberate *Palestinians* from Arab rule, but to "liberate" *Palestine* from Jewish rule. Its founding documents state this explicitly. The PLO's objective was the destruction of the Jewish state, not the formation of a historic national entity in lands then under Egyptian and Jordanian control.

The PLO's own charter explains the logic. Article 1 defines Palestine as part of "the large Arab homeland." The flag adopted by the movement is modeled directly on the banner of the 1916 Arab Revolt—as an emblem of pan-Arabism. Even the organization's creation was an initiative of the Arab League. The PLO itself was not an expression of a long-standing nationalist project, but of a modern Arab political project.

Its leaders admitted as much. In 1956, Ahmad Shukeiri, the PLO's first chairman, told the UN Security Council that Palestine was simply "southern Syria." In 1977, senior PLO commander Zuheir Muhsin stated openly: "Only for political reasons do we carefully underline our Palestinian identity." As if to avoid confusion, he added: "The existence of a separate Palestinian identity is there for tactical reasons." Once the political objectives of destroying Israel were achieved, the very distinction that drove their cause would fade back into the broader Arab nation that created it.

It was only in the 1960s—after the collapse of pan-Arabism and the shock of Israel's victory in the Six-Day War—that a distinct "Palestinian" political identity began to take shape. In that moment, Soviet strategic aims and regional Arab politics converged in an effort to reshape global opinion. Within this environment, Yasser Arafat and the PLO—assisted by Soviet advisers and regional propagandists—recast their struggle. What had long been framed as part of a wider Arab nationalist project was rebranded as the fight of a "native" people against "foreign settlers," a narrative carefully calibrated to resonate with Western audiences already torn over Vietnam and decolonization debates.

The tactic succeeded powerfully. It enabled a large, regionally dominant Arab world to present itself to Western audiences as an embattled minority, allegedly struggling against a foreign "settler" project, when in fact the Arab world remains one of the largest contiguous cultural, linguistic, and political blocs on earth. The men who launched the war on October 7 did not see themselves as a fragile ethnic tribe. They drew strength, doctrine, money, and weaponry from a broad Arab and Islamic universe that spans continents.

None of this denies that many Arabs today sincerely understand themselves as "Palestinians," or that they have built a meaningful identity around that term. Identity can be powerful even when its political form is relatively recent. Most importantly, recognizing how a term emerged is not the same as denying the humanity of those who choose to adopt it.

If anything, the exploitation of that label—its weaponization into a forever war against Israel—has inflicted far greater harm on Arab communities than any historical clarification ever could. While the popularization of the term "Palestinian" proved remarkably effective for terror groups like the PLO and Hamas, for many ordinary Arabs living in the land, it did not bring liberation. It brought decades of instability, corruption, and recurring cycles of violence from which they, too, have suffered deeply. For this book, we will therefore use a clearer, more historically grounded, and more peaceful term: "Arab."

The terms we use matter. "Judea and Samaria." "Arab." "Refugee" in its plain meaning. These are not semantic games. They are essential to telling a story rooted in history rather than in the propaganda of those who wish Israel erased.

Casualties: Tragedy as a Strategy

The war launched by Hamas on October 7 spelled catastrophe for civilians in Gaza. Every single innocent man, woman, and child is a child of God. They bear the image of God. And their deaths are tragic beyond description.

And yet, Hamas planned the war to produce precisely that tragic outcome. It embedded its arsenals in homes, mosques, schools, and hospitals. It dug a vast tunnel network beneath city streets and residential neighborhoods—not to shelter families but to shield its own operatives.

Not one tunnel was ever used as a bomb shelter for civilians. Not one was reserved for patients in hospitals or children in schools. The entire underground city exists to protect Hamas while the people above absorb the blows on their behalf.

From the moment the first rocket left its launcher that morning, Hamas ensured that civilians would suffer. It had placed them directly in harm's way. This was not just the use of human shields; it was rank human sacrifice. And for this unconscionable crime against humanity, Hamas alone bears full responsibility.

Throughout this book, we will not be tallying civilian casualties in Gaza according to the daily numbers issued by Hamas. We will not treat their claims as neutral data. We will not accept their claims at face value. The reason is simple: the numbers are tainted at their source.

Hamas is not a neutral census bureau. It is a terror group. It is, in every fiber of its organization, deceitful and propagandistic. It celebrates lying as a tool of holy war. It has every motivation to inflate, distort, and weaponize casualty figures to isolate Israel internationally. More crucially, it is the architect of the very strategy that places its people in danger. To treat its numbers as authoritative rewards to a scheme that knowingly endangers civilians.

Yet, from the earliest weeks of the war, major news organizations, NGOs, academics, and even Western governments treated charts from the Hamas-controlled "Gaza Health Ministry" as if an independent auditing body had produced them. The US Secretary of Defense quoted them. President Biden repeated them in a State of the Union address.

This book will not. Not because suffering should be minimized, but because suffering should not be manipulated.

The problems with Hamas casualty data are not minor. They are structural.

The failures in Hamas's data are structural, not cosmetic. Even the UN's Office for the Coordination of Humanitarian Affairs admitted in late 2023 that it did not actually know how Hamas calculated its toll, calling its methodology "unknown." Yet it continued to circulate the numbers.

But what is "known" is even worse. Hamas also refuses to distinguish between combatants and civilians. Its tallies collapse terrorists and noncombatants into a single figure designed for maximum emotional and political impact. Democratic militaries painstakingly attempt to separate those categories; Hamas erases them. Hamas also refuses to say what kind of death the deceased suffered—for example, whether it was caused by war or natural causes. Anyone who died in Gaza over the course of the war was considered—automatically—to have been killed by Israel.

There are super-massive holes in the data. When Hamas announced more than thirty-four thousand deaths at the war's two-hundred-day mark, it simultaneously admitted that only around twenty-four thousand were "known martyrs" with identified names. Nearly one-third of the alleged fatalities were unidentified—no names, no ID numbers, no independent way to verify who they were, how they died, or whether they ever existed.

The Al-Ahli Hospital incident revealed the stakes of this distortion. Hamas immediately blamed Israel and claimed nearly five hundred deaths. Protests ignited worldwide. But within days, multiple independent investigations showed the blast was caused by a misfired terrorist rocket. Nonetheless, Hamas folded those deaths into its tally of Israeli "atrocities," long after the facts were established. Beyond blaming Israel for their own crimes, they also inflated the number of casualties—according to a European intelligence source—by as much as 500 percent.

Serious statisticians have likewise scrutinized the data. Abraham Wyner of the Wharton School showed that Hamas's cumulative-death graph increased with mechanical, "metronomic regularity"—something seen only in fabricated datasets, not in real wartime casualty patterns, which spike and dip with combat intensity.

Other anomalies were blatant. United Nations updates based on Hamas data reported days on which almost every newly counted death was listed as a woman or child—ratios so implausible that they read more like narrative objectives than neutral counts. One update even recorded more women and children killed than the total people killed on the same day.

Eventually, even the UN was forced to backtrack. On May 8, 2024, OCHA cut its casualty numbers by half—*half*—due to internal contradictions between Hamas-run offices. Yet the "revised" number also came from Hamas—and so remained unverifiable.

All this would already be enough to cast serious doubt on Hamas statistics. Then we add the simplest fact of all.

Hamas controls Gaza with an iron grip. There is no independent press roaming its streets. No rival ministry maintains separate registries. No opposition party cross-checks the death toll. Journalists who want access to Gaza know that if they challenge the narrative too aggressively, they will lose access, or worse. NGOs operate under the same shadow. A regime that criminalizes dissent cannot be treated as a trustworthy source of data, especially not on the most emotionally explosive question in the war.

Even in open societies, casualty accounting is hard. The United States, with all its investigative capacity and internal criticism, has repeatedly undercounted civilians killed by its own operations, only for outside journalists and analysts to later reveal higher numbers. In Iraq, one careful reconstruction of airstrikes found that the ratio of civilians to combatants killed was far higher than official US figures had claimed. But there is a difference. In democracies, those revelations lead to corrections, inquiries, sometimes even prosecutions. There are mechanisms, however imperfect, to drag uncomfortable truths into the light. In Gaza, there is no such mechanism. Hamas can say whatever it wants. No one inside its territory can publicly contradict it and remain free.

Independent analyses offer a different picture. Based on Israel's own data, the ratio of civilians to combatants killed is estimated to be between 1:1 and 1.4:1. In dense urban combat against an enemy built under civilian infrastructure, that ratio is tragic—but internationally unprecedented in its restraint.

None of this lessens the human pain. Every civilian death is a world destroyed. As Prime Minister Netanyahu put it: "For Israel, every civilian death is a tragedy. For Hamas, it is a strategy." This book will not reward that strategy. It will not use the tools of a terror organization as the baseline for historical judgment. It will rely on verifiable evidence—not on the press releases of the terrorists who started the war and hid behind their own people.

We intend to tell the truth as clearly as possible. But that does not mean we must forfeit compassion, and it certainly does not require pretending to be neutral in a struggle defined by such stark moral contrast.

We will be honest—without being naïve; humane—without blurring the lines between those who target innocents and those who risk everything to save them. To paraphrase Martin Luther King Jr., this book will do what the moral universe has always done—and what Israel's story in these years so powerfully confirms:

It will bend toward justice.

CHAPTER ONE

EXODUS FROM OSLO: THE THIRTY-YEAR HIGHWAY TO HELL

We hoped for peace, but no good came;
For a time of relief—instead, there is terror!
Jeremiah 8:15

On August 1, 2023—just over two months before the worst massacre of Jews since the Holocaust—Maj. Gen. (res.) Tamir Hayman went on a podcast and delivered a message that, in hindsight, reads like an epitaph. "We are not on the verge of a multi-front war," he declared with confidence. "We are not on the eve of war. There is no need to look at intelligence signs. You just need to look at the interests."

Hayman was no ordinary officer. He had served as Israel's chief of military intelligence, entrusted with the nation's deepest secrets. At the time of the podcast, he was directing the Institute for National Security Studies, Israel's most prestigious think tank. His words carried weight. His predictions shaped perceptions. And they did not age well.

To the man once tasked with guarding Israel's survival, Hamas's stockpiles of rockets, its open calls for jihad, its rehearsals for raids on Israeli towns—all of it was dismissed as irrelevant. What mattered, he insisted, were "interests." And who defined those interests? He did. The logic was circular, almost childish. *If I do not want war, my enemy must not want war either. If I prize comfort, my enemy must prize comfort too. If I value life, surely my enemy values life the same.*

With those words, the blindness of Israel's security elite was laid bare. Intelligence reports, intercepted sermons, enemy declarations, the weapons amassed in Gaza, Lebanon, and Tehran—none of it outweighed Hayman's hunch. Analysis was replaced by assumption. And the assumption was simple: if we seek self-preservation, so do our adversaries.

This was not just an intelligence failure. It was the fruit of decades in which Israel's elite military and cultural figures tried to trade their indigenous identity for borrowed illusions. They swapped the realism of Jewish history for the optimism of think tanks, the mandate of survival for the applause of foreign capitals. They wanted to fold the Jewish state into the stream of "normal nations."

October 7 shook Israel out of that dream state. It stripped Israel of its fantasies and forced the nation to confront the ancient truths it had tried to forget. That day was not only a descent into horror, but the start of an awakening. In the aftermath, Israel began to rediscover itself. Mourning turned into resolve. Long-held illusions fell away, replaced by a clearer sense of purpose. In that clarity lay the foundation for Israel's greatest comeback—the transformation from a nation on the brink of annihilation into the dominant power in the Middle East.

Hamas, for its part, was never coy about its genocidal intent. It proclaimed its ambitions at every rally, from every pulpit, and across every broadcast. Its leaders glorified martyrdom and sanctified bloodshed. They boasted openly of their dream to erase Israel from the map. Its founding charter left no room for ambiguity: Islam would "obliterate" Israel, and the day would come when "the Jews will hide behind trees and stones, and each tree and stone will say: 'Oh Muslim, oh servant of Allah, there is a Jew behind me, come and kill him.'" There was, according to the document, one exception: "Except for the Gharqad tree, for it is the tree of the Jews."

The charter was explicit on another point as well: there could be no negotiations, no coexistence, and no peace process. "There is no solution for the Palestinian question," it declared, "except through Jihad." The words were not hidden. They were not whispered in secret caves or buried in encrypted messages. They were shouted from mosque loudspeakers, printed in official documents, repeated for decades without apology. Yet Israel's security elite—schooled in the theology of Oslo and entranced by the delusion of a "New Middle East"—refused to take them seriously. They fatally mistook Hamas's hatred of the Jewish people in general, and of Israel in particular, as transactional rather than ideological. Admitting Hamas meant what it said would have forced Israel's top officers to acknowledge the failure of their own ideology. And so, they chose not to see.

The absurd assessment offered by Tamir Hayman—that Hamas had an "interest" in keeping the peace—was soon eclipsed by an even more astonishing miscalculation from his successor, Maj. Gen. Aharon Haliva. Barely a year before the greatest wholesale slaughter of Jews in Israel's history, Haliva asserted that Israel's greatest threat was not genocidal terrorist armies or rogue regimes pursuing nuclear weapons. The greatest danger was the climate crisis. Repeat: one of Israel's most senior commanders was concerned that summer heatwaves and rising tides posed a greater immediate threat to Israel than Hamas, Iran, Hezbollah, Islamic Jihad, and ISIS.

This was not an offhand comment. According to Moshe Feiglin—former deputy speaker of the Knesset and one of the key thinkers whose insights lay the basis for much of this chapter—Haliva argued in senior forums that climate change was a defining factor in Israel's long-term strategic picture. The far more immediate dangers posed by Hamas and its Iranian-backed allies, he dismissed with chilling ease: "We are in control." In practice, Haliva succeeded in steering the intelligence community's attention away from the enemy's preparations and toward a set of abstract ecological forecasts. Haliva would serve as head of IDF Intelligence on October 7.

Prime Minister Benjamin Netanyahu would later confirm the story, recounting to his ministers a shocking anecdote told to him by Col. Richard Kemp, a former British commander. During the years Netanyahu sat in the opposition, Kemp visited IDF intelligence and was shown a briefing listing Israel's "top ten threats." At the very top, ranked number one, was climate change. According to Netanyahu, Kemp "couldn't believe it."

The misalignment of priorities was impossible to ignore. Unit 8200 was the crown jewel of Israeli intelligence. It was known for cracking enemy codes, mapping terror networks, and intercepting plots before they unfolded. And yet its agents found themselves tasked with side projects far removed from the sacred mission of protecting the Jewish homeland. Instead of focusing on stopping deadly attacks, recruits were kept busy creating a calculator that collects data on carbon emissions. While Hamas tunneled beneath Gaza, Israel's brightest cyber minds were designing software to calculate the solar energy potential of rooftops across Israel. While Hezbollah stockpiled missiles in Lebanese villages, Israel's elite cyber hackers were building models to measure vegetation dryness to predict forest fires. The unit even launched an environmental initiative named "Eco 8200." They hosted "climate hackathons" and formed an internal "Green Forum" devoted to environmental activism. Had it not ended in death and catastrophe, this would all sound comical.

The fixation on the climate went far beyond intelligence units; it seeped into the institutional bloodstream of the IDF itself. In the decade leading up to October 7, the Israeli military proudly expanded a sweeping environmental initiative known as the Nature Defense Forces, led by the IDF's Technology and Logistics Directorate in partnership with Israel's leading environmental organizations. More than sixty-five projects were rolled out across military bases nationwide, channeling time, manpower, and senior command attention into climate resilience, biodiversity preservation, light-pollution reduction, rewilding efforts, and nature-based infrastructure planning. Guy Selai, director of Nature Defense Forces, described these programs as "a multi-year plan within the IDF," explicitly framed as "part of the national effort to mitigate and adapt to climate change." His enthusiasm was shared at the highest levels of the IDF chain of command. Shortly after the launch of the initiative in 2013, then–Maj. Gen. Gadi Eizenkot, who would soon become chief of staff of the IDF, eagerly endorsed the Nature Defense Forces. He called it an effort of "the utmost importance," and pledged that "together with the chief of staff and the entire General Staff, I will ensure that this commendable activity is incorporated into the IDF's multi-year plan."

At the Ramat David Air Force Base, which oversees aerial operations across Syria and Lebanon, soldiers were tasked with creating refuge gardens for endangered species and building designated wildlife crossings. IDF naval bases in Haifa and Ashdod collected environmental data to protect sea life and set out to deepen sailors' knowledge of the marine ecosystem. The IDF's Engineering and Construction Directorate focused on establishing green classrooms and reducing light pollution deemed harmful to birds. Its Foreign Military Liaison Unit diverted personnel and resources to converting dried fishponds into wetlands designed to attract wildlife. The Ground Forces Training Command painted trail markers as a part of a project reimagining live-fire zones as regulated hiking preserves. Even cadets at the IDF's officers' school—the future commanders of Israel's wars—were trained not only in tactics and command, but in ecological ethics and sustainability doctrine. The officers' training base itself also joined the campaign, installing ecological toilets and creating bird gardens with watering points. Most alarming was the initiative's penetration of the Soreq Nuclear Research Center, where officers entrusted with Israel's most sensitive weapons were diverted to preserving ecological corridors and designing seasonal ponds to increase biodiversity.

The insanity was neither peripheral nor abstract. It reached Israel's fighters while they were deployed on the front lines, charged with defending the country's citizens. The 653rd Engineering Battalion was drafted to help "save" the Negev iris—surveying and mapping its growth patterns in the desert, just minutes from the Gaza border. Even in Judea and Samaria—amid a ghastly wave of terror attacks in 2022–2023—border-defense units were required to use surveillance systems designed to detect terrorists to document wildlife sightings. The Samaria Regional Brigade, responsible for the safety of hundreds of thousands of Israelis, devoted manpower to cultivating an Atlantic pistachio grove. The Duvdevan Unit—Israel's elite undercover counterterror force—was assigned to cut and mark hiking trails for civilian visitors and to conduct surveys of the region's red falcon population. Classified units, so sensitive their names cannot be published, were compelled to embed environmental impact assessments into their operational planning cycles. Nowhere was the madness more grotesque than in the Gaza Division itself. As Hamas prepared slaughter just beyond the fence, commanders were forced to tend streams, restore archaeological sites, and conduct seminars on "landscape values."

This was nothing less than a dereliction of duty—criminal negligence bordering on treason. It amounted to the wholesale abuse of Israel's young soldiers, conscripted to defend the state but diverted into an ideological crusade they never enlisted to serve. This was the woke mind virus in its deadliest, most mutated form.

The Israeli military's drift into fashionable ideology, however, was not unique. In September 2025, President Trump's Secretary of War Pete Hegseth stood before America's generals at Quantico and named the same disease. And he moved decisively to remove it. He announced that the Pentagon would be renamed, and more importantly reoriented: no longer the Department of Defense, but the Department of War. "From this moment forward," Hegseth declared, "the only mission of the newly restored Department of War is this: warfighting, preparing for war and preparing to win, unrelenting and uncompromising in that pursuit." Condemning decades of decay in which the military had been pushed to focus on "the wrong things," he declared it his mission to "uproot the obvious distractions" and mocked the ideological capture that had turned the armed forces into what he called "the Woke Department." There would be no more identity months, no more DEI offices, no more climate-change worship. "This is combat," he said. "This is life or death."

Crucially, Hegseth explained how reform would be enforced: by replacing the leaders who had created—or prospered within—the culture he was dismantling. "It's nearly impossible to change a culture with the same people who helped create or even benefited from that culture," he said. In the American system, that authority exists. Backed by President Donald Trump, Hegseth could fire generals, rewrite the rules of promotion, and realign the officer corps with its core mission. He proved both the willingness and the capacity to do so, relieving multiple senior commanders, including the chairman of the Joint Chiefs of Staff. As he put it bluntly: "Personnel is policy."

Unfortunately, Benjamin Netanyahu did not have that freedom. In Israel, senior security appointments—from the IDF chief of staff to the heads of Shin Bet and Mossad—are all subject to judicial review by the Supreme Court. Mere petitions can freeze or void decisions even after cabinet approval, and Supreme Court rulings are effectively final. As described by Ido Norden, the author of *The Invisible Rulers: The Story of Israel's Deep State*, "Netanyahu cannot fire the chief of staff . . . elected officials are weaker than senior officers." Lacking control over personnel, Israel's prime minister—and the voters who empowered him—lacked full control over policy as well.

As in the United States, Israel's security establishment had replaced vigilance with virtue signaling. But unlike Washington, the problem was far harder for Netanyahu to uproot. Judicial and bureaucratic constraints left little room for decisive correction, even as the climate crisis expanded from a background concern into an institutional obsession—complete with budgets, doctrine, partnerships, and prestige. "Especially in an era of climate crisis," said Iris Hann, CEO of the Society for the Protection of Nature in Israel in 2022, preserving the environment was "critical to our lives. The IDF is a central partner in this effort." What she—and many others—could not imagine then became brutally clear on October 7: while the IDF was busy taking on projects better suited to Greenpeace or the World Wildlife Fund, a crisis of an entirely different order was forming just over the border—one that would soon prove far more "critical" to the lives of thousands of Israelis.

This disastrous misalignment of priorities was possible because of another false assumption: in September 2022, Haliva declared with confidence that Hamas was deterred and that Gaza would be quiet for another five years. This was more than a poor forecast. It was the wholesale abandonment of the Jewish worldview. The Talmud commands: *If someone comes to kill you, rise and kill him first.* But Israel's generals, many with certificates from Western think tanks and scholarships from American universities, rewrote it as: *If someone comes to kill you, make sure to focus on recycling.* The hard-earned Jewish realism forged through exile, persecution, and war was abandoned in favor of imported illusions.

And so, despite being encircled by genocidal enemies, Israel chose to deploy its best intelligence officers not strictly against terrorist threats, but also against carbon footprints. The sacred core of intelligence—providing early warning of a preemptive attack—no longer seemed to command serious attention. Veteran intelligence officials later described their frustration in stark terms. Unit 8200 commander Brig. Gen. Yossi Sariel appeared distracted, absorbed in pursuits far removed from Gaza. "He spent a considerable amount of his time," one agent recalled bitterly, "on things that had nothing to do with gathering intelligence. Certainly not with gathering intelligence in Gaza." Another was even more blunt. Sariel, he explained, was dealing with "writing a book, the climate crisis . . . Where do you find time for this?"

In April 2022, Unit 8200 intercepted a forty-page operational blueprint detailing Hamas's plan for a full-scale invasion of Israel. The document—code-named "Jericho Walls"—was written in meticulous Arabic across dozens of pages. It outlined, step by step, the very attack that would later unfold on October 7: an opening barrage of thousands of rockets; drones to blind IDF cameras and disable automated machine gun positions; and a mass infiltration of terrorists by paraglider, motorcycle, and on foot. Every one of those elements occurred exactly as written.

And yet, Sariel and other senior intelligence officers concluded that Hamas lacked either the capability or the will to execute an operation of such scale. The document was quietly filed away. Israel's most senior commanders—the IDF chief of staff, the head of operations, the air force commander—would not see or even hear of the document until after the massacre. Neither would Prime Minister Netanyahu, his defense minister, nor the Knesset's Foreign Affairs and Defense Committee. Even the Mossad, which might have matched the blueprint with overseas Hamas activity, was never informed of its existence. Brig. Gen. (res.) Yaron Rosen later revealed that the air force had prepared "no scenario" for a multi-point mass breach like the one Hamas executed and therefore had "no relevant orders" ready to activate that morning. Lacking a preplanned response, the IAF was forced to improvise.

The night before October 7, scattered elements in Israel's security system detected signs of an imminent attack. Still, Haliva and Sariel remained incapacitated by their own flawed perceptions. Inside Southern Command, an intelligence officer known only as "Aleph" noticed "something extremely unusual going on—heightened readiness on the other side [in Gaza]." By that time, other intelligence agents had already observed dozens of Hamas operatives activating Israeli SIM cards, a telltale sign of an impending invasion. But the indications were dismissed. "Aleph" attempted to force his message up the command chain, contacting Haliva directly. But Haliva was on vacation in Eilat and, despite the troubling reports, did not return to work. "Aleph" also reached out to Sariel, requesting intelligence from a secret system that monitored Hamas activity. Sariel told him the system he was seeking had been nonfunctional for hours. It only came back online at roughly the moment the invasion began.

After the Yom Kippur War, the IDF swore it would never again be caught off guard. It became Israel's unwritten Eleventh Commandment, the bedrock of its military creed: that vigilance and preparedness must never, ever be compromised again. And yet, the IDF ended up blinded all over again, less by enemy deception than by the distractions it had dealt itself. Yet the worldview of Haliva and Sariel was no aberration. It was the logical outgrowth of the doctrine voiced by Haliva's predecessor and the very man who appointed Sariel to his position, Maj. Gen. (res.) Tamir Hayman. Hayman had exhibited the same stunning obliviousness shortly before the massacre, when he waved off concerns of a multifront war with a single phrase: "What matters are interests."

These two claims—that Hamas could be restrained by "interests" and that climate change posed the single greatest threat to Israel—were not random lapses of judgment. They were twin expressions of the same creed that had seeped deep into Israel's elite institutions: progressivism.

At its core, progressivism rests on a single assumption: that all human beings are ultimately driven by the same material impulses—comfort, prosperity, and self-preservation. From that belief flows a dangerous illusion: that even terrorists are, deep down, "just like us." It supposes that their brutality is a distorted cry for help. If they murder innocents, it must be because of an injustice that can be corrected. If they slaughter children, it must be poverty that drives them to desperation. If they blow up a bus or a café, surely it must be some legitimate protest that can be negotiated away.

As a result, many today find themselves endlessly searching for a silver lining of legitimacy in terrorism. There's always a grievance to appease, a wound to heal, a policy to change. What they cannot bring themselves to accept is the possibility that their adversary is not animated by deprivation at all, but by devotion to an ideology that sanctifies death. Not a hunger for bread, but a thirst for blood. And so, Israeli generals and officials trained in progressive paradigms projected their own assumptions onto Hamas. They assumed prosperity would tame fanaticism. They believed jobs and trade would curb jihad. They thought air-conditioned offices and foreign investments would weigh more heavily than visions of paradise gained through barbaric acts.

It was these ideas that motivated the absurd Israeli policy of allowing more than a billion dollars in Qatari cash to be shuttled into Gaza, passing through Israeli soil on the way. They assumed it was in Hamas's "interest" to dedicate that money to cost-of-living essentials to pacify the public and stay in power. In reality, the money simply allowed Hamas to invest more in building rocket manufacturing facilities and networks of terror tunnels. IDF generals and leading Israeli policymakers had blinded themselves to the ideology that drove Hamas: a theology of annihilation and genocide, not a strategy of negotiation or coexistence.

The same logic drove Haliva's fixation with climate change. If Hamas could supposedly be pacified by prosperity, then Israel's true threats must lie not in tribal hatreds but in transnational trends. In the progressive worldview, the first duty of any nation is not to defend its citizens but to serve global goals: to fight for the planet and advance abstract "universal values." Israel's own cause mattered less than those celebrated in European capitals and at the UN. Consequently, Israel's top brass began measuring their relevance not just by their ability to protect Sderot or Kfar Aza, but also by their fluency in the language of international confabs. It was as if TED Talks took their place alongside terror alerts, as if Israel was situated closer to Davos than Damascus.

Meanwhile, Western states taken in by these ideas were unraveling. Civic nationalism—the Enlightenment inheritance that once provided solidarity, meaning, and the will to defend borders—eroded into post-modern progressivism. Borders became obstacles. National identity became suspect. Patriotism became a form of prejudice. In this global pincer, militant Islam rose on one side while progressivism hollowed out the West on the other. Many of Israel's most influential citizens and officers were swept up in the trend. On the ground, the change was painfully obvious.

In its first decades, Israel had fought wars state against state. Egypt. Syria. Jordan. Clear adversaries. Clear battlefields. Clear victories. To win meant destroying enemy armies, capturing enemy territory, and breaking the enemy's will to fight. Israel never lost those wars. After 1973, however, Israel's enemies shifted shape. Israel's foes were no longer nation-states but movements: Hamas, Hezbollah, Islamic Jihad, ISIS, and Iranian militias. They fought not for territory but for theology. Their calculus was not material resources but divine reward. Their measure of success was not just territory seized, but the number of Jews murdered, the amount of fear sown, and the number of martyrs dispatched to the afterlife.

Israel's elites did not adapt. They continued filtering reality through the progressive canon, doubling down on foreign doctrines that confused more than they clarified. As much an enemy as Hamas's tunnels or Hezbollah's rockets was the false doctrine that guided Israel's generals: the belief that all cultures calculate "interests" in the same way, and that the global cause of climate mattered more than Israel's cause of survival.

October 7 shattered that illusion. It revealed that Hamas's only interest was annihilation. That Iran's only ambition was domination. That jihad is not a negotiating position but a lethal creed. It proved that Israel could not go with the flow of the European Union and still survive the furnace of the Middle East. Israelis were forced to look back and trace the roots of the catastrophe. And they found them not in the sands of Gaza, but on the polished tables of conference rooms in Norway. There, some thirty years before, Israel had sown the seeds of its own disaster.

Fear and Loathing on the White House Lawn

The Oslo Accords of the 1990s were celebrated by Israel's political and ideological elites as a new dawn. Negotiated in Norway and signed on the White House's South Lawn, they were cast as a bold leap into a Middle

East supposedly reborn in the optimistic glow of the post–Cold War utopian dream.

In negotiating a settlement with the Palestinian Liberation Organization, Israel was carving away its own flesh. A brand-new, twenty-second Arab state would be created. It would be led by Israel's bitterest enemies and situated atop Judea and Samaria—Israel's very biblical heartland. This was where Abraham, Isaac, and Jacob had settled; where Joshua had conquered; where the Tabernacle had stood for an astonishing 369 years in Shiloh; where Jewish kings had ruled for half a millennium; and where Jewish prophets had lived and preached. It was land wrested in war, reconquered with the blood of Israel's soldiers, and consecrated with the tears and eternal grief of their families.

The deal would leave Israel with indefensible borders. At its narrowest point, the Jewish state would be nine miles wide. The deal promised peace, but it guaranteed strategic weakness: even a small enemy army would be able to cut through Israel like a hot knife through butter. In the salons of Tel Aviv and the corridors of Washington, the accords were celebrated as a historic turning point, the moment when blood and faith would be replaced by pragmatism and reconciliation. But Oslo was no dawn. It was a mirage—a disaster dressed as diplomacy, a self-inflicted wound that would bleed for decades.

For the first time in its history, Israel did the unthinkable: it legitimized a mass murderer whom it had tried to eliminate for almost thirty years. Yasser Arafat—the man who pioneered airline hijackings, who oversaw the murder of schoolchildren in Ma'alot, who stood behind the slaughter of Israeli athletes in Munich—was transformed almost overnight. Oslo did not punish him; it crowned him. And it did not change his bloodthirsty ideology; it reinforced it. After all, decades of mass murder had paid off: the once-hunted terrorist was made a world leader, welcomed with hugs and handshakes by the President of the United States.

In that moment, Israel's government told the world—and its enemies—that terror works. That spattering Jewish blood across buses, schools, and eateries was not a disqualifier for leadership but a pathway to power. His name, once synonymous with bombings and massacres, was now printed in Western newspapers beside words like "partner" and "chairman." Soon, he was also a bona fide billionaire. With the signing of the agreements, billions of dollars in international aid began to fatten Arafat's coffers. His top officials followed suit: the Palestinian Authority, meant to be a governing body, became a kleptocracy that diverted aid into villas for its elites and explosives for its murderous militias. But the most appalling grant that Arafat would receive would come from none other than Oslo itself, the seat of the Norwegian Nobel Committee. Arafat, once a pariah, was awarded the Nobel Peace Prize. Looking back, it's hard to believe that the founder of modern terrorism and airline hijackings was awarded humanity's highest prize for coexistence. He will forever tarnish that once coveted award. And until they repudiate that putrid nominee, the hollow and amoral Norwegian Nobel Committee will live forever in disgrace.

But for all the money and acclaim Arafat pocketed in the Oslo years, nothing was as dangerous as the arms—indeed, the army—that would now be at his disposal. Arafat's Palestinian Authority was given tens of thousands of fully automatic rifles, hundreds of tons of ammunition, and whole convoys of armored vehicles. It was all for the arch-terrorist's newly minted "police force," which was in fact a radical militant army waiting for the order to strike. In doing so, Oslo did not restrain the threat—it supercharged it, arming the very monster it claimed it would tame.

More than arming Israel's enemies, the Oslo Accords also disarmed Israel of its own warrior spirit. Before Oslo, Israel's security doctrine was clear: victory. Israel fought to win. The goal was to destroy the enemy and establish deterrence by force of arms. After Oslo, that doctrine was abandoned. Victory was replaced with conflict management. Terror was no longer an evil to be purged but a grievance to be negotiated. Instead of eradicating the PLO, Israel signed deals with it. Instead of erasing its terror infrastructure, Israel gave it an airport in Gaza and a runway in Ramallah.

The reckless Oslo agreement was bitterly contested in Israel. Rabin could barely muster a majority of Knesset members to vote for it. Too many Jews remembered Yasser Arafat not as a "peace partner," but as the architect of hijackings, massacres, and a flood of Jewish blood. Too many Israelis saw the peril of entrusting the future of Israel to a man who personified terror. At the time, Benjamin Netanyahu stood against the tide—carrying the voices of millions of Israelis who bitterly opposed the disastrous deal. He denounced the illusion at its inception, warning that peace built on self-deception would become a curse. His opposition to Oslo was not fringe, but a reflection of the deep dismay felt by a massive share of the Israeli electorate. In 1996, their anger and disappointment propelled Netanyahu to the premiership. It was a clear sign that millions of ordinary Israelis recognized the truth: that the "peace process" was in fact a process of surrender.

But even Netanyahu's rise to Israeli leadership would not mitigate Oslo's devastating costs. Terror had become incentivized. Bus bombings were rewarded with more calls for more Israeli concessions. Stones and Molotov cocktails ignited more international sympathy for the supposed "freedom fighters." To Arab youth, murderers and martyrs became the equivalent of celebrity athletes and pop stars. Arab parents eagerly indoctrinated their infant children in the cult of Jihad. They got the memo, and its message was clear: violence is worth the risk.

Just as dangerous as Oslo itself was the psychology behind it. This too constituted an invasion—one aimed at Israel's very sense of identity. The target was Israel's leading political, cultural, security, and business figures. Seeking a more prominent role on the world stage, they sought to model the Jewish state on stylish ideologies—for Israel to be secular, progressive, and unmoored from its spiritual destiny. To them, Israel's survival was no longer anchored in its faith or history. It would be secured by international applause and the embrace of fashionable values.

The starkest symbol of this rupture came in 1993, when Prime Minister Yitzhak Rabin signed the Oslo Accords. In his speech, he declared: "No longer will the nation dwell alone." With that phrase, Rabin consciously inverted the Torah's description of Israel as "a people that dwells alone" (Numbers 23:9). What had once been a proud affirmation of Israel's uniqueness became, in Rabin's framing, a liability. He and those like him insisted that Israel should no longer stand apart but must blend into the global order. The Jewish nation, they argued, must detach itself from the very covenantal core that had sustained it across millennia. The future of the Jewish state would rest not on its own faith, courage, identity, and peoplehood—but on the approval of foreigners.

More than redrawing borders, the Oslo Accords sought to rewire Israel's national consciousness, to realign it on the template of a progressive false faith. And like every false deity, it demanded sacrifice—not in theory, but in blood.

In the five years after Oslo, more Israelis were murdered by terrorists than in the fifteen years before. In the Second Intifada, the toll of buses torn apart and cafés reduced to carnage buried the "peace process" beneath a mountain of funerals. Yet even that was not the final reckoning. The full price of Oslo was tallied only on October 7. On that dark day, the illusions were swept away. The bill for decades of self-deception came due in fire and blood.

The passage of the Oslo Accords marked the triumph of progressivism. Its principles were embraced not just as policy, but as dogma. They were accepted in blind faith. And the consequences were profound. This new ideology seeped into Israel's highest institutions, especially the IDF itself. Having surrendered their very minds, Israel's generals would no longer pursue total victory. They would "manage the conflict," keep the flames low, and stop the pot from boiling over.

Promotion to the IDF General Staff required adherence to this creed. Religious Zionist officers—a core component of Israel's combat forces—were blocked by a glass ceiling that prevented them from reaching the highest echelons of command. Simply put, Jewish faith and conviction were disqualifiers. Only those who had thoroughly absorbed the Oslo gospel were deemed fit to lead. Programs like the Wexner Foundation's scholarships, launched just a few years before the Oslo process, reinforced these beliefs. They offered master's degree training at the Harvard Kennedy School to leading IDF officers and government officials, exposing Israel's top brass to the frameworks of Western liberalism, rather than the realism of Jewish history. They were schooled to measure security in climate reports and economic "interests," rather than in the genocidal sermons of Hamas or the apocalyptic ambitions of Iran.

Slowly but surely, the IDF was rebuilt in Oslo's image. Tank battalions and infantry brigades, which are required to conquer large swaths of territory, were gradually trimmed down or scrapped entirely. Instead, the IDF began to shift its focus toward airpower, intelligence, and special units that would engage in limited, pinpoint raids. The sword was replaced with the scalpel, and the one-time army of decisive wars began to resemble a bloated police department with an air force. Unsurprisingly, Israel stopped winning wars decisively. Instead, conflicts were put on pause with negotiated ceasefires—each inevitably breeding another round of conflict.

The Oslo Accords also advanced a fashionable but dangerous idea: the so-called "right to self-defense" framework. In the 1967 Six-Day War, Israel achieved its greatest triumph precisely because it struck first. By launching a preemptive assault, Israel turned potential annihilation into one of the most decisive victories in modern history. In 1973, by contrast, Israel nearly perished because it waited for the enemy to attack. Bound by hesitation and the desire to avoid appearing the aggressor, it gave its enemies the luxury of the first strike—and paid the price in thousands of lives.

This shift was not military but political. Beyond stockpiles of arms and numbers of soldiers, senior IDF officials began to speak of "legitimacy reserves"—the belief that Israel possessed a finite store of moral and diplomatic credit in the eyes of the world, which could be spent only sparingly. Every strike depleted that reserve. Every operation risked condemnation. Therefore, force had to be delayed, limited, and carefully choreographed—not to defeat the enemy, but to maintain approval. Thus, a generation of Israeli generals came to believe that the real battlefield was not in Gaza or Lebanon but in the court of world opinion. Victory would be measured not only in territory or deterrence, but in how justified Israel appeared on CNN and at the UN. And to satisfy *that* quota, Israel could not strike enemies in their planning phase. It had to wait until Jewish lives were threatened—or worse, until Jewish blood had already been spilled.

The Iron Dome is the clearest expression of this mindset. Yes, it is a technological marvel, and yes, it has saved lives. But it embodies a perilous philosophy. Missiles in the hands of terrorists should never be allowed to launch at all. They should be destroyed in their warehouses—or better yet, on the assembly line. Instead, Israel built a system that waits until rockets are already in the sky, already arcing over Ashkelon and Sderot, before it responds. This is not a strategy born of strength, but of submission—the conviction that Israel's right to strike exists only after it has already absorbed blows. It marked a betrayal of the ancient Jewish legal injunction: "If someone comes to kill you, rise and kill him first." Deterrence gave way to signaling. Survival gave way to optics. The doctrine of preemption, which had once ensured Israel's survival, was abandoned in favor of a hollow pursuit of international approval. And in that pursuit, the Jewish state accepted the intolerable: living under constant fire, so long as the world applauded its restraint.

The change in tactics marked a change in spirit. The generals who led Israel's early wars carried a raw Zionist nationalism—imperfect, but fierce, mission-driven, and laden with a strong sense of identity. On the other hand, the generals of the Oslo generation were plagued by an identity crisis. They craved normalcy and the warm embrace of the world. Seeking to replace Jewish destiny with secular acceptance, Israel's generals gradually gave in to fantasy. They trained themselves to see the world through Harvard seminars instead of through the lens of Hamas's charter. They became fluent in the language of interests, moderation, and "conflict management"—but were blind to the reality of radical jihad.

All the while, Israel's enemies never boarded the "Peace Train." Terrorists in Gaza dug miles of tunnels and manufactured thousands of rockets; Hezbollah turned southern Lebanon into an invasion staging ground; and Iran openly plotted Israel's nuclear annihilation. Even Arafat himself—the supposed partner in peace—never laid down his bloodstained ways: he orchestrated the murders of hundreds more Jews *after* he signed the Oslo Accords. The political alignment of Arab populations in Israel reflected the same failure: while Israel's leaders shook hands at negotiating tables, many Arabs in Judea, Samaria, and Gaza were shifting their loyalties to radical Islamists like Hamas.

And still, Israel's military elite remained shackled to the Oslo mindset. They could not accept the regional reality screaming before them. They refused to believe that terrorists were exactly what they openly declared themselves to be: bloodthirsty killers animated by a violent ideology. Instead, they convinced themselves that Hamas and Fatah were moderates-in-waiting who secretly longed for jobs, trade, and prosperity. No matter how many buses exploded in Tel Aviv, no matter how many families were slaughtered in Jerusalem cafés, the generals clung to the fiction that "shared interests" would tame fanaticism. It was a worldview divorced from both Jewish law, which demands the eradication of mass murderers, and from the obvious realities of the Middle East. In truth, Oslo was not merely a diplomatic gamble. It was an ideological surrender that sought to reinvent Israel's very sense of self.

The disaster of October 7 was the bitter fruit of that surrender. Israel's failure was not, at its core, a failure of technology. The drones, satellites, and sensors were in place. Nor was it a shortage of resources. The IDF was funded, well-equipped, and strong. The failure was a flawed conception and an erroneous worldview. A conscious decision to trade in Jewish identity and values for secular illusions, to exchange the hard-boiled realism of Jewish history for the impractical, popular doctrines.

In a way, the war for Israel's identity prepared the ground for the physical assault that would follow. October 7 was the visible eruption of a struggle that had been raging silently for decades—the war for Israel's soul.

Following America's Lead

October 7 was not a bolt from the blue. It was the inevitable endpoint of Israel's decades-long infection with a diplomatic flesh-eating disease: the doctrine of "land-for-peace." While the Oslo Accords handed Gaza to terror and empowered Hamas, they did not create the pathology. Long before Oslo, Israel was pressured into amputating vital strategic territory in exchange for the illusion of coexistence with enemies who never abandoned their war aims—only adjusted their tactics.

To understand why Israel dismantled Jewish communities, collapsed its strategic depth, and boxed itself into borders that invite attack rather than deter it, one must look to Israel's growing dependency on the United States and its faith in the peace process. Over time, Israel's security culture was hollowed out, replaced by a reliance on American guarantees, American weapons, American vetoes, and American permission to act.

America was always linked to the Zionist cause and, under President Harry S. Truman, played a decisive role in Israel's birth. Yet for the first two decades of Israel's existence, Washington—with rare exceptions—refused to arm the Jewish state. Military aid was unthinkable.

Paradoxically, those were the years of Israel's greatest victories. In 1948, Israel beat back five invading Arab armies with salvaged Messerschmitts and Spitfires, plus Czech rifles smuggled in crates stamped "farm equipment." In 1956, it seized the entire Sinai Peninsula in roughly one hundred hours using a patchwork force of French Mystère jets and AMX tanks. In 1967, the IDF faced more enemy tanks than Hitler threw at Stalin in 1941. And still, Israel shattered three Arab armies and tripled its territory, relying mainly on French Mirage jets, British and French armor, and homegrown audacity.

That independence began to erode after 1967. As Israel emerged as a regional power, Washington saw an opening. A year later, the United States approved the sale of advanced Phantom fighter jets to Israel. American weapons began to flow, and with them came American leverage.

After the War of Attrition, Washington pressed Israel into a ceasefire with Egypt that barred Cairo from advancing surface-to-air missiles toward the Suez Canal. Egypt violated the agreement openly. Israel documented the breaches. Washington looked away. Under diplomatic cover, Egypt built a dense missile belt that would exact a devastating toll in the Yom Kippur War.

In 1973, Israel fought with American weapons and under American constraints. On the eve of war, US officials pressed Israel not to preempt. Golda Meir complied. Hundreds of Israeli soldiers died in the opening hours. The aircraft Israel had long sought from the United States were shot down by missiles that could have been destroyed had Israel not been restrained. Only after catastrophic losses did Washington authorize a massive resupply—paid for by Israel—which further embedded American leverage over Israeli decision-making.

Just as the United States shaped how the war began, it dictated how it ended. Israeli forces crossed the Suez, encircled Egypt's Third Army, and stood within striking distance of Cairo and Damascus. With both the Egyptian and Syrian armies effectively neutralized, the IDF was poised to conquer the capitals of the states that had sought its destruction—an outcome that would have cemented Israel's position as the dominant regional power. But just as decisive victory came within reach, Washington intervened. Israel was pressed to halt, resupply its enemy, and accept a ceasefire.

A senior US official recalled Prime Minister Golda Meir's anguished question to America about the war: "Why did you force us to end it?"

After the ceasefire, American demands intensified. Egypt became the centerpiece of US regional strategy. Washington believed that pulling Cairo into its orbit would expel Moscow from the Middle East and redeem America's failures in Vietnam. But Israel would pay the price.

That price was Sinai.

In 1975, the United States suspended delivery of Phantom jets to pressure Israel into withdrawing from western Sinai. Under President Jimmy Carter, the pressure hardened into an uncompromising demand for full withdrawal. Sinai was not symbolic land. It was strategic depth Israel had never possessed before. It placed vast terrain between enemy armies and Israel's cities. It absorbed shock, bought time, and saved lives in 1973. It was the barrier between survival and destruction. Sinai also housed ten Israeli airbases and thirteen Jewish communities. It gave Israel control of maritime chokepoints and oil fields that promised energy independence. Prime Minister Menachem Begin understood this. One of the great heroes of Jewish history, he opposed withdrawal, warned it would invite attack, and pledged to live in Sinai himself. Yet he was pressed to surrender it to a regime that had launched a surprise war against Israel on the holiest day of the Jewish calendar.

Begin initially resisted Carter's demands. But when negotiations moved to Camp David, the American presidential retreat in Maryland, the pressure intensified. Carter warned that the United States had exhausted its patience and that if talks broke down, Israel would be blamed before Congress and the world. As historian Lawrence Wright later said, Begin "began to realize he was going to have to agree to something in order to preserve the relationship with the United States." After thirteen days of relentless negotiations, Carter's arm-twisting succeeded. Begin agreed to give up the Sinai. He did so not because the Israeli public demanded it, but because America and the world did. Defending the decision before the Knesset, Begin explained that Israel could not survive being held responsible for the failure of the peace process. "The State of Israel could not stand up in the face of this," he said. "Not in America. Not in Europe. . . . All the blame would have befallen us." Fear of isolation overcame strategic logic. It was the gravest mistake of Begin's career—and one of the most consequential errors in Israel's history.

The consequences were swift and enduring. Normalization with Egypt proved illusory. Egypt became a factory of anti-Israel and antisemitic incitement. State-controlled newspapers, television channels, mosques, and schools churned out conspiracy theories and grotesque, Nazi-style caricatures of Jews. What Israel received was not peace, but institutionalized hostility: propaganda, boycotts, frozen relations, and military rearmament funded by American aid. Sinai, surrendered as a buffer, became a potential launchpad.

In the north, facing Syria, Begin chose the opposite path. Instead of bartering the Golan Heights, Israel annexed the high ground and anchored its defenses there. The outcome spoke for itself. The Syrian border—despite formal hostility—remained more stable than the Egyptian frontier supposedly secured by peace. The contrast exposed an uncomfortable truth. There was little practical difference between a cold peace and a cold war. But there was an enormous difference between holding land and surrendering it.

The futility of the land-for-peace formula was exposed even before Israel had finished evacuating the Sinai. In 1981, Egyptian President Anwar Sadat was assassinated in full view of the world while reviewing a military parade celebrating Egypt's supposed "victory" in the Yom Kippur War. The moment captured the delusion at the heart of the bargain: Israel was surrendering permanent territory to a regime that could not even protect its own head of state. The Arab Spring of 2011 further underscored the mistake. Egypt lurched through revolution, mass unrest, and the brief rule of the Muslim Brotherhood before settling under the authoritarian grip of Abdel Fattah el-Sisi. Israel had gambled away permanent territory on a roulette wheel of Egyptian regimes.

Worse still, Sinai became the main artery through which Hamas smuggled weapons and materials into Gaza. Tunnels, stockpiles, and infrastructure that enabled October 7 were assembled under Egyptian sovereignty while officials looked away.

After the agreement with Egypt, Washington began formalizing large-scale, recurring military aid. Jimmy Carter approved roughly $3 billion, spread over several years. Under Ronald Reagan, Israel began receiving an average of $1.8 billion annually. That figure rose to $2.4 billion under Bill Clinton, to $3 billion under George W. Bush, and to $3.8 billion under Barack Obama. The aid was meant to offset Israeli concessions and the simultaneous explosion of US arms sales to Arab states. But as the sums grew, so did the strings. American aid was always tethered to American interests.

For Israel's domestic arms industry, the results were impossible to ignore. Israel's homegrown Lavi multirole aircraft program was scrapped in part under American pressure. The largest weapons development effort in Israel's history, the Lavi was a genuine breakthrough: a fighter-bomber that was lighter and cheaper than the American F-16. But fearing competition, Washington lobbied hard for cancellation. In 1987, Israel complied. The decision forced Israel Aerospace Industries to lay off more than four thousand workers, including over 1,500 engineers, after Israel had already spent $2 billion on the program. "Nearly a decade of our lives was wiped out in a single moment," recalled production manager Dov Benjamini. "We left our families day and night, devoted every bit of time we had to this project—and in one morning, it was all over." Aviation analyst Dario Leone later described the decision as a "tacit acceptance of American dominance of Israeli defense procurement." Moshe Arens, the project's chief political sponsor, said in 2013 that had the Lavi not been canceled, the Israeli Air Force "would be operating the world's most advanced fighter."

The pattern extended far beyond the Lavi. Israel was barred from selling its own locally produced weapons to countries Washington opposed. President Clinton vetoed a $1 billion Israeli sale of Phalcon reconnaissance systems to China; President Bush blocked a $700 million deal for Harpy missiles. But the most dangerous gamble was offshoring much of Israel's arms industry to the United States. Production lines for Israeli systems were shifted to factories in the United States, giving any American president the potential power to leverage Israel's own intellectual property against it.

Alongside its arms industry, Israel's military sovereignty was itself steadily eroded. Even the appointment of senior officials increasingly came with an implicit American veto. Caroline Glick, an adviser to Prime Minister Netanyahu and a leading analyst of US–Israel relations, warned after October 7 that American aid "reduces and even erases our strategic discretion and cancels the initiative and creativity of our generals, who in any case are mostly appointed only with Washington's approval." Dr. Mordechai Kedar, a veteran Middle East scholar and former lieutenant colonel in IDF intelligence, made the same point even more bluntly. In February 2024, he said on Channel 14 in Israel: "The appointments of senior officials—Chief of Staff, Shin Bet chief, Mossad chief, and police commissioner—are not determined in Israel, but in Washington. IDF Chief of Staff Herzi Halevi is an American appointment." American pressure reached even the prime minister's cabinet. President Joe Biden informally blocked the appointment of MK Bezalel Smotrich as Israel's defense minister. As its military leadership increasingly absorbed American doctrines, Israel's operational independence was steadily hollowed out by the quiet corrosion of external control.

With the onset of America's "war on terror," it became clear that Israeli and American officers were operating under the same illusions—and repeating the same mistakes. Both countries could crush conventional states with overwhelming force. But once the fight shifted from uniformed armies to jihadist insurgencies, that advantage evaporated.

The doctrines first imposed on Israel through Oslo soon crippled Washington as well: conflict management, nation-building, development aid, counterinsurgency manuals, and endless troop surges. These approaches did not end wars. They prolonged them, draining blood and resolve across Iraq and Afghanistan. American planners assumed economic growth and political reform would pacify societies already radicalized by religion and grievance. Instead, Baghdad and Kabul ended up in the hands of extremists, despite decades of effort to prevent exactly that outcome.

In Iraq, the pattern was clear. In 2003, American forces toppled Saddam Hussein's regime in a matter of weeks. Yet when the enemy was no longer a uniformed army but a fanatical network that sanctified death and drew strength from religious zeal, America sank into the sand. An insurgency turned US bases into targets and streets into battlefields. And from the wreckage emerged the Islamic State, which at its peak controlled territory the size of Britain.

Afghanistan exposed the illusion even more starkly. After twenty years, trillions of dollars, and the training of a three hundred thousand-man army, the Taliban swept back into Kabul in just eleven days. General Mark Milley later claimed, "There was nothing I or anyone else saw that indicated a collapse of the Afghan army in eleven days." Yet the collapse was not only foreseeable; it was inescapable. America assumed Afghans would fight for a government they did not believe in. It misread tribal loyalties and jihadist convictions and built a house of cards on imagined "interests" shaped by Western assumptions rather than Afghan reality.

That same failure of imagination shaped America's Iran policy. The belief that Iran's clerics could be bribed into moderation—with cash, sanctions relief, and international respect—rested on the fantasy that ideological regimes ultimately think like Western states. They do not. To Tehran, nuclear weapons were never bargaining chips, just as they were never negotiable to Kim Jong Un of North Korea. They were destiny: a divine guarantee of survival at home and expansion abroad. These were not "Westerners at heart," but religious fanatics with imperial ambitions, convinced of a sacred mission to spread Islam by force. Believing otherwise was a fantasy—the same fantasy that imagined Hamas would trade its tunnels for access to trade routes.

In the Middle East, America had walked itself into the very Oslo nightmare it had imposed on Israel. It adopted a framework built on the belief that concessions, time, and money could tame enemies driven by radical ideology. Like Israel before it, Washington mistook process for progress. And like Israel, America became trapped in the same endless negotiations, partial withdrawals, and temporary "stabilizations" that strengthened its enemies while draining its own resolve.

By October 2023, Israel was still acting on a script already bloodied and broken in Iraq and Afghanistan. Like the United States, it retreated from hard ground, outsourced security, and bet its future on local actors who despised it.

In May 2000, Prime Minister Ehud Barak ordered a sudden unilateral withdrawal from southern Lebanon. Israel abandoned the South

Lebanon Army—loyal allies who had fought and died alongside it—and left them to Hezbollah's vengeance. In Tel Aviv, much of the political and media elite applauded. Israel, they said, had escaped the Lebanese "mud." Meanwhile, Hezbollah claimed victory. Six years later, Hezbollah carried out a cross-border raid and kidnapped three Israeli soldiers, sparking a war that cost the lives of 121 IDF soldiers and forty-four Israeli civilians. When it ended, Israel again withdrew from southern Lebanon and Hezbollah again declared victory. In 2022, Prime Minister Yair Lapid capitulated to Hezbollah's maritime ultimatum, transferring sovereign waters and gas fields in exchange for American "guarantees." Within a year, Hezbollah rockets falling on northern Israel revealed what those guarantees were worth: nothing.

Gaza followed the same tragic script. Israel's unilateral withdrawal in 2005 was hailed internationally as a bold step toward peace. Hamas hailed it as victory—and proceeded to drag Israel into five wars in less than two decades. Where the Afghan army that America spent billions building collapsed in days, on October 7, Israel's southern border collapsed in minutes.

The failure was consistent. A religious war was misread as a managerial challenge, while concessions were interpreted not as goodwill but as weakness. Winston Churchill's warning to Prime Minister Neville Chamberlain after the 1938 Munich Agreement—an accord that empowered Hitler and paved the way to world war—echoed across the decades: "You were given the choice between war and dishonor. You chose dishonor, and you will have war."

Again and again, Israeli policymakers chose dishonor. On October 7, war chose them.

To be clear, none of this is an indictment of the United States. No country has done more than America to defend the Jewish state diplomatically, militarily, or economically. The US–Israel alliance remains one of the most successful partnerships in modern history. But America is also a sovereign power with its own interests—as it should be. American presidents and diplomats are paid to advance American goals, not Israeli ones. Inevitably, that means Washington will sometimes press Israel to make concessions that serve American strategy, even when those concessions carry grave—sometimes existential—risks for Israel. There is nothing sinister in this. It is simply how states behave. The failure lies elsewhere. While American leaders may feel compelled to ask, Israel is not compelled to agree. Yet time after time, it did.

A well-known anecdote from the Reagan years captures the imbalance. During Israel's war against the PLO in Beirut, the US president was urged by advisers to call Prime Minister Menachem Begin and demand a halt to the bombing. Reagan did not expect compliance. He understood Israel was fighting a terrorist force under Yasser Arafat embedded in a civilian city. Still, he made the call. Begin, seeking to preserve goodwill, agreed. Afterward, Reagan reportedly turned to his aides and said, astonished, "I didn't know I had that kind of power."

Israel is not a supplicant in its relationship with the United States. For roughly $3.8 billion a year, Washington receives extraordinary returns: intelligence that saves American lives, missile-defense and cyber technologies that protect US forces, real-world testing that accelerates American weapons development, and a forward position against adversaries who openly target the West. As early as 1986, US Air Force intelligence chief George Keegan said Israeli briefings gave him insights he "could not have procured with five CIAs." In the decades since, that advantage has only deepened.

Other American allies draw red lines. Saudi Arabia relies on US arms and hosts American bases that protect it, yet it refuses pressure it views as threatening regime survival. Egypt takes massive US aid but flatly rejects American requests to absorb refugees from Gaza. When asked to cross lines that threaten its existence, Israel, too, could have said no. America pursued its interests, as great powers always do. Israel's tragedy was believing it had no choice but to comply.

The Fantasy Detonates

As Hamas finalized its plans for slaughter in 2023, the streets of Tel Aviv filled with protests. Week after week, Israel's main boulevards became arenas of internal rupture, crowded with flags, chants, and rioters. The immediate trigger was Prime Minister Netanyahu's judicial reform program.

In the decades leading up to October 7, unelected actors in Israel's judiciary and legal bureaucracy amassed powers found nowhere else in the democratic West. Sitting judges effectively vetoed appointments to their own court and could strike down laws passed by Israel's parliament—including foundational legislation—without any formal mechanism for legislative override. Unlike in the United States, Israel's attorney general often functioned not as the chief executive's legal advocate but as an internal adversary, monopolizing authority over what the government could legally do. Through binding legal opinions and conflict-of-interest rulings, the office exerted decisive influence over cabinet appointments and the practical reach of executive power. In a state with no formal constitution and few effective checks on judicial authority, the Supreme Court evolved into a hybrid super-legislature—or, as journalist Gadi Taub described it, a "judicial junta."

This concentration of power was sharpened by ideology. A largely left-leaning court repeatedly nullified the preferences of an electorate that, for decades, had voted predominantly for right-wing or centrist governments. To Netanyahu's supporters, the Court had become an unchecked authority, routinely overriding elected leaders. More problematic was the fact that the Court claimed final say not only over law, but over war—constraining the IDF and security services and substituting legal doctrine for strategic judgment. The result was a profound inversion of civilian control: although Benjamin Netanyahu was Israel's head of state, his authority over military and security policy was increasingly filtered, constrained, and at times overridden by unelected legal actors.

For Israel's deterrence doctrine, the consequences were devastating. During the Second Intifada, judicial standards imposed on targeted killings produced a prolonged freeze on such operations in Judea and Samaria and severe restraints in Gaza—forcing Israel into riskier ground incursions or the abandonment of actions that could have neutralized terrorists before they struck. The Court's sustained intervention in punitive home demolitions—one of the few effective deterrents against suicide terrorism—followed a familiar pattern: petitions, injunctions, partial sealing orders, and years-long delays, during which deterrence steadily eroded. Israeli justices also repeatedly intervened on behalf of terrorist murderers held in Israeli jails, imposing excessively generous standards on living-space requirements, nutrition, medical care, and visitation rights.

In practice, these measures softened the costs of violence and reinforced a growing perception among would-be attackers that the personal consequences of terrorism would be limited. Astonishingly, this pattern did not end on October 7. In September 2025, the Supreme Court intervened to mandate improvements in the food provided to the deadliest terrorists held in Israeli prisons—including the very perpetrators of the massacre. They did so while Israeli hostages were still being deliberately starved in Hamas tunnels.

Moreover, the Court asserted an ever-expanding right to second-guess military necessity in real time, inserting judicial standards into operational decisions and security policy. In 2005, it rerouted the security barrier in Judea and Samaria on abstract "proportionality" grounds, overruling military planners in the midst of an active terror campaign. In 2008, despite Hamas's recent takeover of Gaza, the Court required Israel to provide fuel and electricity to the Strip, obligating the Jewish state to sustain a genocidal enemy. A decade later, the Court compelled the government to grant medical entry permits to patients in Gaza who were first-degree relatives of Hamas operatives, overriding security efforts to condition those permits on the return of Israeli hostages then being held by Hamas.

The Court also became a preferred venue for human rights organizations seeking not merely to challenge government policy, but to force its revision. In 2018, petitions arising from riots along the Gaza border prompted the Court to reshape Israel's rules of engagement so that verbal warnings and nonlethal means became the default response, with lethal force confined to a last resort—even amid coordinated, violent assaults. The result was court-ordered restraint that allowed Hamas to test defenses, map vulnerabilities, and refine its assault plans in full view of Israeli troops. The pattern repeated in 2020. Petitions challenging Israel's restrictions on the entry of construction materials and fuel into Gaza compelled the government to reverse course, reopening supply lines that strengthened Hamas's grip on the Strip.

Over time, judicial intervention distorted Israel's strategic judgment. And it forced the Jewish state to litigate its survival not only abroad in The Hague, but at home in Jerusalem. To Netanyahu's supporters, judicial reform was not partisan politics, but a security imperative: an effort to restore civilian authority over war, counterterrorism, and national defense. A state fighting existential enemies, they warned, could not afford a system in which unelected jurists, insulated from the consequences of their rulings, held veto power over life-and-death decisions.

And yet, opponents of judicial reform saw something entirely different. To them, it was not a constitutional dispute but an existential threat to Israel's image, its standing in Western capitals, and its acceptance within the liberal international order. What began as a political protest quickly escalated into a rolling campaign of chaos nationwide.

In March 2023, protest leaders declared a "National Day of Resistance." Demonstrators blocked highways, ports, and major intersections. On March 26, following the announcement of Defense Minister Yoav Gallant's dismissal, hundreds of thousands of protesters shut down roads in more than 150 locations nationwide. Histadrut labor federation head Arnon Bar-David announced a general strike, joined by universities, banks, airlines, and major corporations. Leaders from Israel's high-tech sector declared a near-total shutdown. Airport workers halted operations at Ben Gurion Airport. The doctors' union announced a freeze of much of the healthcare system. Even Israel's embassies in the United States and Britain closed for the day. Under mounting pressure, Netanyahu agreed to delay the legislation.

The pause did little to still the storm. Through the summer and into the fall, the protests intensified—and so did the language. Former President Reuven Rivlin warned publicly of an approaching civil war. Former Supreme Court President Aharon Barak declared that Israel was facing a "grave national disaster." On July 23, the Israel Business Forum, representing the country's 150 largest companies and a large share of its private-sector workforce, declared an emergency strike.

Israel is a robust democracy, and even many on the right accepted the right of citizens to protest, strike, or temporarily withdraw their labor. But in 2023, the protest movement crossed a decisive line: an organized refusal campaign by a few IDF reservists, who publicly announced they would no longer report for duty.

In March 2023—six months before the gravest security failure in Israel's history—a protest group calling itself Brothers in Arms announced it would begin collecting signatures from reservists pledging to refuse service if the government proceeded with judicial reform. The first to act were eighty members of the IDF Special Operations Command. The contagion began to spread. By April, roughly two hundred senior Israeli Air Force pilots informed their commander that they were "freezing" reserve service and halting training. In June, graduates of Unit 8200 issued a warning signed by more than one thousand alumni: "As the destruction of democracy continues, our people will abandon the system." The crisis peaked in July, when 1,142 air force reservists announced they would cease reporting for duty if the legislation advanced, including 235 fighter pilots. That same month, Brothers in Arms claimed that as many as ten thousand reservists across the IDF had declared their intention to refuse voluntary service.

It was telling, moreover, where the refusals came from. The movement was led not by the rank and file, but by elite formations: special operations units, the air force, and Unit 8200. That fact exposed how deeply the Oslo-era mindset had penetrated Israel's security establishment. The logic was implicit and unmistakable. These units saw themselves—not the broader citizen army—as the true pillars of national defense. They believed Israel's security, and therefore its future, rested primarily in their hands.

Like so many of the dangerous ideas that shaped Israel in the years before October 7, this belief was itself a product of the Oslo era. In the decades that followed the Accords, the IDF underwent a quiet but profound transformation. Once built around mass—armor, infantry, engineers, and artillery designed for decisive victory—it evolved into a "sting" army optimized for precision: intelligence, airpower, and special operations. Within this framework, elite technological and intelligence units came to see themselves as the state's "broad shoulders." Security, in their view, rested less on soldiers than on specialists. From there, the leap was easy. If they were the true guardians of Israel's survival, then they were also entitled to judge when the state itself had lost legitimacy.

The refusal campaign simply gave political expression to that worldview. It reflected the core assumptions of the Oslo mindset that produced it: that Western approval, legal abstractions, and international legitimacy mattered more than hard power; that Israel could afford moral posturing in place of deterrence; that self-image outweighed survival; that it was better to be admired than feared—better to be in vogue than secure.

Within their own moral universe, the refusers believed they were acting responsibly—even heroically. They cast themselves as Israel's last line of defense: enlightened, progressive Israelis holding the country together while carrying the religious, the "settlers," and the "pro-Netanyahu" camp on their backs. In that story, refusal to serve in the reserves was an act of civic virtue.

The refusal campaign was not an act of civil courage. It was an assertion of ideological supremacy—placing a political worldview above the state itself. As Moshe Feiglin observed, it revealed a consciousness in which "the party comes before the state . . . a consciousness characteristic of totalitarian regimes, where the symbols of the ruling ideology overshadow the state flag." Those supposedly fighting for "democracy" were hawking the very logic of democratic breakdown. Prime Minister Netanyahu issued a similar statement: "In a democracy, the army is subordinate to the government; the government does not bend to its will. When officials in the army try to dictate the government's policy using threats . . . that is the end of democracy."

Even if the figures put forth by Brothers in Arms were exaggerated, the refusal campaign still involved only a small fraction of the IDF's reserve forces. But the signal mattered far more than the numbers. To Hamas, Hezbollah, and Iran, those refusing service were advertising social fracture. They were signaling that Israel's cohesion was conditional, that its military reliability was questionable, and that its will to fight was susceptible to internal pressure. They made Israel appear to its enemies like an open door.

Israel's leaders warned, urgently and repeatedly, of the danger of refusing service. IDF Chief of Staff Herzi Halevi pleaded publicly: "The IDF needs you—only together will we protect our common home." Netanyahu warned that calls for refusal endangered national security and urged the military to stay out of politics. But the damage was done.

While Israelis argued in the streets, Hamas prepared in plain sight. Assault courses were built and filmed. Simulated kibbutz raids were rehearsed. Gliders, motorcycles, drones, and explosives were tested. Hamas leaders delivered speeches and sermons announcing their intentions. Parades celebrated Israel's upcoming demise. Every intelligence signal pointed in the same direction. And yet many of Israel's senior commanders reassured themselves. Hamas was deterred, they insisted. It wanted jobs, permits, tourism, and stability. For too many at the top, the primary threat was no longer a jihadist army across the fence, but the judicial agenda of Prime Minister Netanyahu's government. The overriding priority became the defense of Israeli "democracy," not the defense of Jewish lives. As Israel debated itself into paralysis, Hamas moved methodically toward execution.

At dawn on October 7, the illusions collapsed, replaced by a reality more savage than anyone had been willing to imagine. As thousands of terrorists tore through the border wall, it became clear that the real threat had never been the "climate crisis," international integration, Israel's standing abroad, or the abstract debates over democratic norms. The real danger was right across the border: the terrorists foaming at the mouth while openly plotting a genocide of Jews on Jewish soil. Israel's security elites, who for so long had their heads in the clouds, were slammed into the earth by war. The doctrine of "shared interests" imploded amid mass rape, execution, and abduction. The myth of "deterrence for five years" came crashing down in the smoke of burning homes and the blood of murdered children. The progressive creed met the reality of RPGs.

On October 7, Israel was shaken awake from the Oslo-era dream state. The facts were simply undeniable. At its core, the failure was not a matter of intelligence, strength, or technology. The IDF still possessed overwhelming power. Israel's satellites still orbited. Its drones still flew. The warnings were everywhere. The failure was, first and foremost, a matter of identity.

For three decades, Israel's elites had tried to become something they were not. They attempted to build a state on borrowed Western values, a hollow imitation of progressive Europe. They sought normalcy, acceptance, and applause—to blend in rather than stand apart. October 7 proved, with brutal clarity, that in Israel such a state—and such a state of mind—cannot stand.

The massacre forced the question back onto the table: What is Israel? A hollow replica of other nations, absorbed in fashionable causes while its enemies sharpen their swords? Or a people ancient and enduring, commanded to fight for life even in the valley of death? In the very hours of October 7, the answer began to emerge. As Hamas breached the border and death swept through kibbutzim, a transformation took hold within Israel itself. Those who had been shouting at one another in the streets of Tel Aviv dropped their placards and ran toward the front. Reservists who had vowed not to serve reported for duty. Protesters who had accused their brothers of destroying democracy found themselves fighting beside them. Even at the highest levels of power, political divisions collapsed. Within days of the war's outbreak, opposition leaders set aside rivalries and joined Prime Minister Benjamin Netanyahu in an emergency unity government that included his most prominent political opponents.

Stories poured in from that black morning. IDF soldiers storming homes to save the families trapped inside announced themselves not with call signs or commands, but with the cry of *Shema Yisrael*—the ancient declaration of faith that has carried Jews through centuries of exile and persecution. From inside sealed rooms and bomb shelters, terrified families shouted back the same words. Rescuers and rescued united through an ancient biblical verse.

Thousands of young secular soldiers asked their chaplains to help them obtain tefillin, the small black leather boxes containing verses from the Torah, which are bound to the arm and the head during prayer. Army bases reported soaring requests for tzitzit—the ritual fringes worn on a four-cornered garment, commanded in the Bible as a constant reminder of Jewish identity and obligation. Soldiers sought to clothe themselves not only in helmets and flak jackets, but in the ancient garments of ritual prayer. Synagogues overflowed. Soldiers across the ranks began wearing patches emblazoned with the word *Messiah*.

A longing for Jewish connection—long buried beneath layers of cynicism, self-doubt, and identity crisis—suddenly surged to the surface. A nation fractured by politics and ideology began, almost instinctively, to knit itself back together. Israelis rediscovered that their uniqueness was not a weakness, but their deepest source of strength. Amid the most painful crisis in a generation, Israelis joined Jews around the world in embracing their Jewishness. Out of mourning came a renewed will to live, not as a hollow imitation of Western progressivism, but as the people of Israel—rooted in history, bound by faith, and united under the ancient and miraculous banner of God.

Ultimately, Israel's historic comeback did not begin in the skies above Iran or in the movement of divisions on a map. Israel's change of fortunes began with a change of heart.

After the October 7 massacre, Israelis came to understand not only themselves more clearly, but their enemy as well. Terror was no longer misread as a bargaining position or a distorted form of political protest. Hamas, Palestinian Islamic Jihad, Hezbollah, the Houthis, Iran, and Arafat's Fatah were finally seen for what they are: modern Nazis engaged in a sustained campaign of murderous extermination. Terrorists were no longer imagined as partners to be persuaded, but as enemies to be destroyed.

Even left-leaning Israelis were irrevocably changed, a transformation especially striking among the survivors of Kibbutz Be'eri. Once a bastion of Israeli liberalism, Be'eri's residents overwhelmingly believed in coexistence and accommodation. They employed Gazans in their homes and fields, welcomed them onto the kibbutz, and trusted that economic opportunity and human decency would soften hostility. Instead, that trust was weaponized. Workers gathered intelligence, mapped routines, and passed information directly to Hamas—information later used to facilitate the massacre.

In one interview, Be'eri resident Avida Bachar, whose wife and son were murdered on October 7, articulated the moral reckoning with devastating clarity: "Before October 7, I loved them. They worked for me. I believed that if I gave them everything—money, time, opportunities—if I took them to the hospital and drove them, they wouldn't want to kill me." October 7 proved those beliefs were naïve—and lethal.

Once Bachar reached clarity about the nature of the problem, his strategic conclusion followed with equal clarity: "We need to change strategy in Gaza. Anyone who wants to lay hands on your land—you should take their land." This was the precise inverse of the Oslo paradigm. Where Oslo rewarded violence with territory and legitimacy—fueling a tidal wave of terror—this doctrine insisted that aggression must carry irreversible costs. Where concessions had failed catastrophically, an uncompromising war on terror opened the path to recovery from October 7—and to redemption from the Oslo Accords.

CHAPTER TWO

POWER FROM THE GROUND UP: THE IDF ON OCTOBER 7

One man of you would chase a thousand, for the Lord your God, He it is that fights for you, as he has promised you.
Joshuah 23:10

Captain Bar Zonshein was twenty-three years old, a tank commander in the 77th Battalion of the IDF's legendary 7th Armored Brigade. Fifty years earlier, under the command of Avigdor Kahalani, that same battalion had stood in Israel's hour of annihilation and held the line in the Valley of Tears—the greatest tank battle since the Second World War's clash at Kursk. Outnumbered but unbroken, they had saved the state. On October 7, Zonshein stepped into that legacy—and carried it forward under fire.

At dawn, Hamas's Nukhba Force tore through the border fence, pouring into Israel in wave after wave. Zonshein, then attached to Golani's 51st Battalion, was stationed at the tiny Mars outpost along the Gaza border. He received a single order: *There's a terrorist raid near Nirim—Move there!* It was the last command he would hear. From that moment on, Zonshein and his men fought alone.

Improvisation became survival. Near Ein HaShlosha, he cut down a squad of terrorists. At Nirim, he destroyed two more—crushing some beneath his treads. A report of fighting at Kissufim sent him charging onward, where he wiped out two anti-tank teams at close range. Then came the desperate call: a disabled tank, its turret dead, its crew bleeding inside. Zonshein found them, ordered them to follow, and drove straight back into the fire. "At that stage we were surrounded by hundreds of terrorists," he recalled. "I fired with MAG [machine guns] and tank shells, running over dozens. Eight or nine tried to climb onto the second tank—I killed them." His radio barely worked. All he caught were fragments: *Kissufim—squad. Nirim—two squads. Ein HaShlosha—respond.*

Two direct missile strikes tore into his tank. Fuel gushed out in streams. Still, he fought on—until the vehicle finally broke down near division headquarters. Zonshein abandoned it without hesitation and resolved to continue the fight on foot. He leapt into the open trunk of a speeding jeep carrying special operators, then dismounted and sprinted through fields crawling with terrorists to reach the Mars outpost and mount another tank. He fought without pause. "I spotted three terrorists on motorcycles, killed them near the memorial garden. At the kibbutz perimeter fence, another squad—I killed all five. Two fled into the fields; I killed them too." For two days, he battled on. From Saturday noon until Sunday afternoon, when reinforcements finally broke through, his tank was the only operational armored vehicle across a nineteen-kilometer sector. By the end, he and his crew had personally killed between seventy and ninety terrorists—a nearly inconceivable tally for a single tank in modern war.

"True, we were surprised," he acknowledged afterward. "But we recovered. I'm telling you with confidence: our army's ability to withstand this is assured. We will win the war one hundred percent, wherever it is—south or north."

Zonshein's solitary struggle was only one thread in a vast tapestry of desperate heroism woven along the Gaza border that morning. Wherever the enemy struck, small bands of defenders—cut off, outnumbered, and outgunned—threw themselves in the breach. Their courage was not summoned by command nor born of orders. It rose by instinct alone. It was raw, unyielding, and elemental. The will to shield comrades, to defend their communities, and to hold the line for their nation—whatever the cost.

For decades, Israel's security had been entrusted to an oligarchic elite, managed from war rooms and command centers. But on October 7, the nation's defense was suddenly democratized. Its salvation came not from the top down, but from the ground up, delivered by salt-of-the-earth Israelis whose courage became the final barrier between slaughter and survival. On that day, when the need was greatest, that unvarnished heroism did more than save lives. It saved the Zionist dream itself.

The attack of October 7 marked the lowest point in the history of the State of Israel—and the darkest hour for the Jewish people since the Holocaust. Beginning at 6:29 a.m., more than six thousand terrorists, led by Hamas, burst through the border fence. Their invasion was synchronized with the launch of nearly 4,300 rockets, an operation so vast and meticulously coordinated that it stunned Israel's entire defense establishment into paralysis. They struck everywhere at once—overrunning dozens of kibbutzim and towns, storming IDF bases, and descending on the Nova Music Festival, where nearly four thousand young men and women had gathered to dance and celebrate life. For some twenty-four hours, Hamas controlled territory inside Israel—an area four to five kilometers deep, and in places far beyond that—turning sovereign Israeli communities into killing grounds.

The result was slaughter on a scale that beggared belief. Roughly 1,200 Israelis were butchered with firearms, grenades, axes, knives, and cleavers. The atrocities carried the marks of medieval savagery: men and women mutilated, decapitated, burned alive; parents executed before their children; women raped and brutalized, their bodies deliberately desecrated. The killers did not hide their crimes. They flaunted them, using their victims' phones to livestream indescribable atrocities on their victims' own social media accounts. Another 251 men, women, and children were dragged across the border into Gaza, their abduction inaugurating one of the most agonizing and protracted hostage crises in history.

Entire communities were erased in a matter of hours. Kibbutzim that had stood for generations—Be'eri, Kfar Aza, Nir Oz, and others—were turned into charnel houses. Thousands were wounded, including more than six hundred by gunfire. An entire nation was scarred and forever traumatized.

Relative to Israel's population, it was the deadliest terrorist attack anywhere in the world in at least half a century, and among the deadliest ever recorded. Until that day, Israel's worst single terror attack—the 1978 Coastal Road Massacre carried out by Fatah—had claimed thirty-eight lives. October 7 was more than thirty times deadlier. Speaking in the days that followed the attack, President Biden said that, "for a nation the size of Israel, it was like fifteen 9/11s." His ambassador to Israel, Tom Nides, further clarified the magnitude: "It would be the equivalent of forty thousand to fifty thousand Americans dying." For Israelis, the scale surpassed that of the entire Second Intifada, which lasted five years and claimed more than a thousand lives, compressed into a single morning.

But October 7 marked more than a military failure; it struck at the very foundations of Zionism itself. Israel was founded on a single, irrevocable promise—that Jews would never again stand defenseless. The IDF, the Border Police, the Shin Bet, the Mossad: these were never merely security organs. They were expressions of sovereignty, pillars of Jewish rebirth, and the embodiment of Israel's modern Maccabee ethos. Barely a generation after Auschwitz, the Jewish people had done what history deemed impossible. They had forged the strongest military in the Middle East and one of the most formidable fighting forces in the world.

Yet on that morning, IDF reinforcements failed to arrive for long, desperate hours. The political echelon was paralyzed. The air force—long regarded as Israel's decisive edge—came too little, too late. The Shin Bet, entrusted with stopping terror before it stirred, was utterly blindsided. The Mossad, legendary for its reach abroad, was caught flat-footed at home. As Israel's gravest military failure since 1948 unfolded in real time, the burden of defense fell not on institutions but on people—rank-and-file soldiers, neighborhood defense squads, and ordinary citizens—left to face the storm alone.

And yet, on that day of darkness, something astonishing occurred. Often without orders, without heavy weapons, and without a plan, Israel's citizens became soldiers. Strangers became comrades. The spirit of 1948 returned to the land. They stormed forward with nothing but an unbreakable will to shield their brothers, defend their homeland, and preserve the Jewish dream. In that defiance, they inscribed a chapter of courage that history will forever remember and revere.

On the darkest day in its history, the State of Israel was not saved by cutting-edge jets, advanced technology, or decorated generals. It was saved by soldiers who seized the moment; by commanders who leapt from tank to tank as each was disabled; by reservists who grabbed their rifles and raced south without waiting for the call; by kibbutzniks who stood guard with pistols, knives, and their bare hands. By local security squads who held the line just long enough to avert wholesale slaughter. By fathers who fought for their children, mothers who shielded their families, and teenagers who ferried the wounded under unrelenting fire.

In a region crowded with kings flaunting showpiece arsenals, purchased in multibillion-dollar shopping sprees, Israel revealed that it lives in a different league. Its power was not bought in the global arms bazaar. It was certainly not, as its enemies sneer, merely a by-product of American aid. Israel's strength flowed from a deeper source: the heart of its people. In those critical hours, ordinary Israelis fought street by street, house by house, and room by room against trained terrorists who often came in greater numbers and with heavier weapons. Many survived. Many fell. But all revealed the superhuman strength of spirit that has carried the Jewish people through the inferno of their history.

The miracles that followed—the rallying of the nation, the reversal of the war, the rediscovery of Israel's inner strength—did not begin with the massive counterstrikes that came later. Nor did they originate in the halls of power. Israel's comeback began that very morning, amid chaos and terror, when ordinary men and women fought with lionlike ferocity—each a warrior on par with King David himself. Through them, October 7 will be remembered not only as a day of massacre and collapse, but as a day of defiance, sacrifice, and unconquerable courage. It was the day the Jewish people, assailed by a savagery they believed belonged to the past, rose with a valor worthy of the giants of their history.

October 7 marked the beginning of Israel's second War of Independence—and the heroism it unleashed would prove no less awe-inspiring than the first.

Where Was the IDF?

That morning, a single question burned through every shelter, every besieged army base, and every targeted home: Where is the IDF? How could the most powerful army in the Middle East—battle-hardened by decades of counterterrorism, armed with cutting-edge intelligence, shielded by billions of dollars in advanced defenses—take so long to arrive? How could communities less than a kilometer from Gaza be left to fight for their lives for three hours, for ten, even for twenty-four? Those questions never faded. They likely never will.

No answer can ease the agony of that day. No explanation can restore the lives that were taken or mitigate the horrors endured. But amid the grief, it's important to counter the conspiracy theories claiming that Israel allowed the attack to happen, or that a stand-down order was issued from above. Those claims are false. And they obscure a harder, more sobering truth. The collapse of Israel's defenses that morning was not the product of betrayal, but of failure—systemic, cumulative, and catastrophic. It was a perfect storm.

First, there was time—or rather, the lack of it. Even under ideal conditions, mobilizing Israel's reserves takes hours. October 7 offered no such conditions. It was Shabbat and Simchat Torah, the most joyous day on the Jewish calendar. Soldiers were at home or in synagogue. Units were dispersed, their equipment unprepared and scattered. And as the attack unfolded, the fog of war descended almost instantly.

Second, there were other fronts. To Israel's north loomed Hezbollah—far larger, far better armed than Hamas, with tens of thousands of rockets aimed at Israel's cities. One of Defense Minister Yoav Gallant's first orders was to rush forces north. "My assessment," he later explained, "was that Hamas would not launch such a war without Hezbollah in the background, providing backup." Israel's border with Lebanon is more than twice the length of its boundary with Gaza, and places far larger cities within range of a potential Hezbollah assault. Israel could not afford to leave the northern front exposed. As a result, a substantial share of its forces—and its focus—was directed toward the north.

Third, there was the sheer scale of the assault. Hamas's onslaught was unprecedented: terrorists breached the border at 119 separate points and launched simultaneous attacks across dozens of locations—kibbutzim, IDF bases, highways, even the Gaza Division's own headquarters at Re'im. Command and control disintegrated almost immediately. The Southern Brigade commander, Col. Asaf Hamami, was killed shortly after 7 a.m., along with many of his company and platoon commanders. Within hours, the very officers meant to coordinate the response were gone. By midday, Israel's southern command was reduced to relying on civilians with cellphones to report where the attacks were still underway.

The IDF was left with only fragments of the battlefield picture. Reports arrived late and incomplete. Priorities were confused. Hundreds of simultaneous hostage situations paralyzed Israel's greatest advantage: overwhelming firepower now risked killing its own civilians. The result was indecision at the top, chaos in the field, and a deadly vacuum—one that forced ordinary soldiers, local defense squads, and unarmed civilians to absorb the first shock of the war.

But none of these explanations reaches the heart of the matter. Israel knew how long it takes to mobilize its reserves. It knew that the northern front with Hezbollah is perpetually one miscalculation away from war. It knew that border command posts and bases would be among the first targets—and that any serious war plan must include redundancy, with backup headquarters ready to assume control if the forward command is overrun. So, the question remains: why was Israel not prepared for contingencies well within the realm of possibility?

The answer lies, most likely, in a fatal miscalculation at the very top. Israel's senior leadership—from the Ministry of Defense through the IDF General Staff—had constructed a strategic worldview so rigid that it blinded them to reality. They persuaded themselves that Hamas was deterred, weakened, and absorbed with governing Gaza; that it would not—and therefore could not—risk a large-scale invasion. Hamas's true intentions, broadcast openly and without shame, were dismissed as bluster and propaganda. Its genocidal ambitions were treated as performative rhetoric rather than operational doctrine. Much as Hitler's early declarations of a German-dominated Europe were once waved away as theatrical exaggerations meant to rally a crowd, Hamas's promises of annihilation were discounted as crude terrorist posturing. In both cases, the catastrophe lay not in secrecy but in the refusal to take the enemy at his word.

Instead of preemptively dismantling Hamas's war machine, Israel's leadership chose to manage it, believing it would never be fully deployed. Action on that flawed assumption, they offered economic incentives: permitting the delivery of Louis Vuitton suitcases stuffed with Qatari cash into Gaza and issuing tens of thousands of work permits granting Gazans access to Israel. Instead of purchasing stability, the cash financed Hamas's arsenals. Instead of fostering coexistence, the work permits supplied the terror organization with eyes and ears inside Israeli communities. The problem was not strategic, but psychological. As former US Defense Secretary Robert McNamara later confessed about the errors that dragged America into Vietnam: "You see what you want to believe."

Under the perilous spell of groupthink, Israel's senior military leadership convinced itself that Hamas did not want war. That assumption hardened into certainty—and certainty displaced preparation. There was no plan B. No second line. No fallback. There was no malfunction of technology, nor a shortage of manpower. It was a failure of leadership. A failure of imagination. A failure of the mind. It was a flawed strategic dogma, worshiped by Israel's generals as an article of faith. In Israel, it has a name.

Conceptzia.

Few words in Hebrew carry the weight of Conceptzia. It does not mean merely a "conception," but a hardened worldview—so rigid, so self-assured, that no contrary evidence is permitted to disturb it. The term is seared into Israel's national memory as shorthand for the fatal assumptions that nearly cost the country its existence during the Yom Kippur War.

The roots of that tragedy lay in the intoxicating confidence born of Israel's stunning victory in 1967. That war had been decided almost before it began. Prime Minister Levi Eshkol was warned repeatedly by US President Lyndon B. Johnson: "Israel will not be alone unless it decides to go it alone." Eshkol is barely remembered today, but he should be. Though unassuming in stature, he was formidable in resolve. He essentially told the most powerful man in the world, "Go to hell." When Egyptian President Gamal Abdel Nasser closed the Straits of Tiran, an unmistakable act of war, Eshkol ordered the Israeli Air Force to destroy the Egyptian and Syrian air forces on the ground. The war was decided within hours. In six days, Israel crushed the armies of Egypt, Syria, and Jordan. But from that lightning victory emerged a dangerous conclusion: that Israel's enemies had been permanently deterred.

Six years later, on Yom Kippur 1973, Egypt and Syria exploited that impression to strike in a coordinated surprise assault. Hundreds of Israeli soldiers were killed in the opening hours. The nation buckled and almost broke. Israel was saved only by desperate battlefield heroism—by commanders like Avigdor Kahalani, whose armored brigade held the line in the north, and Ariel Sharon, whose audacious crossing of the Suez Canal turned the tide of the war in the south. In retrospect, Israel had not grown weaker between 1967 and 1973. Its leaders had simply sealed themselves inside a Conceptzia that dismissed Arab preparations as noise, bluster, and bluff. They clung to that illusion until it nearly ended the Zionist project itself.

That same overconfidence shaped Prime Minister Golda Meir's fateful decision not to strike first in 1973. Like Eshkol before her, she faced pressure from Washington—this time from Richard Nixon and Henry Kissinger. But unlike Eshkol, she complied. She did so even though Egyptian President Anwar Sadat had made his intentions unmistakably clear. In April 1973, Sadat told *Newsweek*: "Everything in this country is now being mobilized in earnest for the resumption of the battle . . . The time has come for a shock." Soon after, he announced "the stage of total confrontation." He shouted his intentions to the world. Israel heard—and chose to ignore and dismiss him.

Instead, Israel placed its faith in concrete, sand, and water. Instead of eliminating the threat, they would box it out with a barrier. The Suez Canal, Israel's generals assumed, would serve as a perfect tank trap. Behind it rose the Bar-Lev Line: a hundred-mile fortification of towering sand ramparts, reinforced bunkers, tank firing positions, minefields, barbed wire, booby traps, and massive oil reservoirs meant to set the canal itself on fire. Israel trusted the Bar-Lev Line so completely that it scarcely bothered to man it.

On the morning of the attack, only 436 Israeli soldiers, 3 tanks, and 70 artillery pieces defended the line. A few kilometers behind them stood 8,000 troops and 277 tanks. They faced 10,000 Egyptian soldiers and 1,550 tanks. At 2:05 p.m., Egyptian artillery unleashed a barrage exceeding 10,000 shells per minute. Bridges went up. Water cannons dissolved the sand walls. Within hours, 60 breaches tore through the Bar-Lev Line. The fortress collapsed almost instantly. Israel survived—but barely.

Fifty years later, history repeated itself. Once again, Israel's leaders convinced themselves the enemy would not dare. Warnings—from analysts, intelligence officers, even civilians monitoring Hamas activity—were brushed aside. And once again, rather than preempt the threat, Israel chose containment. It built a barrier eerily reminiscent of the Bar-Lev Line—another technological answer to a human enemy. This time, it was the Gaza border fence.

Completed at a cost exceeding a billion dollars and upgraded just two years before October 7, the barrier was hailed as a marvel of modern engineering. Twenty feet high, bristling with cameras, radars, seismic sensors, remote-controlled gun turrets, and unmanned ground vehicles. Beneath it ran a massive subterranean concrete wall designed to block tunnels. Observation towers punctuated the border at intervals as short as five hundred feet. Maj. Gen. Eran Ofir, who oversaw its construction, boasted in 2021: "Today I can inform the residents of the Gaza border area that there is a barrier, both underground and above ground, with advanced systems, that will prevent infiltration into Israel in the best possible way." In a cruel case of historical déjà vu, the generals' faith in this fortress of steel and concrete proved so absolute that, on the morning of October 7, Israel's entire fifty-nine-kilometer border with Gaza was defended by just 767 soldiers.

History is littered with the ruins of "impenetrable" walls. Jericho's fortifications sank into the earth. France's Maginot Line was bypassed by Hitler in 1940. And Hitler's Atlantic Wall collapsed before the Allies in 1944. Barriers, it seems, are made to be broken. Israel would relearn the same brutal truth: no wall, no technology, no theory of "deterrence" can stop a terrorist army massed at your border. When a bloodthirsty enemy presses a knife to your throat, offense is not just the best defense—it is the *only* defense. Yet to Israel's security elite, the fence was considered impregnable. The threat was seen as contained. Then, on Simchat Torah 2023, the wall and the Conceptzia collapsed together.

It was both Shabbat and a festival. Alert levels were low, soldiers were home on leave, and police were undermanned. At 6:29 a.m., the sky filled with rockets. At 6:37 a.m., the first reports of infiltration came in: 3,800 Nukhba commandos crossing under the cover of 1,400 rockets. By 7:00 a.m., waves of thousands more followed, with still more rockets screaming overhead. The billion-dollar border barrier was exposed for what it was: utterly worthless. Hamas blew open thirty-seven gates in the barrier and breached it at more than a hundred points. Nearly every sensor and remote-controlled machine gun was disabled by commercial drones dropping explosive charges with chilling precision. Bulldozers tore through steel. Paragliders sailed overhead. At IDF headquarters, paralysis reigned. Their entire defense posture had been built on assumptions that, like the Gaza border wall, now lay in ruins.

So where were the reinforcements? They existed—but they were hours away. Israel's strength lies in its reserves, and reserves take time to summon, equip, and deploy. Hamas did not wait. Within minutes, terrorists poured through dozens of breaches. Within an hour, they were rampaging through towns. By midmorning, they were livestreaming massacres. Border bases fell. Outposts were overrun. Soldiers were murdered in their bunks and barracks. Police stations came under siege. Civilians hid in safe rooms for hours—some for a day. For some, help never came. Israel's vaunted air force scrambled jets, but close air support against dispersed terrorists was nearly impossible. Hostages made overwhelming firepower too dangerous. Drones were scarce. Ground forces were still mobilizing.

By the night of October 7, the IDF had finally regained control of the border, killing more than 1,600 terrorists and capturing 149. The cost, however, was catastrophic. In the starkest possible terms, Israel's security elite had fulfilled the warning of the Book of Psalms: "They have eyes, but do not see; ears, but do not hear." Yet Israel survived—not because of its generals, but despite them. It survived because low-ranking soldiers held their ground, because reservists without orders rushed north and south, and because civilian defense squads refused to yield. Like the ragtag militias of 1948, they charged into a battlefield tilted impossibly against them. Knowing Israel had no one else to turn to, they fought as though numbers meant nothing.

Might of the Maccabbees

Like the Maccabees twenty-two centuries ago, Israel's defenders stood few against many. At the Sufa outpost, that ancient pattern took modern form in one of the war's most desperate stands.

A small group of soldiers from the Nahal brigade first heard fragmented radio reports of infiltrators, followed by the crack of incoming fire. They could not yet grasp the truth: terrorists had already reached the outpost, and they were surrounded. "Then I saw four pickup trucks and dozens of motorcyclists racing in," recalled Lieutenant Amir, who commanded one of the teams. "They started shooting at us." Terrorists surged forward by truck, by motorcycle, and on foot. Mortars slammed into the compound. Bullets ripped through the air. The outpost was under attack from three directions at once.

Corporal Eshal of Nahal's 50th Battalion remembered reaching his position and being hit immediately. "I took a bullet to the neck," he said. "I fell, and I was choking." Corporal Amit, also wounded, described the strange, adrenaline-fueled clarity of combat: "A bullet shattered a bone in my head. It didn't hurt—you just keep fighting." Then they heard the cry they all recognized: *Allahu Akbar.* The attackers breached the gate. The defenders fell back, barricading themselves inside the fortified dining hall—bracing for what they understood might be their last stand.

The defenders were outnumbered, their radios were jammed, and casualties were mounting. From the cramped room, they watched the assault close in. "I saw the terrorists with my own eyes—five, four meters away," Rotem recalled. "Every few minutes, they shoved a grenade through. One exploded beside me and shredded my right leg. A comrade tied a tourniquet and we kept going." Supplies vanished quickly. Radios crackled, then fell silent. Magazines dwindled to single rounds. Water ran out. Medical gear was exhausted. Men scavenged rifles from the fallen and rationed bullets like currency. They shifted firing positions, sprinting from one corner to another, to create the illusion of numbers and keep the attackers guessing.

Grenades kept coming. "One exploded and I felt my body burning—like I was on fire," Amit recalled. The back door of the dining hall was blown open. Once again, the defenders repelled the breach—but each assault exacted a higher price in blood and energy. Outside, the memorial near the post became a makeshift casualty point: five dead, six wounded at that single site alone. Inside, the remaining fighters huddled on the upper floor, exhausted, isolated, and running out of time. "I knew I was going to die," Matan later said. "I decided I'd take as many as I could with me." That shared resolve to hold the line at any cost bought the outpost the time it needed.

Relief finally arrived that afternoon. At 2:30 p.m., combat helicopters evacuated the wounded from the memorial site. Shayetet naval commandos, backed by Caracal infantry, stormed the post. It took three brutal hours to clear Sufa and restore control. When the smoke cleared, the truth was unambiguous: a handful of Nahal reconnaissance fighters had held the position against impossible odds long enough for reinforcements to break through. Had they faltered, Sufa would almost certainly have fallen. Their stand was raw and relentless—the small, stubborn hinge on which a far larger battle turned.

Avi Kassa, a son of Israel's Ethiopian-Jewish community and a staff sergeant in Golani's 51st Battalion, led his sniper squad against terrorists storming into Kissufim on trucks and motorcycles. Like the soldiers at Sufa, he and his men were vastly outnumbered. "They were dozens, and we were five," he recalled. "We decided we would fight whatever came. It was clear to us that if they got past us, Kissufim would be left exposed."

He was on patrol when the sirens wailed and rockets streaked across the sky. "In the middle of the patrol, the sirens started. We saw rockets and intercepts overhead. My sergeant and I decided to drive to the nearest fortified shelter near the entrance to Kibbutz Kissufim." Moments later, the terrorists arrived in waves. The squad opened fire. In the chaos, one of Avi's soldiers was hit in the arm. Avi heard him scream. "When you reach command, your soldiers become your children," he said. "I knew I would do everything, every day, to keep them safe. Even when bullets were whizzing past, I knew in my heart that if necessary, I would take the hit for my soldier." As he rose to shield his wounded comrade, a bullet struck him in the head. He collapsed, unconscious. His men dragged him into a jeep and raced toward the command post, leaving two soldiers behind to hold the line. Alone, they fought on until their deaths. Kassa would survive, after two brain surgeries, a medically induced coma, and six months in the hospital.

When he finally awoke, his first words were not about himself, but about his soldiers. Two were gone—but the man he shielded lived. "Often we operate under terrible conditions," Avi later said, "but we know the only thing we truly have is each other. These were the people I felt safest fighting beside. Even the decision to drive toward Kissufim and fight, when we didn't know how many terrorists were there, was a joint decision by all of us. We knew it wouldn't be easy and that maybe not all of us would return."

The capacity to fight while outnumbered was again starkly displayed at the site of the day's worst massacre. The Nova Music Festival became a slaughter etched into the nation's memory: 378 murdered, 44 kidnapped, thousands hunted like prey through open fields. For hours, the grounds were a killing zone—soaked in blood, fear, and chaos. And yet Nova was not liberated by battalions, or even platoons, but by twelve soldiers of the Shaked Battalion—guided in by a nineteen-year-old off-duty soldier hiding among the carnage.

The first IDF regulars arrived at 11:20 a.m., almost five hours after the massacre began. On their approach, they encountered two terrorist squads. "We began scanning the forest," one recalled. "We hadn't gone more than fifty or sixty meters before we encountered a squad. We charged—and killed them." From the festival gate, they saw hundreds of bodies. Survivors lay bleeding, hiding in trash bins, toilets, even beneath the dead. Dozens of terrorists still prowled the grounds. "The site was abandoned. Terrorists were roaming freely, armed, and still slaughtering civilians. We saw them with our own eyes." Reinforcements were nowhere in sight. Staff Sergeant Bar Kakon recalled that, for the twelve of them, the choice was clear: "We decided to go in ourselves."

They broke through the fence and came under massive fire. For thirty minutes, the twelve advanced relentlessly—maneuvering, flanking, cutting terrorists down one by one. As they fought through the grounds, they shouted "IDF!" so civilians would know help had finally arrived. "Slowly, we saw the wounded crawl out from containers, from under trailers, from Coca-Cola bins scattered around the site." Kakon opened a yellow container. Inside were dozens of civilians—some dead with horrific wounds, others still alive, hiding among the bodies. Though they were a tiny force facing scores of terrorists, the Shaked soldiers gathered survivors into a makeshift triage point, held it for two hours without backup, and kept fighting.

They were the first to secure the grounds, but they soon understood how many police officers and security guards had already fallen in its defense. Uniformed bodies were strewn across the site. Hours later, reinforcements finally came. By then, the Shaked fighters had already pushed on—killing two terrorists on a motorcycle, capturing Gazan looters with pockets stuffed full of phones and cash stripped from the dead, and plunging into fresh battles at Kissufim. Kakon was himself wounded by a grenade and multiple bullets. "They came prepared—with vests, magazines, RPGs," he said. "But they were not at the level of our soldiers."

These acts of peerless heroism were not measured merely by numbers—by how few stood against how many. They were also measured by how far Israel's warriors were willing to go: by the conscious choice of so many to lay down their lives for their comrades, to storm forward under fire while facing conditions that defy human comprehension.

Among those who made that choice was Colonel Roi Levi, to whom this book is dedicated. We first met Roi in the summer of 2014, as he was recovering from a critical battlefield injury sustained in Gaza just weeks earlier. By then, he had already fought through the defining campaigns of the IDF in the twenty-first century—Defensive Shield, the Second Lebanon War, Cast Lead, Protective Edge, and Northern Shield. During Operation Protective Edge, in the Gaza neighborhood of Shuja'iyya, an anti-tank missile struck the building where he and his men were positioned. Two commanders fighting beside him were killed, and Roi was critically wounded. Doctors fought for his life. His rehabilitation took months.

And yet when we met him—still recovering—he was already back in uniform, doing everything possible to command, inspire, and lead. We saw him near the Gaza border, where he remained close to his troops. Then again, at a ceremony for his soldiers who had just emerged from the fighting. We met a third time later that week at a hospital, where he continued to receive treatment. He made an immediate impression: soft-spoken, every word measured and deliberate—and beneath it all, the unmistakable steel of a man who was a warrior to his core.

Though he had already spent fifteen years in the IDF and could easily have retired, Roi clawed his way back into combat leadership. He returned to command the IDF's elite Egoz Unit, and later the Bar'am Brigade, which hunted and neutralized Hezbollah tunnels along the northern border. In the summer of 2023, he assumed command of the elite Multidimensional Unit—a role he would hold for barely two and a half months before October 7 arrived. That morning, Roi grasped faster than most what was unfolding. By then, he was married and the father of five. Yet without a moment's hesitation, he began assembling his soldiers and preparing to head south. One officer recalled being told the unit would move straightaway to confront the enemy: "I made a quick calculation about where it would be best for me to go in order to link up with the first force, receive equipment, and head down. I put on my uniform . . . Within fifteen minutes, we were already on the move."

By mid-morning, a force from Roi's unit reached Kibbutz Re'im. "From the media, we understood this wasn't a lone cell," Roi's radio operator recalled. "This was a major event." They advanced on foot for two kilometers through terrain crawling with terrorists until they found a way into the kibbutz. Inside, chaos reigned. Armed Israeli civilians were fighting to hold back the invasion, while police officers worked to evacuate the wounded. One of Roi's officers remembered: "There were all kinds of people in the area whose identities I didn't know—who arrived independently, took whatever they had, with or without weapons, with or without uniforms. It was hard to tell who was a terrorist. The fear of friendly fire was high. The chaos was real."

It was at this stage, with his soldiers already engaging the enemy while trying to enter the kibbutz, that Roi Levi arrived. "When we entered the kibbutz, they fired at us," Roi's radio operator recounted. "Stones exploded next to us—you're scared out of your mind. But Roi tells us: *we charge toward the fire.* I said to him, 'Are you crazy?' And then he gets up—and you follow him. If he's doing it, who are you not to?" Roi and his soldiers linked up with the kibbutz's security squad and began to advance house by house, engaging in fierce combat with terrorists. "The place looked like a war zone," the operator said. "They fired at us, we eliminated terrorists—grenades, explosives, massive gunfire. We were inside an Israeli community: houses riddled with bullets, vehicles on fire." At the fourth line of houses, shrapnel from a grenade tore into Roi, and blood began pouring from his arm. His radio operator tried to pull him back and apply a tourniquet. Roi refused. "He told me to put on a personal bandage so he could keep fighting. Then he told me, 'Wash the blood off me—I don't want it to lower the fighting spirit of the soldiers.'" Despite having shrapnel lodged in his wrist and elbow, Roi continued to fight.

Moments later, terrorists barricaded inside one of the houses opened fire at Roi's team. Responding to the new threat, he split his forces—sending one team to flank the building while he remained with another to provide cover. He asked for the radio handset and stepped forward to check on his men. As he began to deliver his orders, a bullet struck him in the heart. "I understood he'd been killed, but I wasn't ready to give up," the operator recalled. "I shouted, 'Roi, get up! Get up—we need you!' He didn't get up. A few seconds of confusion, and then I tell myself: get a grip, you have a mission. Finish it." Even without their commander, Roi's soldiers kept on fighting until nightfall, when the last terrorists in Re'im were eliminated.

Roi Levi fell as he had lived: leading from the front. In one of Israel's darkest hours, he ran toward the fire without a thought for himself, guided only by his duty to his men and to everything they fought to defend. His sacrifice was not born of rank, nor was this caliber of leadership confined to Israel's commanders. That day, across the south, the same instinct recurrently rose in Israel's soldiers: to place oneself between death and others, and to fall so that others might live.

On the road to Nir Am, a Namer Armored Personnel Carrier from Golani's 13th Battalion came under siege by more than fifty terrorists. Grenades rained down, and one was hurled inside the vehicle. Among the soldiers inside was nineteen-year-old Sgt. Matan Abergil. "We were surrounded with no way out," recalled another soldier who was there. When the grenade landed, Abergil tried to hurl it back, but failed. Then he made his choice and threw his body over the grenade. It exploded beneath him, his body absorbing the blow. For nine minutes, Abergil hung on to life despite being mortally wounded. His last words were, "I did all I could to try and protect the Israeli people." Because of his sacrifice, six soldiers lived.

At the Zikim training base, ninety recruits, only weeks into their service, suddenly faced dozens of terrorists. On duty was Staff Sergeant Eden Alon Levi, nineteen, a basic training instructor. She ordered her trainees into shelter and took up the defense herself. At 8:00 a.m., she sent one final message to her family WhatsApp group: "I love you guys." She and five other instructors were killed, along with one trainee. Two other bases in Zikim were overrun. But Eden's base was not. Her sacrifice saved the lives of ninety recruits.

Alongside such selfless sacrifice stood an equally relentless tenacity. Israel's soldiers fought not only to the last bullet, but often beyond it—fighting until the fight consumed them.

Commanding an IDF outpost near Kibbutz Magen, Lieutenant Shila Rauchberger forced his soldiers into the fortified hall to shield them from Hamas artillery fire. He then took position at the entrance with two others, bracing a refrigerator against the door. For four relentless hours, wave after wave of terrorists attacked. Rauchberger was wounded in the arm, bleeding heavily—but he kept firing. He fought on until he collapsed from his wounds. His stubborn leadership held the outpost and tied down attackers who might otherwise have joined the wider massacre. He was posthumously promoted to captain.

One of the soldiers who fought beside him was Corporal Amichai Rubin. Twenty-two years old, he had spent four years studying in a religious seminary before enlisting in the Golani Brigade. When the rocket fire began, he ran barefoot to the reinforced area for protection—then refused to stay there. He charged out with his commander. He kept fighting after being wounded in the arm. He kept fighting after a bullet shattered his leg. From his knees, he continued firing. Shot in the head, unable even to rise, he fought on for twenty more minutes from the floor. Declared brain dead, his organs gave life to five Israelis. These men became the shield between a defenseless company and extermination.

These are only a few of the countless acts of heroism that marked October 7. Each, on its own, is extraordinary. Taken together, they reveal something far greater: that on Israel's darkest day, the backbone of its defense was not advanced weapons systems, not senior commanders, not intelligence or bold strategy—but the raw courage of individuals cut off from orders, abandoned by circumstance, and still unwilling to stop. This was not the polished heroism of ceremonies and parades. It was the desperate, defiant heroism of survival: clawing forward inch by inch against an overwhelming enemy, saving civilians house by house, and shielding comrades with their own bodies. On October 7, amid the gravest failure in Israel's history, IDF soldiers wrote a testament of courage so fierce and unyielding that it belongs among the rarest chapters of heroism the modern world has ever known.

Rise of the Security Squads

In a country that has always lived on the edge of danger, Israelis knew long before October 7 that their security could never rest solely in the hands of the state. From that knowledge emerged a uniquely Israeli institution: the *kitat konenut*—the civilian security squad.

In the American Constitution, the right to bear arms was never about sport or hunting. It was rooted in a deeper idea: the citizen militia—ordinary individuals ready to take up arms at a moment's notice to defend their home, hearth, and republic. In the United States, that concept has long since receded into abstraction. In Israel—hemmed in by enemies, forged in war, and steeped in a warrior ethos—it never became obsolete.

Across the country, in towns and kibbutzim, these security squads quietly stood watch. By day, they were farmers, teachers, factory workers, and retirees. By necessity, they were riflemen and combat medics. They trained together, kept weapons within reach, and shouldered a responsibility that most modern societies could scarcely imagine: to serve as the first line of defense when everything else fails. Their mission was always stark and demanding: to hold the line in the deadly gap between the opening shots of an attack and the arrival of the army. On October 7, that gap yawned wider than ever before.

As border defenses collapsed and reinforcements did not come, the burden fell on these citizen militias. They were not battalions or brigades. They were neighbors with rifles. Parents who doubled as protectors. Reservists who slept with helmets by the door. Armed with little more than standard-issue weapons and a handful of magazines, they took their positions at the gates of their communities—and fought.

They were never meant to face an invading force. But when the army did not arrive, they held anyway. They held long enough for families to barricade themselves in safe rooms, for civilians to flee through fields and back roads, and—hours later, sometimes a full day later—for soldiers to finally reach them. In some places, they bought minutes. In others, entire lifetimes. And in dozens of communities across Israel, it was the kitot konenut that forestalled total annihilation.

At Netiv HaAsara, most members of the security squad were veterans of Israel's elite units. They had trained for infiltrations, rehearsed ambushes, and prepared for scenarios few civilians ever confront. Even so, nothing in their experience fully prepared them for what was to come. More than ten terrorists stormed the moshav, six of them descending by paraglider into its very center.

Squad commander Ziv Wolk sensed the magnitude of the rupture the moment the sirens sounded. Minutes later, a security official confirmed his dread: "Aircraft" were inbound. Then came the rockets, the burning vehicles, the flying fragments of debris. From sealed safe rooms, terrified families called Wolk and whispered descriptions of terrrorists moving freely through their streets. With calm precision, he divided his men into fire teams and sent them from one home to the next. For more than ten hours, until the army finally arrived after 5:00 p.m., the squad fought almost entirely on its own. Some wore sandals. Some carried only pistols. They were joined by a Yamam counterterrorism operative who lived in the moshav, a Border Police officer, and civilians who grabbed rifles from their homes. Together, they clawed back Netiv HaAsara, room by room, street by street.

At one moment, a terrorist crouched behind a neighbor's door, poised to strike. An unlikely ally intervened: a massive Dogo Argentino. The dog hurled himself at the terrorist, forcing him into the open. The terrorist killed the dog, but the sacrifice bought precious seconds—long enough for the squad to cut him down. Their defiance saved the community from being overrun. The cost, however, was staggering. Twenty residents were killed, among them five members of the security squad itself: Amit Vaks, Gil Ta'ase, Danny Wobek, Oren Stern, and Adi Baharav. Their names are now inseparable from the story of Netiv HaAsara, the men who drew a line in fire and refused to let their community be erased.

Just north along the Mediterranean, Kibbutz Zikim faced its own trial. At dawn, the Navy warned of infiltrators approaching from the sea. Unlike other communities caught unaware, Zikim's security squad had minutes of forewarning—and they used them. Rifles in hand, they fanned out along the kibbutz's perimeter fence, resolved to meet whatever emerged from the surf.

What appeared first was an IDF jeep racing toward the gate. Within seconds, the truth snapped into focus. This was no rescue. The vehicle had been captured, commandeered by six Hamas terrorists who had come ashore on the beach. They gambled on disguise. Instead, they drove straight into the sights of Zikim's defenders. The firefight was immediate and ferocious. Automatic bursts ripped through the morning air, echoing across the coastal fields. For nearly an hour, a dozen Israelis fought trained terrorists at close range. One by one, the terrorists fell, until all six lay dead. Still, the squad did not stand down. For the next twenty hours, until 2:30 a.m. the following morning, they held their positions. Rifles trained outward, they shielded the kibbutz as families were evacuated under cover of darkness. No reinforcements arrived. The army was tied down elsewhere, stretched thin, reeling beneath the enormity of the invasion.

In Moshav Ein HaBesor, the security squad's ability to properly confront the Hamas terrorists came about almost by accident. Only a month before the war, residents had formed a local unit to deal with a spike in car thefts. Seventy-eight people volunteered, far more than the usual eight or ten. Each night, five of them patrolled the perimeter fence, not against terrorists, but thieves.

Then came that Shabbat morning. When the first mortars fell, the security coordinator made a split-second decision: mobilize everyone. Within minutes, vehicles packed with Hamas terrorists roared toward the gates. Against overwhelming firepower, farmers turned fighters held their ground. At the center of the battle was Professor Yiftach Gefner, a physician from Tel Aviv University, abruptly cast as a combat medic for his own brother. Elad, one of the squad members, was gravely wounded. Yiftach loaded him into a car and sped toward Soroka Hospital. On the road, they drove straight into a massive Hamas convoy of trucks, motorcycles, and some thirty armed terrorists. The air exploded with gunfire. Elad was hit again. Yiftach slammed the car into reverse, bullets tearing past as he hurtled back toward the moshav at one hundred miles an hour.

Only later did they manage a second attempt, this time with an ambulance and an armed escort. The journey took nearly two hours, weaving through fields crawling with terrorists. In the passenger seat, Yiftach fought to keep his brother alive, stemming the bleeding as rounds cracked against the vehicle. Elad survived because his brother refused to let him die. The community survived by the same dogged determination. A security squad built to stop car thieves had become a fighting force overnight. By chance, courage, and resolve, Ein HaBesor had what it took to survive.

In nearby Nir Am, the fate of an entire community hinged on the split-second intuition of a single woman. Inbal Rabin-Liberman, the kibbutz security coordinator, heard the low hum of drones along the border that morning and sensed what was coming. When the power went out, she made a decision that would prove decisive: she ordered the electrician not to activate the backup generator. Darkness, she judged, could be their shield. She moved at once. Sprinting from house to house, Inbal unlocked the kibbutz armory, pressed rifles into the hands of her squad, and deployed them to preplanned ambush positions along the fence. Her timing proved providential. When the terrorists arrived, they found the gate still locked, held fast by the very blackout Inbal had enforced. Deprived of power, visibility, and access, the attackers were forced to turn back.

Less than half a kilometer away, Yamam commandos in Sderot were locked in a ferocious firefight against dozens of terrorists. But Nir Am, against every expectation, was spared. An entire community lived because one woman turned instinct into strategy and darkness into defense. One woman's leadership and intuition had saved a kibbutz.

Forty-eight members of Israel's civilian security squads, the kitot konenut, were killed defending their communities on October 7. These men and women were never meant to carry the weight of a nation. They were not trained to win wars or repel invading armies. Their mandate was modest and specific: hold the line for minutes, perhaps an hour, until the army arrived. But when the army did not come, they became the front line of Israel itself.

Tragically, they might have been even more effective had the government not stood in their way. In the aftermath of October 7, members of the security squads recounted a grim truth. When the terrorists came, many members of the kitot konenut had no weapons. The rifles meant to arm them in precisely such emergencies had been collected by the IDF two years earlier, ostensibly to curb a rise in armories being broken into and looted by Bedouin criminals. One squad member described the result without ornament: "The IDF took our rifles and left us with just a handful. We faced Hamas commando squads with pistols."

At a kibbutz in the Sha'ar HaNegev Regional Council, the situation was scarcely better. A squad member recalled: "We opened the armory, began distributing rifles—and seven were defective, completely unusable. One of our men, with full combat training, had no weapon at all. We sent him home, at least to be with his wife and kids. Others had no helmets." Bini Kfir, commander of the security squad in Moshav Tekuma, west of Netivot, later recounted that he had warned a senior officer about the removal of the weapons. The response was chilling in its complacency. There was no need to worry, the officer assured him. "Now that the barrier is built, there is no threat." In a merciless irony, the billion-dollar barrier of concrete and steel had not stopped the enemy. It had stopped Israelis from being able to defend themselves.

And still, the security squads fought with what they had. With a few magazines of ammunition and intimate knowledge of their own streets and fields, they improvised under rocket fire. They confronted swarms of terrorists larger, better armed, and more ruthless than anything they had ever trained for. They dragged families into safe rooms, covered evacuations through orchards and fields, and shielded children with their own bodies. They became a thin human wall holding back a Holocaust.

What unites their stories is not courage alone, but the way they held the very fabric of the country together. On October 7, while brigades faltered and entire outposts fell, it was the kitot konenut who stood ready. They held long enough for a nation in shock to gather itself. They kept massacres from becoming total annihilation. In that hour, they were not merely guards at the gates of their communities. They were the guardians of Israel itself.

CHAPTER THREE

DAWN OF THE GREAT GENERATION: ISRAEL'S CIVILIAN DEFENDERS

The craftsmen draw near and come;
Each one helps the other, Saying to his fellow, "Take courage!"
The woodworker encourages the smith;
He who flattens with the hammer, him who pounds the anvil.
Isaiah 41:6-7

Aner Shapira served in the Nahal Brigade's elite reconnaissance unit. But on October 7, he was off duty, enjoying a music festival while on break for the holiday. He was unarmed, wearing sandals and a T-shirt.

Twenty-two years old and the eldest of seven, Aner was a Jerusalem boy from a family steeped in Israel's story. His great-grandfather, Haim Moshe Shapira, stood among Israel's founders; he was a signatory of Israel's Declaration of Independence and later served as a minister. Aner and his great-grandfather were linked by more than lineage. The two shared a birthday, and in an eerie foreshadowing, the elder Shapira had once been gravely wounded by a grenade thrown into the Knesset. Facing grenades hurled by terrorists, Aner would earn his own place in Israel's history alongside his illustrious ancestor.

By the time the first bursts of gunfire tore through the Nova festival, Aner's commander had already ordered him to report to the Sufa outpost. He gathered his friends and fled the festival grounds. But the battlefield had already closed in. On the road to Re'im—later known as the "highway of death"—his car came under heavy fire. With his friends, including Hersh Goldberg-Polin, he sprinted to the nearest shelter. Twenty-seven people crammed inside. Aner stood guard at the entrance, clutching a broken glass bottle as a makeshift weapon. He knew Hamas fighters prowled outside and that the concrete walls would not hold forever. Still, he did his best to comfort those panicking inside. "I'm in the army," he told them. "I spoke with my commander. They're on their way."

The army did not come. Hamas did.

The terrorists began throwing grenades into the crowded shelter. Aner had already declared what he would do: "When they throw grenades inside, I'll grab them and throw them back out." A photo released later showed the scene—people lying on the floor, shielding their heads, while Aner stood alone at the doorway.

The first grenade clattered in. Aner seized it and hurled it out before it exploded. Then a second, a third, a fourth—seven in succession—each one he grabbed and flung back. Each blast shook the shelter; each time, those inside were spared. Survivors remembered the blur of his rapid movements, the impossible composure of a young man standing between them and certain death. The eighth grenade came in. Aner caught it as he had the others, but it detonated in his hands. The blast tore through the shelter, killing him instantly. Hersh Goldberg-Polin lost his arm, managed to apply a tourniquet, and was dragged into captivity. Terrorists stormed the shelter, killing more and seizing others. In all, sixteen were murdered, and four were kidnapped. Seven survived in the shelter, and two of those seized would be released in a hostage release deal later on.

Dashboard camera footage would soon confirm what the survivors had already testified: a young man intercepting grenade after grenade and tossing them out of the shelter, each time saving the lives behind him. His parents, Shira and Moshe, learned the full story from those he saved. "Aner saved our lives," one survivor said, "he was the angel who kept us safe." Jewish tradition teaches that "whoever saves a single life is considered by scripture to have saved the whole world." Aner saved nine worlds, seven times over.

Aner was in the IDF, but on leave. In that moment, he had no uniform, helmet, or vest. There was no rifle across his chest, no team covering his back. And yet, faced with the ultimate test, he did not retreat. He stood fast and held firm, a Jewish warrior to his core. His strength summoned the memory of Samson, the Israelite judge who devastated the Philistines in Gaza, not far from that shelter in Re'im. Like Samson, Aner fought alone, laying down his life to give life to a nation. Soon, Aner's name appeared across Israel: on stickers, painted on walls, etched on bus stops and city benches. For the people of Israel, a hero was born.

Aner's courage illuminates one of the central truths of October 7. When the sirens wailed and terrorists poured across the border, the IDF could not hold the front. Into that void stepped civilians. Parents and paramedics. Farmers and bus drivers. Medics and musicians. Ordinary people who shouldered the burden that Israel's generals had dropped. Across the South, municipal police became infantry and convoy commanders, clearing buildings and securing intersections under fire. Fathers armed with pistols, and some with nothing but kitchen knives, swept stairwells and safe rooms. Medics treated the wounded between volleys of bullets. Teenagers ferried families through kill zones. And some, like the young man at Re'im who hurled grenades back out of a shelter, held death at the doorway so others could live.

Aner and so many others understood their chances. They were not fighting as part of an organized and coordinated military force. They knew they were unlikely to survive. They did not know whether fighting would save anyone—or whether it even could. And yet they fought anyway, willing to pay the ultimate price.

Throughout most of history, Jews did not have armies. And yet, even as civilians, they fought—not because victory was possible, but because surrender was not. Defiance often took forms so small they barely registered as resistance at all. It could mean continuing to live openly as a Jew despite the mortal danger that choice entailed: wearing Jewish dress, bearing a Jewish name, speaking Yiddish, Ladino, or Hebrew in streets seething with hostility. At other times, it meant laying down one's life.

At Masada, Jews clung to a sun-scorched mountain fortress and defied the greatest empire on earth, knowing the end from the beginning and choosing death over submission. In the Warsaw ghetto, Jews rose in armed revolt amid ruins and starvation, fully aware they would not survive, yet resolved that they would not die on their knees. They fought so that the Nazis would pay a price, so that history would record that Jews resisted even when it guaranteed annihilation. And in countless forgotten moments between antiquity and the Holocaust—moments without monuments, memorials, or names—Jews made the same choice. Alone, unarmed, and abandoned, they chose dignity over submission. For that choice they paid with persecution, pogroms, and genocide. And yet they chose struggle anyway—if only for its own sake. In doing so, they revealed the hidden logic of Jewish survival: that those who refuse to bend the knee deny their enemies the final victory. They lived—and died—by the truth later captured by Winston Churchill: "Nations that went down fighting rose again, but those who surrendered tamely were finished."

This instinct—the refusal to submit even when defeat was assured—did not perish in the gas chambers or in the ruins of the Great Revolt against Rome. It was carried forward, generation to generation, into those who built the State of Israel and those who still sustain it.

Menachem Begin famously described himself as a "fighting Jew," a man without "trembling knees"—and he meant it literally. As commander of the Irgun and later as prime minister, Begin embodied a defiance rooted not in bravado, but in memory, and in an unyielding conviction that Jewish survival required Jewish strength. He once traced his strength to its source. It came from his father, Ze'ev Dov Begin.

One day in prewar Poland, Ze'ev Dov was walking with a rabbi when a Polish police officer swaggered over and cut off the rabbi's beard—an act Begin described as a popular sport among antisemitic bullies. In those days, a Jew who struck a policeman risked far more than arrest. He risked a pogrom. Begin would later recount what happened next to President Jimmy Carter. Despite the mortal danger, "My father did not hesitate," he said. "He struck the sergeant's hand with his cane." Both Ze'ev Dov and the rabbi were beaten brutally. But they escaped something worse. There was no pogrom. Begin remembered the aftermath vividly. "My father came home that day in terrible shape," he recalled, "but he was happy. He was happy because he defended the honor of the Jewish people and the honor of that rabbi." Begin then told President Carter that two things from his youth had never left him: the persecution of helpless Jews, and the courage of his father in refusing to accept it. He said he shared this story with Carter because he wanted the president to know "what kind of Jew he was dealing with."

Ze'ev Dov never knew what that moment would become. But the courage he displayed in a single fearless blow forged one of the toughest Jews in history—and a founding father of the first Jewish state in millennia.

An even more harrowing inheritance was forged in Auschwitz. Rachel Zini was imprisoned there with her mother, Elisheva. One day, amid the endless grind of slave labor, a Jewish woman lost all strength and was unable to stand. A Nazi SS officer demanded she return to work; she was too depleted to comply. Enraged, the SS officer set an attack dog on her. The animal tore into her flesh as the guard looked on, screaming. Rachel's mother, Elisheva, decided she had seen enough. She stepped forward, walked right up to the Nazi officer, and slapped him across the face—twice. The officer reflexively drew his pistol and trained it on Elisheva, a young mother willing to die for the honor of her fellow Jew. He pulled the trigger, but the gun jammed. So he chose another method: a brutal flogging of ninety lashes—more than enough to kill a body broken by starvation and exhaustion. She was beaten savagely, her body dragged back to the barracks nearly lifeless. She lay unconscious for nine days. When she awoke, the first words that came out of her mouth were: "*It was worth it.*"

Later, Elisheva and her daughter Rachel were forced onto a 650-kilometer death march to Innsbruck, Austria, along with two thousand other Jewish women. Only two hundred survived. At the end of the march, they were liberated by American soldiers. One of them would later marry Rachel. From that union came an esteemed rabbi in Ashdod. From that rabbi came a son who would enter Sayeret Matkal, Israel's most elite unit, rise through the ranks of the IDF, and become a general. His name was David Zini. On October 7, he personally fought entire squads of terrorists in the South. In 2025, he would be appointed by Prime Minister Benjamin Netanyahu to lead the Shin Bet, becoming one of the guardians of the State of Israel.

Rachel's mother could not have known where her defiance would lead. She only knew that submission was intolerable. That dignity was worth dying for. Yet, what began as a slap in Auschwitz did not end there. It crossed generations and returned—armed—to defend the Jewish state.

October 7 thrust Jews back into conditions hauntingly familiar from earlier catastrophes of Jewish history. Once again, ordinary men and women were pushed onto the front lines of survival—forced to fight without coordination, equipment, reinforcements, or command. Often, they fought with no realistic hope of saving themselves. They fought anyway. They did so knowing that even if they fell, they would go down fighting. Commanded by God to "choose life," Jews never seek death. But across thousands of years, Jewish history has proven something sterner still: when death is forced upon them, there is no sacrifice Jews will not bear to preserve dignity, defend one another, and refuse the quiet erasure of submission. On October 7, in the shadow of massacre and collapse, that ancient resolve did not merely endure. It surged to the surface, revealing itself once more as the engine of Jewish survival.

The struggle of heroes like Aner belongs firmly to the lineage that helped shape Israel's national ethos: Samson in Gaza; Elazar Ben-Yair at Masada; Mordechai Anielewicz and Paweł Yaakov Frenkel in the Warsaw Ghetto. Like them, Aner and so many other heroes of October 7 did not fight with a soldier's kit or in a battle group. They did not fight believing they could win. They fought to answer an ancient summons that has bound Jews to one another across centuries of exile, siege, and slaughter: *Kol Yisrael arevim zeh lazeh*—all Israel is responsible for one another. In the spirit of that timeless code, ordinary Jews raced forward into fire so that their nation might yet live.

However, between October 7 and every earlier trial in Jewish history, there was one terrible difference. In 2023, the Jews had a world-class army. And in the first, fatal hours, it failed them. Aner seemed to sense this even before he fell. A gifted painter, musician, composer, and writer, he left behind hundreds of pages of lyrics and dozens of unfinished songs. One line, written before the massacre, now reads like prophecy—an indictment of the complacency that sealed his fate:

> We fell asleep while standing,
> While they sharpened their knives . . .

The Thin Blue Line

Every pillar of Israel's security apparatus is essential: the IDF, the intelligence services, and the police. Historically, it was the IDF that met enemy armies on open battlefields or beyond Israel's borders. But on October 7, the war erupted inside Israeli towns and neighborhoods. While the army mobilized and held other fronts, much of the earliest contact with the invaders fell to those already embedded among civilians: patrol officers and station commanders, dispatchers, and traffic cops.

They fought a soldier's battle without a soldier's loadout. Many had only sidearms and whatever protective gear they could grab. They improvised checkpoints, organized evacuations, established perimeters, cleared buildings room by room, shielded families in safe rooms, and held intersections under fire until reinforcements arrived. Police Commander of the Negev Region Eyal Azulai later said:

> This is why I keep repeating it again and again: the police saved the State of Israel. This is not a cliché. I was there. I almost paid with my life—me and our officers. Not a single one ran away. Everyone, the entire district, the entire region, and even officers from outside came and fought. They joined the battle.

On October 7, Israel's defenders wore not only the legendary olive-green uniforms of the IDF. They were also wearing blue.

At dawn on the day of the massacre, thousands were still dancing at the Nova festival near Re'im when the rocket sirens began to sound. Lt. Col. Nivi Ohana, commander of the Ofakim police station and the officer in charge of security at the festival, had just finished his night shift. Seeing the rockets streaking overhead, he made a split-second decision: "I decided to stop the music," Ohana recalled. "I told the people that the party was over, and we needed to leave quickly." He also set up fast lanes on a nearby highway to expedite the evacuation. Most of Nova's nearly four thousand attendees and personnel managed to escape. According to a later investigation, Ohana's decision likely spared some two thousand lives.

Ohana had tried to warn the IDF of the dangers of holding a party so close to Gaza. He was rebuffed. The IDF even dismissed his requests for soldiers on site, promising only "spatial" security from a distance. So, he acted on his own. He placed forty-two officers at the festival, including eight from the anti-riot police unit, Yasam.

When the invasion began, those reinforcements would form the battle line holding back legions of terrorists. By 7:00 a.m., as terrorists poured across the border, police and private security formed a makeshift checkpoint at the festival gate. Outgunned and outnumbered—handguns against assault rifles, grenades, and RPGs—they fought for hours to slow the attack. Sgt. Maj. Aaron Arthur Markovich was shot but kept firing until his ammunition was gone; only then was he killed. Sgt. Maj. Yulia Vakser, still holding the line, phoned the IDF Southern Command: "The remaining revelers are about to be killed," she warned. Half an hour later, she herself was dead. Elsewhere, two police officers and an IDF officer clustered near a disabled tank, defending fifty trapped partygoers for hours until rescue came.

Hearing that Ofakim was under attack, Ohana had already rushed back to the city—straight into another battlefield. He joined his officers in the streets. "I recognized my police officers, some of them wearing flip-flops or in their underwear, and next to them were civilians armed with knives who joined them—they just jumped out of the house," he recounted. Wounded by shrapnel and knocked unconscious, he was evacuated to a hospital. Within hours, Ohana returned with his shoulder dislocated and wounds still fresh. He took command. He only later discovered the impact of his earlier insistence on additional police presence at the party—and that so many of those very officers had been killed fighting Hamas. The toll at Nova was devastating. Yet amid the failures of that day, the police stood and fought. Their courage blunted the massacre and saved countless lives.

In Nahal Oz, providence placed a small, elite team of Israeli police officers inside the kibbutz. All would be killed or wounded, but their struggle would save the kibbutz from being completely overrun. When 180 Hamas terrorists stormed into Nahal Oz, the community's security squad was nearly defenseless. Their rifles were locked in the kibbutz armory, inaccessible because of the power outage. But eleven undercover officers from the Border Police's elite Yamas unit were stationed inside the kibbutz in preparation for the weekly riots on the Gaza border.

On their way to link up with security chief Eyal Fiorentino, the Yamas officers encountered terrorists outside the fence. The unit split up. Six engaged the enemy directly, while five pressed forward. At 7:15 a.m., terrorists broke into the kibbutz. The Yamas fighters met them head-on, killing many in close combat. In the fierce exchange, Fiorentino and First Sgt. Shlomo Yaakov Krasniansky were killed, and the rest of the team was wounded. For three hours, the surviving Yamas officers joined the deputy security chief, fighting street by street. They managed to block most of the first wave of terrorists and slow the assault.

Their resistance prevented an immediate massacre. But some terrorists broke through and targeted the homes of its elderly residents. Shlomo Ron, one of the kibbutz founders, sacrificed himself to save his wife, daughters, and grandson: he sat in his living room, giving the appearance that he was alone, while his family hid in the safe room. The terrorists shot him dead but did not search further, leaving his family undiscovered. By 10:00 a.m., a second wave of terrorists forced their way in. Over the following hours, they carried out murders and abductions, livestreaming their crimes on stolen phones. Seventeen-year-old Tomer Arava Eliaz, a resident of the kibbutz, was coerced at gunpoint to lure neighbors from their homes by telling them it was safe to come out. Hamas repeated this tactic across the communities they overran—forcing hostages to trick fellow residents into exiting their safe rooms.

At 12:05 p.m., a Jeep carrying five Israeli soldiers encountered a group of terrorists on the approach to the kibbutz. They engaged immediately, killing at least five of the attackers. Outnumbered and exposed, three soldiers—Maj. Chen Buchris, Lt. Yiftach Yavetz, and Staff Sgt. Afik Rosenthal of the elite Maglan commando unit—were killed holding their ground against overwhelming force. The two surviving soldiers continued to fight and radio for backup, buying precious time. Together, the soldiers delayed the attackers long enough for reinforcements to arrive. At 1:15 p.m., a force of seventy Maglan troops finally reached the kibbutz.

By day's end, thirteen civilians were murdered in Nahal Oz, including two members of the security squad and two foreign nationals, along with four police. Eight civilians were taken hostage. Tragic as this toll was, it would have been far greater without the courage of the Yamas officers, the local defenders, and the Maglan commandos who refused to abandon their posts. According to the IDF investigation, an estimated eighty terrorists were killed in and around Nahal Oz. Though Hamas succeeded in murdering and abducting residents, their plan to overrun the kibbutz was thwarted by determined resistance. At no point was Nahal Oz fully under their control.

Perhaps the most consequential battle fought by Israel's police on October 7 took place in Sderot, the largest city to be infiltrated. With thirty five thousand residents, Sderot is the urban heart of the Gaza border region. Though only 1.2 kilometers from the border fence, the city was unprepared for a terrorist incursion.

Within half an hour of breaching the border, Hamas terrorists surged into Sderot. The IDF's warning of infiltration arrived virtually at the same moment as the terrorists themselves. The city's security squad had not trained for two years, and like other local units, its rifles had been taken away by the army over fears of theft. They faced an invasion with pistols. City officials sent an SMS warning of the infiltration, but many Sabbath-observant residents never saw it in time. As late as 9:00 a.m., worshippers were still walking to synagogue, even as death squads roamed the streets. Forty-one terrorists entered the city, murdering civilians at will—including thirteen retirees on their way to the Dead Sea. They were gunned down beside a locked shelter that had malfunctioned and failed to open.

Because Sderot was the largest town breached, word spread rapidly across social media. More than 1,000 armed Israelis from across the country rushed to the city. It was a remarkable show of solidarity, but it also caused chaos, clogging roads while complicating command and control.

The fiercest fighting in Sderot occurred at its police station. Twenty-six terrorists stormed the building. An officer on the roof shot four, but the rest charged inside, killing anyone they encountered and driving the survivors to the roof. Two rescue attempts failed. Eventually, Yamam commandos seized the first floor of the police station, evacuating the wounded. The officers trapped on the roof were lifted off by a firefighting crane. With the building cleared of all police, an urban siege began. The terrorists, entrenched inside, turned the reinforced station into a firing point. Police commanders, coordinating with IDF elements, imposed a cordon and initiated Yamam's "pressure-cooker" procedure—escalating fire to smoke out the terrorists barricaded inside. Breakout attempts were cut down with anti-armor rockets and precision fire. Near midnight, with terrorists still dug in, the order was given to level the station. Drones, tanks, helicopter strikes, and finally bulldozers brought the building down. By the next morning, the station and the city were cleared.

To the west, two separate battles prevented hundreds of additional terrorists from entering Sderot. According to investigations, those forces had planned a mass slaughter in the city and a push north toward central Israel.

The cost was grievous. Over October 7 and the days that followed, Sderot lost seventy-three residents. Yet of the forty-one terrorists who infiltrated the city, all were killed or captured. The stand at Sderot kept the massacre from spreading and stopped roaming death squads from driving farther north.

In the months that followed, the shattered police station was transformed into a memorial: eighteen pillars built from its ruins, enshrining the day when police officers held the line for a city under siege.

Plainclothes Heroes

The Hamas assault on Kibbutz Nahal Oz—the same community where the eleven Yamas officers had made their intrepid stand—began with an artillery barrage. Miki—a member of the kibbutz, armed with a pistol and seven magazines—put his wife and young daughter in the safe room. When word spread that terrorists were inside the community, he loaded his weapon and prepared for the worst. Terrorists were soon breaking into his home.

The first window shattered. Miki fired through the glass, cutting down the men trying to force their way in. Another squad tried a second entry. Again, Miki was faster. Then came the escalation: an RPG slammed into the front door, ripping it from its frame. A dozen armed men stormed inside. Miki positioned himself behind a small concrete wall at the entrance to the safe room, firing with an icy calm that belied the chaos. "The volume of fire directed at me was enormous," he recalled. "Something unbelievable." For ninety minutes, he held the line, killing or wounding every fighter who tried to reach the shelter.

"You have this feeling that no one is coming," he remembered. "You don't know what's happening around you. All you hear are the screams of your neighbors."

When a stun grenade went off, Miki was forced into the safe room with his family. Crawling through smoke and glass, he dragged himself inside, pistol still in hand, clinging to the door handle to keep it closed as gunfire raked the walls. The terrorists tried a different tactic. They brought hostages, including neighbors, who were forced to tell Miki that it was safe to come out. One refused to play his part. Risking his life, he told the truth: it was a trap. The terrorists then shifted tactics, offering a bargain—Miki's surrender in exchange for his family's lives. "They told me, 'Come out, we don't touch women and children—you can be sure of that,'" he recalled. Miki stalled, feigning weakness: "I told them I was bleeding, that I needed to bandage myself." In truth, he was buying time and setting a trap of his own.

Peering through a crack, he saw a terrorist standing outside with an RPG. Miki challenged him: "Why are you holding an RPG if I'm about to come out? That's not what we agreed." The man hesitated, then said, "You're right. I'll start putting it down when you open the door." Miki rattled the handle, making noises as if unlocking it. The terrorist bent to set aside his weapon. In that instant, Miki threw open the door and unleashed a storm of fire. The terrorist fell. The rest fled. When IDF forces finally reached the kibbutz that afternoon, Miki, his wife, and their daughter were alive. On his own, Miki had taken down twelve to fourteen terrorists.

On October 7, Israel's civilians joined soldiers and police to defend their families. As Miki proved, they fought no less ferociously.

In the same kibbutz, another tale of valor began to unfold. Noam Tibon had retired from the IDF. He was a major general in the reserves, so he had a background in combat operations. But on that day, he was a father trying to save his son. That morning, his phone buzzed with a desperate call: his son and his family were trapped, surrounded by dozens of terrorists. Tibon told them to stay silent. He set off in his car. When he told other IDF generals about the situation, they told him they were aware and were on the way. That phrase—"on the way"—surprised Noam, because Israel's vaunted military should already have been there. "Something in my heart told me, 'Noam, you have to go there.'" At the entrance to the kibbutz, he stumbled into a battle between the Maglan soldiers and Hamas terrorists. Without hesitation, he took a rifle and helmet from a fallen soldier and joined the fight. In an instant, the retired general was once again a warrior.

He fought his way toward his son's home, but along the road, he found two wounded men. He stopped, evacuated them, and went back into the fire. Meanwhile, his family's pleas kept flashing on his phone. Still, he pressed on, joining a paratrooper unit in the grueling task of clearing houses, room by room. Only when the area was secured did he unlock his son's safe room and free his family. For him, the line between father and commander was blurred, but his instinct was clear: first the mission, then himself.

The stories of Miki and Noam are stunning examples of the latent strength that lives within the people of Israel. When entire towns were left to fend for themselves, it was ordinary civilians—farmers and fathers, mothers and teenagers, even retirees—who rose to the fight. In defending and rescuing their friends, families, and neighbors, they did more than save lives. They shouldered the very survival of the nation.

In Kibbutz Be'eri, one of the hardest-hit communities on October 7, just twenty-six armed Israelis faced an onslaught of some 340 terrorists. Half were members of Shaldag, one of the IDF's most elite units. The other half were civilians. Ordinary Israelis fought shoulder to shoulder with commandos—and fit right in. Outnumbered by more than ten to one, they held the line as long as humanly possible. But within a few hours, much of the kibbutz lay overrun. In those hours of terror, as homes burned and shelters were breached, it was neighbors, medics, and citizens from across the country who fought to save lives in the most horrific circumstances imaginable.

In an act of unparalleled valor, Captain (res.) Elhanan Kalmanson, an off-duty Mossad agent, and his brother Menachem traveled to Be'eri from central Israel to help the struggling kibbutz. Their nephew, Itiel, later joined them. Finding an abandoned IDF armored vehicle, the trio used it to make an ad hoc family rescue team. Over the next fifteen hours, they evacuated more than one hundred residents from burning homes and shelters, often under direct fire. Itiel recalled the fighting:

> It was insane—volleys of shells from our tanks, their anti-tank missiles, rockets falling, attack helicopters firing, grenades. Usually, you first take out the threat and then evacuate people, but Elhanan . . . understood immediately that the situation was different and we couldn't wait until the fighting was over.

A survivor would later write of Elhanan: "He arrived like an angel and immediately instilled confidence in us. His face will remain etched in my heart forever." The next day, Elhanan stayed to finish the fight. Leading the way into the last house to be cleared, he was killed in action—sealing his mission with his life.

In Be'eri, where 10 percent of the community was massacred that day, Elhanan's story became a symbol of selfless courage. He and others in Be'eri were not ordered to risk their lives. They were compelled only by the conviction that, in Israel's darkest hour, there was no choice but to serve. In the depths of death and destruction, they understood that their duty was to rescue and to heal.

Amit Mann was a twenty-two-year-old medic with Magen David Adom living in Be'eri. For seven hours, she fought a different kind of battle—keeping hearts beating and lungs breathing while the walls shook around her. When the attack began, she rushed to the kibbutz clinic under fire to help care for the wounded who had been brought there. Caring for others was her calling; she had dreamed of becoming a paramedic since childhood. In the clinic, she worked the radios, calling repeatedly for relief and reinforcements, refusing to abandon her post even as the explosions drew closer. All the while, she sent short, urgent text messages to her sisters, a mixture of medical updates and pleas for help. Her final text was simple and devastating: "They're here, in the clinic. I don't think I'll make it out of here. I love you." At 2:00 p.m., the terrorists burst in. They shot the patients on their beds, the staff at their stations, and Amit herself. She died as she had lived—in service to others, her hands still stained with the work of saving lives.

Another heartbreaking story occurred at the Nova festival, where Liron Barda, a bar manager, stayed at the scene of the massacre to help tend to the wounded. Her friends begged her to flee. She refused, saying she had to stay behind to tend the wounded. She tied tourniquets, started IV lines, and poured everything she had into saving those around her. The last photo taken of her shows her bending over an injured young woman who was lying on a stretcher. As the terrorists closed in on the makeshift command post where they were sheltering, people shouted at her to run. Liron turned to the woman she was caring for and told her, "I'm staying with you." Liron and the woman were both killed. Like Amit in Be'eri, Liron gave up her life to be the last line of care for those who could not move on their own.

As in Be'eri and at Nova, so too across Israel, ordinary civilians stepped forward as the nation's first responders. One was Rami Davidian, a farmer from Moshav Patish. That morning, he received a call from a friend begging him to rescue his son trapped at the music festival. Rami jumped into his pickup truck and drove straight toward the inferno. Along the way, he began scooping up others—dazed, bleeding, stumbling through orchards. Survivors waved from the fields, desperate for rescue. Rami loaded them in, then turned back again. Soon, neighbors joined him. Together, they improvised a command post amid the chaos. His pickup truck became an ambulance. The roads weaving through local farms became evacuation routes. Wave after wave of young men and women were ferried out of the killing fields.

At one point, he came face-to-face with the terrorists. "I got a call from a young woman named Amit who begged me to save her. When I reached her, she was already surrounded. I spoke to them in Arabic, told them my name was Abu Rami and that soldiers were on the way." Incredibly, they believed him. He sped her to safety. That same day, his niece, eighteen-year-old soldier Ofir Davidian, was killed fighting terrorists. Even amid incomprehensible grief, her father—Rami's brother—kept working the improvised rescue line. Even mourning could not stop the mission. Even as families bled, they fought to save others.

Other civilian heroes who emerged that day were barely adults. Eighteen-year-old Noam David, a student in a pre-military academy, had nothing but a white T-shirt, an old helmet from the Yom Kippur War, and a battered pickup. At 7:00 a.m., when rockets screamed overhead, his headmaster shouted that Hamas was on the move. By 7:30 a.m., Noam was driving south, directly into the storm.

He had no training, no armor, and no orders. What he did have: grandparents who fled the Holocaust, parents who built a life in Israel, and a brother who had recently sworn his IDF oath at the Western Wall. Noam felt all of it converge into one instant. "This is why I was raised," he thought. "This is why I was taught. For this moment." Over and over again, he drove commandos into battle and ferried the wounded back out. He saved a rabbi's wife. He rescued a soldier shot through the face. He transported the bodies of fishermen murdered on Zikim beach. He picked up a Kalashnikov from a dead terrorist just to feel less naked on the roads. "A year ago," he would recall, "I did the Shayetet [Naval Commando] tryout carrying sandbags. This time, it was corpses."

His truck became an unstoppable lifeline. On one run, he helped evacuate a pregnant woman already in labor, her family packed into the truck. A little boy asked his father, "Why did the bad men do this to us?" The father whispered, "Sweetheart, I don't know." Noam drove on through fire and smoke. At eighteen, in a white shirt, he became what Israel has always depended on in its darkest hours: an ordinary kid transformed into a hero because there was no other choice.

Across the south that day, such stories multiplied—civilians diving headfirst into danger to help strangers. These were not isolated flashes of heroism. On the ground, they were becoming the overarching and emergent theme of the day.

Eyes on the Ground

For decades, Israel's intelligence services wore legend like armor. The Mossad and the Shin Bet were spoken of as invisible giants. They slipped into enemy capitals, intercepted plots across distant borders, and ran agents in hostile territory. Israelis grew up with a quiet confidence: in a bunker or a command center somewhere, someone was always watching. Someone always knew. Someone was in control.

On October 7, that confidence came crashing down. The most sophisticated intelligence apparatus in the Middle East, and possibly the world, failed to foresee the deadliest attack in Israel's history. When fences were breached and the skies filled with rockets, no satellite or drone or whispered tip delivered the warnings that should have come. For the first time in a generation, those sworn to guard Israel found themselves unable to respond.

When Israel's intelligence agencies faltered, ordinary people filled the void. Neighbors with no agent networks and no formal training became the country's eyes and ears when it mattered most. They interrogated captives, cracked enemy communications, and pulled vital information from the chaos. It was not elegant. It was urgent, improvised, and human. And in those first chaotic hours, it was a game changer.

At the start of their attack, Hamas troops broke into the Gaza Division headquarters, cutting off all communications. The division commander, besieged within the base with his family, could not speak with other units. Nor could he communicate with his superiors or the air force. In those first crucial hours, the higher echelons—at Southern Command headquarters in Beersheva and the IDF General Staff headquarters in Tel Aviv—were not aware of the extent of the attack or where it was unfolding. Instead, they relied on civilian calls for help to understand where the Hamas invaders were carrying out their massacres.

One of the most remarkable of them was Druze mother Nasrin Yosef of Moshav Yated. That morning, she and her family huddled in the safe room as gunfire closed in. Her husband told her, "No one leaves." He put on his uniform and slipped out the back to join the security squad, even though he had a broken leg in a cast. Members of the squad managed to capture some of the attackers alive, and Nasrin decided to use her fluent

Arabic to interrogate them. She grabbed one by the neck, looked him in the eyes, and demanded, “Look at me. I’m not afraid of you. Where did you come in from?” Stunned by her audacity, the attacker pointed toward a section of the fence where they had broken in.

Switching from fury to cold composure, she used a bluff to bargain. “You have a wife, children—don’t you want to see them again? Tell me where the others are.” She promised the terrorist that she would give him money, food, and gold. He broke: the others were hiding in nearby caravans. Nasrin passed the tip to the security squad, and they swept the area. They captured more terrorists, bound their hands, and brought them to her garden.

Then, as darkness fell, a terrorist’s phone rang: the contact read “El-Ayyash.” Nasrin demanded the code to his phone, seized the device, and answered the call herself. Calmly, she posed as an ally: “This isn’t Mohammed. This isn’t Wadiya. It’s Nasrin. I’m one of you. I have a safe house. Your men are here with me.” A Hamas commander on the line pressed her for proof. She handed the phone to the terrorist, who reassured him: “She’s protecting us, hiding us from the army.” Convinced, the caller spilled locations in Rafah, boasting of hundreds more joining the invasion, and added a chilling line: “Tonight we will conquer Israel.” Every word went straight to the IDF officer beside her.

“I choked up and hung up,” she said later. “I told the officer, ‘I can’t do this anymore.’ Even in my worst nightmare, I never imagined I would be speaking on the phone with a Hamas man in my own language.”

Nasrin’s garden had become a makeshift intelligence post. A mother, untrained and improvising under fire, produced the actionable intelligence the nation’s agencies had failed to provide. By doing so, she helped save her community. She lost close friends that day, yet her courage saved hundreds. “If I hadn’t gone outside, interrogated and talked,” she said, “most of our community would not be here now.”

The city of Sderot witnessed another kind of improvisation: an off-duty Shin Bet officer who turned a terrorist’s own radio into the intelligence weapon that decided the battle. The man, identified only as A., was a field operations officer in the Southern District. He had no orders that morning and no chain of command guiding him. He simply heard the sound of war and ran toward it. What he found was carnage: bodies on the pavement, a soldier fleeing for his life, a group of elderly civilians massacred on their way to the Dead Sea. At the heart of it all, the Sderot police station was under siege—terrorists barricaded inside with explosives at the doors and snipers covering the exits.

Clusters of civilians, medics, and scattered soldiers stood paralyzed. A. took charge. He deployed them in a perimeter around the station, determined to keep the attackers boxed in. They fought to reach the wounded, among them the Southern District's own police commander, bleeding but still fighting. Reinforcements trickled in—another Shin Bet agent and a medic from United Hatzalah. The medic was shot by a sniper while trying to treat a casualty. Trying to help the medic, A. noticed an abandoned terrorist pickup truck down the street. Thinking it might contain medical equipment, he sprinted through fire and rifled through the wreckage. He brought back bandages for the medic—and a radio the terrorists left behind. The bandages saved the medic's life. The radio helped save the city.

He passed the radio to a colleague fluent in Arabic. Together, they tapped into Hamas's live chatter. Suddenly, the fog lifted. Every movement, ambush, and maneuver was being broadcast in real time. For the first time since dawn, the defenders of Sderot knew exactly what they were facing. "That intelligence was the game changer," A. said later. "We gathered information from the terrorists' own radio. It broke the battle in our favor." With that stolen channel, they cut off reinforcements, anticipated ambushes, and managed to keep the terrorists boxed inside the police station until Israeli reinforcements arrived. The crucial intelligence that escaped drones, satellites, and analysts alike was uncovered by a lone field officer, wrested from the wreckage of a truck.

Where Nasrin and A. provided insight in the heat of battle, another civilian delivered warnings that could have stopped October 7—if anyone had listened. His name was Rafael Chayon, a forty-year-old resident of the southern city of Netivot. For more than a decade, he had run a volunteer network of twenty-six civilians who listened, decoded, and tracked enemy signals along Israel's borders. He drew no salary and held no badge. But time and again, he picked up signs that others missed.

Already in 2019, he had warned: Hamas is preparing to seize Israeli communities. Repeatedly, he raised the alarm. But officials dismissed him. "Impossible," they told him. "They're not capable of it. Pure fantasy." In May 2023, the Communications Ministry even stripped him of the radio gear he had been using. It was the same gear the ministry had previously approved. Inspectors came to his home a few weeks before October 7 to ensure he wasn't interfering with their own surveillance. On September 12, 2023, less than a month before the invasion, Chayon outlined the details of a possible Hamas naval commando raid—exactly, step for step, the kind of assault that would unfold weeks later in Zikim. Nobody listened.

Then came the day itself. Even without his equipment, Chayon became a one-man war room. He spoke with desperate families in Be'eri, Nahal Oz, and Kfar Aza. He connected rescue forces to Kibbutz Holit, enabling an evacuation that saved everyone there. He was on the phone with the deputy commander of Maglan just three minutes before the officer was killed. Under fire, he guided troops to trapped civilians. By nightfall, he had personally helped direct the rescue of thirty-one people, including a senior security official. "I lost thirty-seven friends," he said later. "People I had spoken to minutes before. The line just went dead."

For Chayon, the tragedy was doubled: not just the massacre itself, but the knowledge that it could have been prevented had his warnings been heeded. "If I had my gear," he said bitterly, "this event could have been prevented." In the days after, the state came back to him. His equipment was returned. Ministers visited. The army reconnected. Today, he commands a network of more than forty volunteers, monitoring not just Gaza but Lebanon, Jordan, Egypt, and Iran.

October 7 revealed a brutal paradox: the larger and more sophisticated the system, the more complete its failure. Intelligence headquarters froze. Command chains stalled. Screens filled with data, but no one moved fast enough to translate knowledge into action. And so the burden shifted downward. On the ground, in backyards and on burning streets, ordinary individuals filled in for senior intelligence chiefs. They acted without clearance and without waiting for someone to tell them what to do. They read the moment, trusted their instincts, and moved. Because of them, entire towns and neighborhoods were spared, and dozens lived to be reunited with their families.

Israel's enemies had hoped to prove that the Jewish state could be caught off guard, to strip its once-mythic guardians of their aura of invincibility. But Hamas also discovered something it had not anticipated. Even without the full machinery of its famed intelligence agencies, Israel could still generate intelligence as raw as it was potent. It came not from headquarters, but from the fearless work of plainclothes heroes—mothers, off-duty officers, and citizen spies. Their work was unofficial and off the books. But it was decisive. It saved towns. It saved lives. And it proved a final truth: when Israel's institutions failed, its people did not.

CHAPTER FOUR

MOBILIZE, O ISRAEL: A NATION GOES TO WAR

Hark! a tumult on the mountains,
As of a mighty force . . .
God of Hosts is mustering,
A host for war.
Isaiah 13:4

On the morning of October 7, as the first images of slaughter from Israel's south spread across phones and television screens, Prime Minister Benjamin Netanyahu addressed the nation. He spoke directly into the lens, without ornament or hesitation. "Citizens of Israel," he said. "We are at war. Not an operation. Not a round." He then repeated the word that reorients a nation's soul.

"War."

Fighting major wars roughly once every decade, Israel is a nation forged in conflict. So was the man who now led it. From early in life, Netanyahu's instincts were shaped by Israel's struggles—brutal wars of survival, waves of murderous terror, the hypocrisy of global censure, and the unrelenting lesson that Jewish sovereignty endures only so long as it is ferociously defended.

His father, Benzion Netanyahu, one of the world's foremost historians of antisemitism, raised his sons on sober, hard-learned truths: that the world is chronically hostile to Jews, that Jewish weakness invites catastrophe, and that the world's sympathy evaporates at the first sign of pressure. Benzion had served as secretary to Ze'ev Jabotinsky, the founder of Revisionist Zionism, who preached Jewish strength, military independence, and the necessity of standing alone when needed. In the Netanyahu household, the excruciating lessons of Jewish history were not an abstraction. They were an inheritance and a mandate. In 1967, Benjamin Netanyahu was a high school senior in the United States when the Arab world closed in to destroy Israel. He watched his father's creed converge with reality. He flew to Israel and volunteered to dig trenches.

In the years that followed, Netanyahu experienced the unresolved trauma and ruthless realities of Jewish history firsthand. He enlisted in the IDF, gaining acceptance to Sayeret Matkal, Israel's most elite commando unit. Already in training, he bore the costs of war. Two close friends were killed in a training accident; one died in Netanyahu's arms in the back of a command vehicle racing toward the hospital. He saw combat early and would be wounded on multiple occasions. In March 1968, he fought PLO terrorists led by Yasser Arafat in the blistering Battle of Karameh in Jordan, where as many as thirty-three IDF soldiers were killed. Later that year, in response to repeated attacks on Israeli civilian airliners, his unit carried out a daring operation at Beirut International Airport, destroying fourteen Arab-owned aircraft after ensuring they were empty. It was an act of calculated deterrence, intended to spare innocents while making clear that terror would be answered beyond Israel's borders, regardless of the outrage it provoked abroad. During Israel's War of Attrition with Egypt, Netanyahu took part in repeated cross-border raids. In one operation in May 1969, Egyptian fire hurled him into the Suez Canal. Dragged down by his gear, he nearly drowned before being pulled ashore—only to be blasted backward moments later by an Egyptian RPG. Survival, he learned, was never guaranteed. It was seized, moment by moment, under fire.

In May 1972, Netanyahu was shot in the shoulder during the rescue of Sabena Flight 571. Disguised as aircraft technicians in white coveralls, he and his team stormed the hijacked plane, killing both male terrorists within two minutes, capturing the female hijackers, and rescuing all ninety passengers alive. A year later, having completed his active service, Netanyahu interrupted his studies at the Massachusetts Institute of Technology to return to uniform in the Yom Kippur War. Within three years, the agony and real meaning of Jewish sacrifice would be seared into him forever: his brother Jonathan "Yoni" Netanyahu was killed while leading the Entebbe rescue mission. "The death of his brother affected him immensely," said journalist David Remnick. "But it also enlarged his sense of purpose . . . his sense of destiny, his sense of mission."

Graduating from MIT, Netanyahu entered another battlefield: global politics and the war of perception. At the helm of a counterterrorism institute founded in his brother's memory, he carried Israel's case onto the airwaves and into the public eye. As Israel's ambassador to the United Nations, then as a deputy foreign minister and prime minister, he confronted Israel's diplomatic isolation, watching international institutions excuse terror, normalize antisemitism through procedure, and demand restraint from the Jewish state alone. He came face-to-face with the hard truth that Israel's survival would be contested not only with bullets and missiles, but with cameras, resolutions, and condemnations.

As US President Barack Obama pursued a nuclear agreement that many believed would clear Iran's path to nuclear weapons—even as Tehran openly threatened Israel with annihilation—Netanyahu stormed the stage of history, determined to stop it. In March 2015, he strode into the US Capitol and denounced it before a joint session of Congress, defying a sitting American president on his own turf. "The days when the Jewish people remained passive in the face of genocidal enemies," he declared in the Capitol, "those days are over." Relations with the White House plunged to what some considered an all-time low. Netanyahu accepted the cost. "History will not give us another chance," he said. And if isolation was the price of preventing a second Holocaust, he was willing to pay it. His national mission also carried a deeply personal dimension. As one of his former advisers once observed, "The Prime Minister has a messianic sense of himself—as someone called upon to save the Jewish people." The millions of Israelis who returned Netanyahu to office, election after election, appeared to share that belief.

On October 7, the long arc of Benjamin Netanyahu's life appeared to converge into a single, terrible moment. The lessons drilled into him in childhood, the wars he fought as a young commando, the brother he buried, the decades spent defying terror, isolation, and international pressure—all of it crystallized on that dark morning. The instincts, resolve, and defiance that had defined his rise were suddenly demanded at full scale. Netanyahu had already become one of the most consequential Jewish leaders of the modern era. Now he faced a war that would not be confined to Israel's borders but would press against the entire world. With a seven-front conflict tightening around a nation of under ten million, this seemed to be the moment his life had been preparing him for—the moment Benjamin Netanyahu was summoned to carry the full weight of Jewish history and the Jewish future.

Like their prime minister, Israelis lived with national responsibility woven into the fabric of ordinary life. They understood instinctively that routine in Israel is provisional and carried a quiet awareness that the national posture could shift, in a single moment, from normalcy to a wartime footing. With little or no warning, any school run, workday, or family dinner could abruptly tilt into a state of emergency. Even as they went about their daily lives, Israelis always knew that at any moment, history might suddenly enter the room. And when it did, they would be ready. So, when their prime minister declared war, looking straight into the camera lens, Israelis felt him speaking directly to them personally. Had they stood with him in that room, a chorus of millions might well have answered with the same three words: "Say no more."

In a cadence of perfect clockwork, they moved. Within hours, the IDF had placed roughly 360,000 reservists on call—the largest mobilization since the Yom Kippur War, almost exactly fifty years before. Men and women leapt from beds, left synagogue mid-prayer, cut short their morning runs. Almost instinctively, they yanked uniforms from closets, stuffed socks and dog tags and battered field gloves into rucksacks, and snapped open long-kept combat kits from under beds or on shelves in their garage. They loaded up their cars, slammed their trunks, and drove. The sleeping giant of Israel's citizen-army stirred from its slumber and surged into the fray.

Until October 7, many Israelis viewed the reserve army as a theoretical concept—a relic from the era of cataclysmic conflicts fought between nation-states. Reserve soldiers usually served for between one and three weeks a year, mostly training, hardly imagining they'd be summoned to save the country as their fathers had during Israel's early decades. Large-scale land wars felt like long-gone history.

But on that day, that figment of wishful thinking—along with so many other illusions that had settled over Israel's psyche—went up in the smoke of the smoldering kibbutzim. A river of reservists flowed fervently toward their operational bases. Workers shelved their projects; students abandoned their studies; fathers and mothers kissed their children goodbye. Men and women in uniform streaked north and south across Israel's highways, each startled by the same sight: every car beside them seemed to be driven by someone dressed in olive green. As they drove, they noticed how the approach roads to every IDF base were jammed with cars. With parking lots at bases overflowing, the highway shoulders became ad hoc car parks. Miles of parked vehicles coiled along the margins of Israel's roadways marked the nation's return to arms.

The staggering figure—360,000 soldiers—represented roughly 6 percent of Israel's adult population, abruptly trading civilian life for the battlefield. It was more than a matter of statistics. It was bakers and bankers, engineers and entrepreneurs, rabbis and teachers, who all walked away from businesses, classrooms, and living rooms to pick up rifles and set everything else aside. Over the course of that day, Israel transformed from a nation under attack to a society at war.

This was not a phased recruitment campaign or a careful buildup. It was a tidal wave of sacrifice charged with a singular purpose. Men and women in sandals, suits, hospital scrubs, and start-up hoodies who suddenly became soldiers again. The choreography was raw but almost flawless: call-up, muster, kit-up, deploy. The machinery of mobilization immediately roared to life. In hours, the Jewish state was combat-ready.

Service in the reserves is not a modern Israeli invention. It stretches back to the very genesis of Jewish nationhood. In the Bible, the phrase "Nation of Israel" did not describe a cultural abstraction but a military force: it meant those able and ready to serve. When 603,550 Jews marched out of Egypt, they were counted not as individuals but as "all who go out in the army for Israel"—men of fighting age, twenty years old and up, enrolled by their very existence in the defense of the people.

As Chaim Herzog notes in *Battles of the Bible: A Military History*, written with Mordechai Gichon, in the age of King David, every able-bodied Israelite was obligated to serve periodically—roughly one month each year—creating a rhythm of regular, universal service that made national defense a shared civic duty. Scripture itself preserves the specialized military character of Israel's tribes: the Benjaminites, "armed with bows," were famed for ambidexterity—"[they] could use both the right hand and the left in hurling stones or shooting arrows out of a bow" (1 Chr. 12:2); the Gadites "could handle shield and buckler," their faces "like the faces of lions," "swift as gazelles upon the mountains" (12:8); the Judahites "bore shield and spear" (12:24); Naphtali fielded forces "with shield and spear" (12:34); and Zebulun produced warriors "expert in war, with all instruments of war . . . able to keep rank" (12:33). Most strikingly, Issachar is portrayed as the kingdom's "intelligence" tribe—men "that had understanding of the times, to know what Israel ought to do" (12:32). In David's kingdom, regular reserve duty and differentiated tribal competencies fused into a single national ecosystem of defense. Discipline, specialization, and shared responsibility were woven into the fabric of society.

This martial tradition, carried intact across millennia, was reborn in the modern State of Israel. Defense was never outsourced. Israel's security rested not on standing armies alone but on the citizen-soldier, summoned when duty called and returning to civilian life when the watch was done.

Before October 7, reserve duty was still demanding, disruptive, but contained—limited to a few weeks a year. The Hamas massacre shattered those boundaries and rewrote the very meaning of service. Reservists were no longer called for weeks but for months on end. Families were split, careers were suspended, and lives were placed on hold indefinitely. The ancient covenant of national service was stretched to what some feared would be its breaking point. What had been a shared burden measured in days became an open-ended ordeal. And it echoed an old truth: survival demands more of the Jews than of any other nation.

Battle Stations

"In that moment when I saw the pictures on my TV, I knew there was going to be a war," one reservist recalled. He packed his uniform, socks, and essentials, then rushed to answer his brigade commander's call. As early as 9:30 a.m., many in his brigade had already reported for duty. A process that normally takes thirty-six hours—issuing weapons, drawing supplies, organizing logistics—was compressed into ten. By nightfall, they were pushing into communities whose fences had been torn down in the onslaught.

The mission was as stark as it was simple: defend. "When [a terrorist] comes to the fence with guns and vehicles, we just need to destroy them," the reservist said. "We do it at day, at night, during Shabbat, whenever. We are here. We are ready."

Reservists deployed to frontline towns—Netiv HaAsara, Magen, Kissufim—holding inner positions because the perimeter itself had collapsed. They dug in on street corners, built ad hoc strongpoints inside synagogues and schools, and spread troops through the night to catch infiltrators crawling toward holes in the border fence. The work was relentless. Soldiers were lucky if they slept two hours in broken shifts. Communications rooms buzzed with live feeds of terrorists sneaking through gaps, forcing split-second decisions that meant life or death for the communities behind them.

David Citron, a thirty-two-year-old venture capitalist turned combat medic, described the scene by phone from near Gaza as Iron Dome interceptors boomed overhead. "Thousands and thousands of soldiers, everyone just making their way onto base. A lot of anger, a lot of frustration, a lot of shock," he related. "A lot of people were completely blindsided, myself included." But shock quickly calcified into determination. "If [a terrorist] gets through, after the border, he can just wander into the [nearby Israeli] cities," a reservist explained. That unvarnished arithmetic sharpened focus and fueled endurance. There was no time for theories, no appetite for blame. The only question was whether and how the line would hold.

Israel's reserve system is unique. Military service is compulsory for most Israeli citizens at the age of eighteen. Before October 7, men and women typically remained in the reserves after active duty until age forty for enlisted soldiers and forty-five for officers. Periodic call-ups and training keep the structure alive. Yet October 7 tested it as never before. And the soldiers surpassed all expectations. Within forty-eight hours, three hundred thousand reservists had already mobilized. IDF spokesperson Daniel Hagari stated that the speed was unprecedented: "Israel has never mobilized so many reservists so quickly." Defense analyst Franz-Stefan Gady put it bluntly: "In terms of cold start capability, the IDF remains unmatched by the rest of the world."

Some reserve units saw turnout surpassing even their full rosters. The 252nd Brigade, for example, reported an extraordinary 120 percent attendance, as veterans who had already completed their service showed up alongside those officially called. In the week following October 7, the IDF received some 1,500 applications from men in ultra-Orthodox communities—long hesitant about military service and largely exempted—who now sought to don the uniform and stand shoulder to shoulder in defense of Israel. Some who had aged out of formal duty volunteered anyway. "I lost my father, uncle, and cousin in the Yom Kippur War," said Noam Lanir, a fifty-six-year-old entrepreneur. "Now it is my time." He joined his two sons at the front. Such generational echoes became common: fathers and sons serving side by side, old soldiers donning uniforms to serve alongside teenagers fresh from basic training. "Of course, we are scared," said Dan, a thirty-five-year-old reservist en route to his base. "We are afraid, but we are focused."

On the ground, reservists performed tasks that contemporary combat doctrines rarely envision for them. They weren't merely backfilling logistics or manning checkpoints. They were holding the perimeters of towns where defenses had collapsed, running emergency medical units under fire, building makeshift intelligence networks, and in some cases, launching offensive thrusts to clear villages. The compression of time—from call-up to combat in hours, not days—meant training cycles vanished. Maintenance routines were jettisoned. What replaced them, in large part, was improvisation: carpenters welding barricades, coders configuring comms gear, farmers driving armored personnel carriers with the same steadiness they used to drive their tractors. Reservists understood instinctively what was at stake. As one communications officer said, "To everybody in the world, every terrorist group, every organization that wants to test us: we are here, we are doing our job, and the job is to protect the Israeli people."

It wasn't only men who answered the call. Across Israel, women stepped forward, trading their daily routines for the grueling demands of national service. Keren Sokolov, a mother of seven living in Efrat who immigrated from the United States, left a house bedecked for her daughter's bat mitzvah to report to the Home Front Command in Jerusalem. "I received the call-up order a few days after the fighting began—just two days before my daughter's bat mitzvah," she said. "We'd planned a Shabbat celebration, ordered balloons, I'd been cooking all week. On Thursday, I went to base, left in uniform just so I could celebrate with her." The mass mobilization, she added, "reminds me exactly why I am here."

In Tel Aviv, Ran Peretz, twenty-four, watched her partner—a plastic surgeon—be drafted and retrained as a combat doctor. She soon got her own summons. She had worked as a marketing manager for a bridal gown brand; in uniform, she served as a sniper instructor. "The war caught me on vacation in Italy for my partner's birthday—he was born on October 7," she recalled. "At first we tried to disconnect a little, to avoid sinking into despair, but by the next day we realized the magnitude and knew we were needed back home." From Givat Koach, thirty-one-year-old Isabella, a mother of two and a logistics NCO in the Hoshen Battalion, rejoined service as her husband deployed to the south. She did her best to balance the needs of her family with those of her nation. "Since we were both drafted, I make sure to come home to the kids at the end of each day. We are in a state of emergency, and there's no time to think about the private self."

The mobilization revealed something fundamental about Israel's security model: it is as much a matter of social infrastructure as military infrastructure. The reserve system is not just a list of names in a file; it is a living lattice of skills and identities that runs through much of Israel's population. Business administrators became platoon leaders, healthcare professionals became medics, tech engineers became communications specialists, and supply chain managers turned into logistics coordinators. The system drew on every skill Israel's civilian economy had produced, and in doing so reminded the country that national survival depends on more than weapons. It depends on people.

This diffusion of responsibility produced speed and flexibility. It also exposed strain. Families lost breadwinners overnight. Supply chains buckled as managers disappeared into uniforms. Businesses from Tel Aviv to Haifa shuttered or limped along with skeleton crews. And every family asked itself the same unspoken question: how long can this go on?

The first weeks of mobilization were carried by a spirit of urgency and improvisation, but the grind soon followed. Reservists, enduring open-ended deployments, felt the mounting pressure of not knowing when they would return home. And beyond that uncertainty lay the most brutal truth of all: that, tragically, many never would. The deepening fatigue was matched by financial strain at home. Maj. Gen. (res.) Itzik Ronen observed that the conventional challenges of reserve duty were compounded by the particulars of the unprecedented struggle: "The scale of conscripts, the multiple arenas, the initial operational failure, the length of the campaign, and the intensity of the fighting."

Even upon release, many left with an "order in hand," already notified that their next call-up was only a few months away. Salaried workers faced uncertain job security. Self-employed reservists watched their careers waste away, with clients lost, ventures collapsing, and years of work jeopardized by months in uniform. The price of service was paid not only on the battlefield, but in bank accounts, households, and the inner lives of those who answered the call. Yet through exhaustion and uncertainty, solidarity endured. Stockbrokers, teachers, and even top TV producers, who days earlier had nothing in common, shared foxholes and combat rations.

Asael, a reservist serving in the northern sector, told a reporter, "I left behind a wife, a child, a job, academic studies—and it is clear to me that the people of Israel and the IDF have a once-in-a-lifetime opportunity to erase and eliminate evil from the south and the north. I am highly motivated to stay here until we complete the mission." Nadav, a twenty-six-year-old student from Gush Etzion drafted to the Gaza border, agreed: "I've never had such a level of motivation in my life . . . everyone wants to do it to the end and not take their foot off the gas." He described the strength of the warriors: "The army is strong. All the guys who go out [do so] with a smile and high morale. Even the wounded really want to go back inside Gaza and fight."

The story of Israel's October mobilization is both immediate and ongoing. It was immediate in the blitz of return flights, the midnight convoys, the home-to-frontline scramble. And it remains ongoing in the harder grind: broken families, shuttered businesses, and prolonged deployments. But the mobilization was not just of bodies, but of an unbreakable will—the collective resolve of a people refusing to lie down in their graves.

As the dust settled on those first chaotic days, one truth became undeniable: without reservists, there is no state. The reserves did more than fill ranks; they ringed the country with a living rampart of unflinching courage, buying Israel time to think, room to maneuver, and the confidence to breathe again. Ordinary lives, stopped mid-stride, stepped up with extraordinary service. And in stepping into uniforms and danger, the people rewrote Israel's social contract: that when the nation's survival is at stake, it is ordinary citizens who come to save the state.

Globetrotting Home

"Everyone is coming. No one is saying no," said Yonatan Steiner, a twenty-four-year-old reservist who closed his laptop in New York and flew back to rejoin his army medical unit stationed near Lebanon. For Steiner, the decision was instantaneous. Work, life, convenience—all of it dissolved in the shadow of war. "This is different, this is unprecedented, the rules have changed."

He was not alone. From New York to Vilnius, from Bangkok to Buenos Aires, Israelis abroad made the same calculation: friends, family, and the nation mattered more than whatever civilian pursuit had occupied them hours earlier. Nimrod Nedan, a twenty-three-year-old medical student in Lithuania, had lost friends and relatives in the attack. "I cannot sit here and study medicine while I know that my friends are fighting and my family needs protection." He added, "This is my time."

The departures became a kind of roll call of the global Jewish community. Start-up founders in New York tucked away their children with a simple story—"Daddy's going on a business trip"—while quietly booking tickets to Tel Aviv. Students ditched their travels, and professionals quit their business trips.

It took more than individual willpower to move an entire diaspora home. Israel's military dispatched C-130 Hercules transport planes to European capitals to scoop up stranded soldiers. Meanwhile, airlines—national, private, and makeshift—became first responders of a different kind. El Al, Israir, and Arkia airlines added flights, opened new routes, and bent every rule in the book to accommodate the rush. Soon, would-be soldiers were being ferried back to their homeland from across the world, lying on cots meant for flight attendants, or sprawled across the floor in the kitchens at the back of the airplane. El Al upended its decades-old policy of not flying on the Jewish Sabbath. It was a rule enshrined in a cabinet decision made in 1982. But now the calculus shifted. The rabbis gave their blessing, the board authorized the change, and Sabbath flights lifted off from New York, Bangkok, and other cities packed with reservists. In the words of one executive, saving lives outweighed everything else. The decision, once politically radioactive, became a moral imperative.

At the El Al check-in counters in airports across the world, staff shouted instructions into restless lines of travelers. "Military first," one agent said firmly, pulling soldiers out of the crush of people desperate for seats. In Athens, the scene looked like a wartime evacuation: hundreds of Israelis, many ticketless, pressed forward for hours, clutching papers and phones. Meanwhile, security officers patrolled, and volunteers handed out apples, bananas, and bottled water.

Technology helped smooth the chaos. WhatsApp groups sprouted across continents, functioning as a new civic nervous system. Soldiers shared updates on which airlines were still flying, which gates still had tickets, and which cities might offer the last route home. Rumors became lifelines. "We set up WhatsApp groups almost everywhere in the world," said Yedidya Shalman, who cut short his honeymoon in Thailand. "We slowly worked to bring as many reservists as possible back to Israel." Sometimes the improvisation took on almost biblical proportions. US media reported strangers at El Al counters in New York offering to buy tickets for reservists they didn't know. Others raised hundreds of thousands of dollars for charter flights to assist the IDF cargo planes ferrying soldiers back from hubs across Europe. The patchwork of commercial schedules, military logistics, and private generosity stitched together a vast air-bridge back to Israel.

Whole NGOs were remodeled, and grassroots groups were created to help out. The Israel Reserve Fund sprang into being in the first days of the crisis, founded by actress Swell Ariel Or and fellow activists. "I felt helpless," Or said, recalling the guilt of watching events unfold from Los Angeles. "I wanted to give the reservists the feeling that someone has their back." The group started by raising money on social media to buy tickets for stranded soldiers. Soon it was supporting hundreds across the globe—combat troops, intelligence officers, logistics personnel. Yoni Benzacar, one of the organizers, ticked off the list of origins: Thailand, South America, Australia, India, the UAE, the United States, and Canada. In each case, donations from Jews and non-Jews alike transformed into boarding passes. What began as off-the-cuff activism hardened into infrastructure: a network of volunteers operating like a civilian logistics arm of the IDF. Other organizations joined in. La'aretz, a Jewish nonprofit, secured flights for young Israelis caught in India after their post-army travels. The result was a surge of bodies into Ben Gurion Airport, each one a testament to civic energy filling the gaps left by institutions overwhelmed by scale.

Not everyone returning was on the official list. Hundreds of reservists who had not been formally called up nonetheless packed their bags and booked tickets. They simply couldn't stay away. Yaakov Swisa, a forty-two-year-old father of five in Los Angeles, hadn't been called. But when his old army roommate was killed at the Nova Music Festival, he booked a ticket anyway: "I've been crying for two, three days. Enough. That's it. I am ready to fight." Others came to volunteer in noncombat roles. Adam Jacobs, an eighteen-year-old college student from New Jersey, had lost a cousin in the massacre. "I couldn't live with myself if I stayed here," he explained. He boarded a flight to Tel Aviv, intending to shuttle supplies and assist logistics teams. "It's never been this bad," he said, his voice a mixture of determination and disbelief.

For many, the journey itself became part of the story. "It was probably the best flight I was ever on in the worst possible circumstances," said Yehuda Brownstein, a twenty-four-year-old Israeli American. He hadn't been called, but he bought the first ticket available from Los Angeles after hearing the news. Before landing in Tel Aviv, passengers spontaneously rose and sang "Hatikvah," Israel's national anthem, in memory of those who had died. "There really was this connectedness between everyone in that cabin—everyone there for the same cause," Brownstein recalled. Some even deployed their own resources. Noam Lanir, the entrepreneur who had lost three relatives in the Yom Kippur War, used his private jet to ferry reservists and bereaved families from Italy and Greece. Lanir, a leader of the Brothers and Sisters in Arms protest movement, had spent the past year rallying against the government's judicial overhaul. Now he was flying soldiers home. "I'm sending my private jet to whoever needs it," he said. "We survived Auschwitz, we survived the Yom Kippur War. We will survive this."

The contrast was striking. Those who days earlier had urged reservists to withhold service were now working to mobilize them. In the aftermath of the massacre, ideological divides dissolved into the single overarching mission of Jewish survival.

For all reservists, mobilization carried a human cost that extended far beyond the battlefield. But for those coming from overseas, the burden was especially heavy. They shouldered the financial and emotional toll of leaving behind jobs, start-ups, and families—not a few hours' drive away, but across oceans and continents. Fathers in New York wondered how long their families could endure their absence. Professionals in Europe closed office doors without knowing whether they would ever reopen them. Unlike Israeli reservists, there would be no weekend leave, no short drive home, no fleeting return to normalcy. Spouses at home bore the heaviest load—explaining disappearances to young children, managing households without primary incomes, and spending sleepless nights waiting for messages from a distant war.

These were not secondary effects. They were the intimate and daily costs of modern Jewish existence. When tens of thousands vanish from the global workforce to reappear on the battlefield, the ripples are vast. Payrolls go unmet, ventures stall, and households buckle under strain. Yet for those climbing into their cars and boarding international flights, the calculation was clear: Jewish survival mattered most.

What unfolded in the weeks after October 7 was more than military mobilization. As the Jewish diaspora poured its sons and daughters out toward the homeland, it demonstrated how a people dispersed across the earth can still beat with a single heart. As the spirit of volunteerism blurred the line between civilian and soldier, so too did it erase the distinction between citizen and expatriate. When survival was at stake, these distinctions all melted away. The global call-up became a chorus of voices and actions: Americans, Europeans, Australians, South Americans—some active in reserves, some not; some better trained, some less so; but all converging on the same small strip of land.

It is no exaggeration to say that Israel's turnaround began not only with the men and women on its bases, but with the jet-lagged students, exhausted entrepreneurs, and wide-eyed volunteers who answered the call from across oceans. In the words of one reservist—a fighter pilot who bolted from his apartment on Manhattan's Upper West Side: "There is no other place in the world I would rather be."

The Nation's Embrace

From the first hours of the war, Israelis understood that the burden of defense could not rest on soldiers alone. Alongside the fighters, civilians stepped forward as logistics coordinators, caregivers, and sustainers—providing food and equipment to deployed units and even childcare for soldiers' families. The line between military duty and civilian support quickly blurred, until the entire society functioned as a single emergency network.

Already on the morning of October 7, local "command centers" sprang up in towns, neighborhoods, and community halls. Volunteers coordinated rides for reservists, organized warehouses of donated goods, and fielded calls for urgent supplies. Synagogues and schools filled with toiletries, blankets, and hygiene kits. Families set up roadside stands offering soldiers fresh food, warm clothing, and even tactical equipment—all free of charge. Businesses rolled out donation drives. Supermarkets introduced charity options at checkout that let shoppers purchase essentials to be transferred directly to troops or displaced families. What began as individual acts of altruism soon grew into a civilian logistics corps. Civilians managed transportation, procurement, and morale. Soldiers heading south found not just convoys of armored vehicles on the roads but convoys of ordinary Israelis handing out sandwiches, socks, and words of encouragement.

Alongside these grassroots networks, Israel's business sector rapidly transformed itself into a parallel support system. Major corporations redirected capital, logistics, and infrastructure to sustain the home front and support fighting forces in the field. The tech giant Salesforce, which maintains a large presence in Israel, committed $3 million to emergency relief organizations, including United Hatzalah and Save the Children. At CloudZone, employees converted their offices into a fully operational support hub for a paratrooper unit, ensuring that more than one thousand regular and reserve soldiers received everything from tactical equipment to basic supplies. Retail companies also filled critical gaps. Ricochet, Israel's leading outdoor supplier, provided thousands of items ranging from socks and kneepads to headlamps and tactical uniforms. Icon Group, the distributor of Apple and Lenovo products in Israel, donated thousands of portable chargers to field units. Incredibuild purchased sleeping bags, socks, and hygiene kits. Coffee chains joined in: Roladin sent mobile carts to staging areas with free coffee and pastries; Café Greg distributed thousands of light meals; and Biga ensured gluten-free provisions for celiac soldiers.

Across the food industry, restaurants, cafés, and delivery platforms turned their kitchens into arteries of the war effort. McDonald's converted five branches in the south into donation hubs, producing thousands of meals each day for soldiers, evacuees, and hospitals, while offering a 50 percent discount to uniformed personnel nationwide. The BBB burger chain gave free hot meals to security forces, sent daily deliveries to IDF units and displaced families, and used its restaurants as collection points for donated supplies. Wolt, Israel's leading food delivery app, introduced a donation option within its platform, allowing customers to send packages to evacuees. The company pledged one thousand packages of its own and doubled every customer contribution. Independent restaurants, too, cooked in bulk for soldiers and evacuees, often at their own expense. Food—hot, abundant, and freely served—became one of the most tangible expressions of solidarity.

While businesses supplied goods and meals, civilians also took responsibility for one another's families. Informal childcare arrangements, errand-running, and temporary housing solutions emerged everywhere. Neighbors looked after each other's children; communities pooled resources and collected secondhand clothing for evacuees. Volunteer EMS groups such as United Hatzalah continued their lifesaving work under intensified conditions, rushing to treat rocket victims and bolster the stretched emergency system.

The most dramatic pivot came from Brothers and Sisters in Arms. Known before the war as the foremost arm of the protest movement tearing Israel apart over judicial reform, the organization redirected its energy overnight. Leasing a hangar in Tel Aviv, its volunteers amassed mountains of donated gear, from socks and helmets to tactical vests. The hangar became a magnet for ministers, Knesset members, and even foreign dignitaries, all eager to witness how quickly ordinary citizens had organized an improvised supply network.

As Israelis offered time and goods, Jews abroad contributed what they could from afar. Mainly, that meant money. And they gave in extraordinary measure. JGive, an online charity platform, reported that in October 2023 alone, about ₪102 million were donated through its platform—ten times the amount of the previous October. The share of donations from abroad leapt from 21 to 71 percent. The Jewish Federations of North America (JFNA), the umbrella organization for a network of more than 141 local Jewish Federations, raised an estimated $1.4 billion for civilian relief.

But perhaps most striking was how much money flowed not to the established charities but to the new grassroots networks inside Israel. WhatsApp groups became fundraising channels; small NGOs managed budgets once reserved for national organizations. With speed and flexibility, they filled gaps left by Jewish communal giants and even the state itself. Nowhere was it clearer than in the mad scramble to kit out Israel's troops. From the start of the war, shortages in the IDF became clear. Soldiers often lacked thermal clothing, proper boots, and modern helmets. Regulations technically barred units from accepting direct donations, but many commanders felt they had no choice but to bend the rules. Requests for gear circulated widely, and civilians responded with astonishing speed.

Formal and informal groups sprang up to meet these needs. Yashar LaChayal expanded operations to provide toiletries, warm jackets, and rest corners. Boots for Israel distributed over 46,000 pairs of tactical boots. Unit 11741 delivered eleven thousand helmets. Chayal's Angels went even further, sending holistic care teams—massage therapists, acupuncturists, yoga instructors—to transform bases into makeshift healing centers. Israeli business leaders abroad also stepped in to fill the gear gap. Few did so more prominently than Eran Efrat, an Amsterdam-based entrepreneur who recognized the emerging shortages in the war's earliest days. "In the first week, there was panic," he recalled. "Nobody knew what to do. We just sent gear to Israel and hoped they would take it." Drawing on private networks and social-media fundraising, Efrat raised approximately $40 million and adopted an unusually direct approach—bypassing traditional channels to contract US-based manufacturers to produce tactical equipment for Israeli soldiers. "The fact that we brought so much," he noted, "helped us get their attention."

These efforts soon coalesced into more structured frameworks. Dotan Sofer, a tech executive, helped unify nearly ninety separate initiatives under the umbrella of Forum Hachamalim—"the War Rooms Forum." With warehouses as large as fourteen thousand square feet and thousands of full-time volunteers, these groups managed thousands of daily requests for supplies. Sofer estimated that together, grassroots groups delivered more than $1 billion in gear within six months—rivaling the sums raised by global Jewish charities. Historians of philanthropy noted how unusual this was. In modern states, civilian donations for combat gear are virtually unheard of. Benjamin Soskis, a scholar of philanthropy, observed that while such efforts existed in the US Civil War and World War II, they were eventually replaced by centralized systems. Israel, he said, had put forth a revolutionary model: smaller grassroots charities had replaced the larger mainstream institutions.

This was especially clear with the Friends of the Israel Defense Forces (FIDF). For decades, FIDF had been the premier international charity supporting Israeli soldiers, raising hundreds of millions annually in glitzy galas featuring A-list celebrity honorees. Yet after October 7, the organization's magnitude became its greatest limitation. Bound by legal advice and institutional caution, FIDF refused to provide combat gear of any kind—even as soldiers at the front lacked boots, helmets, and thermal clothing. Its donations went instead to welfare projects, family support, and infrastructure, all important but far from the urgent needs in the field. In light of what many viewed as a failure, FIDF would eventually be rocked by scandal. A leaked internal report alleged financial mismanagement, cronyism, lavish spending, and a toxic culture, prompting donor backlash and frozen contributions. Within weeks, both the board chair and the CEO stepped down, and the organization rushed to install interim leadership to steady the ship. It was an extraordinary comedown for the marquee charity that had long styled itself as the IDF's flagship US fundraiser. One of the world's top Jewish charities, it seemed, had taken the path of Israel's top brass.

Meanwhile, small volunteer groups—some born overnight in WhatsApp chats—delivered exactly what FIDF failed to provide. For soldiers in the field, the lesson was searing: the most effective support did not come from the philanthropic elite, but from ordinary Jews in Israel and abroad, moving with a speed and freedom no boardroom or bureaucracy could match.

In equipping Israel's soldiers, mom-and-pop charities had not only outperformed legacy giants; they had surpassed the state itself. Just as October 7 exposed the cracks in Israel's military leadership, the ensuing shortfalls in equipment exposed the failings of the military bureaucracy. At the IDF General Staff, high-ranking officers were willing to admit vaguely to "some shortages." Meanwhile, brigade commanders were pointing to significant gaps. Farther down the chain, the truth was presented even more starkly. Battalion commanders were reporting, "I have nothing." Company commanders were claiming bluntly, "We don't even have enough to drink." The gaps were not only logistical but cultural: a military ethos of "winging it" discouraged admissions of need. As one soldier put it, "If you say you're short on night-vision goggles, you're told, 'So you have two instead of four? Make do.'"

In their budgets as in their imagination, the civilians of the Jewish world were under no such constraints. They identified the shortages, raised the money, and delivered the goods. In the same way that reservists had stepped forward on the battlefield when the army faltered, ordinary Israelis and Jews abroad stepped forward on the home front to provide what the system could not. The cumulative effect was extraordinary. Soldiers fought in Gaza and on the northern border, but their lifelines stretched through kitchens, warehouses, synagogues, and smartphones. Families in Tel Aviv supplied battalions at the front; donors in New York and London paid for helmets and boots; cafés in Jerusalem served coffee to troops waiting for buses.

In this sense, October 7 marked not only a military mobilization but a national one. The people of Israel—and the Jewish people worldwide—refused to separate front from rear, battlefield from home front. They understood instinctively that survival was collective, and that in crisis, the nation itself must become the army's embrace.

CHAPTER FIVE

THE GATES OF GAZA: YEAR ONE OF THE SOUTHERN CAMPAIGN

God goes forth like a warrior,
Whipping up rage like a fighter—
Yelling, roaring aloud,
Then charging upon the enemy.
Isaiah 42:13

In the decades leading up to the October 7 massacre, far smaller terrorist attacks had been sufficient to send Israel to war. In March 1978, PLO terrorists hijacked a bus on Israel's coastal road, killing thirty-eight civilians, among them thirteen children. Within seventy-two hours, the IDF launched Operation Litani, invading southern Lebanon to drive the terrorists away from Israel's border. The Coastal Road Massacre, then the deadliest terrorist attack in Israel's history, triggered a major campaign with consequences that would shape Israel's northern front for years. In March 2002, months of relentless suicide bombings culminated in the Passover Massacre at Netanya's Park Hotel, where thirty civilians were slaughtered as they sat down for the Seder. Israel responded with Operation Defensive Shield, a sweeping campaign that retook terrorist strongholds throughout

Judea and Samaria. So too, in the summer of 2014, the kidnapping of three Israeli teens by Hamas—coupled with the discovery of cross-border attack tunnels from Gaza—triggered Operation Protective Edge, in which Israel invaded the Strip. With every such tragedy, the pattern was clear: large-scale terror brought full-scale war.

This dynamic defines one of the enduring tragedies of Israel's modern history: waiting for catastrophe to confront dangers that were plainly visible long before they turned lethal. Time and again, Israel has required massacres—immutable, undeniable atrocities—to justify actions that prudence and experience should have dictated earlier. The threshold for response has been set disastrously high, as though legitimacy must be purchased with oceans of blood.

This hesitation stands in stark contrast to one of Judaism's oldest strategic and moral principles: that even small provocations can justify decisive action, precisely in order to prevent larger calamities. The source of this principle is King David himself. When David was informed that the Philistines were "plundering the threshing floors" of the Israelites—stealing grain, not lives—he turned to God for guidance. The answer was immediate and unequivocal: "Go and attack the Philistines" (I Sam. 23:1–2). No one had been killed. No village had been razed. The offense was economic, limited, and easy to overlook. And yet it was enough.

The logic was clear. Predation, once tolerated, does not remain small. What begins with stolen grain ends with stolen land, and what begins with harassment ends with slaughter. David did not wait for widows and orphans to accumulate before acting. He understood that restraint at the wrong moment is not mercy, but negligence.

This principle is not confined to biblical narrative. It is codified in Jewish law. The Talmud rules that if an enemy approaches Jewish border towns even to collect straw or hay, Jews are obligated to desecrate the Sabbath to drive them off. The law is rooted not in militancy, but in foresight. Of course, the straw itself is negligible. But what matters is the precedent. Allow the enemy to take the hay today, and tomorrow he will take the harvest. Allow him the harvest, and soon he will take the town itself. Crucially, this lowering of the threshold for casus belli is not rooted in a love of war. It is rooted in a hatred of it. By nipping threats in the bud, it aims to avert the far greater violence that inevitably follows unchecked aggression.

The modern world learned this lesson the hard way in the 1930s. Long before the first shots of World War II were fired, Adolf Hitler announced his intentions openly—and violated international norms repeatedly, incrementally, and deliberately. In 1933, Germany withdrew from the League of Nations. In 1935, Hitler reintroduced conscription, openly defying the Treaty of Versailles. That same year, he announced the creation of the Luftwaffe—again in direct violation of international agreements. In 1936, German troops marched into the demilitarized Rhineland, a brazenly illegal act that Hitler's generals feared would fail had France, supported by Britain, militarily intervened. Sadly, they did not. Then came the Anschluss, Germany's illegal annexation of Austria in 1938. Again, no response. Then the dismantling of Czechoslovakia—first the Sudetenland, then Prague itself. Each violation lowered the cost of the next. By the time Germany invaded Poland in September 1939, Hitler no longer led a fragile regime testing boundaries. He commanded a rearmed, mobilized war machine. The moment for early, limited intervention had passed. What remained was a one-way road to world war.

The year leading up to October 7 was anything but quiet on the Gaza front. Along the border fence, violent demonstrations became routine. Riots flared. Explosives were detonated, tearing holes in Israel's billion-dollar border fence. Incendiary balloons drifted into southern Israel, igniting fires that consumed agricultural fields and livelihoods. In September 2023, just one month before the massacre, the Erez border crossing was closed for nearly two weeks after sustained rioting and violence along the fence. No serious country would tolerate such a reality. If explosives were planted on the American border, or foreign militants repeatedly breached it, or incendiary devices were used to set American fields ablaze, negotiation would not be the response. And yet Israel chose a different path. Rather than confront escalating aggression, it attempted to purchase quiet with concessions.

Behind the scenes, Israel negotiated with Hamas through intermediaries, offering diplomatic bribes in exchange for quiet. According to officials familiar with the talks, Israel increased the number of work permits issued to Gazans, expanded the fishing zone off Gaza's coast, eased export restrictions, and considered reopening crossings previously closed due to violence. As little as ten days before October 7, Israel was reportedly weighing an increase in labor permits for Gazans from 17,500 to 20,000. At the same time, with Israel's consent, Qatar continued distributing monthly cash payments—hundred-dollar bills to roughly one hundred thousand Gazan families—flowing through a system fully controlled by Hamas. Each concession lowered the cost of escalation and raised the price of restraint. Tolerating the intolerable was not a policy for stability. It was a path to disaster—and it led directly to October 7.

Israel's problem has never been that it acts too forcefully. On the contrary, it is that it so often acts too late—and is therefore compelled to act with a severity that earlier resolve might have spared. Jewish tradition grasped this truth millennia ago: lowering the threshold for response is not an invitation to war. It is the surest way to prevent one.

Tragically, Israel once again chose to absorb blow after blow until restraint was no longer possible. Once again, the reckoning arrived only after a massacre left no alternative but full-scale war. In a single Shabbat morning, Jews suffered nearly as many deaths as Israel endured through two Intifadas. War was no longer a matter of choice. It was imposed. The only question that remained was how far the fire would spread.

The answer came within twenty-four hours. On the morning after the massacre, Hezbollah, Iran's most powerful proxy, opened fire. As smoke still rose from Israel's southern communities, rockets and mortars rained down on the north. The IDF struck back with artillery and drones, targeting Hezbollah observation posts across southern Lebanon. A day later, the border was breached. A squad of terrrorists, later claimed by Palestinian Islamic Jihad, crossed from Lebanon into Israeli territory and ambushed an IDF patrol. In the ensuing firefight, Lt. Col. Alim Abdallah, deputy commander of the 300th Brigade, was killed—one of the first officers to fall in the northern campaign. Within days, Hezbollah escalated. Antitank missiles began striking Israeli communities, forcing the evacuation of nearly one hundred thousand civilians living within five kilometers of the border. Ghost towns appeared overnight. Schools, shops, and synagogues stood silent as artillery thundered through the empty valleys of Galilee.

Hezbollah's entrance confirmed what Israeli intelligence had long dreaded: this would not be a single-front war. Hamas in the south, Hezbollah in the north, Iranian-backed militias in Syria and Iraq, Houthi missiles from Yemen, and threats from Iran itself—all converging toward the same goal: the destruction of the Jewish state.

This was the nightmare scenario every strategist seeks to avoid, and the defining lesson of both world wars: that even the strongest nations fall when forced to fight on too many fronts. In 1914, Germany's Schlieffen Plan sought to sidestep that predicament precisely: to crush France within weeks in the west, before the Russian army could mobilize in the east. When the plan failed, Germany was caught between two giants and dragged into a multi-front quagmire that bled its armies to exhaustion. In 1939, Adolf Hitler resolved not to repeat Germany's old mistake. Before striking Poland and risking a simultaneous war with France and Britain, he secured his eastern flank by signing a pact with the Soviet Union—buying time to deal with his western enemies first and the Red Army later. After overrunning Poland, Germany crushed France in 1940. Only then did Hitler turn east, launching his invasion of the Soviet Union the following year. For a few years, the strategy appeared to be working. But by 1943, the limits of sequencing had caught up with Hitler. The Allies were advancing through Italy. A year later, they stormed the beaches of Normandy. Germany once again found itself fighting on multiple fronts, its strength stretched beyond endurance. The Third Reich collapsed under the same strain it had sought so carefully to avoid. Every serious student of military history understands the lesson: fight one war at a time—or risk losing them all.

When Hezbollah's rockets tore across the sky on October 8, it was clear Israel would not have that luxury. But Israel had survived such wars before. In 1948, Israel fought against five invading Arab armies and survived. In 1967, it faced Egypt, Syria, and Jordan simultaneously—and prevailed in six days. In 1973, during the Yom Kippur War, Egypt and Syria attacked in concert; Israel nearly collapsed but ultimately turned the tide. Yet none of those wars resembled what began in October 2023. This was not a conflict against states but against networks—transnational, asymmetric, and ideologically fused. By the night of October 8, as the scope of the attack became clearer, Prime Minister Benjamin Netanyahu gathered his war cabinet. The plan he began to formulate was more ambitious than any in Israel's history. Israel was preparing not merely to retaliate, but to reshape the strategic landscape that had allowed such an assault to occur. Addressing the mayors of the devastated southern border towns on October 8, Netanyahu delivered a resolute message that would define the campaigns yet to come. Israel, he declared, would "change the Middle East."

But exactly how Israel would achieve that goal remained unclear. Within the cabinet, tempers flared. Defense Minister Yoav Gallant, a former general in the IDF, urged an immediate strike on Hezbollah, unleashing Israel's pre-planted deterrents: vast networks of hidden explosives and dormant intelligence operations designed to cripple Hezbollah's infrastructure in the event of war. Gadi Eizenkot and Benny Gantz, both former IDF chiefs of staff, argued that the north would have to wait. Netanyahu sided with caution. Israel would defend itself on every front, but it would begin with an offensive against the enemy that started the war. The decision to focus first on Gaza was not merely emotional; it was strategic. As Netanyahu later explained, "After we suffered the massacre by Hamas, if we were to get sucked into a war on two fronts, we would have drowned. I felt it was better to deal with Hamas before heading north." That choice carried a cost. It meant absorbing the blows from every other front—every missile from Lebanon, every drone from Yemen, every provocation from Iraq or Syria—without losing focus.

Already on October 7, Israeli jets were in the air, striking targets across the Strip. Wave after wave of aircraft thundered overhead, their engines rolling through Gaza as command centers, rocket launch sites, and ammunition depots erupted in pillars of fire. In the first day of the war alone, the Israeli Air Force struck more than eight hundred targets in Gaza. On October 8, the cabinet formally declared war. It was the first official declaration of a state of war since 1973. The campaign was also given a name: Swords of Iron.

Initially, Defense Minister Yoav Gallant announced a "complete siege." Electricity, fuel, food, and water—all were cut off. At the first cabinet meeting after the attack, Gallant told the generals that there would "be no conversation and no messages to Hamas. No negotiations . . . They'll only talk to us when they're on the floor with their heads under water." The mood of the nation was steel. But the blockade of water, food, and fuel entering Gaza would be brief.

In the war's opening weeks, Israel carried out one of the most rapid and comprehensive decapitations of terrorist leadership in modern warfare. Nearly one hundred Hamas operatives were eliminated, spanning every echelon of command: members of the political bureau; heads of military intelligence, manpower, production, weapons, and military industries; the chiefs of Hamas's rocket, aerial, and naval forces; and dozens of senior field commanders, including nearly thirty brigade and battalion commanders and more than twenty Nukhba assault commanders who led the October 7 massacre.

On October 10, IDF aircraft struck down the head of Hamas's office for internal relations and its minister of economy. Days later, Ali Qadi, a senior Nukhba commander directly involved in orchestrating the massacre, was killed in a drone strike. Qadhi was no newcomer to terror. In 2005, he had been arrested for his role in the kidnapping and brutal murder of an Israeli businessman who employed him at a sweets factory near Jerusalem. He was later released as part of the Gilad Shalit exchange and deported to Gaza—where he promptly returned to terrorism. Announcing his death, the IDF issued a blunt warning: "All Hamas terrorists will meet the same fate." That same day, Israel eliminated Asem Abu Rakba, head of Hamas's aerial array and a senior operational commander of the October 7 attack. Abu Rakba was responsible for developing Hamas's drone and airborne capabilities—an increasingly central component of its assault doctrine. His replacement would be killed later that month. A day after Abu Rakba's assassination, Israeli forces killed Bilal al-Qadra, the Nukhba commander responsible for the massacres at Kibbutz Nir Oz and Nirim, two of the communities most savagely hit on October 7.

On October 17, Israel struck Ayman Nofel, commander of Hamas's Central Gaza Brigade and a member of its general military council, in Bureij. Nofel was not merely a battlefield commander. He was the architect of Hamas's "Joint Operations Room," the coordinating framework that unified nine major terrorist organizations in Gaza under Hamas leadership. That umbrella structure proved essential to the scale, synchronization, and lethality of the October 7 assault. Described by the IDF as "one of the most dominant figures" in Gaza, Nofel was the highest-ranking Hamas leader eliminated at that point in the war. On October 26, IDF fighter jets struck Hamas's Deputy Head of Intelligence, Shadi Barud. Not content with destroying infrastructure, Israel was methodically dismantling the human architecture of terror—closing accounts left open for years, and removing the men who had planned and coordinated the massacre.

But Israel knew airpower would not be enough. Within a week of the massacre, the IDF issued an extraordinary order: one million Gazans were instructed to evacuate Gaza City and move south. It was a final, irrevocable signal that this would not be another limited round of conflict, nor another calibrated exchange. The IDF was going in, on the ground, to dismantle Hamas at its core. From the smoldering ruins of Israel's southern communities, armored divisions rolled toward the border while artillery units set up howitzers behind them. Reservists flooded bases in numbers nearly unseen in Israel's history. Behind the uniforms stood a nation traumatized yet unified, bound together by grief, fury, and resolve. None doubted the cost or the complexity of what lay ahead. But every soldier, commander, and citizen understood that Israel would not survive another multi-front war by standing still. It would survive only by changing the game entirely.

Few places haunt the Israeli imagination like Gaza. Since before Israel's founding, Gaza proved itself a poisoned well—its hatred spilling outward in a steady drip of infiltration, murder, and terror against the Jewish communities that dared live within reach of its border. In 1956, a young kibbutznik named Roi Rotberg—just twenty-one years old—was murdered and mutilated by infiltrators from Gaza near his home in Nahal Oz. At his funeral, IDF Chief of Staff Moshe Dayan delivered a eulogy that would become famous, less for its consolation than its cold clarity:

> *Have we indeed forgotten that this young group in Nahal Oz carry on their shoulders—like Samson of old—the heavy gates of Gaza—and that behind those gates live hundreds of thousands of hate-ridden people*

who pray that we be weakened so that they may then tear us apart? We are the biblical generation of the settlement, following the Joshua conquest, and the helmet and the sword are the essential requirements. Our children will have no life if we do not dig shelters, and without barbed wire and a machine gun, we will not be able to pave roads or dig for water. Millions of Jews who were annihilated without having had a country look to us from the ashes of Israeli history, commanding us to settle and build a land for our people. But beyond the furrow border, a sea of hatred and vengeance swells, waiting for the day that calm will dull our vigilance, the day we listen to ambassadors of scheming hypocrisy who call on us to lay down our arms . . . This is the choice of our lives—to be prepared and armed, strong and resolute, or let the sword fall from our fist and our lives be cut down.

From the beginning, Israel's founders saw Gaza for what it was: a serpent coiled at the edge of the map, waiting to be ignored so it could strike. More than seventy years on, Moshe Dayan's question—have we indeed forgotten?—remained painfully relevant, and its answer painfully clear. Israel had forgotten the depth of the hatred it faced. Gaza had not.

As in the days of Dayan, Gaza remained a reminder of the terrible arithmetic of Jewish sovereignty: that Israel would either live by the sword—or die by it. This time, Israel would not content itself with absorbing the blow and restoring deterrence at the margins. This time, it would take the fight into the very "sea of hatred" Dayan had described. Gaza had spent nearly a century testing Israel's strength. Now, it was going to face it.

The Coastal Pain

From the earliest recorded history, Gaza was marked as a source of trouble. Already in the opening pages of Scripture, this narrow coastal strip loomed large as a gateway and a fault line. It appears as a staging ground for invasion, a breeding ground for hostility, and a recurring thorn in Israel's side from the very dawn of its national story. In Genesis, Gaza is identified as a boundary point of the land of Canaan: "The borders of the Canaanites were from Sidon toward Gerar, as far as Gaza, toward Sodom" (10:19). It is presented not merely as a place, but as a threshold—a point of entry into the land itself. In Deuteronomy, Gaza reappears with a darker inflection. A people known as the Kaftorites are described as overrunning another nation, the Avvites, "who lived as far as Gaza, destroying them and settling in their place" (2:23). From that moment, Gaza was already synonymous with encroachment—a bridgehead through which foreign invaders pressed into the heart of the land.

When Joshua led the conquest of Canaan, the tribe of Judah "captured Gaza and its territory," fulfilling the command to "possess the land." Yet the Judeans failed to maintain control. They "could not drive out the inhabitants of the plain, because they had chariots of iron" (Judg. 1:18-19). In the twelfth century BCE, waves of Philistines arrived from the Aegean Sea, transforming Gaza and its neighboring cities—Ashkelon, Ashdod, Ekron, and Gath—into a Philistine city-state confederation. From those strongholds, they harassed the tribes of Israel, raiding border villages, seizing harvests, and carrying off captives. In the biblical record, the Philistines are not portrayed as occasional raiders but as a persistent affliction: organized, relentless, and cruel. From the coastal plain around Gaza, Philistine columns advanced toward the Judean hills, striking deep into Israelite territory.

The Book of Judges recounts their domination and how it was broken by the miraculous rise of Samson. A Nazirite warrior of supernatural strength, Samson waged a one-man insurgency against the Philistines. He burned their fields, slew their soldiers, and shattered their pride. But his saga reached its tragic climax in Gaza itself. Betrayed, blinded, and chained, Samson was dragged into the temple of Dagon, the Philistine god, before thousands of revelers who mocked him. There, standing between the pillars of Gaza's great temple, he cried out, "Let me die with the Philistines" (Judg. 16:30). With one final surge of divine strength, "he pulled with all his might," and the temple collapsed upon Samson and his enemies alike. It was vengeance—but also prophecy. Gaza would endure as a place where Israel's suffering would resound, and where those who sought its destruction would ultimately be buried beneath the wreckage of their own designs.

Gaza and its neighboring Philistine cities continued their onslaught throughout the time of the prophet Samuel and King Saul. In one of Israel's darkest moments, the Philistines captured the Ark of the Covenant after the Battle of Eben-Ezer (1 Sam. 4). The Ark—the holiest symbol of Israel's covenant with God—was carried triumphantly into Philistine territory, placed in the temple of Dagon in Ashdod. From there, it was sent to Gath, and finally to Gaza's sister city, Ekron. Yet the victory became a curse. Plagues broke out in every city that harbored the ark, with infestations of rats and outbreaks of painful "hemorrhoids." Terrified, the Philistines returned the Ark to Israel. Along with it, they sent a bizarre tribute: "The following were the golden hemorrhoids that the Philistines paid as an indemnity to the LORD: For Ashdod, one; for Gaza, one." They also sent golden rats, symbols of the plague that had struck them. Still, despite their strange reparations to the God of Israel, the Philistine menace endured.

The Philistines would go on to slay the first Jewish king, Saul, and his would-be heir, Jonathan, at the battle of Mount Gilboa. It was only under King David that their power would finally be broken. The king who had once slain the Philistines' champion Goliath also conquered their cities, subdued their rule, and ultimately brought the Ark back into Jerusalem. His son Solomon, inheriting a kingdom at peace, ruled "from Tiphsah to Gaza, over all the kings west of the river" (1 Ki. 4:24). For a fleeting generation, Gaza was part of the Jewish realm—not a threat, but a frontier. But the peace would prove short-lived. The Philistines reemerged, and Gaza once again became a symbol of rebellion. During the reign of Hezekiah, king of Judah, he "struck the Philistines as far as Gaza" (2 Ki. 18:8), restoring Israelite control to the southern frontier. But greater powers were on the march.

The empires of Egypt, Assyria, Babylon, and Persia would take turns sweeping across Israel's coastal plain. Gaza, perched astride the ancient Way of the Sea—the Via Maris—became their prize. Whoever held Gaza held the crossroads between Africa and Asia, and the gateway to the Land of Israel. The ten northern tribes were carried away by the Assyrians, vanishing into history. The tribes of Judah and Benjamin were later exiled by the Babylonians—yet they were destined to return. When they did, under the Persian king Cyrus the Great, they rebuilt their temple and their nation. But Gaza would remain beyond their reach.

Throughout later antiquity, Gaza remained one of the most contested military prizes of the ancient world. When Alexander the Great marched south from Tyre in 332 BCE, Gaza was the last Persian stronghold barring his path to Egypt. Its commander, Batis, refused to surrender. Alexander besieged the city for two months, constructing vast earthen ramps and pounding its walls with catapults. When Gaza finally fell, he ordered it sacked. Thousands were slain, and the survivors were sold into slavery. The world's most powerful man had to bleed for Gaza before he could pass into Egypt. In the centuries that followed, Gaza's soil was trampled by the armies of Alexander's Hellenistic successors. The Battle of Gaza (312 BCE) pitted Ptolemaic Egypt against the forces of Antigonus. A century later at Rafah (217 BCE), 120,000 soldiers clashed in one of antiquity's largest battles between the Ptolemies and Seleucids.

After the Maccabees wrested control of Israel from the Seleucids, Gaza proved a persistent source of pain for the Jews. Around 96 BCE, the Hasmonean king Alexander Jannaeus destroyed the city for resisting Jewish rule. When Pompey's legions arrived half a century later, Gaza was rebuilt under Roman patronage and restored to its independence as a Hellenistic city loyal to Rome. During the Great Revolt of the Jews against Rome (66–70 CE), Gaza sided with the empire and massacred its Jewish inhabitants. In reprisal, Jewish forces later struck back. Empires came and went, but Israel's conflict with Gaza was there to stay.

During the Middle Ages, Gaza once more became a pivot of holy war, reemerging as the scourge of the crusader states. In the Barons' Crusade of 1239, Theobald I of Navarre led a Christian army southward but was ambushed near Gaza by Ayyubid forces and crushed. Only five years later, in 1244, at nearby La Forbie, a combined crusader-Syrian coalition was annihilated by Egyptian troops and their Khwarezmian mercenaries, marking the collapse of Christian power in the Holy Land. The final Christian dream of retaking Jerusalem died amid the blood and sand of Gaza.

The city's fortunes rose and fell with each new empire—Mamluks, Ottomans, and briefly, the French. In February 1799, Napoleon marched through Gaza on his way to Jaffa and Acre, using it as a staging ground for the ill-fated Syrian campaign that ended his Middle Eastern ambitions. Yet even in his failure, Gaza again played its ancient role: the gateway—and graveyard—of conquerors. World War I, Gaza became a battlefield once more. British and ANZAC forces launched three major assaults on Ottoman-held Gaza in 1917. The first two, in March and April, ended in bloody stalemates. The third, in November, finally broke the Ottoman line and opened the road to Jerusalem. That month, the British Foreign Secretary Arthur Balfour would issue his famous Balfour Declaration, declaring his nation's support for the establishment of a "national home for the Jewish people" in the Land of Israel. Gaza, Israel's oldest battleground, became the threshold of its modern resurrection.

From its birth, the modern State of Israel found itself drawn into Gaza's gravitational pull—the strip of land it could neither hold nor abandon. Jews had lived in the strip almost continuously for millennia, but the modern Jewish community was driven out in 1929 during the wave of antisemitic Arab pogroms that swept the British Mandate. Once the Jews built their army, the familiar dynamic quickly set in. Israel would repeatedly conquer Gaza and then relinquish it, paying the price for both. One small town captured the pitiful progression. In 1946, Jewish pioneers founded Kfar Darom, a lonely outpost on Gaza's edge. It was a declaration of Jewish presence amid a sea of Arab hostility. Two years later, during the War of Independence, Egyptian forces overran it and wiped it from the map. After the Six-Day War, Israel returned, rebuilt, and resettled it. And in 2005, Israel returned once more—this time to dismantle Gaza's Jewish communities and uproot their inhabitants.

As it had since time immemorial, Gaza figured prominently into Israel's wars. In 1956, alongside Britain and France, Israel launched the Sinai Campaign, capturing Gaza and the entire Sinai Peninsula in a matter of days. Yet within a month, under US pressure, Israel withdrew—relinquishing what it had won. Gaza was handed back to Egypt. Terror again erupted from the enclave, striking across the border as if nothing had changed. Then came 1967. Once again, Israel conquered Gaza—this time in a stunning, six-day whirlwind. In the decades that followed, Israel held it, governed it, even mingled with it. Tens of thousands of workers from Gaza crossed daily into Israel; Israelis crossed into Gaza to buy its wares, sip coffee by its beaches, and fill their homes with wicker furniture from its markets. For a fleeting generation, it seemed the pendulum had paused. But Gaza never stays still. With the outbreak of the First Intifada in 1987, the cycle of violence began anew.

Over the years, thousands of Israelis chose to live in the Strip. They built twenty-one Jewish communities across its dunes, known collectively as Gush Katif. Each one stood as a promise that this time, Israel would stay. Yet the old patterns of withdrawal were carved too deeply into Israel's psyche. The Camp David Accords of 1979, meant to achieve peace with Egypt, planted the seed of retreat: Israel withdrew from the Sinai Peninsula, setting a precedent that would echo decades later. In 1994, as part of the catastrophic Oslo Accords, Israel handed over Gaza's major cities and population centers to Yasser Arafat and the PLO. In August 2005, under Prime Minister Ariel Sharon's disengagement plan, Israel's departure from Gaza was made complete. IDF soldiers—some with faces soaked in tears—dragged fellow Israelis from their homes, synagogues, and schools. Torah scrolls were carried out from sanctuaries; the Jewish dead were torn out of their graves. Bulldozers leveled what had been built, destroyed, and rebuilt again. The dream of a Jewish presence in Gaza was again swept away in dust and tears.

Predictably, what was heralded as an "act of peace" became the opening chapter of a new series of wars. Within two years of Israel's withdrawal, Hamas violently seized control of Gaza, executing rivals and consolidating absolute rule. The territory was no longer shaped for civilian life but repurposed for conflict. Agricultural fields gave way to rocket launch sites. Legitimate commerce was displaced by an underground economy of smuggling tunnels, weapons depots, and command bunkers. From that point forward, Gaza entered a grim and repetitive cycle. Each confrontation—2008, 2012, 2014, and 2021—followed the same choreography. Hamas initiated violence, launching rockets at Israeli cities and embedding its forces among civilians. Israel responded with airstrikes and, at times, ground incursions aimed at restoring deterrence. Yet each campaign ended the same way: Israel withdrew, and Hamas remained in power. Meanwhile, Hamas used every ceasefire as an opportunity to rearm, rebuild, and refine its tactics, ensuring that the next round would be deadlier than the last.

To describe this pattern of limited, half-baked campaigns, a new language emerged. Officials spoke of "rounds of conflict," a sort of forever war waged in installments. Others, more bluntly, called it "mowing the lawn"—periodic operations designed not to defeat the enemy, but merely to keep it temporarily in check. The phrase captured the futility of the strategy. In Gaza, the grass always grew back, thicker and more dangerous than before.

Gaza was integrated into Israeli consciousness as what it had always been: a chronic pain, familiar enough to be normalized. A burden Israel had carried for thousands of years, and quietly assumed it would carry for thousands more. But some pains are not meant to be borne. With the launch of its largest-ever ground campaign in Gaza in the fall of 2023, Israel was no longer looking for relief. It was looking for a cure.

The Assault

Hamas had spent fifteen years preparing to meet an Israeli invasion, transforming the dense coastal enclave into a death trap. The Strip bristled with tens of thousands of assault rifles, anti-tank missiles, mortars, and improvised explosives. Beneath its streets ran a labyrinth of tunnels, command posts, and weapons factories. Aboveground, ordinary life was deliberately weaponized. Homes and narrow alleys were engineered as ambush sites. Schools and hospitals were converted into hardened fighting positions—places from which Hamas could fire with impunity, knowing that any Israeli response would draw not only bullets, but instant international condemnation. Hamas understood it could never defeat the IDF in open battle. So it redesigned the battlefield, turning Gaza into a massive, spike-studded Iron Maiden, engineered to dole out death by a thousand cuts. Wherever Israel advanced, it would bleed.

But Gaza had tried laying traps for Jews before. Millennia earlier, the Philistines had surrounded Samson in Gaza, waiting to kill him at dawn. Yet Samson rose at midnight, tore Gaza's massive gates—posts, bar, and all—from their foundations, hoisted them onto his shoulders, and carried them to a hill facing Hebron, miles away. It was an act both miraculous and symbolic: Samson ripped open Gaza's defenses, humiliating the Philistines and proving that nothing could contain the spirit of Israel. It was a lesson Gaza would relearn the hard way.

Just under three weeks after the massacre, on October 27, the order came. At 6 p.m., columns of tanks rolled across the border. Infantry units advanced behind them. Drones circled overhead and artillery thundered. Simultaneously, Gaza experienced a complete communications blackout. Unsurprisingly, the United Nations General Assembly passed a resolution calling for an "immediate and sustained" humanitarian truce. But Israel would not be fooled again.

The ground campaign was accompanied by a renewed wave of high-level targeted assassinations. On October 31, Ibrahim Biari—the commander of Hamas's Central Jabalia Battalion and a key planner of the October 7 atrocities—was eliminated in a massive airstrike, along with roughly fifty other terrorists. Senior Israeli officials later disclosed to *The New York Times* that Biari had been located using a newly deployed, highly sophisticated artificial-intelligence system developed by Unit 8200, which used phone surveillance to pinpoint his whereabouts. Biari was no stranger to Israeli intelligence. He had been responsible for the 2004 suicide bombing at the Port of Ashdod, in which thirteen Israelis were murdered, and had remained on Israel's most wanted list ever since. Nearly two decades later, the reckoning finally arrived. Justice, long deferred, was at last delivered.

The assassinations soon moved decisively up Hamas's command hierarchy. On November 8, Israel announced the killing of Mohsen Abu Zina, Hamas's head of weapons development and military industries. Two days later, Ahmed Ghandour—the commander of Hamas's Northern Gaza Brigade and a senior member of its political bureau—was eliminated. Ghandour was regarded by Israel as one of Hamas's "aces": a veteran commander who had overseen the kidnapping of Gilad Shalit in 2006 and survived two previous assassination attempts, in 2002 and 2012. In the same strike, Israel also killed Ahmed Siam, a Hamas commander who days earlier had personally blocked the evacuation of roughly one thousand civilians sheltering at Rantisi Hospital, holding them there as human shields. The campaign did not pause. Days later, the IDF eliminated Mohammed Khamis Dababash, a senior member of Hamas's political bureau, who had directed the 2002 terror attack in Atzmona that killed five Israelis. One by one, figures who had evaded justice for decades were being removed from the battlefield.

By November 3—less than a week after the ground offensive began—Israeli forces had encircled Gaza City from multiple axes. Three days later, they fought their way to the sea, cutting the Strip in two. What had begun as a frantic defensive response was rapidly becoming a relentless offensive. The objectives were unmistakable: destroy Hamas's military infrastructure, dismantle its tunnel network, and recover the hostages. The cost was severe. By the end of the first month of fighting, eighty-three IDF soldiers had been killed, many in anti-tank ambushes or by improvised explosive devices buried in the ruins. Combat engineers and sappers—the quiet heroes of the campaign—advanced house by house, clearing buildings rigged with explosives and uncovering tunnel shafts by the dozen. Yet despite the ferocity of the resistance, the pace of the advance was striking. Within a month, Israel had seized vast swaths of northern Gaza—territory Hamas had ruled unchallenged for seventeen years. Entire Hamas brigades collapsed in the face of IDF firepower, with terrorists either being killed, or fleeing and vanishing underground.

Urban warfare is among the most demanding forms of combat, defined by close quarters, chaos, and unremitting pressure. Yet the IDF adapted with striking speed, fusing intelligence, airpower, and ground maneuver in real time. Units deployed drones to scan the ruins, used AI-assisted targeting to map tunnel entrances, and pushed small infantry teams block by block through Gaza's neighborhoods. By late November, Hamas was approaching operational breakdown. Then, on November 24, Israel agreed to a brief ceasefire to secure the release of hostages. For Hamas, it was a lifeline; for Israel, an opportunity to reunite 105 hostages with their families. When the truce unraveled a week later, the IDF shifted south, resetting the campaign and entering an even more challenging phase.

Through December and January, the IDF pushed into Khan Younis—Hamas's southern stronghold and the hometown of its Gaza leader, Yahya Sinwar. The fighting there was the fiercest of the war: tunnels burrowed beneath schools, ambushes launched from hospital grounds, civilians trapped in a battlefield Hamas had deliberately embedded among them. By late January, Israeli forces had encircled Khan Younis, cutting off the

Strip's southern region. The campaign had entered a phase of measured dismemberment. Hamas's once-cohesive battalions were being shattered into isolated cells, stripped of command and coordination. But the deeper Israel advanced, the higher the cost. Hamas had seeded entire neighborhoods with belts of improvised explosives—hundreds of tons of buried munitions—that destroyed tanks, bulldozers, and armored personnel carriers.

January also marked the first assassination of a founding figure of Hamas. In Beirut's Dahieh district, Israel killed Saleh al-Arouri, the deputy chairman of Hamas's political bureau and the principal architect of its external terror operations. The explosions sent shards of glass and twisted metal through the streets near one of the neighborhood's famed sweet shops—a visceral signal that Israel's war with Hamas had expanded far beyond Gaza. Like many senior Hamas figures, al-Arouri had spent years in Israeli prisons before being released in a deal Israel would later regret. The United States designated him a terrorist in 2015 and placed a $5 million bounty on his head. His killing was not a surprise so much as the fulfillment of a promise. Just weeks earlier, Prime Minister Benjamin Netanyahu had declared in a nationwide address that he had instructed Mossad to pursue Hamas's leaders "wherever they are." Defense Minister Yoav Gallant was blunter still: Hamas's leaders, he said, were living on "borrowed time"—"marked for death."

Israel's ability to deliver on that warning rested on a long tradition. After the 1972 Munich massacre, Israel launched Wrath of God, a global manhunt that spanned years and continents. Over the course of the campaign, Israeli operatives and special forces assassinated at least a dozen senior terrorists directly linked to the attack and its support network, and disrupted many more. Targets were eliminated in Rome, Paris, Cyprus, and Beirut; some were shot at close range, others killed by remotely detonated bombs. The most audacious strike, Operation Spring of Youth in 1973, saw Israeli commandos infiltrate Beirut by sea—some dressed as women—and kill three top PLO leaders in a single night. The killing of al-Arouri signaled the revival of that doctrine—patient, methodical, and unforgiving. Exile and proxy sanctuaries no longer conferred immunity. Hamas's leadership, wherever it fled, would be hunted down.

The turn into 2024 also brought mounting international pressure over civilian casualties—pressure that increasingly constrained Israel's operational freedom and complicated its access to equipment and ammunition. By mid-January, several Israeli commanders were already warning publicly that delays in US arms deliveries were having tangible effects on the battlefield. Although these disruptions were not widely reported until the spring of 2024, they had begun earlier. Under growing political pressure tied to the fighting in Gaza, the Biden administration reportedly slowed or effectively froze the transfer of several key munitions at the start of the year, including a proposed sale of up to 6,500 Joint Direct Attack Munition (JDAM) kits valued at roughly $260 million. In March, Washington further declined to advance the congressional notification process for an additional weapons package estimated at more than $1 billion. That package included approximately $700 million in 120mm tank ammunition, $500 million in tactical vehicles, and close to $100 million in 120mm mortar rounds. The Pentagon also delayed shipments of JDAM precision guidance kits already in the pipeline. The impact was gradual but real: supply lines tightened, operational planning margins narrowed, and battlefield decisions were increasingly shaped not only by military necessity, but by diplomatic constraints.

As Israel prepared for a potential invasion of Rafah, President Biden issued an unprecedented public warning: if Israel proceeded with a full-scale operation, the United States would withhold certain arms deliveries. What had previously been conveyed through reports, leaks, and diplomatic signaling was now stated openly. Weapons transfers were no longer treated as a standing commitment, but as leverage, explicitly linked to policy compliance. That posture hardened further in October, when the administration again warned that US arms deliveries could be restricted—this time unless Israel significantly expanded the flow of humanitarian aid into Gaza.

For Israel, the timing of these weapons holdups was devastating. As the IDF fought its bloodiest battles in Khan Younis and Deir al-Balah, units on the ground began reporting dwindling stocks of shells, spare parts, and precision munitions. Commanders were forced to ration firepower and prioritize targets with growing caution. Infantry units often cleared buildings with small arms and hand-thrown explosives rather than calling in airstrikes that risked exhausting limited precision ordnance. In some cases, soldiers improvised—filling empty water bottles with gasoline and deploying them from drones when conventional munitions were unavailable. The consequences of these constraints became brutally clear on January 23, when Israel suffered its deadliest single day of the war. Twenty-four soldiers were killed in one day, bringing the death toll of the Gaza ground operation to 210. Most of the casualties—twenty-one reservists—were lost in a single incident in central Gaza as they prepared two buildings for demolition, planting explosives by hand. An anti-tank projectile struck one of the structures, triggering a catastrophic collapse. The scene underscored the risks imposed by limited stockpiles of precision munitions. Tasks that might otherwise have been executed from the air were instead carried out at close range, with soldiers exposed inside booby-trapped urban terrain.

Behind the scenes, frustration mounted. Israel was, as veteran defense analyst Avi Kober observed, "fighting with one hand tied behind its back." Yet the campaign did not halt. Under intensifying political, diplomatic, and logistical pressure, Israel pressed on—absorbing losses, adapting its tactics, and continuing the fight.

By February, the IDF had seized most of central Gaza, and Hamas's presence in Khan Younis was steadily collapsing. The air campaign shifted south to Rafah—the last gateway between Gaza and Egypt. Yet a familiar pattern was reasserting itself. Israel could defeat any force it encountered and conquer any ground it entered, but each new foothold came with the expectation of eventual withdrawal. Ground taken at great cost one week was contested again the next. In classical warfare, victory depends not only on taking territory, but on holding it. When the Allies defeated Nazi Germany and Imperial Japan, they stationed hundreds of thousands of troops to secure, stabilize, and rebuild those societies—garrisons that, in modified form, remain in place more than eight decades later. Territorial control was treated not as a temporary measure, but as the foundation that secured a lasting victory.

Israel, by contrast, was compelled to fight without the option of permanence. Hemmed in by international pressure—and by its own lingering aversion to reentering Gaza—it was expected to dismantle Hamas while simultaneously preparing to leave the ground it had just paid to seize. The result was a strategic contradiction. This was the residue of the "Oslo mentality": the belief that Israel may fight for territory, but must never truly hold it. That assumption proved more stubborn than Hamas itself. The obstacle was not military capability. It was psychological.

Hamas, for its part, could not survive a sustained, full-scale Israeli maneuver. In open battle, it would be annihilated. But Hamas did not need to win set-piece engagements to achieve its aims. A single improvised explosive device buried beneath a road, or a lone sniper firing from the window of a civilian structure repurposed as cover, could halt an advance, inflict casualties, and impose delay. This was not warfare aimed at victory, but at attrition. Each Israeli casualty echoed far beyond the battlefield, rippling through a small society bound tightly by family and reserve service. Time, rather than territory, became Hamas's ally. The goal was to bleed Israel—physically, psychologically, and politically—until pressure mounted to stop, withdraw, and begin the cycle again. Hamas did not need to defeat the IDF. It needed only to endure, and to make every step forward cost enough to be questioned.

By March, Israel controlled a majority of the Strip. In a major blow to Hamas's command-and-control apparatus, Israel reported the killing of Marwan Issa, the deputy commander of the Izz al-Din al-Qassam Brigades, alongside Ghazi Abu Tama'a, the head of Hamas's administrative and combat support staff. The March 10 strike hit both operational command and the logistical backbone of the war effort. Hamas's organized resistance was fracturing, its leadership steadily cut down. Yet the cycle of clearing and re-clearing districts like Shuja'iyya, Zeitoun, Jabalia continued to drain the morale of Israel's soldiers. As the campaign wore on, the IDF began rotating brigades to recover. Thousands of reservists were released to tend to families and livelihoods left on hold for months. The war had become more than a contest of firepower. It was a test of willpower—of vigilance under exhaustion, of resolve under repetition, of endurance against an enemy that survived not by winning battles, but by refusing to disappear.

Through April, the war sank deeper underground. Combat engineers collapsed tunnel after tunnel, while intelligence officers and special units hunted Hamas commanders through vast subterranean networks burrowed beneath hospitals, mosques, and dense civilian neighborhoods. Each week uncovered new revelations: underground weapons factories, hardened command centers, and sprawling complexes stocked with Iranian-supplied munitions. The toll continued to climb. By late spring, more than 242 IDF soldiers had been killed and thousands wounded. The figures were lower than early projections—but in a country as small and tightly knit as Israel, each loss carried an unbearable weight. Casualties were not statistics; they were sons, fathers, neighbors, and reservists pulled from ordinary life into extraordinary danger. By May, ground forces followed the air campaign's shift south to Rafah, Hamas's final stronghold.

The advance on Rafah unfolded under extraordinary international pressure. For weeks, Israel's allies—chief among them the United States—warned publicly against a ground operation in the city, citing the dense concentration of displaced civilians sheltering there. Diplomatic cables, press briefings, and presidential statements all carried the same message: do not go in. Rafah, Israel was told, was a red line. But for Israel's leadership, Rafah was also the last military reality standing between Hamas and survival. Intelligence assessments were unequivocal. Hamas's final fully constituted brigades—its last intact maneuver formations—were concentrated in and around Rafah, along with senior commanders, remaining tunnel hubs, and the remnants of its smuggling and resupply networks tied to Egypt. Leaving Rafah untouched would have preserved Hamas's core fighting force. Prime Minister Benjamin Netanyahu understood the stakes. Having already paid the costs of half measures for nearly two decades, he concluded that stopping short now would amount to strategic failure.

In the end, the dire predictions proved vastly overstated. Rafah did not become a humanitarian catastrophe, in large part due to Israel's painstaking efforts to evacuate more than half a million civilians from the area. Israeli forces secured the Rafah crossing within days, severing Hamas's access to the principal artery through which weapons, cash, and supplies had flowed for years. The operation unfolded far more narrowly—and far more effectively—than critics had claimed was possible. And it was there, in Rafah, that the war delivered its most consequential blow. In October 2024, Israeli forces killed Yahya Sinwar, Hamas's leader in Gaza and the chief architect of October 7. Ultimately, Israel's Rafah offensive underscored a recurring lesson of its history: restraint imposed from abroad brings disaster; sovereign resolve brings victory.

By June and July, the war had shifted into a campaign of raids and rolling strikes. The IDF consolidated control of the Netzarim Corridor, which bisected Gaza, and launched large-scale operations to widen and secure its flanks. On July 13 came one of the most consequential blows of the war. An Israeli airstrike in the Khan Younis area killed Mohammed Deif, the commander of Hamas's military wing, along with Rafa Salama, head of the Khan Younis Brigade. With Deif's death, Hamas lost the chief architect of its modern war machine—the figure who, beginning in the early 2000s, transformed the organization from a crude insurgent network into one of the most lethal terror groups on earth. At the time of his killing, Deif ranked second on Israel's threat list, behind only Yahya Sinwar—the "Butcher of Khan Younis." He had been on Israel's most wanted list since 1995 for orchestrating a wave of bus bombings that tore through Israeli cities. Though briefly detained by the Palestinian Authority in 2000 at Israel's request, he escaped within months and vanished once more into the shadows.

Few targets in Israel's history proved as elusive. According to Amir Avivi, Israel attempted to kill Deif at least seven times. A strike in 2001 missed him. Another in 2002 cost him an eye. Further attempts followed in 2003 and 2006, leaving him gravely wounded. He narrowly escaped again in the 2014 Gaza war, when Israel initially believed him dead, and survived two more attempts in 2021. This time was different. On July 13, 2024, Israel employed eight two-thousand-pound bombs to ensure finality. Hamas denied Deif's death for more than five months before finally conceding it on January 30, 2025—bringing to an end one of the longest and most consequential manhunts in Israel's history.

By August and September, as the war neared the end of its first year, a hard truth had settled in. Hamas was broken—but not gone. Reduced to ambushes, sniper fire, and sporadic rocket attacks, it no longer resembled an army, yet it still resisted eradication. Israel could dominate the battlefield, but the return of the captives and a decisive victory remained out of reach. At home, the country was changing. Among soldiers at the front, there remained a powerful sense of resolve and cohesion. But within Israeli society, the political consensus was fraying. As 2024 gave way to 2025, public confidence in the political and military leadership eroded among parts of the population. Prime Minister Netanyahu's promise of "total victory" divided the nation. Support for a ceasefire grew. Protests demanding a deal to bring the hostages home swelled. After a year of continuous war, exhaustion—emotional, economic, and psychological—was setting in.

And yet, the war had also revealed that even under severe diplomatic constraints, Israel could mobilize with extraordinary speed, fight with astonishing precision, and adapt with grit and ingenuity. A tiny Jewish state had accomplished what once required massive Western coalitions: the conquest of a dense, fortified urban enclave ruled by a terrorist army. Gaza had been penetrated, mapped, and dismantled in ways many thought impossible.

Still, amid the ruins, the central question lingered. Every tunnel destroyed revealed another nearby. Every cleared stronghold threatened to regenerate from the rubble. Israel had proven—again—that it could enter Gaza and crush whatever stood in its path. But history whispered its familiar question: could it stay? Could Israel finally plant its flag in Gaza—or was it bound to the old pattern, where every conquest carries a withdrawal in its wake? Israel's largest foray into Gaza demonstrated that its most difficult battle was not for territory, but for clarity. Not how to fight—but how to finish.

Gaza forced a reckoning over the meaning of victory itself. Israel was no longer fighting only an enemy, but an idea: whether it would continue to administer conflicts endlessly, or reclaim the strategic will to win once and for all. In that struggle, Israel was fighting for its soul. Breaking free from the Oslo-era doctrine of permanent indecision would require more than tanks and troops. It would require the courage to define victory without ambiguity—and the resolve to pursue it without apology, hesitation, or retreat.

Why Hamas Survived

Two years into the war, even after the last living hostages were brought home, Hamas still dominated approximately half of Gaza. The same organization that carried out the worst massacre of Jews since the Holocaust remained entrenched at the doorstep of the most formidable Jewish military force in history. For many Israelis, that reality was intolerable. How could it be that after Hamas's battalions were shattered, its senior commanders erased, thousands of fighters killed or captured, and vast tunnel networks detonated—Hamas still survived?

The answer had little to do with firepower or battlefield competence. It lay elsewhere: in policy choices, psychological constraints, and a war conducted under irrational rules that tethered every Israeli advance to an enemy revival. Three words defined the paradox that kept Hamas alive:

Aid. Breaks. Hostages.

When Israel declared war on October 7, its response was immediate and absolute. A total siege was imposed. Gaza would be sealed—no electricity, no fuel, no food, no water. The objective was stark and simple: destroy Hamas, rescue the hostages, and nothing more. Providing goods for Gaza was not the mission. Within days, however, Joe Biden arrived in Tel Aviv. The visit was framed as an embrace of solidarity, but it carried a warning. Behind the public displays of friendship came private demands. The siege, Washington insisted, could not stand. Food and water had to flow. "Humanitarian relief," the administration argued, was a moral imperative. And so, the siege was breached. Aid convoys began moving through the Kerem Shalom and Rafah crossings, restoring fuel, food, and water to the Strip. The very lifelines Hamas required to survive were reopened, not by force of arms but by force of diplomacy. Israel's leadership consented, naïvely believing that supporting civilians would preserve international legitimacy and secure long-term support. It was a grave miscalculation.

Since the beginning of warfare, victory has turned on one principle above all others: sever the enemy's supply lines. Israel, however, was compelled to do the reverse—to provide and secure the very resources sustaining its enemy. Had fuel remained cut, Hamas's tunnel network would have gone dark and unventilated. Had food been halted, its fighters would have faced rapid collapse. Had water been withheld, organized resistance would likely have unraveled within days. History offers no shortage of precedent. When the United States fought Japan in 1945, it deliberately strangled the island nation's food supply. American B-29s seeded Japan's coastal waters with thousands of naval mines, sinking or crippling nearly seven hundred civilian vessels carrying food to a country dependent on imports to feed its population. American commanders felt no embarrassment about the strategy. They named it plainly: Operation Starvation. It was not cruelty, but clarity—and it helped bring the war to a decisive close, saving countless lives.

Israel required no such distant measures. Gaza was already encircled on three sides; the fourth, bordering Egypt, could have been sealed within days. Hamas was caught in a natural chokehold, its war machine utterly dependent on external lifelines. Yet even while Hamas held 250 hostages, Israel remained bound by foreign impositions of moral restraint. It was compelled not only to fight its enemy, but to feed and fuel it, too.

Even within Gaza, local suppliers had no problem cutting water to Gaza's civilians to put pressure on Hamas. In November 2023, the Abdul Salam Yassin Company—operator of a desalination plant supplying nearly half of Gaza's population—halted its operations in protest over Hamas's detention of a single employee. At the same time, more than seventy trucks transporting water containers across the Strip suspended their work, severing a major supply line to Gaza's residents. The consequences were neither hidden nor denied. A member of the company's board openly told reporters that the shutdown would affect more than one million people who normally depended on its water. He acknowledged the scale of the harm without hesitation. "I know it is catastrophic," he told Reuters, "but protecting our employees is a sacred issue." And yet his company did this over one detained worker. Israel did not do so after 251 innocents were abducted and 1,200 more savagely butchered.

Once aid began flowing, Hamas no longer faced a logistics problem. Food and goods were quickly seized by its operatives—often in brazen daylight raids—then resold at extortionate prices. The proceeds funded payrolls, sustained recruitment, and kept the organization alive. Through a perverse inversion of humanitarian intent, Israel became the quartermaster of its enemy. The same fuel meant to power hospitals ventilated tunnel networks. Truckloads of food sustained Hamas fighters while Israeli hostages were deliberately starved to the brink of death. Aid that was meant to relieve suffering instead prolonged the war—feeding the very force responsible for it.

The results were predictable. What might have been a short, decisive campaign became a two-year grind of raids, breaks, and recurring airstrikes. This outcome did not spare Gaza's civilians. It condemned them. Far more people died over two years of intermittent bombing, displacement, and collapse than would likely have perished in a concentrated, weekslong siege designed to end the war outright. The logic was ancient, and the warning older still. As Rabbi Elazar cautioned nearly two millennia ago: "He who is compassionate to the cruel will ultimately become cruel to the compassionate." In Gaza, that ancient truth was replayed in modern form. Compassion extended to a terror regime only empowered the abusers and multiplied the suffering.

Ultimately, the most moral way to wage war is to end it swiftly—an insight as old as strategy itself. Sun Tzu, the foundational theorist of military thought, warned with brutal clarity: "There is no instance of a country having benefited from prolonged warfare." The same truth was articulated centuries later amid America's greatest national catastrophe. Early in the Civil War, Frederick Douglass argued that the Union must free and draft enslaved men into the war effort, insisting that anything less would constitute a fatal half measure. To withhold the full force available to Lincoln's armies, Douglass warned, was not restraint but misguided leniency toward the structures that sustained the enemy. Such leniency would only postpone the achievement of victory. And in war, postponement is paid for in lives. As Douglass predicted with grim precision, a "lenient war" would become "a lengthy war—and therefore the worst kind of war."

The second reason for Hamas's survival was the endlessness of its pauses. By November 2023, less than a month after the launch of Israel's ground invasion, the IDF had achieved what few thought possible: Gaza City—the seat of Hamas's power—was surrounded. Command nodes were collapsing, battalion commanders were dead or in hiding, and the organization was bleeding. But then came a pause. On November 24, under US and Qatari mediation, Israel agreed to a temporary truce. It was set to last four days before being extended in increments. In exchange for the release of terrorists from Israeli prisons and a surge of "humanitarian aid," Hamas agreed to release Israeli hostages. The first day brought miracles: brothers and sisters reunited, children running into their parents' arms, elderly women embracing grandchildren they feared they'd never see again. The nation of Israel rejoiced. Unfortunately, Hamas did too. For the first time in weeks, supply convoys poured in, tunnels reopened, units regrouped, and command links reconnected. Like a boxer saved by the bell, Hamas was able to breathe and bounce back.

And it happened again—and again. When Donald Trump returned to the Oval Office in January 2025, his administration brokered another temporary ceasefire to accelerate hostage talks. Another came that autumn. Each pause followed the same pattern: Hamas on the ropes, the world intervenes, Hamas recovers. The IDF—unmatched in speed, discipline, and precision—was fighting an enemy the world refused to let it finish. The result was not peace, but paralysis. Israel was waging a war it could fight but never win. The IDF was fighting in an arena of perpetual interruption—a theater where every advance triggered a call for restraint. Wars end when one side loses the will to fight. But every truce gave Hamas exactly what it needed: time. Time to rebuild tunnels. Time to regroup. Time to rally the world against Israel.

The third—and most agonizing—constraint was the hostages scattered through the tunnel networks beneath Gaza. From the first hours of October 7, Hamas understood the leverage it had seized. By abducting the elderly and the wounded, women and children, soldiers and civilians alike, it obtained its most powerful weapon: Israel's conscience. No commander could authorize a full airstrike knowing that Israelis might lie beneath. No armored unit could flatten a block knowing that one wrong calculation could kill one of their own. This was Hamas's most cynical and effective strategy—weaponized empathy. Major tunnel complexes housing senior Hamas leaders—from Yahya Sinwar's bunker in Khan Younis to Mohammed Deif's redoubts beneath Rafah—were routinely assessed as possible hostage sites. Israel could locate them, track them, even reach them. But it could not strike them.

By mid-2025, in parts of southern Gaza where the IDF was operating, entire compounds were deliberately left untouched—neither entered nor bombed—because intelligence suggested hostages were inside. Hamas quickly learned the lesson. These sites became sanctuaries. From within them, operatives launched attacks on Israeli troops encircling the area, retreating afterward into zones they knew were off-limits to airstrikes. From one such compound alone, terrorists repeatedly emerged, struck, and withdrew unharmed. In one instance, nearly a dozen Israeli soldiers were killed by terrorists operating from a single location, holding one hostage.

This was the cruel arithmetic of the war in Gaza: the enemy hides among innocents—and the innocents, unbearably, include your own. The hostage dilemma penetrated every level of strategy. Even when intelligence pinpointed Sinwar himself, operations were delayed or aborted. Hamas endured not because Israel lacked power, but because its leaders were shielded by Israeli captives and its fighters by the civilians around them.

Aid. Breaks. Hostages. Each reinforced the others. Aid sustained Hamas's logistics. Ceasefires restored its morale. Hostages restrained Israel's firepower. Together, they produced a war fought without finality. The irony is bitter. By the fourth month, Hamas was militarily defeated—its brigades shattered, its command fractured. Yet politically, diplomatically, and psychologically, it survived. Gaza became a theater of stalemate, with the world as its audience. By the second year, Hamas controlled barely 40 percent of the Strip. Sadly, that was enough. Enough to claim survival. Enough to deny Israel closure.

The IDF had proven what it must—that when unleashed, it could conquer any terrain, crush any foe, and obliterate any terrorist stronghold. What it could not do—what it was not permitted to do—was finish the job.

The cost of that restraint was staggering: nearly a thousand soldiers killed, fifteen thousand wounded, billions spent, families stretched between pride and exhaustion. And still Hamas endured—because the war in Gaza was never only against armed terrorists, but against an ideology indulged by the world. Israel had the means to end the war in months. But it fought under rules written by others—by diplomats thousands of miles away, by television anchors counting inflated casualties, by agencies that sent flour to feed terrorists, and by an ally that demanded limits in the name of mercy. Why did Gaza take so long? Because Israel fought not only

Hamas, but its own conscience and the world's expectations. Because each time victory neared, it was deferred—for optics, for politics, for morality misapplied. History's verdict, however, is unforgiving: wars do not end when the world feels comfortable. They end when evil is broken beyond recovery.

CHAPTER SIX

PRELUDE TO THE TERROR: THE WAR ON TERROR IN JUDEA AND SAMARIA

Gather on the hills of Samaria
And witness the great outrages within her . . .
Thus said the Sovereign God:
An enemy, all about the land!
Amos 3:9, 11

Though it drew relatively little attention during the war, the crisis began on Israel's most overlooked front: Judea and Samaria. Long before October 7, the catastrophe that would combust in the south was seeded in Israel's central hills.

Judea, Samaria, and East Jerusalem—territories held by Jordan until Israel liberated them in 1967—have long formed a cauldron of violence and terror. Though Jewish life flourished there for centuries, the region was rendered *Judenrein* after Jordan's conquest during Israel's War of Independence. Following the Six-Day War, with the land restored to

Jewish control, Jews returned once more to build homes in these hills—at the very crossroads of Jewish history, faith, and national survival.

Today, across this sprawling hill country, roughly half a million Israelis live amid millions of Arabs—about 150 Jewish communities encircled by more than 450 Arab towns and villages. While the Arab population is often inflated to more than three million, demographer Yoram Ettinger places the figure closer to two million. Even so, ever since Israel ceded control over large portions of these lands to the Palestinian Authority under the Oslo Accords, the threat to Jewish life has intensified sharply. The region became a persistent incubator of terror—a frontline where stone-throwing attacks metastasized into waves of firebombings, stabbings, car-rammings, shootings, IEDs, and organized terrorist cells aimed directly at Israel's heartland. And yet, despite the danger, a growing number of Jews continue to build lives in Judea, Samaria, and East Jerusalem—for two reasons: one ancient, and one urgently modern.

First, Judea and Samaria are the Jewish biblical heartland—the very stage on which most of the Bible unfolds. Nearly four-fifths of the biblical narrative is set among the region's valleys and ridgelines. Hebron's Cave of the Patriarchs, Shiloh's site of the Tabernacle, and Rachel's Tomb near Bethlehem are only a few of the places that anchor the deepest roots of Jewish nationhood. It is precisely this profoundly Jewish landscape that the diplomatic shorthand "West Bank" is designed to obscure. As noted earlier, the term is not neutral geography but a linguistic weapon, coined to amputate three thousand years of Jewish history with a bureaucratic flick of the pen. Calling Judea and Samaria the "West Bank" is as absurd as renaming Pennsylvania the "West Bank" of the Delaware or French Alsace the "West Bank" of the Rhine—and at least those are real rivers. The Jordan, at most points, is little more than a stream. The purpose is not description but erasure: to recast Jews as trespassers in the very cradle of their civilization, to murder Jewish memory and then claim the land it sanctifies. Jews, on the other hand, returned to these hills because they knew the truth—Judea and Samaria are the most Jewish lands on earth.

Second, and no less decisive, Israeli control over Judea and Samaria is a matter of Jewish survival. Without these lands, the State of Israel contracts to a nine-mile waist at its narrowest point, providing any hostile invasion force with a corridor it can sever in minutes. But with Israel in control of these lands, it commands the ridgeline and the Jordan Valley: a natural defensive barrier any sober strategist would fight to the last man to hold. States that intend to survive seek depth, elevation, and lines of approach they can defend. Judea and Samaria provide all three.

And yet, even as they safeguard Israel, Judea and Samaria also embody its most complex security dilemma. They are where demography, theology, and topography converge—and collide. It was there, in the contested footholds of Israel's central hill country, that the newest doctrines of multi-front, existential terror first took root. The method was incremental. Stones and Molotov cocktails became drive-by shootings and roadside bombs; lone-wolf assaults hardened into organized, networked cells; neighborhoods once secure turned into logistics hubs of terror. Each incident was small enough to file and forget, yet together they formed a pressure campaign that forced Israel to disperse its focus, scatter its elite manpower, and accept a steady bleed as the price of temporary calm. Judea and Samaria were the original battleground—the terrorists' rehearsal space and Israel's earliest warning.

The IDF's Central Command is charged with counterterrorism and maintaining control over Israel's administered zones in Judea and Samaria. But its Judea and Samaria Division, composed of six regional brigades, still could not contain what was coming. In the two years leading up to October 7, the region would erupt in the fiercest wave of terror since the Second Intifada.

At the start of 2022, things were calm. Six months earlier, Benjamin Netanyahu had been removed from office for the first time since 2009. Under its new prime minister, Naftali Bennett, Israel still imagined it had relative control. Relative—because in the six months from August 2021 through March 2022, there were still hundreds of terrorist actions perpetrated against Israelis. Still, they had resulted in only one Israeli death. But the illusion of "relative calm" collapsed in the spring of 2022, when a sequence of mass-casualty attacks struck Israel's heartland in rapid succession.

In March 2022, the terror wave erupted with shocking brutality. An Israeli Bedouin carried out a roaming killing spree in Beersheba—stabbing a woman at a gas station, ramming and killing a rabbi on a bicycle, and then murdering two more civilians at a shopping center before being shot by a bus driver. Days later, two Israeli Arab cousins opened fire with assault rifles at a bus stop in Hadera, killing two—an attack publicly mourned by officials in their Israeli-Arab hometown. Within forty-eight hours, the violence struck again when a terrorist from the Jenin area rampaged through the Ultra-Orthodox city of Bnei Brak, killing five people, including a Christian police officer who died returning fire. In less than a week, terror moved seamlessly from the Negev to Israel's coastal plain and into the heart of its cities, leaving the sense that something far more dangerous had begun.

Deadly Terror Attacks in Israel in 2022, Largely Originating in Judea, Samaria, and East Jerusalem

Date	Location	Perpetrator	Victims	Attack Description
Mar 22, 2022	Beersheba, Southern Israel	Arab terrorist (34) from Southern Israel	4 killed, 2 wounded	Stabbing, car-ramming, and shooting spree across multiple sites kills Doris Yahbas (49), Laura Yitzhak (43), Rabbi Moshe Kravitzky (50), and Menahem Yehezkel, (67)
Mar 27, 2022	Hadera, Northern Israel	Two ISIS Arab terrorist cousins	2 killed, 10 wounded	Assault rifle attack on bus stop kills Yezen Falah and Shirel Abukarat, both 19
Mar 29, 2022	Bnei Brak, Central Israel	Arab terrorist (27) from Samaria	5 killed	Mass shooting in ultra-Orthodox city kills Amir Khoury (32), Ya'akov Shalom (36), Avishai Yehezkel (29), Victor Sorokopot (38), Dimitri Mitrik (23)

Date	Location	Perpetrator	Victims	Attack Description
Apr 7, 2022	Tel Aviv (Dizengoff St.)	Arab terrorist (28) from Samaria	3 killed, 6 wounded	Shooting at a downtown Tel Aviv bar kills Tomer Morad (28), Eytam Magini (27), Barak Lufan (35)
Apr 29, 2022	Ariel, Samaria	2 Hamas Arab terrorists from Samaria	1 killed	Murder of security guard Vyacheslav Golev (23), who used his body to shield his fiancée from the hail of bullets, saving her life
May 5, 2022	Elad, Southern Israel	Arab terrorists (19 and 20) from Samaria	3 killed, eight injured	Axe attack and shooting of Boaz Gol (49), Yonatan Havakuk (44), Oren Ben Yitfah (35) in a park on Israel's Independence Day
Sep 20, 2022	Holon, Central Israel	Arab terrorist (28) from Samaria	1 killed	Shulamit Ovadia (84) beaten to death with a metal bar
Oct 25, 2022	Near Kedumim, Samaria	Arab terrorist from Samaria	1 killed	Stabbing attack mortally wounds Shalom Sofer (63)
Oct 29, 2022	Kiryat Arba, Judea	Arab Hamas (35) terrorist from Judea	1 killed, 3 wounded	Shooting attack kills Ronen Hanania (49). The terrorist was an elementary school teacher.
Nov 15, 2022	Ariel, Samaria	Arab terrorist	3 killed, 4 wounded	Stabbing attack in Ariel industrial zone kills Tamir Avihai (50), Michael Ladygin (36), Motti Ashkenazi (59)
Nov 23, 2022	Jerusalem	Arab terrorist	2 killed, 22 wounded	Two explosions at a bus stop near the entrance to Jerusalem kill Aryeh Shechopek (15) and Tadese Tashume Ben Ma'ada (50)

These massacres happened against the backdrop of the Negev Summit, where foreign ministers from Egypt, Bahrain, Morocco, and the UAE joined Israel's leadership under US sponsorship to chart a new regional peace. The symbolism was unambiguous: while diplomats toasted reconciliation, jihadists declared war. Like the onslaught of October 7, these attacks were aimed squarely at derailing the Abraham Accords. But even after the summit ended, the killing did not. In April, a terrorist infiltrator from Jenin opened fire on Tel Aviv's Dizengoff Street, murdering three Israelis and wounding six before being shot dead in Jaffa. Over the next month, four more Israelis were murdered in two shooting attacks. In a matter of weeks, eighteen Israelis had been murdered.

Israel's response strove to project strength. The IDF launched Operation Breakwater, its largest counterterror campaign in Judea and Samaria since the early 2000s. Fifty-six reserve battalions were mobilized, and nightly IDF operations swept across northern Samaria. A new forty-five-kilometer segment of the security barrier began to rise along the Green Line, sealing infiltration routes from Jenin and Tulkarem. Within weeks, Israeli forces intercepted 150 vehicles and detained over six hundred suspects attempting illegal crossings. The government poured $57 million in emergency funding into the police, even as civilian demand for firearms licenses skyrocketed by 2,500 percent.

In August 2022, Israeli forces captured the Islamic Jihad commander in Jenin. Two months later, a dramatic October raid killed five terrorists, including the founder of a rising brand of terror: the Lions' Den. Modeled on Hamas and rooted in northern Samaria, the group rapidly became a cult phenomenon. By the end of 2022, its Telegram channel had soared to 239,000 followers, eclipsing even Hamas's al-Qassam Brigades. By year's end, Israeli forces had made more than two thousand arrests. Without the scale of Operation Breakwater, the toll would have been far higher. As Shin Bet Director Ronen Bar revealed, Israeli security forces foiled 312 major terror attacks during that period—stabbings, shootings, and bombings that never came to pass.

And yet, the trajectory was obvious. In 2020, there were just nineteen shooting attacks in Judea and Samaria. In 2021, that number climbed to ninety-eight. By 2022, it had exploded to 167. And that was only the gunfire. According to IDF Central Command, an additional 3,780 non-shooting attacks took place that year—an average of 315 per month—including 646 assaults with Molotov cocktails or improvised explosive devices. The escalation reached the capital that November, when two sophisticated, coordinated, and remotely detonated bombs ripped through Jerusalem bus stops, killing two and wounding twenty-three. Between 2021 and 2022, there was also a more than fivefold increase in the number of shooting incidents targeting IDF forces entering Palestinian Authority-controlled cities. The numbers told the story plainly: a region sliding from unrest into open insurgency.

At the very end of 2022, just days before the new year, Benjamin Netanyahu returned to power after the brief Bennett–Lapid interlude. His campaign promise had been blunt: restore deterrence and drive terror back underground. Within weeks, he authorized the deadliest raid on Jenin in nearly two decades, targeting Islamic Jihad cells preparing imminent attacks. The terror group answered with rockets from Gaza—a reminder that Israel's traditionally separate fronts, South and East, were beginning to merge into one. Netanyahu's new government sought to reassert control, but events were already outpacing his hawkish agenda.

In early 2023, Jerusalem was hit by a rapid succession of brutal attacks: a mass shooting on International Holocaust Remembrance Day that killed seven, a child-led shooting the following morning that wounded two, and a car-ramming in February that murdered three more—including two young brothers—signaling a sharp and disturbing escalation in the terror wave. Then terror turned toward the roads. The Jewish areas of Judea and Samaria are stitched together by vulnerable arteries like Route 60, Route 443, and Highway 90 in the Jordan River Valley. In 2023, these roads, weaving through Arab villages and terrorist hotspots, became kill zones. Rocks, Molotov cocktails, roadside bombs, and ambush gunfire turned daily commutes into daily gambles. None of these flashpoints carried more symbolic weight than Huwara, the village that had already seen dozens of attacks over the years. On February 26, brothers Hallel and Yagel Yaniv, aged twenty-one and nineteen, were shot dead while stuck in traffic there. That night, enraged Israelis stormed Huwara, torching homes and cars—a glimpse of the growing chaos that unchecked terror was beginning to unleash.

The Explosion of Deadly Terrorist Attacks in the Year Leading Up to October 7

Date	Location	Perpetrator	Victims	Attack Description
Jan 27, 2023	Jerusalem (Neve Yaakov)	Arab terrorist (21) from East Jerusalem	7 killed, 3 wounded	Mass shooting on Holocaust Remembrance Day; victims include Eli (48) and Natalie Mizrahi (45), Rafael Ben-Eliyahu (56), Asher Natan (14), Shaul Chai (68), Irina Korolova (59), and Ilya Sosonsky (26)
Jan 28, 2023	Jerusalem	Arab terrorist (13) from East Jerusalem	2 wounded	Shooting attack
Feb 10, 2023	Jerusalem (Ramot)	Arab terrorist (31) from Issawiya	3 killed, 4 wounded	Car-ramming; victims include newlywed Alter Shlomo Lederman (20) and brothers Yaakov Yisrael (6) and Asher Menachem Paley (8)
Feb 26, 2023	Huwara, Samaria	Arab terrorist (41) from Nablus, aided by his son	2 killed	Drive-by shooting of brothers Hallel (21) & Yagel (19) Yaniv
Feb 27, 2023	Beit HaArava Junction, Samaria	Arab terrorist (44) from Jericho	1 killed	Elan Ganeles (26) shot dead on a highway between Jericho and the Dead Sea
Mar 9, 2023	Tel Aviv (Dizengoff street)	Arab terrorist from Nil'in	1 killed, 2 wounded	Or Eshkar (32) killed in shooting attack in central Tel Aviv
Mar 19, 2023	Huwara, Samaria	Arab terrorist	1 wounded	Drive-by shooting; victim, a former US Marine, returned fire, forcing attacker to flee

Date	Location	Perpetrator	Victims	Attack Description
Mar 25, 2023	Huwara, Samaria	Arab terrorist	2 wounded	Drive-by shooting targeting IDF soldiers
Apr 7, 2023	Hamra Junction, Samaria	Arab terrorist cell from Hamas	3 killed	Massacre of British-Israeli Lucy Dee (48) and her daughters Maia Dee (20) and Rina Dee (15)
Apr 7, 2023	Tel Aviv (Boardwalk Promenade)	Arab terrorist (45) from Kafr Qasem, Northern Israel	1 killed, 7 wounded	Italian tourist Alessandro Parini (35) killed in car-ramming on Tel Aviv promenade
May 30, 2023	Hermesh, Samaria	Arab terrorist from Islamic Jihad	1 killed	Meir Tamari (32) shot while driving on a road near his home
Jun 20, 2023	Eli, Samaria	Arab terrorist with Hamas	4 killed	Shooting at a restaurant kills Ofer Fayerman (64), Harel Masood (21), Elisha Anteman (17), and Shmuel Mordoff (17)
Jul 4, 2023	Tel Aviv	Arab terrorist	Unborn child killed	Ramming and stabbing
Aug 5, 2023	Tel Aviv	Arab terrorist from Jenin	1 killed	Shooting of Israeli security Guard Chen Amir (42)
Aug 19, 2023	Huwara	Arab terrorist from Nablus	2 killed	Execution of Aviad Nir (28) and his father Silas (Shai) Nigreker (60)
Aug 21, 2023	Hebron area, Judea	Arab terrorist	1 killed, 1 wounded	Murder of Batsheva Nigri (40), a mother of three, in front of her daughter (12) while driving to Beit Hagai
Aug 31, 2023	Modi'in (Maccabim Junction)	41-year-old Arab terrorist from Samaria	1 killed, 6 wounded	Stabbing and car-ramming. Lone soldier Cpl. Maksym Molchanov, 20, killed

By March 2023, the terror campaign was fully entrenched, with shootings striking both Tel Aviv and the arteries of Judea and Samaria—killing civilians in the heart of Israel and repeatedly targeting soldiers and motorists in Huwara, which had become a persistent flashpoint of violence. By early April, Israel struck back. In a raid on Nablus, security forces arrested the terrorists responsible for the attack on the soldiers and killed both a senior Fatah official and a member of the Lions' Den. The reprisal made headlines but did little to stem the tide.

The fuse then burned its way to the powder keg on Jerusalem's Temple Mount. On April 5, after evening Ramadan prayers, hundreds of Arabs barricaded themselves inside the Al-Aqsa Mosque. Ostensibly, the spark was a rumor—Jews preparing to sacrifice a goat. Far more likely, Hamas had orchestrated the provocation. Israeli police stormed the compound, as those holed up inside hurled fireworks and bricks to repel them. More than four hundred were arrested. Within hours, rockets were launched from both Gaza and southern Lebanon—yet another mingling of the fronts. Two days later—April 7, 2023—came the attack that would scar Israel's collective conscience. A Hamas terrorist ambushed a British-Israeli family near Hamra, murdering Lucy Dee and her two daughters, Maia and Rina. CNN's Christiane Amanpour would later describe the indiscriminate killing of three unarmed women as a "shootout." In truth, it was a massacre perpetrated by Hamas. As if that weren't enough for a single day, that night a forty-five-year-old Arab Israeli citizen rammed his car onto Tel Aviv's beachside boardwalk.

By May, Israel's counterterror campaign extended to Gaza, where a sweeping offensive targeted the leadership of Palestinian Islamic Jihad. In Operation Shield and Arrow, Israeli airstrikes eliminated five PIJ commanders in the Strip, even as nightly raids continued across the central hills. Yet terror did not relent. On May 30, a Jewish father of two was shot dead near his hometown of Hermesh. Three weeks later, on June 19, Israeli troops clashed with terrorists in Jenin, where a massive improvised explosive device crippled an armored vehicle and forced a perilous evacuation under fire. The extraction required a rare Apache helicopter strike—the first aerial intervention of its kind in Judea and Samaria since the Second Intifada. The explosives were not the only new threat emerging from Judea and Samaria that summer. By mid-2023, terrorists there had begun launching primitive, locally made "Qassam" rockets toward nearby Jewish communities. Judea and Samaria were now mutating into an embryonic rocket front.

A day after the operation in Jenin, two members of Hamas murdered four Israelis at a hummus restaurant in Eli. And then came the largest Samaria operation in two decades. Before dawn on July 3, 2023, Israel launched Operation Home and Garden in the Jenin refugee camp—Samaria's foremost terrorist stronghold. Drones struck weapons factories and explosives caches before a brigade-size force of two thousand soldiers swept in. For fourteen hours, firefights raged in the alleys. The IDF killed nine terrorists and lost one of its own, Sergeant-Major David Yitzhak of the elite Egoz unit. The IDF declared it had accomplished its goals, but Jenin's symbolism only grew. Beyond the reach of the Palestinian Authority and too diplomatically fraught for the IDF to hold, Jenin had become a sovereign enclave of terror.

By the summer of 2023, terror had become unrelenting and intimate. Attacks struck cities, roads, and pedestrian zones in rapid succession: a ramming-stabbing in Tel Aviv that killed an unborn child; mass gunfire in Ma'ale Adumim; the daylight murder of Tel Aviv city inspector Chen Amir on a crowded pedestrian mall; the execution of a father and son in Huwara; and the drive-by shooting that killed preschool teacher Batsheva Nigri as her twelve-year-old daughter watched from inside the car. August ended as it began—with bloodshed—with a stabbing on Jerusalem's light rail and a car-ramming that killed Maksym Molchanov, a lone soldier from Ukraine who volunteered for the IDF. Terror was no longer episodic. It was omnipresent, personal, and inescapable. In the nine months before October 7, thirty-one Israelis were murdered in terror attacks emanating primarily from Judea and Samaria.

In late August, shortly after Batsheva Nigri's murder, Netanyahu addressed the spiraling chaos: "We are in the midst of a terrorist wave. This wave is encouraged, directed, and financed by Iran and its proxies . . . We are using defensive and offensive measures to deal with the murderers and their dispatchers from near and far." That same day, Maj. Gen. Yehuda Fuchs, head of Central Command, publicly acknowledged: "Israel is in the midst of a major wave of terror." The IDF reinforced units across Judea and Samaria. Yet none seemed to realize that the violence emanating from Judea and Samaria might itself be part of a larger strategy—a diversion meant to exhaust Israel's forces and dull its focus while the real storm gathered in Gaza.

The Conflict-Management Mirage

In early October 2023, the trend repeated itself. On October 5, an Arab terrorist again opened fire on an Israeli couple and their baby as they drove through Huwara. The bullets tore into the car's frame but, miraculously, not its passengers. Within hours, IDF troops tracked the shooter down and killed him after he fired on Israeli troops. To Israelis, it looked like another entry in the long and familiar ledger of violence in the territories—a tragedy narrowly averted, an incident to be "contained." But in hindsight, it marked the final note in a dreadful melody that had been building for two years.

Israelis have long learned to live with "a low flame" of violence. Sporadic shootings, stabbings, and Molotov attacks blended into the background noise—each a tragedy to be tolerated as the "price of doing the Zionist business." Every incident was quickly localized as a "settler problem," an unfortunate feature of life in Judea and Samaria. Then came the familiar ritual: a limited operation to catch the perpetrators, a terse statement from the IDF, and a flurry of tweets from pundits and politicians. Almost as soon as the attack had occurred, it would be forgotten. Over 2022 and 2023, thousands of separate terror incidents were recorded across Judea and Samaria. Most caused no casualties. But the cumulative effect was corrosive. Ordinary Israelis, IDF commanders, and political leaders alike—all grew accustomed to the constant stream of terror. What should have been a national crisis had become the nightly news.

The normalization of dead Jews—the belief that there is such a thing as a "tolerable" level of terror—exacted a ruinous price. What began as pragmatism hardened into habit. Israelis learned to live with terror the way city dwellers learn to live with the hum of traffic or the wail of distant sirens: tuning it out until silence itself feels unnatural. Israel's strategic awareness dulled. The IDF, once defined by its doctrine of preemption and renowned for decisive, unmistakable victories, became increasingly reactive—policing instead of preventing, responding instead of shaping. Each week brought another shooting on a highway, another ambush in an alleyway, another stabbing at a checkpoint. Each incident was small enough to contain, none large enough to force a reckoning. But terrorism is a science of patience. Its strength lies not only in the lives it takes, but in the mindset it molds—training its victims to accept the next blow as inevitable. By tolerating "low intensity" terror, Israel unwittingly allowed its enemies to gain followers, fame, and the confidence to raise the stakes with every new attack. What Israel called containment its enemies called momentum.

This mindset was clearest in Israel's approach to terror on the roads of Judea and Samaria, where Israel chose to accommodate danger by rerouting around it instead of eradicating it. In 2022, six Israeli civilians were murdered in attacks on highways across the region. By the first half of 2023, that toll had more than doubled to thirteen. The simple fact that the sovereign state's main arteries had become kill zones should have justified an all-out war on terror. Israel did not pour out vengeance; it poured out concrete. The government built a network of bypass roads to help Jewish residents skirt terrorist hotspots rather than secure the zones themselves. Over the seven years before October 7, Jerusalem allocated ₪576 million for those detours—an engineering fix for a moral and strategic failure.

The most critical of these, the Huwara Bypass Road, tells the story in miniature. Construction first began in 1992, yet the project stalled for decades, even as the same stretch of road saw hundreds of ambushes and drive-by shootings. It was finally completed—symbolically, almost mockingly—in 2024. For far too many families, that thirty-two-year delay proved fatal. The broader lesson was that, by trying to go around its problems, Israel only deepened them. Terror cannot be bypassed; it must be broken. Instead of diverting traffic, the state should have mobilized reserves, swept the region, and restored deterrence not only in Judea and Samaria but across Gaza and Lebanon as well. In those crucial years, Israel had its best chance to demonstrate zero tolerance for terror—to remind its enemies that no Israeli life is negotiable, and that no red line is

The Boteachs in uniform. From left to right: **Chana Boteach,** serving in an IDF military diplomacy unit; **Dalia Boteach,** serving as an IDF social worker; **Yosef Boteach,** shortly after receiving his beret while serving the Golani Reconnaissance Company; and **Mendy Boteach,** serving in Gaza in 2024 with the 8th Brigade Reconnaissance Company, holding the tefillin his great-grandfather Yosef Elchanan Valent, carried with him as he endured the camps during the Holocaust.

IDF units deployed to Israel's beaches, 2021, to clean and salvage stretches damaged by tar pollution. In the decade leading up to October 7, while Israel's enemies prepared for war, the IDF expanded a sweeping environmental initiative known as the Nature Defense Forces, led by the Technology and Logistics Directorate in partnership with major environmental organizations. More than sixty-five projects were launched nationwide, directing significant time, manpower, and senior command focus toward climate resilience and sustainability—a strategic misjudgment whose costs would become clear on October 7. (IDF Spokesperson's Unit)

Benjamin Netanyahu addresses the Knesset against the Oslo Accords, 1995. Then leader of the opposition, Netanyahu stood against the tide, giving voice to millions of Israelis who opposed the agreement. He warned from the outset that peace built on illusion would become a curse. His stance reflected deep public dismay, which in 1996 carried him to the premiership—proof of how many believed the so-called "peace process" risked becoming a process of surrender. Yet even his rise to power could not undo the far-reaching consequences of Oslo. (Dan Hadani Collection, National Library of Israel)

Palestinian militants drive back to the Gaza Strip with the body of Shani Louk, a German-Israeli dual citizen, on Saturday, Oct. 7, 2023. (Source AP News) "In the early hours of October 7, 2023, my beautiful daughter Shani, who lived vibrantly through dance and song, became the symbol of Hamas savagery and Islamist butchery . . . Today, Shani's love of life is a symbol of Israel's collective and eternal fight to survive and is beautifully captured in the words 'we will dance again.'" —Nissim Louk, father of Shani Louk and a close friend of the authors.

Hamas terrorists abduct elderly civilians from Kibbutz Be'eri, October 7, 2023. The killers did not conceal their crimes—they flaunted them, filming the the massacre and kidnappings with bodycams and GoPros.(Bodycam footage)

Hamas terrorists fire into the bomb shelter near the Supernova Festival, October 7, 2023, where Aner Shapira and twenty-seven others were hiding. Inside, Aner seized and hurled back seven grenades in succession before an eighth detonated in his hands, killing him. His heroic self-sacrifice saved nine lives. (Dashcam footage)

An IDF Caterpillar D9 armored bulldozer, essential for clearing IEDs, in Gaza in November 2023. For fifteen years, Hamas prepared for an Israeli ground assault, transforming the densely populated enclave into a fortified battlefield. Tens of thousands of rifles, anti-tank missiles, mortars, and improvised explosives were stockpiled. Beneath the streets lay a vast tunnel network of command posts and weapons workshops. Above ground, civilian infrastructure was embedded within the fighting: homes and alleyways rigged as ambush sites, schools and hospitals used as defensive positions. Unable to defeat the IDF in open battle, Hamas reshaped the terrain itself—engineering a battlefield designed to exact a relentless toll. (IDF Spokesperson's Unit)

Unit 669, the IDF's elite search-and-rescue unit, evacuates wounded soldiers in Gaza, February 2024. As of this writing, 925 Israeli soldiers have laid down their lives since October 7. Of them, 472 fell in combat in Gaza after ground operations began on October 27, 2023. More than 3,000 have been wounded in the fighting. (IDF Spokesperson's Unit)

Soldiers of the Netzah Yehuda Battalion, an all-religious unit in the Kfir Brigade, operating in Beit Hanoun in northern Gaza in May 2024. Throughout the war, the IDF returned again and again to Hamas strongholds such as Beit Hanoun and Jabalia. Each time Israeli forces cleared IED fields and dismantled terrorist infrastructure before withdrawing—and each time the areas seemed to rise from the rubble, reconstituting themselves into renewed threats to Israeli towns just across the border. Hamas rebuilt with ruthless efficiency, recruiting new fighters and booby-trapping buildings, turning the campaign into a brutal test not only of firepower, but of endurance and resolve.

Fighters of the Haruv Reconnaissance Unit of the Kfir Brigade operate in northern Samaria during Operation "Summer Camps," August 2024. For more than two years before October 7, Tehran funneled weapons, funding, and direction into Judea and Samaria, turning refugee camps and neglected neighborhoods into an active front against Israel's heartland. After the war began, the area became a central arena of combat. The IDF and Shin Bet launched sweeping arrests, raided IED workshops, seized weapons, and dismantled the financial and logistical networks sustaining terrorist cells. (IDF Spokesperson's Unit)

Fighters of the 282nd Fire Brigade during the ground maneuver in Lebanon, October 2024. Approximately 12,500 targets were struck, including 1,600 command centers and 1,000 weapons depots. Seventy to eighty percent of Hezbollah's short-range rocket launchers were destroyed, and its UAV arsenal was reduced to roughly thirty percent of its prewar strength. Israeli fighter jets logged 14,000 flight hours and 11,000 sorties over Lebanon, while the Navy recorded 25,000 operational sea hours. Hezbollah's indirect fire dwindled to sporadic volleys, and the Radwan Force was rendered incapable of launching a broad offensive. Along the contact line, troops uncovered and destroyed some 1,500 subterranean assets, including every offensive tunnel network—preventing an "October 7 in the north." (IDF's Spokesperson's Unit)

Reserve soldiers of the 6th Etzioni Brigade operate during the ground maneuver in southern Lebanon, November 2024. In the campaign, the IDF temporarily seized territory on the Lebanese side of the northern frontier to a depth of roughly five kilometers. The scale of the operation was reflected in its toll: Hassan Nasrallah and thirteen members of Hezbollah's senior command forum were eliminated, along with four division commanders, twenty-four brigade commanders, twenty-seven battalion commanders, sixty-three company commanders, and twenty-two platoon commanders. An estimated 4,000–5,000 Hezbollah operatives were killed, and approximately 9,000 more were rendered non-operational. (IDF Spokesperson's Unit)

Eight Israeli Air Force F-15I Ra'am strike fighters of 69 Squadron "Hammers" depart Hatzerim Airbase, June 2025, en route to strike Iran. From the opening salvo, the barrage did not relent, hitting ballistic missile facilities, nuclear enrichment sites, military research centers, and enemy airfields in rapid succession. The pilots undertook one of the longest-range and most perilous missions in Israel's history—flying 1,500–2,000 kilometers into hostile airspace, often at night, under tight fuel and munitions constraints, where a single miscalculation could prove catastrophic. (IDF Spokesperson's Unit)

Bislaḥ Brigade combat team forces operate in the Tel al-Sultan neighborhood, October 16, 2024—shortly before the discovery and identification of Hamas leader Yahya Sinwar, architect of the October 7 attacks. As the war entered its second year, Israel transitioned to a grinding campaign intended to pressure Hamas on the hostage issue. The pivotal moment came not from a special forces raid but from a tank crew maneuvering through the ruins of Rafah. In a firefight in Tel al-Sultan, IDF troops killed several militants. Only afterward did they realize that one of them was Sinwar. His identity was confirmed the next day through dental records. (IDF Spokesperson's Unit)

An Arrow 3 interceptor launches in June 2025 to engage incoming Iranian ballistic missiles. By striking threats during their exo-atmospheric flight phase, Arrow 3 provided Israel with a critical upper layer of defense against strategic missile attacks and positioned it among the world's most advanced air defense powers. Its operational use against Iranian missiles marked the first confirmed combat interceptions beyond the atmosphere. For the first time, warfare had reached outer space. (IDF Spokesperson's Unit)

Israeli infantry operate in Gaza, June 2025. On May 16, Israel launched Operation Gideon's Chariots, among the largest IDF maneuvers of the war—a coordinated assault by air, sea, and ground, with up to five divisions advancing into northern and southern Gaza. Designed to exert overwhelming pressure on Hamas to secure the release of the remaining hostages, the operation marked a strategic shift: no longer raid and withdraw, but seize, clear, and hold. Under Chief of Staff Lt. Gen. Eyal Zamir, forces moved deliberately, securing each area to prevent Hamas's return and establish sustained control. (IDF Spokesperson's Office)

An IDF UH-60 Black Hawk helicopter takes part in the operation to bring home the last remaining living hostages, October 2025. After two years of war, Israel secured the return of the final 20 living hostages abducted on October 7 and held in brutal Hamas captivity in Gaza for 738 days. The operation took place under the first phase of US President Donald Trump's 21-point plan to end the Swords of Iron war. (IDF Spokesperson's Unit)

elastic. Instead, the government paved detours around danger—and the enemy read that as permission to keep paving the road to the Jewish state's destruction.

Israel's policy of containment was, in fact, a slow surrender of initiative. A rolling emergency became the new normal. What so few yet grasped was that the so-called "low flame" was itself the enemy's strategy of war: a controlled burn designed to keep Israel perpetually on defense until the day the fire stormed over the fence. Israel's tragedy on October 7 did not begin with rockets; it began with arithmetic—with the quiet calculus of tolerated terror. For two years, attacks in Judea and Samaria multiplied at a rate unseen since the Second Intifada. Yet every car-ramming that went unavenged, every shooting met with only a localized response, delivered the same message to Israel's enemies: the threshold of Israeli pain had risen, and the price of Jewish blood had plunged.

Israel also failed to grasp just how synchronized its enemies had become even before October 7. Gaza, Lebanon, and the central regions—once separate battlefields—were already moving as parts of a single organism, animated by Iranian design. Tehran's doctrine was brutally simple: keep Israel perpetually stretched, morally exhausted, and strategically distracted.

The chaos had assumed a sort of choreography. In August 2022, the arrest of Bassam al-Saadi, the Islamic Jihad commander in Jenin, lit the fuse for Operation Breaking Dawn. Terrorists in Gaza unleashed rockets while Israeli forces were still flooding Judea and Samaria. The result was a nation on a treadmill—launching airstrikes in Gaza while raiding Jenin, policing one front while bracing for the next. In January 2023, after Israel's deadliest Samaria raid in years, Gazans fired rockets "in solidarity." Three months later, when riots gripped the Temple Mount in April 2023, rockets rose not from one horizon but from three—Gaza, Lebanon, and Syria. Over thirty projectiles were fired from Lebanese soil, the largest barrage since 2006. They were launched by Hamas and Islamic Jihad under Hezbollah's protection, barely a day after a public meeting between the Hamas leader Ismail Haniyeh and Hezbollah's Hassan Nasrallah in Beirut. Israel struck targets in both Gaza and Lebanon, but the point was clear: in a future conflict, no one front would stand alone.

The same pattern repeated in May 2023, when the death of Khader Adnan, an Islamic Jihad figure in the territories, triggered another Gaza rocket storm and the brief war known as Shield and Arrow. Even as Israel struck PIJ command posts in Gaza, militancy in the central region surged—the Lions' Den and Jenin Brigades continuing their attacks, keeping Israeli brigades tied down long after the Gaza ceasefire. Hamas, for its part, stayed deliberately in the background, letting PIJ take the blows while it preserved strength for the larger war it knew was coming. Meanwhile, Israel was locked in a deadly rotation—like a fighter surrounded, forced to turn his back on one opponent every time he faced another.

The coordination was not only operational but logistical. From 2022 onward, Israeli intelligence tracked a surge in weapons smuggling into Judea and Samaria—an Iranian- and Hezbollah-directed enterprise running through Syrian and Jordanian corridors. Israeli border units, together with Jordanian forces, repeatedly intercepted rockets, explosives, and rifles traced back to handlers in Lebanon and the IRGC. Those pipelines explain the sudden leap in the quality and quantity of weaponry in Judea and Samaria throughout 2023. In the months leading up to October 7, the pattern was unmistakable: each front was being fueled by the others. Gaza, Lebanon, and Judea and Samaria were no longer isolated flashpoints but coordinated instruments in a single, Iranian-designed symphony of attrition—keeping Israel's sword drawn in every direction until the day came when all fronts would converge.

By mid-2023, the pressure had achieved results. For months, intelligence briefings from Judea and Samaria monopolized command attention. Jenin, Nablus, and Huwara dominated the nightly situation reports. Intelligence assets that once monitored Gaza were diverted to tracking micro-cells in the central territories. Aerial surveillance hours that could have been used over the Strip were reduced to accommodate daily drone coverage of Jenin and Nablus. Israel's gaze was drawn away from Gaza, toward the hills where blood was already being spilled. Tragically, Israel would not look back in time.

On October 5—the same day that a lone terrorist tried to murder a family in Huwara—two companies from the IDF Commando Brigade were redeployed from the Gaza border to Israel's central hill region. On paper, the transfer was a standard procedure: reinforce Central Command for the holiday season. Yet the relocation of roughly one hundred elite soldiers symbolized something far deeper—Israel's fatal misreading of the battlefield. The north was tense but quiet; Even Hezbollah seemed in no hurry for escalation. Hamas in Gaza, seemingly contained by deterrence and intoxicated by cash infusions from Qatar, appeared to have accepted the status quo. So, when the army's most capable commando companies were sent to Samaria, it was done with the confidence of a nation that believed it understood its enemies. The assumption proved catastrophic. While Israel stared into the smoke of "small" fires, a volcano was forming just beyond the fence. Just two days before the Hamas onslaught, the front Israel feared most was not the one that would erupt.

Judea and Samaria During the War

On the evening of February 20, 2025, twenty-six-year-old Adi Jegna climbed onto a Bat Yam commuter bus and noticed a suspicious bag. Inside, she saw rolls of toilet paper and a canister of yellowish liquid. She wasn't sure whether to tell the driver, but then she shifted the bag slightly and saw Arabic lettering. "Then, I understood I could not ignore it." She informed the driver. He ordered all passengers off and deposited the vehicle at the bus depot while the bomb squad raced in. Minutes later, a massive explosion tore through the bus. Almost at that exact moment, two other booby-trapped buses nearby burst into flames. Two other buses had been rigged—bringing the total number to five—but the devices failed to detonate. No civilians were killed. Only by a miraculous stroke of luck—and one woman's instinct—did the carnage not reach the level the bombers intended.

It was the largest coordinated terrorist bombing attempt since October 7, and it originated in Judea and Samaria. The devices—four to five kilograms each, timed and loaded with nails and screws—were designed to maximize casualties during morning rush hour. One device bore the message "Revenge from Tulkarem." Hamas's Tulkarem battalion appeared to claim responsibility, calling it a "jihad of victory or martyrdom." The man who planted the bombs fled into Samaria, where, over months in hiding, he manufactured new devices and plotted a suicide bombing in Tel Aviv—until an accidental detonation near Nablus exposed him. He was arrested on July 23, five months after the failed attack.

If the attack revealed the lethal imagination of terror emanating from Judea and Samaria, Israel's response revealed its own mindset: decisive in execution, but still bound by a doctrine of containment. Israel was still managing threats it needed to remove. Defense Minister Israel Katz answered with tall orders: not only would Israel's forces pursue the perpetrators "to the bitter end," but they would also "destroy the terror infrastructure in the camps that serve as forward outposts of the Iranian axis of evil." Meanwhile, Security Minister Ben-Gvir, who had resigned over the January 2025 ceasefire and terrorists-for-hostages deal, blamed political leaders. In a radio interview, Ben Gvir insisted, "This failure is on the political leadership that chose to release terrorists." But his most pressing point was this: "We must launch an all-out war in Judea, Samaria, and Gaza."

As the minister in charge of internal security—and a longtime resident of Judea—Ben Gvir understood that Judea and Samaria were an essential component of the war unleashed on Israel on October 7. For more than two years, Tehran had been funneling weapons, cash, and directives into Judea and Samaria, transforming neglected neighborhoods and refugee camps into a full-scale front aimed at Israel's heartland. From the first days of the war, Judea and Samaria ceased being a backburner flank and instead became an epicenter of kinetic warfare. The IDF and Shin Bet moved with urgency and breadth: mass arrests, sweeping raids, and seizures of weapons. The campaign reached deeper—disrupting terrorist inciters and financiers, while severing the logistical arteries that kept their cells fed, funded, and supplied. In the year following October 7, the state reported over two hundred arrests for incitement alone. Suspected currency exchanges and funding channels were raided, suspected bank accounts were frozen, and workshops churning out rockets and munitions were methodically dismantled.

But the main feature of Israel's actions in Judea and Samaria was large-scale military raids, which began almost immediately after the Gaza border massacre. On October 12, 2023, the IDF raided Jenin. On October

19, intense clashes near Tulkarem claimed the life of an Israeli officer; the fighting included a rare drone strike against an armed cell. By October 27, a massive column of over one hundred armored vehicles reentered Jenin, with the IDF announcing the detention of scores of suspects and the elimination of senior PIJ operatives. In that first month alone, the IDF detained roughly 1,030 suspected Arab terrorists in Judea and Samaria—about 670 affiliated with Hamas.

But throughout the war that erupted on October 7, terror still raged on the ground in Israel's cities. Already in the first weeks after the massacre, an Israeli reservist was gunned down while driving home from a deployment. In late November 2023, two Hamas terrorists from East Jerusalem opened fire at a bus stop in the capital, leaving four Israeli civilians dead—including a twenty-four-year-old woman and her unborn child—and sixteen wounded. Amid the chaos, an armed bystander who had heroically engaged the terrorists was mistakenly shot and killed by an IDF soldier who thought him one of the attackers. More than a month after the IDF had cleared southern Israel of a Hamas invasion, terrorists were still spilling innocent blood on Israel's streets.

Meanwhile, IDF operations continued. In January 2024, during a sweep in Tulkarem, the IDF searched roughly one thousand buildings, arrested dozens, uncovered five explosive-manufacturing labs, and seized more than four hundred improvised explosive devices. In follow-up operations, Israeli forces eliminated senior commanders from Hamas, PIJ, the Jenin Brigades—and even Fatah-affiliated terror cells. Terrorist activity in Judea and Samaria increasingly mirrored Gaza's model: operations hidden within civilian infrastructure—mosques, workshops, and even schools. And as in Gaza, Israeli airstrikes became a routine tool of war: drones, helicopters, and fighter jets operating in places where that kind of firepower had once been unimaginable. According to the IDF's own statements, by January 2025, at least 165 armed terrorists had been eliminated in about 110 aerial strikes in Judea and Samaria.

Despite major gains, terror surged through the first half of 2024. In January, two were killed in a shooting spree on a highway in Samaria. In mid-February, a shooting attack in southern Israel saw two more civilians murdered. Days later, terrorists from the Bethlehem area sprayed cars stalled near a military checkpoint, killing one and wounding six, among them a pregnant woman shot in the chest who survived with her baby. A week after that, a Palestinian Authority police officer opened fire at a gas station near Eli—the same site of a deadly attack months earlier—killing two Israelis before being shot dead by the manager of the hummus restaurant they had attacked.

Terrorism in the Israeli Heartland Throughout the First Year of the War

Date	Location	Perpetrator	Victims	Attack Description
Nov 2, 2023	Near Einav, Samaria	Arab terrorist from Samaria	1 killed, 4 wounded	Elhanan Ariel Klein (29) shot by a terrorist as he drove home from reserve duty.
Nov 30, 2023	Givat Shaul, Jerusalem	2 Hamas Arab terrorists (30 and 38), brothers from East Jerusalem	4 killed, 16 wounded	Shooting attack at a crowded bus stop; victims included Liviya Dickman (24) and her unborn child; Hanna Ifergan (67), Rabbi Elimelech Wasserman (73), and Yuval Kestelman (38), an armed civilian who engaged the terrorists and was mistakenly killed amid the chaos.
Jan 7, 2024	Near Ofra, Samaria	3 Arab terrorists from Samaria	2 killed	Amar Mansour (32), Dr. Lara Tannous (42) killed after terrorists blocked the road with their car and fired upon approaching vehicles.
Feb 16, 2024	Re'em Junction (Southern Israel)	Arab terrorists (37) from East Jerusalem	2 killed, 4 wounded	Uri Yaish (27), Ishay Gertner (23) killed in shooting attack at a major junction in southern Israel.

Date	Location	Perpetrator	Victims	Attack Description
Feb 22, 2024	Near Maale Adumim, Judea	3 Arab terrorists from Bethlehem, Judea	1 killed, 6 wounded	Terror squad opened fire on vehicles trapped in traffic killing Matan Elmaliah (26) and wounding a pregnant woman, who was shot in the chest but survived along with her baby.
Feb 29, 2024	Near Eli (gas station)	Arab terrorist from Qalandiya, Samaria	2 killed	Shooting attack at a gas station kills Uria Hartum (16), Yitzhak Zeiger (57); terrorist was killed by the manager of the hummus restaurant that was attacked.
Mar 14, 2024	Beit Kama Junction, Southern Israel	Arab terrorist from Rahat, Southern Israel	1 killed	Stabbing attack; IDF NCO Uri Moyal (51) was mortally wounded but managed to neutralize the attacker.
Apr 1, 2024	Gan Yavne (shopping mall)	Arab terrorist from Dura, Judea	1 killed, 2 wounded	Stabbing attack; Lidor Levy (34) mortally wounded.
Apr 12, 2024	Near Malachei HaShalom, Samaria	Arab terrorist (21) from Nablus, Samaria	1 killed	Benjamin Achimeir (14) stabbed to death while shepherding near his community.
Aug 4, 2024	Holon, Central Israel	Arab terrorist (34) from Salfit, Samaria	2 killed, 2 wounded	Stabbing attack in a public park kills Rina Daniv (66), Avraham Soumichi (77)
Aug 11, 2024	Jordan River Valley, Samaria	Arab terrorist (31) from Qabatiya, Samaria	1 killed	Shooting attack; victim was a recently discharged IDF soldier driving to visit his fiancée.

Date	Location	Perpetrator	Victims	Attack Description
Aug 18, 2024	Bar-On Industrial Park, Samaria	Arab terrorist from Nablus, Samaria	1 killed	Workplace attack; security guard Gideon Peri (38) murdered with a hammer by an Arab colleague.
Sep 8, 2024	Allenby Crossing, Judea	Arab terrorist from Jordan	3 killed	Shooting attack at the Israel-Jordan border kills Yohanan Shchori (61), Yuri Birnbaum (65), and Adrian Marcelo Podzamczer (57)
Oct 1, 2024	Jaffa, Central Israel	2 Hamas terrorists (19 and 25) from Hebron	7 killed, 17 wounded	Mass casualty shooting attack in a crowded urban area kills Victor Shimshon Green (33), Shahar Goldman (30), Inbar Segev-Vigder (33), Nadia Sokolenco (40), Revital Bronstein (24), Ilia Nozadze (42), and Ionas Chrosis (26). One of the deadliest attacks of the war.
Oct 6, 2024	Beersheba, Southern Israel	Arab terrorist (29) from Southern Israel	1 killed, 9 wounded	Shooting attack at Beersheba bus station kills Cpl. Shira Chaya Suslik (19)
Oct 10, 2024	Hadera, Northern Israel	Arab terrorists (36) from Umm al-Fahm, Northern Israel	1 killed	Stabbing attack mortally wounds Rabbi Rafael Mordechai Pishoff (35), a father of eight
Oct 15, 2024	Near Ashdod	Arab terrorist (28) from Samaria	1 killed, 4 wounded	Shooting attack kills Adir Kadosh (30), a police officer from Yavne, murdered one month before his wedding
Oct 27, 2024	Glilot, Central Israel	Arab terrorist (21) from Central Israel	1 killed, 40 wounded	A truck-ramming attack kills Bezalel Carmi (72) and wounds dozens. 8 people were found pinned down under the vehicle.

Over the next few weeks, a brutal wave of stabbings claimed three more lives. In mid-March, an IDF noncommissioned officer was fatally stabbed, killing his attacker before collapsing. In the weeks that followed, a thirty-four-year-old engineer was stabbed to death in a Gan Yavne mall, and a fourteen-year-old boy was found knifed to death after vanishing while herding his sheep.

For terrorists operating from Judea, Samaria, and East Jerusalem, the objective was to infiltrate across the Green Line and into Israel's major cities. Yet even within Judea and Samaria itself, the scale of violence was staggering. In the first six months of the year, first responders recorded 3,272 acts of terrorism—including 456 Molotov cocktail attacks, 299 explosive charges, and 109 shootings. That amounted to more than five hundred Arab terrorist attacks each month in Judea and Samaria alone.

The terror attacks were relentless—and so were the counterterror operations launched to stop them. Yet both sides were only at the opening stage of a grinding contest. In August 2024, Israel initiated Operation Summer Camps, described by the IDF and Shin Bet as a "full-fledged war" aimed at uprooting entrenched terror infrastructures in Tulkarem and Jenin. Bulldozers, infantry, and armor—backed by air cover—rolled into camps where terrorist rule had been allowed to calcify over the years. The campaign eliminated dozens of high-value terrorists and destroyed laboratories, weapons caches, and observation posts. By year's end, the Shin Bet reported 1,040 attacks foiled during the conflict's first ten months—689 shooting plots, 326 explosive attacks, and two attempted suicide bombings. Yet despite the scale of success, the verdict from many analysts was sobering: the networks were disrupted, not dismantled. Terrorists scattered into the surrounding hills, regrouped, and rearmed. Each airstrike that killed the leader of a terror cell was followed by another, striking his successor. Israel, it seemed, was once again mowing the lawn: cutting back the visible blades of terror but leaving the roots intact.

For Israelis, the price of an unfinished strategy kept mounting in blood. In the fall of 2024, a recently discharged soldier was shot dead on Route 90 while driving to visit his fiancée, an Israeli security guard was murdered by an Arab coworker who attacked him with a hammer at an industrial park, and then a Jordanian terrorist gunned down three Israelis at the

Allenby Bridge border crossing near Jericho. The violence peaked when two Hamas terrorists opened fire on crowds in Jaffa, killing seven civilians and wounding many more. Before October ended, four additional Israelis were murdered in separate attacks across the country.

Beginning in early 2025, the IDF switched tactics—no longer limited to lightning raids but shifting to prolonged stays. In response to a new wave of attacks and the failed bus bombings in Bat Yam, the government launched Operation Iron Wall—a directive to establish sustained control inside the refugee camps identified as terror strongholds: Jenin, Tulkarem, and others. Within days of its launch, Israeli forces had eliminated eighteen terrorists, arrested sixty suspects, and dismantled more than one hundred IEDs, defusing another thirty buried along access roads and alleys. Over the following months, the numbers swelled: more than one hundred terrorists killed, three hundred detained, 450 weapons seized, and hundreds of explosives uncovered. It was during this operation that Merkava tanks returned to Judea and Samaria for the first time since Operation Defensive Shield in 2002. Their arrival demonstrated that, far beyond counterterror raids, Israel was fighting a ground war on its own soil.

But even spectacular raids, armored deployments, and pinpoint airstrikes did not end the problem; they reshaped it. Terrorists adapted. Smuggling and weapons manufacturing proliferated, while a new market for cheap arms flooded Judea and Samaria. In February 2025, the IDF uncovered a weapons-smuggling network along the Jordanian border, seizing dozens of handguns and four long-barreled rifles, as well as repair and manufacturing workshops producing improvised "Carlo" submachine guns. Security officials warned that Iran and its proxies were deliberately "flooding the market" with low-cost weapons—enabling terrorist cells to arm themselves without the need for significant funding. Three months later, in May 2025, Israeli forces seized $2 million in terror financing routed to operatives in Judea and Samaria—funds traced not only to Iran, but also to Turkey. A weapons pipeline was still feeding a steady stream of arms to the camps and cities where Israel now fought nightly.

All the while, the terror did not abate. It cut through cities, highways, and ordinary civilian spaces across the country. A twelve-year-old boy was shot to death on a public bus near Maaleh Adumim in December.

Weeks later, a three-man terror cell ambushed a bus and passing cars near Kedumim, murdering three more Israelis. The violence only intensified. Over the spring of 2025, four separate attacks claimed five additional lives—including a pregnant woman mortally wounded in a drive-by shooting as she traveled to give birth. Doctors performed an emergency cesarean section, but her newborn son later died from his injuries.

Terrorism in the Israeli Heartland Throughout the Second Year of the War

Date	Location	Perpetrators	Victims	Attack Description
Dec 11, 2024	Near Maaleh Adumim, Judea	2 Arab terrorists from near Hebron, Judea	1 killed, 4 wounded	Shooting attack on a public bus kills Yehoshua Aharon Tuvia Simcha (12)
Jan 6, 2025	Near Kedumim, Samaria	3 Arab terrorists from Jenin	3 killed	Shooting attack kills Rachel Cohen (73), Aliza Reiss (69), and Elad Yaakov Winkelstein (36)
Mar 3, 2025	Haifa, Northern Israel	Arab terrorist (20) from Northern Israel	1 killed, 4 wounded	Stabbing attack at the Central Bus Station in Haifa kills Hassan Dahamsha (70)
Feb 27, 2025	Karkur Junction, Northern Israel	Arab terrorist from Judea and Samaria	1 killed, 13 wounded	Ramming attack mortally wounds Yaheli Gur (17)
Mar 24, 2025	Yokneam, Northern Israel	Arab terrorist (25) from Northern Israel	1 killed, 1 wounded	Shooting attack kills Moshe Horan (85)
May 15, 2025	Peduel Junction, Samaria	Arab terrorist from Samaria	2 killed	Tzeela Gez (30) was mortally wounded in a drive-by shooting while on her way to deliver her fourth child. The baby, Ravid Haim, succumbed to his wounds two weeks later

Date	Location	Perpetrators	Victims	Attack Description
Jul 10, 2025	Gush Etzion, Judea	2 Arab terrorists (both 23) from Judea and Samaria	1 killed	A combined shooting and stabbing attack in a shopping center kills Shalev Zvoloni (22). The terrorists were two Palestinian Authority police officers who had just completed studying abroad in Qatar
Sep 8, 2025	Jerusalem (Ramot)	2 Hamas Arab terrorists (20 and 21) from Samaria	6 killed, 21 injured	Shooting attack on a bus kills Yaakov Pinto (25), Rabbi Levi Yitzhak Pash (57), Yisrael Matzner (28), Yosef David (43), Sarah (Sarita) Mendelson (60), and Rabbi Mordechai Steinsteg (79)

In the summer of 2025, a shooting attack at a shopping center in Gush Etzion killed another Israeli; the perpetrators were Palestinian Authority police officers who had just returned from training in Qatar, erasing the distinction between terrorists and the local Arab police meant to stop them. The year's deadliest attack came in September 2025, when Hamas terrorists opened fire on a Jerusalem bus, killing six and wounding twenty-one more. By the end of two years of war—from October 2023 through October 2025—stabbings, beatings, shootings, and car-ramming attacks inside Israel had claimed the lives of forty-nine Israelis, including twenty-four in Judea and Samaria alone. Even as Israel fought its enemies on its borders, the war on its streets never truly stopped.

The multi-front strategy that Israel had faced before October 7 was now playing out in reverse. Then, when Israeli operations intensified under its Central Command, rockets would rain from Gaza or Lebanon. Now, while Israel fought a full-scale war in Gaza, terror cells in Judea and Samaria pulled at its flank, forcing large-scale deployments of IDF forces to the east. The dynamic was crystal clear—each front helped the other. One glaring example: the Jerusalem attack that claimed four lives in November 2023 occurred just hours after Israel and Hamas agreed to extend the first ceasefire of the war. And still, Hamas shamelessly claimed responsibility. Even in a negotiated pause, Hamas played its multi-front game—dispatching terror from one front while the other rested.

The attempted bus bombing in Bat Yam—which could have killed hundreds of Israelis—made one thing frighteningly clear: Judea and Samaria were no subsidiary theater. They had become a primary front in the war. Over time, its dangers seemed likely to rival—and perhaps exceed—those of Gaza and Lebanon. Tunnels, weapons workshops, explosives labs, and smuggling routes were gradually transforming a region once known for sporadic attacks into an industrial engine of terror. Israel's response—more than one hundred airstrikes, thousands of raids and arrests, and the evacuation of forty thousand residents from terrorist strongholds—underscored the scale of the threat.

For all the fury of Israel's counteroffensive, the strategic question remained: could Israel make its military achievements permanent? Beyond the temporary suppression of terror, could it secure a lasting victory? The answer demanded more than soldiers; it required political clarity and a doctrine that treated Judea and Samaria as a theater of war—not a policing problem to be managed, but a battlefield to be won. Operation Iron Wall and the deployment of heavy armor signaled the necessary seriousness, as did the arrest and elimination of high-value operatives. But the terrorists adapted quickly—melting away, reconstituting cells, and replacing fallen leaders. And every time Israel conquered, it withdrew—constrained by its own adherence to the Oslo framework that had provoked the very instability the IDF sought to uproot. All the while, weapons kept flowing in, and incitement continued to spread.

When Adi Jegna peered into a bag on a quiet bus and acted, she performed a small, human act of frontline courage. Her instincts, combined with good fortune, saved lives. But no nation can survive on luck alone. Judea and Samaria demanded the full measure of a state at war: unflinching force, sustained presence, and the political will to treat the front as the principal theater it had become. In his radio interview after the botched bombing, National Security Minister Itamar Ben Gvir put it bluntly, invoking the timeless words of the Jewish sages: "God has mercy on us, but how many times can we rely on miracles?

The Unfinished Front

Even after the operations of 2023–2025, the danger facing Israel from Judea and Samaria remains larger, closer, and more perilous than the threat from Gaza ever was. Gaza's fence with Israel is thirty-six miles; the barrier with Judea and Samaria is roughly two hundred miles. Gaza holds two million Arabs; Judea and Samaria contain up to three to three-and-a-half million. Sderot, the largest Israeli town on the Gaza line, has about thirty-six thousand residents; Gush Dan—the economic and demographic heart of Israel—sits right up against Judea and Samaria with nearly four million people.

The scale—and the proximity to Israel's largest population centers—makes the terror threat from Judea and Samaria feel extreme. But it is the barrier's porousness that makes it existential. If Gaza's vaunted "high-tech fence" proved worthless in stopping a terrorist invasion, the aging concrete wall separating Qalqilya and Tulkarem from the suburbs of Tel Aviv is already faring even worse. By official estimates, forty thousand Arabs cross the Green Line into Israel's heartland every month. Many come to work. But Israel must assume that not all do. The fact that entire battalions of potential combatants can penetrate the barrier each month underscores what October 7 made unmistakably clear: when confronting terrorists, one cannot simply "build a wall."

In October 2025, a single night near Lachish exposed the scale of the failure. Security patrols captured 122 Arabs from Hebron crossing illegally into Israel. Boaz Shlomo, head of the regional council, called it what it was: "a complete collapse of the army in its mission." He didn't mince words. "Any such infiltrator could be a combatant coming to carry out an attack. Every such attempt must be treated that way." It wasn't. And that is the point. Israel continues to sleepwalk through a front that's already been blown wide open.

In Judea and Samaria, the threat runs deeper still. It emanates not only from terrorist factions armed by Iran, but from the preachers, teachers, and curricula funded by the Western world. The Palestinian Authority, far from serving as a moderating force, has become an ideological incubator for the same jihadism that erupted in Gaza on October 7. Schools, summer camps, textbooks, mosque sermons, and social media messaging have codified a worldview that sanctifies terror—and therefore inevitably breeds terrorists. In classrooms built and financed with international aid, children are taught to revere killers as heroes. Streets bear the names of "martyrs." Songs glorify suicide bombings. After October 7, those narratives found fresh oxygen. As long as teachers radicalize and societies celebrate bloodshed, terror ceases to be an aberration—it becomes an aspiration.

Another deep-rooted part of the problem lies in Israel's system of justice. Israel has no death penalty for terrorists who murder Israelis. Even its "life sentences"—or, in the case of mass murderers, "multiple life sentences"—are rarely for life. Too often, they end prematurely in hostage swaps or political deals for terrorists' release. Those who remain behind bars often enjoy conditions that border on privilege: academic programs, premium healthcare, generous visitation rights—sometimes a better standard of living than they had before their crimes. Yahya Sinwar, the mastermind of October 7, was once a prisoner in Israel. Ironically, he would not have lived to commit his atrocities had Israel not saved his life. After a lifesaving brain operation performed in an Israeli hospital, he was released as part of the Gilad Shalit deal. The consequences of that misplaced mercy need no retelling.

Added to the indulgence of imprisoned terrorists is the perverse economy that finances terror itself. While the United States made it a point of national doctrine to eliminate its most notorious enemies—Osama bin Laden, Abu Musab al-Zarqawi, Abu Bakr al-Baghdadi—Israel's most lethal adversaries were often allowed not only to survive, but to prosper. Yasser Arafat died a billionaire. Khaled Mashal and other senior Hamas leaders remain billionaires today, living comfortably abroad while their foot soldiers kill and die. Even low-level terrorists are rewarded. The Palestinian Authority's infamous "pay-for-slay" program guarantees lifetime stipends to convicted murderers and generous pensions to their families—turning mass murder into a salaried profession.

Though Israel passed the Deduction Law in 2018 to penalize such payments, the Palestinian Authority simply ignored it. That same year, the US Congress passed the Taylor Force Act—signed into law by President Donald Trump—with the explicit goal of ending the grotesque "pay-for-slay" system by cutting off American aid. It failed as well. "They haven't stopped paying," said Maurice Hirsch, director of the Initiative for Palestinian Authority Accountability and Reform at the Jerusalem Center for Public Affairs. "Sixty-five percent of the Palestinian Authority's budget comes from Israel. So out of every one hundred shekels a terrorist receives from the PA, Israel itself provided sixty-five." The absurdity is staggering. Through a web of legal fictions and budgetary shell games, Israel is not merely failing to stop the financing of terror—it is effectively paying the men who murder its citizens.

The scale is staggering. According to Israeli Foreign Minister Gideon Sa'ar, the Palestinian Authority dramatically expanded these payments over the past year. In 2024, it paid approximately ₪470 million—about $144 million—to terrorists and their families. In 2025, that figure rose to at least ₪700 million—roughly $214 million—as of October alone. By year's end, the total was almost certainly higher. This is not social welfare. It is a reward system for bloodshed—one that ensures terrorism is not only ideologically encouraged, but economically rational. Where other nations dismantle terror networks by killing their leaders and cutting off their funding, Israel has too often been forced to confront a grotesque inversion: an enemy whose leaders grow rich, whose killers receive pensions, and whose violence is continuously subsidized under the Oslo Accords' banner of "peace."

Those who served the longest sentences—for committing the most heinous crimes—earned the most money. According to a recent report by Palestinian Media Watch, 160 of the 250 prisoners serving life sentences who were released under the October 2025 ceasefire deal with Hamas had become millionaires while incarcerated in Israeli prisons—enriched by the Palestinian Authority's terror-reward system. What followed was obscene. After their release, 154 of these men were photographed by *Daily Mail* lounging at Egypt's five-star Mirage Hotel—relaxing by the pool, drinking at the bar, and eating at the buffet.

Together, the lure of wealth and the absence of any credible punishment have turned jihad from a one-way ticket to prison or the grave into a comfortable career. Terrorism is no longer sustained by ideology alone; it has become an industry—one that draws the youth of Judea, Samaria, and Gaza the way Silicon Valley draws the youth of the United States. For young Arabs in Israel, the signal is not subtle. Violence pays. Kill Jews, go to prison, get rich, and emerge a hero. Meanwhile, Israel tolerates and even subsidizes the very system that incubates the next generation of terrorists. It is sheer insanity—normalized, institutionalized, and paid for in blood.

Israel stands at a crossroads. The same complacency that allowed Gaza to arm and erupt is repeating itself in Judea and Samaria. The impulse to wish danger away—to believe that money and mercy could purchase goodwill—is the very illusion that led to October 7. What must be done is not complicated, but it requires moral clarity and the courage to act upon it.

Israel must abandon half measures and treat Judea and Samaria as the principal theater it has become. That means a permanent security footprint in identified hotbeds—not episodic "in-and-out" raids but sustained presence: bulldozers and armor to deny sanctuary, infantry to hold ground, and a rebuilt security architecture that restores real deterrence over time. Deterrence is not a weekend operation; it is permanence. At the same time, Israel must stop underwriting the problem. Funding to the Palestinian Authority should be cut off until Ramallah halts terror payments and dismantles the educational and social infrastructure that glorifies murder. The illusion that the PA is the antidote to Hamas has died; it has become part of the poison. Money should not feed institutions that lionize killers or subsidize their families.

Israel's justice system must answer to the first duty of any sovereign: to preserve its people. The penal system must never be a rewards program for child-killers, and prisons cannot be universities of jihad or comfort zones for killers. Perks must end; the revolving door must close; stipends and privileges must be stripped. Minor acts of violence cannot be shrugged off as misdemeanors. While Israeli law allows for a maximum sentence of twenty years for stone-throwing, the usual sentence given is about six months. Each rock, each Molotov cocktail aimed at a moving car is an act of attempted murder—and must be punished accordingly. When small crimes go unpunished, greater ones always follow.

Just as punishment must be credible, murder cannot be negotiable. Given Israel's recent history, there is only one way to ensure that: capital punishment for terrorists convicted of murdering civilians. Terrorists are not lawful combatants; blowing up buses and stabbing octogenarians are not acts of war; they are acts of barbarism. Those who plan, execute, or abet the slaughter of innocents should face the ultimate legal consequence a democracy can impose. This is not vengeance—it is prevention: a lawful, proportionate policy designed to make the cost of mass murder intolerable. The alternative is to invite more murders—and guarantee that more civilians will be kidnapped for the sake of another exchange.

Criminal and ideological engines alike must also be named and confronted. This is not "militancy" or "frustration"; it is a totalitarian death cult that teaches children to revere killers. Call it by its name, expel or bar from citizenship those who actively support violence, and refuse euphemisms in public diplomacy. Survival requires blunt language and consistent policy.

Finally, the political framework must change. Another Arab state achieved—or even conceived—through terror would only institutionalize the reward structure that fuels violence. The overwhelming majority of Israelis now recognize what October 7 proved beyond doubt: that a new Arab state inside Israel's borders, in any form, poses an existential danger to the Jewish state. International agreements that restrict Israel's sovereignty over territories it must secure only perpetuate the cycle of bloodshed. President Trump's October 2025 deal to free the living hostages was an extraordinary achievement. Yet by forbidding Israel to apply sovereignty in key areas, it delays the most direct solution to a decades-old problem. And by requiring Israel to acknowledge the Arabs' aspiration for statehood on Israeli soil, it risks sustaining the very logic of terror it sought to end.

The choice before Israel is not between peace and war, but between illusion and survival. We can continue to fund, tolerate, and coexist with the forces sworn to destroy us—or we can draw the moral line. Sovereignty, permanence, honest justice, and the refusal to bankroll one's enemies are not radical ideas; they are the foundation of security itself.

The future of Judea and Samaria will decide the future of Israel. Gaza was the warning. These hills are the test. And this time, the price of delay will not be measured in rockets or borders—but in the lives of the four million Israelis who live beneath the shadow of a front the nation can no longer afford to ignore.

CHAPTER SEVEN

ISRAEL KILLS FIRST: THE LIGHTNING STRIKE OF LEBANON

God's voice breaks cedars;
God shatters the cedars of Lebanon—
making Lebanon skip like a calf.
Psalms 29:6-7

By the fall of 2024, the war had metastasized. What began on October 7 had become, within a year, a seven-front existential struggle. Ballistic missiles flew in from Yemen, drones swarmed from Iraq, and terror cells stirred across Judea and Samaria. But none of those fronts packed a punch like Lebanon. For months, the frontier between the Galilee and southern Lebanon lived on a hair trigger: Hezbollah rockets, mortars, and drones crossing south, Israeli artillery and airstrikes roaring back north. The pattern appeared mechanical, following a sort of ritual—tit for tat, strike for strike. Hezbollah was clearly calibrating its blows to stave off total war, as if strict choreography could protect it while dancing on the edge of disaster. Yet with every passing month, the slow-boiling borderland edged closer to eruption. By mid-summer, nearly one hundred thousand Israelis had been evacuated from their homes in the north. Israel knew the pattern could not hold. It had spent four decades tolerating an Iranian proxy army mobilized on one of its most vulnerable borders. It was time to end the experiment.

In dealing once and for all with Hezbollah, Israel would not just be defending itself. It would be doing the free world a favor: Hezbollah's fingerprints were all over the waves of terror that had battered the West since the 1980s. Hezbollah was not merely a Lebanese faction. It was a transnational hybrid—a global drug cartel, terrorist army, and the Ayatollah's unsinkable aircraft carrier. And just as the Ayatollah's regime was baptized in American blood, Hezbollah was conceived in the same holy war. Both began their crusade the same way: with indiscriminate attacks on America's embassies. In April 1983, a car bomb slammed into the US Embassy in Beirut, killing 63 people, including 17 Americans. The Reagan administration blamed Hezbollah. In October, another truck bomb detonated at the Marine barracks near Beirut's airport, killing 305—among them 241 US Marines. It would mark the single deadliest day for the Corps since the battle of Iwo Jima. A US federal court concluded that Hezbollah and its Iranian sponsors were responsible.

What followed those attacks was a decade of kidnappings and torture. Western hostages vanished into the warrens of Beirut—priests, journalists, professors, diplomats. Among them was CIA Station Chief William Buckley, abducted, brutalized, and ultimately murdered. Between 1982 and 1992, thirty Westerners were kidnapped; US intelligence later confirmed that Hezbollah orchestrated most of them. In 1984, another bomb tore through the new US Embassy annex in Aukar, killing twenty-four, including two American service members. A year later, Hezbollah hijacked TWA Flight 847, holding its passengers hostage for seventeen days. They executed US Navy diver Robert Dean Stethem and dumped his body onto the tarmac. These were not random outrages. They were doctrine—asymmetric war waged through terror proxies to drive America and its allies from the Middle East. Hezbollah's methods became the blueprint for a generation of jihadists, among them Osama bin Laden. In no small measure, the architecture of 9/11—martyrdom fused with global theater—was born in Beirut.

In the 1990s, Hezbollah began exporting its terror worldwide. In March 1992, a suicide bomber destroyed the Israeli Embassy in Buenos Aires, killing twenty-nine. Two years later, on July 18, 1994, a van packed with explosives slammed into the AMIA Jewish community center in the same city, killing eighty-five and wounding three hundred—the deadliest attack on Jews since the Holocaust. Argentine, Israeli, and Interpol investigations all traced the bombings to Hezbollah and Iranian operatives. The carnage carried into the twenty-first century. In 2012, a Hezbollah suicide bomber struck a bus of Israeli tourists in Burgas, Bulgaria, killing six. And through it all, the group never stopped rearming—stockpiling rockets, drones, and precision-guided missiles in open defiance of international law. While its terror reached across continents, its arsenal remained fixed on one target: Israel's northern border.

By 2024, Hezbollah was no longer a militia. It was a terror organization capable of going toe to toe with nation-states—Lebanon's most powerful military machine, and at the same time one of its dominant political parties, complete with a vast social-welfare network. Its Secretary-General, Hassan Nasrallah, ruled from subterranean bunkers with the authority of a head of state. Manpower estimates varied. Nasrallah boasted of one hundred thousand fighters; Western intelligence put the figure closer to forty thousand to fifty thousand full-time soldiers, backed by twenty thousand reservists and thousands of logistical and intelligence operatives. These were not amateurs. They had fought and killed alongside Bashar al-Assad's genocidal forces in the Syrian Civil War, hardening their ranks with years of battlefield experience. At the spear's tip stood Hezbollah's elite Radwan Force, trained in cross-border raids, tunnel warfare, and psychological operations. Behind them loomed an arsenal that dwarfed that of most nation-states: between 120,000 and 200,000 rockets and missiles—from crude Katyushas to thousands of precision-guided weapons capable of striking Tel Aviv, Haifa, and even Israel's southern bases. In an all-out war, analysts estimated Hezbollah could launch three thousand to four thousand rockets per day, overwhelming Israel's Iron Dome and David's Sling defenses. Some of its long-range weapons—the Fateh-110 and M-600 series—could deliver half-ton warheads over 250 kilometers.

This was not a border threat. It was a regional one—a strategic blade held up to Israel's throat.

When Hamas attacked on October 7, Hezbollah watched closely. For years, Hassan Nasrallah had helped shape the "axis of resistance," coordinating strategy with Iran's Revolutionary Guard and Hamas's military wing. But now he faced a dilemma: how to deploy the axis without destroying it. In a conversation shortly after the October 7 attacks, Hezbollah's deputy commander, Ibrahim Aqeel, urged a limited front, deploying small numbers engaging in harassment operations, while avoiding mass incursions. The goal was to tie Israel down in the north without triggering its full fury. Nasrallah agreed. In the same conversation, he issued strict rules of engagement: calibrated provocations that would draw blood but not awaken the bear. He believed Israel would remain predictable, regulated, and restrained. It was the same doctrine he had relied on since he went to war with Israel in 2006—and it would prove fatal.

What neither Nasrallah nor Aqeel realized was how deeply Israel had already infiltrated Hezbollah's inner communications. When Nasrallah spoke to Aqeel about the rules of engagement, Israeli cyber units were listening. And Israel would later turn those very "rules"—the psychological boundaries Hezbollah believed inviolable—into bait. For months, the IDF struck at the edges of Hezbollah's defenses, just enough to sustain the illusion of restraint. Each calculated strike lulled Hezbollah deeper into its own script. Meanwhile, Israel was drawing up plans for another kind of war. When Nasrallah would least expect it, Israel would flip the switch.

Through the winter and early spring of 2024, Hezbollah lobbed sporadic rockets and drones. But summer brought dangerous escalations. On June 11, Israel targeted a Hezbollah command center in Jwaya, killing Taleb Abdallah, the group's senior field commander in southern Lebanon. The next day, Hezbollah fired two hundred rockets at northern Israel; another 150 rockets and thirty drones would follow a day later. On July 3, Israel struck again—this time killing Mohammed Nasser, a key Hezbollah operations officer, in Tyre. Hezbollah answered with one hundred rockets that morning and another two hundred that night. Three weeks later, Israel suffered one of the most horrifying attacks of the war. On July 27, a Hezbollah rocket slammed into a soccer field in the Israeli Druze town of

Majdal Shams, killing twelve children and injuring dozens. Israeli shock turned to fury. Within days, an airstrike leveled a Hezbollah facility in southern Beirut, killing Fuad Shukr, one of Nasrallah's closest military commanders, and the man who had ordered the massacre. Hezbollah vowed vengeance, firing 320 Katyusha rockets in a single day.

By late September 2024, the IDF had reported over nine thousand rockets launched from Lebanon since the start of the war. Meanwhile, Nasrallah clung to his doctrine of "controlled escalation," believing Israel would continue to strike surgically and steer clear of all-out war. He misread the moment completely. Inside the Israeli war cabinet, the argument was over: the north would not be stabilized by deterrence. It would be secured by destruction. On September 16, Israel's Security Cabinet added a new war aim: to restore security in the north and allow displaced Israelis to return home. Nasrallah should have taken note. For years, Israel's intelligence community—AMAN, Mossad, and Shin Bet—had been quietly mapping Hezbollah's terrorist empire. Its bunkers, tunnels, depots, fiber-optic lines, and encrypted communications; everything was cataloged, cell by cell. The mapping was patient, meticulous, and invisible. By the order finally came, Israel's target list was already bursting at the seams. Hezbollah had built its strength over decades. Israel would dismantle it in days.

The plan was not to nibble at the edges. It was to paralyze the core. To annihilate command and control, destroy launch sites, collapse tunnel networks, and decapitate the leadership—a textbook tackle against Hezbollah's center of gravity. It would be a campaign of "systemic unraveling." They would strike fast, in layers, without warning—a modern echo of the Six-Day War, where Israel's air force had erased Egypt's on the ground before it could take off. The logic was ancient and brutal. In the Talmud, there is a famous phrase: "If one comes to kill you, rise early and kill him." In 1967, that principle became state policy. Facing encirclement by Arab armies, Israel struck first and won the Six-Day War. In the Yom Kippur War, Israel neglected the core principle and was nearly destroyed. On October 7, it had made the same mistake, allowing Hamas to fester to the point where it could not be contained. Facing an existential threat in Lebanon, Israel would learn its lesson. Nasrallah—arrogant, insulated, and convinced that Israel would remain trapped by proportionality—never saw it coming.

In the final days of September, Israeli intelligence and airpower fused in a coordinated strike plan that would redefine modern warfare. The assault was not a retaliation. It was a reckoning—a preemptive and surgical strike total that would redefine covert operations and open warfare alike. It would prove that Israel is unstoppable, so long as they wage war in the way that God would.

Beep Beep

Throughout 2024, Israel hunted Hezbollah's hierarchy with surgical precision. One by one, the pillars of the organization vanished from the battlefield. In January, an Israeli airstrike killed Wissam al-Tawil, a senior commander in Hezbollah's elite Radwan Force. In February, his comrade Ali Muhammad al-Debs followed. By June, Taleb Abdallah—commander of the elite Nasr Force—was eliminated. July brought the death of Mohammed Nasser, commander of the "Aziz" Unit. And only weeks later came the crown jewel of the campaign: Fuad Shukr, Hezbollah's most senior military commander. For decades, Shukr had been a ghost—the man the United States had hunted since the 1983 Marine Barracks bombing in Beirut. He lived in shadows so deep that, after his death, Lebanese television mistakenly aired photographs of another man. On July 30, 2024, at 7:00 p.m., Shukr received a phone call instructing him to go to his apartment, five floors above his office. Moments after he stepped inside, an Israeli missile tore through the apartment—and through him.

"Every commander who was killed—his information network died with him," admitted a senior Lebanese official. None more so than Shukr. "He was a source of knowledge," noted Dr. Carmit Valensi, a leading Israeli expert on Hezbollah. "He knew how to work and communicate with Nasrallah. They spoke the same language." According to a Shiite cleric close to the organization, Israel not only decapitated Hezbollah's command structure but also struck its strategic rocket operators, the irreplaceable core of its arsenal. Yet the keynote event—the blow that would finally snap Hezbollah's spine—was still to come.

Hezbollah had always been obsessed with secrecy. In February 2024, Nasrallah, convinced Israeli intelligence had infiltrated every digital signal, issued a stark directive to his terrorist followers: get rid of your cell phones. "Shut it off, bury it, put it in an iron chest and lock it up," he commanded, "The collaborator is the cell phone in your hands, and those of your wife and your children. This cell phone is the collaborator and the killer." To protect his men, he ordered a return to old-school technology: pagers. He didn't know that the order itself would set the trap in motion. Years earlier, the Mossad had anticipated this move. It had created a front company posing as an international pager manufacturer—a firm called BAC, operating out of Europe with a subsidiary in Hungary. On paper, BAC made legitimate communications equipment. In reality, it functioned as a Mossad front—a fact they teased on their website. The company coyly described itself as "agents of change," offering "innovative solutions" for international relations. Hezbollah became its most important client. The pagers produced for the group were built on a separate line, and hidden inside their batteries was a crystalline explosive, PETN: refined, compact, and invisible to the naked eye.

The Mossad had spent a decade perfecting the transformation of everyday communications into weapons. The program began ten years earlier with walkie-talkies engineered to detonate when activated by Israel. "A walkie-talkie was a weapon just like a bullet or a missile," recalled one of the case officers involved. The units were sold to Hezbollah at a "good price"—high enough to seem real, low enough to be irresistible. Over sisxteen thousand were purchased, tested, and distributed throughout the ranks. But there was a flaw with the walkie-talkies—they were made to fit in military vests, worn only in combat. The Mossad wanted something its enemies would carry everywhere, something always within reach. The solution was simple: a pager.

When the Mossad discovered that Hezbollah was ordering pagers from a Taiwanese manufacturer called Gold Apollo, the plan became clear. The Israelis built a perfect replica. They tested it obsessively: first by detonating it inside padded gloves to calibrate just enough explosive to wound the user—but not the people standing near him. "We test everything triple, double, multiple times," one Mossad agent later told *60 Minutes*, "to make sure there is minimum collateral damage." Mossad engineers even cycled through dozens of ringtones to find the precise tone that would compel someone to pull the device from their pocket. They timed the average human response: seven seconds. When the prototypes came out too bulky, they solved the problem with marketing. YouTube ads touted the device as "robust, dustproof, waterproof, with long battery life." Brochures extolled its reliability. The new model—branded as the Gold Apollo AR-924—became one of the most sought-after pagers on the market.

To complete the deception, Mossad established shell companies and even recruited the same Gold Apollo saleswoman Hezbollah had used before. She approached Nasrallah's procurement officers with an irresistible offer: a "free upgrade" on their next shipment. By September 2024, roughly five thousand pagers had been distributed to Hezbollah's senior personnel. The bomb was now in their pockets.

September 17, 2024. At 3:30 p.m., a message flashed across Lebanon. Thousands of pagers beeped at once. Three intelligence officials later said the trigger was an Arabic message crafted to resemble an urgent communiqué from Hezbollah's leadership. Seconds after it appeared, the devices detonated. The effect was instantaneous—and apocalyptic. Pagers exploded in markets, offices, and cars. Operatives riding motorcycles fell lifeless in the streets. Clips depicted men missing eyes and fingers, their stomachs torn open by shards of their own devices. Curiously, Iran's ambassador to Beirut, Mojtaba Amani, was among the injured. The wounded overwhelmed more than 150 hospitals across Lebanon. "Never do you have eye emergencies at this frequency. It's transforming two thousand people into disabled [people] at the same time," one Lebanese doctor complained. The Israeli design had worked exactly as intended: those standing beside were barely touched.

The Mossad called it "the bomb in a pocket." One agent later explained the logic: "The aim wasn't to kill Hezbollah terrorists. If he's just dead, he's dead. But if he's wounded, you have to treat him, feed him, invest resources. And those people without hands and eyes become living proof—walking in Lebanon—of 'don't mess with [Israel].' They're proof of our superiority all across the Middle East." According to Hezbollah officials, the explosions incapacitated some 1,500 fighters through injuries alone—many permanently blinded or dismembered. And that was likely a lowball estimate designed to save face, which was especially necessary at the time. The sheer, almost supernatural reach of Israeli intelligence sent a pulse of fear throughout Lebanon, eroding confidence in Hezbollah's ability to protect even its own.

Panic spread as fast as the blast wave. The day after the pagers exploded, fear gripped Lebanon. People were afraid to turn on their air conditioners. Others unplugged their televisions, terrified they might detonate too. At a funeral in Beirut for those killed in the "pager operation," Hashem Safieddine, head of Hezbollah's Executive Council, vowed revenge: "This aggression will definitely face its special punishment. This punishment is definitely coming." And then, the second wave began—erupting in the crowd right before his eyes. Hezbollah's handheld radios—the walkie-talkies Mossad had seeded a decade earlier—were remotely triggered, killing at least 30 people and wounding 750 more. Hezbollah answered with rocket and artillery fire on Israeli positions at Neve Ziv and Beit Hillel, and launched several drones across the border. But the damage was done. Its communications, its confidence, and its command were in ruins.

That same day, Israel's Shin Bet announced it had foiled a Hezbollah plot to assassinate a former senior defense official using a Claymore mine. Israel seemed omniscient. Yet the IDF maintained official silence regarding its role in the explosions. The following day, Chief of Staff Herzi Halevi offered a thinly veiled hint: "We have many capabilities that we have not yet activated . . . we have seen some of these things." By September 22, Prime Minister Benjamin Netanyahu was less restrained. "If Hezbollah has not understood the message," he warned, "I promise you, it will understand the message."

On September 19, Israel carried out some of the heaviest airstrikes since the war began, striking more than a hundred Hezbollah rocket launchers and fortified positions across southern Lebanon. The next day, Israeli jets hit Beirut's Dahieh suburb, killing Ibrahim Aqil—acting commander of Hezbollah's elite Radwan Force—along with senior officer Ahmad Mahmoud Wahabi and more than a dozen high-ranking terrorists, tearing out what remained of Hezbollah's battlefield command. Inside the organization, recriminations began almost immediately. In the months that followed, senior figures—including interim leader Naim Qassem—conceded that the pager attack had been a catastrophic failure. A formal inquiry committee was convened. "Israel's intelligence-gathering methods were the main factor that caused our casualties," Qassem admitted. "They were far more extensive than we ever imagined." Even Nasrallah, at the time, appeared to agree. He called the operation an "unprecedented blow"—a "test" for Hezbollah, one that, he acknowledged, "could be called a declaration of war." Nasrallah, it seemed, still didn't get the memo—the declaration had been made.

By September 21, the IDF announced it had "almost completely dismantled" Hezbollah's military chain of command. Two days later, Israel carried out more than 1,600 strikes across Lebanon, obliterating the group's stockpiles and aerial arrays. Hezbollah tried to respond, firing 240 rockets toward Israel, Judea and Samaria, and the Golan Heights, injuring five. But the barrages were erratic and uncoordinated—the reflex of a body whose nervous system had been destroyed. On September 24, Israel struck again, killing Ibrahim Qubaisi, commander of Hezbollah's rocket and missile division. By then, it seemed there was only one leader left.

Busted in the Bunker

Hassan Nasrallah's rise was the story of a boy from a dusty Beirut suburb who dreamed of climbing to the top of the world's most wanted list—and did. Born in 1960 in greater Beirut, the eldest of nine in a moderate family, Nasrallah's childhood was unremarkable—until he was seized by a fanatical obsession with jihad. While his friends played football, he devoured Islamist tracts. When Lebanon plunged into civil war in 1975, the chaos became his crucible. His family moved to the southern village of Aaraia, where he discovered the Amal Shiite movement and the messianic teachings of its leader, Imam Musa al-Sadr. The teenage zealot found his bloodstained calling.

While studying at a public school in Tyre, Nasrallah's zeal caught the attention of a cleric who sent him to the Shiite seminary in Najaf, Iraq—the beating heart of Shiite scholarship. There, amid the revolutionary ferment of the 1970s, he met Abbas Musawi, a Lebanese preacher who became his mentor—and would one day serve as Hezbollah's secretary general. Under Musawi's tutelage, the boy from Beirut was remade into a disciple of the Ayatollahs. When Saddam Hussein expelled foreign clerics from Iraq, Nasrallah and Musawi returned to Lebanon, carrying with them a new gospel: Shiite militancy under Tehran's command.

Following the success of Iran's Islamic Revolution, Shiite communities across the region—and beyond—were radicalized. Relocating to Lebanon's Bekaa Valley, Nasrallah rode that wave, preaching, organizing, and plotting jihad. In a lecture during the 1980s, he proclaimed that Hezbollah's blood would be spilled for the Ayatollah, whose rule he envisioned spreading across the entire Muslim world. When Israel invaded Lebanon in 1982, Tehran dispatched hundreds of Revolutionary Guards to train and arm its adherents, laying the groundwork for an Islamic republic on Lebanese soil. From their fusion with radical Lebanese Shiites, Hezbollah was born. In 1985, the group formally announced itself in an open letter to the Lebanese press. Its mission was explicit: to expel Israel, export Iran's revolution, and extend the rule of the Supreme Leader. That same year, Hezbollah began firing rockets into northern Israel—a declaration that Lebanon's south now belonged to the Party of God.

Throughout the 1980s, Nasrallah proved himself both capable and ruthless. He forged alliances, recruited fighters, and crushed rivals—including Amal, the very movement that had once shaped him. After a brief period of study in Iran's holy city of Qom, he returned to Lebanon in 1990 to help command Hezbollah's expanding forces. When Israel assassinated Abbas al-Musawi in 1992, Nasrallah—barely thirty-two—assumed leadership. Under his direction, Hezbollah evolved from a guerrilla faction into a political-military empire: entering elections even as it fortified the border with Iranian-supplied rockets, bunkers, and tunnels. Nasrallah's insurgency against Israel's presence in southern Lebanon bled the IDF in an exhausting war of attrition that ultimately led to Israel's unilateral withdrawal in May 2000. "Thereafter," observed Bruce Hoffman of the Council on Foreign Relations, "Hezbollah effectively supplanted the Lebanese Army as the country's only truly effective military force."

The 2000 Israeli withdrawal made Hassan Nasrallah a legend across the Arab world. To millions, he was the man who had defeated the Zionists;

to the West, Iran's most lethal proxy. He had turned Hezbollah into a state within a state—the dominant power in Lebanon. In 2006, Nasrallah sparked the Second Lebanon War by ordering an unprovoked cross-border assault in which eight Israeli soldiers were killed and two abducted. Ever the performer, he delivered a televised voice message early in the war, urging viewers to look toward "the middle of the sea." The broadcast cut to footage of the Israeli Saar 5 warship INS Hanit—which had been struck by a Chinese-made C-802 anti-ship missile fired by Hezbollah, killing four Israeli sailors. That moment stood among Nasrallah's most potent propaganda victories—a scene that made Israel's cutting-edge weaponry appear powerless. Nasrallah survived the war in bunkers, directing attacks while Beirut burned above him. When Israel accepted a UN-brokered ceasefire, he resurfaced to declare victory once more. From there, his reach only grew—into Syria's war, into global terror networks, and into the mythology of the modern Middle East. For three decades, Hassan Nasrallah stood at the intersection of faith and firepower—the cleric who turned jihad into a brand, and Hezbollah into the most formidable non-state army on earth.

For decades, Israeli intelligence had studied Hezbollah—focusing the full force of its surveillance and analytic machinery on the organization. From weapons stockpiles in the Bekaa Valley to training camps in Nabatieh, from convoys shuttling arms between Damascus and Baalbek to the fiber-optic cables buried beneath Dahieh's streets, Israel mapped out everything it could. Smuggling tunnels cutting through mountains, antennas disguised as minarets—every structure was tracked, photographed, and logged as a target. The result was one of the most exhaustive intelligence efforts in the modern Middle East: a forty-year shadow war fought with spies, wiretaps, and satellites. Nasrallah was not an easy mark. Since 2006, he had lived almost entirely underground. His public appearances were limited to prerecorded speeches projected on giant screens in Beirut's southern suburbs. His convoys ran with decoys; his whereabouts were a mystery even to his closest lieutenants. He trusted almost no one. His communications were hardwired, his bunkers sheathed in concrete thicker than a bank vault. For years, Israel's most sophisticated technologies failed to penetrate the darkness. But in the world of intelligence, patience is a weapon too.

The breakthrough came not from a single clue, but from the convergence of many. Years of signals intelligence—intercepted chatter between Iranian engineers and Hezbollah logistics officers, patterns of encrypted transmissions bouncing across Lebanon—were aligned with reports from human informants. Gradually, Israeli analysts assembled a profile of one site in the Haret Hreik district, buried beneath an unremarkable residential block. Beneath it, they believed, lay Hezbollah's most guarded secret: its primary command bunker—engineered with Iranian technology and concealed even from much of the group's senior leadership. The bunker had been built to survive anything. Israel intended to prove otherwise.

In an operation that would be described as rivaling the exploding beepers, Israel achieved the means for a flawless precision strike against a deeply buried bunker. In a joint project spanning the Defense Ministry's weapons unit, Unit 8200, air force engineers, Rafael, and Elbit, Israeli teams developed what sounded like science fiction: specialized guidance and sensing modules that could talk to penetrating warheads attached to bunker-busting bombs. Like a bespoke kill chain, the system allowed ordnance to "read" the earth and correct its course at depth, enabling real-time precision strikes at varying underground layers. That degree of accuracy was essential: a one-meter deviation could mean the difference between destroying a tunnel and striking beside it—leaving those inside alive, injured rather than dead. At this level of operation there was no room for error. The Mossad had pursued the technology not only with Lebanon in mind but also for a potential strike on Iran's nuclear sites. The project reached completion in 2022, roughly a year before Hamas's October 7 attack. For ten months the devices remained dormant while Israel fought in the south and managed the northern front—until the moment they were needed.

In late September 2024, As Israeli jets pounded Dahieh's skyline, a Mossad team slipped into Beirut carrying packages that appeared innocent until you picked one up and felt the weight. The Mossad team crept through narrow alleys, hugging walls, hoping their handler had coordinated with the IDF so the air force would not bomb the route they were taking. Their destination was a high-rise apartment block; beneath it lay Hezbollah's primary underground command bunker. The Mossad team was tasked with planting devices at preplanned points inside the building directly above the compound. They gave their chances of survival no better than 50/50. If Hezbollah's thugs found them, there would be no prison, no trial. Even if they remained undetected, they still risked death or maiming from shrapnel when Israeli bombs rained down nearby.

Just hours before setting out, the agents held a tense discussion with their handlers. They said they were prepared for the mission but demanded that the air force halt its heavy bombardments during their infiltration. The handler said just the opposite would occur: the raids would not only continue but intensify, forcing Hezbollah guards to take cover and giving the agents a chance to reach the bunker. Running right through a thundering wave of airstrikes, the agents reached their positions and set down what they had carried. The agents exfiltrated the way they came and vanished into the city.

Every hallway, chamber, and ventilation shaft had been cataloged. Every escape route was mapped. Satellite radar confirmed seismic anomalies beneath the building; fiber-optic sensors planted months before were now relaying real-time acoustic data from deep underground. The bunker's hum—generators, relay chatter, footsteps—was being monitored. The picture was complete. Nasrallah, unaware of how exposed he had become, was still trying to rebuild. After the losses of Fuad Shukr, his trusted strategist, and Ibrahim Aqeel, his operational brain, he was attempting to stitch back together a fractured command. Israeli intelligence reported that Nasrallah would be meeting with Ali Karaki, commander of Hezbollah's southern front, and General Abbas Nilforoushan, the Quds Force liaison in Lebanon. The meeting promised certainty—and risk: warn Washington and the opportunity might be lost; act alone and risk facing a regional chain reaction without American support. Gallant and Halevi favored a heads-up to the Americans; Barnea and others argued for speed. The prime minister—en route to the United Nations General Assembly—made his decision midair. "I called on a secure line and decided: We will do it." He also decided not to alert Washington:

"If we had told the Americans that we would target Nasrallah, the news would have leaked within five minutes." After one last call from his hotel room, Netanyahu's order went down the wire.

On September 27, 2024, at exactly 18:21, the order came: Operation New Order. Ten Israeli fighter jets—F-15I Ra'ams and F-16I Sufas—thundered out over the Mediterranean, each loaded with precision ordnance: eighty-three BLU-109 one-ton bunker-busting bombs, nicknamed "Heavy Hail." The air force initially planned to use about half that number. But Gallant insisted they double the payload to ensure Nasrallah's death. Each of the munitions carried warheads equipped with the specialized Israeli guidance systems designed to punch through Lebanon's dense stone with perfect precision. Every bomb was assigned a precise coordinate and a depth calibration measured to the meter.

Beirut's southern skyline erupted in light as the earth beneath it convulsed. Layers of reinforced concrete folded inward on themselves. Within seconds, a bunker complex two decades in the making—the nerve center of Hezbollah's military and political command—ceased to exist. Nasrallah was gone. So were Ali Karaki, Abbas Nilforoushan, and roughly three hundred Hezbollah operatives and officers gathered for the meeting. The subterranean labyrinth that had coordinated thousands of rocket launches and safeguarded decades of Iranian secrets was reduced to a crater of dust and molten steel.

As reports of Nasrallah's death spread, the region trembled. In Beirut, confusion reigned for hours. Hezbollah's television network, Al-Manar, went dark. Spokesmen first denied the rumors, then fell silent. Crowds poured into Dahieh shouting "Labayk ya Nasrallah!"—unaware that the man they invoked was already gone. Across the border, Israel held its silence before confirming a day later that Nasrallah had been killed. Prime Minister Netanyahu hailed the assassination as a decisive step toward "changing the balance of power in the region for years to come," adding, "Nasrallah was not a terrorist—he was the terrorist." Hezbollah's retaliation was furious but unfocused. Within twenty-four hours, the group launched hundreds of rockets, drones, and anti-tank missiles toward northern Israel in a campaign it called Operation Khaybar—a reference to the Prophet Muhammad's conquest of the Jewish tribes of Arabia. But Israel's aerial defenses intercepted nearly all of them. Hezbollah's offensive power had been decapitated along with its leader.

On October 4—just a week later—Israel struck again, killing Hashem Safieddine, Nasrallah's newly appointed successor. Hezbollah hastily named Naim Qassem, its longtime deputy, as acting leader. Capable and loyal but devoid of Nasrallah's charisma, Qassem inherited a shattered movement. Hezbollah's once-feared command structure was gone. "[Nasrallah] was leading us," lamented one Hezbollah supporter. "He was everything to us. We were under his wings."

The IDF later released a brief video of Air Force Commander Maj. Gen. Tomer Bar addressing his officers: "Kudos to all the partners in the neutralization cell. We will get them all. Continue with the same professionalism, the same calm. We are on the right path." Analysts quickly grasped the magnitude of what had occurred. The apex predator of global terror had been cleanly removed. As counterterrorism scholar Bruce Hoffman observed: "Nasrallah's death is a crushing blow. There are no clear successors."

The Crossing

Following Nasrallah's death, Hezbollah was a shell of its former self. Yet the group still retained offensive capabilities—and used them. On September 25, Hezbollah fired a ballistic missile toward Mossad headquarters in Tel Aviv, the first such attack of the war. On October 13, a Hezbollah drone struck the cafeteria at the Golani training base near Giv'at Ada, killing four soldiers and wounding dozens more. About a week later, another drone slammed into the window of the prime minister's residence in Caesarea. Netanyahu was away; there were no casualties. But even these acts of defiance proved futile. They were the spasms of a crippled force, gestures without consequence. For Hezbollah, the writing was on the wall.

But high-level assassinations and exploding beepers were still not enough to eliminate the Hezbollah threat—certainly not its most dangerous component: the prospect of a ground invasion into Israel's north, a mirror of Hamas's assault on October 7. Like Hamas, Hezbollah had spent years preparing precisely such an operation. A lattice of tunnels snaked beneath southern Lebanon, ready to disgorge thousands of Radwan commandos who could cross into Israel within minutes. After the planned massacre, those same tunnels were to serve as holding sites for hostages—a northern replay of Gaza's horror. Vests, weapons, vehicles, and escape routes—everything had been prepared. But Israel would not be caught off guard twice. The threat would be dismantled before it could be deployed. And there was only one way to do that: a full-scale ground campaign.

On October 1, 2024, Israel announced the launch of "limited, localized, targeted ground raids" into southern Lebanon. The crossing was deliberate and methodical. Arabic-language warnings—printed on leaflets and broadcast over radio—urged civilians in the south to evacuate. While ground units moved into southern Lebanon, the air force kept up its strikes. On October 5, Israeli jets hit near Tripoli for the first time, targeting the al-Baddawi camp and killing Hamas's Qassam commander in Lebanon. In the days that followed, a string of precision strikes in Beirut pulverized missile depots and long-term weapons caches concealed beneath residential buildings. By October 7, Israel had extended its operations along the coast and deep into southern command zones, while ground formations advanced into border villages. That night, the IDF carried out a large-scale air assault on Hezbollah's underground command centers in southern Lebanon, killing at least fifty terrorists, including several senior commanders. Among them was Hezbollah's newly appointed Chief of Staff, Soheil Hussein Husseini. Meanwhile, fourteen IDF brigades pressed into the southern Lebanese villages that had long served as Hezbollah's gunsights over Israel's northern border. The next day—October 8, exactly one year after Hezbollah began its assault on Israel—the group's acting leader, Naim Qassem, publicly expressed support for ceasefire efforts.

As five IDF divisions entered thirty towns across Southern Lebanon, what soldiers discovered were not civilian neighborhoods, but a vast network of military installations disguised as civilian neighborhoods. The sheer number of "outposts" that Hezbollah had built in Southern Lebanon came as a shock to anyone who served there. Arms caches were everywhere, along with advanced weapons workshops. Hezbollah flags fluttered from rooftops, and posters of martyrs papered nearly every wall. The ground campaign became an X-ray—exposing, then excising, the layers of Hezbollah's hidden war machine. During the night of October 20–21, the IDF announced Operation Robin Hood, aimed at dismantling Hezbollah's financial infrastructure. Israeli aircraft struck dozens of sites belonging to Hezbollah's al-Qard al-Hasan network, while a senior financial officer was killed in a precision strike in Syria. The next day, October 22, the IDF revealed that beneath Beirut's al-Sahel Hospital lay one of Nasrallah's underground bunkers—stocked with nearly half a billion dollars in cash and gold. After the hospital's director ordered an evacuation, Israel launched a new wave of airstrikes across Beirut, focusing on Hezbollah's precision-missile project.

Muhaibib would become the ground campaign's centerpiece. For more than a decade Hezbollah had tunneled toward a single aim: a forward subterranean base to disgorge two hundred Radwan fighters to seize Kiryat Shmona—the largest Israeli city on the Lebanese border. A heavy iron door concealed the entrance to a labyrinth: 1.5 kilometers of reinforced concrete with side chambers, firing points, oxygen and power supplies, rations, and armories. More than a tunnel, it was a fortress—a staging ground built to spew fighters, missiles, and slaughter into Israel's north.

The IDF paratroopers brigade cleared the complex in brutal, claustrophobic fighting. The battle was measured in silenced shots and short bursts, lasers carving thin lines in the dust. The enemy knew the maze; the Israelis learned it under fire. After thirty-six hours of close-quarters combat in heat and total blackness, the defenders were dead, captured, or sealed behind blast doors they would never open again. Then the engineers went to work. Facing the constant threat of mortars and sniper fire, they hauled in four hundred tons of liquid explosive. Combat teams held the perimeter above while a brigade secured the road used by the tanker trucks bringing the fuel from Israel—one clean hit on a truck could have blown up the whole effort. Below, sappers worked like surgeons: casing charges, rigging junctions, and stringing detonating cords. After nearly two weeks of preparation, the area around the tunnel complex was evacuated and a final sweep was completed.

The fuse was lit. Seismographs in Israel—as far south as Caesarea—jumped. The blast registered as an earthquake. An entire mountain went up in smoke. What Hezbollah had spent years carving, Israel destroyed in seconds. Operationally, the IDF had erased Hezbollah's most significant forward base along the border. "It was a historic mission," one officer recalled. "You cross the fence, see the evil built against your people for years, and tear it out—while the lights of Metula glow behind you." It was the single largest explosive charge ever set by the IDF. As another officer put it: "The biggest explosion we ever made—and the one that buried their war."

In total, the IDF seized the Lebanese side of the northern frontier to a depth of roughly 5 kilometers. But the real scale of the operation spoke through the numbers: Israel eliminated Hassan Nasrallah and 13 members of Hezbollah's senior command forum, along with 4 division commanders, 24 brigade commanders, 27 battalion commanders, 63 company commanders, and 22 platoon commanders. Between 4,000 and 5,000 Hezbollah commanders and operatives were eliminated; around 9,000 more were rendered nonoperational. Some 12,500 targets struck—including 1,600 command centers and 1,000 weapons depots. 70 to 80 percent of Hezbollah's short-range rocket launchers were destroyed, and Hezbollah was said to possess just 30 percent of the UAVs that it did on the eve of the conflict. Fighter jets logged 14,000 flight hours and 11,000 sorties over Lebanon. The Israeli Navy recorded 25,000 operational sea hours. Hezbollah's indirect fire had withered to small, sporadic volleys; coordinated barrages were a thing of the past. Most crucially, the IDF reported that the Radwan Force—once Hezbollah's tip of the spear—had been rendered incapable of launching any broad offensive. Along the contact line, troops uncovered and destroyed some 1,500 subterranean assets, including every offensive tunnel network and one that crossed into Israeli territory. An "October 7 in the north" had been prevented.

The ground war did not erase Hezbollah entirely. Under pressure from the Biden administration, Israel stopped short of a full-scale push. As in Gaza, it was permitted to deliver a blow—but not a death blow. Yet this time, Israel achieved something enduring: it stripped Hezbollah of the one posture it had always relied upon—the illusion of invincibility. On television, *60 Minutes* correspondent Lesley Stahl asked an Israeli operative involved in the beeper operation: "Did you completely destroy and crush Hezbollah?" He didn't hesitate. "The honest answer is no," he said. "But after the tipping point of the beeper operation and the walkie-talkie—and then the IDF attack—Hezbollah is in a very, very difficult situation: no chain of command, no spirit in their soldiers, asking, begging, for a cease-fire." The campaign in Lebanon didn't finish the job. But it proved that when Israel takes the initiative and maintains momentum, the results are bound to be biblical.

CHAPTER EIGHT

AXIS TO ASHES: THE CLAMPDOWN ON SYRIA, YEMEN, AND IRAQ

Damascus has grown weak,
She has turned around to flee;
Trembling has seized her,
Pain and anguish have taken hold of her,
Like a woman in childbirth.
Jeremiah 49:23

They call it the "Shia Crescent"—a geographic horseshoe of clerics and Kalashnikovs running up through Lebanon and Syria, stretching east across Iraq and Iran, and closing its curve in the Arabian Peninsula. In strategic terms, it is far more tangible: a chain of oil fields, refineries, weapons caches, rocket launchers, drone factories, and proxy armies that Iran has spent decades forging into a sword of Damocles poised above the Middle East. The Shia Crescent is more than a demographic contour; in Tehran's grasp, it has become the blueprint of a radical Islamist empire—bound by terrorist militias, financed by oil, and fueled by messianic zeal. Its purpose is nothing less than to remake the balance of power in the region—a mission captured in the name the Iranians use for it: the Axis of Resistance.

From the moment Ayatollah Ruhollah Khomeini and his followers seized power in 1979, their ambitions reached far beyond Iran's borders. Within a year, Khomeini issued his command: "Try hard to export our revolution to the world." The Ayatollah saw encirclement everywhere, warning that "all the superpowers and all the powers have risen to destroy us. If we remain in an enclosed environment, we shall definitely face defeat." A decade later, he declared that "the Iranian people's revolution is only a point at the start of the revolution of the great world of Islam."

Like the communists of the Cold War, Iran's new rulers harbored dreams of global domination and contempt for state sovereignty. The mandate to export the revolution was not a slogan—it was law. The constitution of the Islamic Republic codified it explicitly: Article 154 commits Iran to "the right-seeking struggles of the oppressed against the arrogant everywhere in the world," while the preamble vows "the continuation of the Revolution at home and abroad." This was not a nationalist uprising, but a transnational crusade with imperial intent. And for the next four decades, Tehran worked methodically to export its Shia Islamist creed—arming proxies, cultivating militias, and constructing a new league of rogue regimes spanning continents.

Iran saw its first opening in Lebanon. Amid the chaos of the Lebanese Civil War, the Islamic Revolutionary Guard Corps (IRGC) helped establish Hezbollah in 1985—just six years after Iran's own revolution. What began as a small Shia militia evolved into a terrorist army and political powerhouse, becoming Tehran's most successful foreign franchise.

In Yemen, Iran's expansion unfolded gradually. During the 1990s, members of the al-Houthi family traveled to Qom for religious training under Iranian clerics. In the 2000s, as the Houthis waged an insurgency against the Yemeni government, Tehran quietly funneled weapons, cash, and advisers into the fight. When the rebels seized Sana'a in 2014, Iranian support turned overt, securing a stubborn foothold on Saudi Arabia's southern border. What began as a tribal uprising evolved into a satellite quasi-state—armed, financed, and directed from Tehran.

In Syria, the civil war of 2011 provided the conditions for Iranian intervention. As the Assad regime teetered, Iran rushed to its rescue, deploying Revolutionary Guard units, Hezbollah fighters, and imported Shia militias from across the region. By 2012–13, Iran was heavily engaged in shoring up the Syrian government—an emergency intervention that granted Iran a permanent presence in the country.

But the greatest triumph of the Axis of Resistance came with the collapse of Iraq. After the 2003 US invasion toppled Saddam Hussein—the Sunni strongman who had long brutalized Iraq's Shia majority—the country descended into a sectarian insurgency. Tehran moved swiftly into the void. Immediately after the US invasion, the IRGC's Quds Force began to bankroll, arm, and train Shia militias. Iran's grip tightened further during the war against ISIS in 2014, with these same militias entrenching themselves in Iraq's political, economic, and security apparatus. What began as shadow militias became pillars of the state—their commanders now parliamentarians and ministers, their fighters the soldiers of a parallel army. In the span of a decade, Iraq was transformed from a bulwark against Iranian expansion into its largest imperial outpost.

In every hostile takeover, the Iranian playbook followed a single, ruthless formula: exploit chaos, entrench control. Like a vulture that feeds on dead and dying states, Iran would swoop down onto every civil war or insurgency—weaponizing identity, subsidizing militancy, and converting social and religious ties into strategic reach. By fusing fanaticism with finance and firepower, the regime built durable proxies. Each began as a militia, morphed into a political movement, and ended as a parasite feeding on the very host that gave it life. Over time, this international network of terrorists, smugglers, and tainted bureaucrats transformed Iran from an isolated theocracy into a patron of permanent conflict—and the power broker of the Middle East.

More than battlefield assets, Iran's proxies are instruments of governance. In Lebanon, Hezbollah dominates politics, dispenses welfare, and runs hospitals and schools. In Iraq, Shia militias control ministries, bureaucracies, and infrastructure projects. In Yemen, the Houthis regulate ports, customs, and smuggling routes. Across these fronts, militias collect taxes, issue permits, and distribute aid. Not content merely to be feared, they strive to be needed—embedding themselves into daily life until they become indispensable. In doing so, each has built a parallel state loyal not to its own flag, but to Tehran. An entire region has thus become a laboratory for Iran's hybrid warfare—an intricate fusion of religion, politics, and social welfare engineered into a single system of control.

Iran's reliance on proxies compensates for what it lacks in conventional military power. Its terrorist networks are engineered to thrive in asymmetrical environments. Militias are cheaper than divisions, and insurgencies have repeatedly proven too resilient for any Western coalition to defeat. So instead of invading, Iran infects—cultivating discontent, recruiting militias, and supplying just enough firepower to tilt the balance of a civil war. The result is a slow-motion conquest that feeds on the sectarian fractures woven into the region's political DNA. Through violence, propaganda, and patronage, Iran's proxies transform fear and dependency into allegiance. Meanwhile, Tehran extends its influence at minimal cost: while its proxies bleed on the battlefield, Iran quietly reaps the political reward.

By the eve of October 7, the Ayatollah's terrorist alliance controlled five Middle Eastern capitals: Tehran, Beirut, Damascus, Baghdad, and Sana'a. With Lebanon, Syria, and Iraq firmly in its orbit, Iran had forged a contiguous zone of influence stretching from the Zagros Mountains to the Mediterranean Sea—an unbroken corridor of militias, missile depots, and supply routes linking Tehran to Beirut. With Yemen, it gained something equally decisive: a southern anchor on the Arabian Peninsula and a foothold at the mouth of the Red Sea. From positions near the Bab al-Mandab Strait—one of the world's most vital maritime chokepoints—Tehran could threaten the shipping lanes that feed the Suez Canal. Nurtured by the region's chronic instability, Iran had raised a revolutionary realm from the rubble of failed states.

For all of Tehran's anti-Zionist rhetoric, the true objective of the Axis of Resistance was never Israel's destruction alone. Far more valuable was the encirclement of Saudi Arabia and the neutralization of the Gulf monarchies. Though framed as a coalition against Israel, the axis's deployment pattern tells a clearer truth. Glancing at a map, anyone can see how its geographic footprint encircles the Arabian Peninsula, positioning itself to dominate the Gulf's vital energy reserves.

There is a religious dimension to the Saudi-Persian rivalry. One is Sunni, the other Shia. Together, they represent opposing standard-bearers in a theological divide that had endured for more than a millennium.

Since the days of Khomeini, Iran's leaders have denounced the House of Saud as usurpers of Islam's holiest sites—illegitimate custodians of Mecca and Medina. Yet behind the pious invective lies something far more concrete and combustible: oil. Control of the Gulf's energy arteries is the linchpin of Iran's imperial project—the material foundation beneath its messianic vision.

Saudi Arabia's vast energy wealth lies almost entirely along its Eastern Province, hugging the Persian Gulf—from Dhahran to Abqaiq, from the Ghawar field to Ras Tanura. Directly across the water sits Iran's Khuzestan province, a mirror coastline that has every major Saudi oil facility in range and in its sights. In simple terms, Iran is closer to Saudi oil than Riyadh itself. Tehran's ambitions are also a matter of geography. Roughly twenty million barrels of oil—about one-fifth of global supply—pass each day through the Strait of Hormuz, the narrow maritime chokepoint Iran already commands from its northern shore. Controlling both coasts would enable Tehran to expel foreign forces and single-handedly dominate one of the most critical trade routes on Earth.

In 2014, Quds Force commander Qassem Soleimani articulated Iran's grand strategy with striking candor. Cross-referencing the geography of oil reserves with the map of Shia populations, he described how the vast majority of the world's petroleum wealth lay within a single, Shia-dominated corridor. If Iran could topple the Arab governments along that belt through proxy insurgencies, he said, it could "control seventy percent of the world's oil." Soleimani's words laid bare Tehran's grand design: a Shia petro-empire spanning the oil basins of Basra and southern Iraq, the Eastern Province of Arabia, and the Gulf coastline. If Iran's network of militias and client states could secure these regions, it would stand as the world's dominant energy power—and a marshal of the global economy. What began as a local, theological insurrection would end with the Achaemenids reborn.

But Iran's ambitions soon collided with a rising counterforce: an emerging alignment of moderate, pro-Western states loosely bound under American patronage. The Abraham Accords of 2020 crystallized this new order. By normalizing relations between Israel and key Arab powers, the accords embodied a regional vision built on modernization, trade, and shared security. For Tehran, the accords were not just a diplomatic setback—they were a geopolitical barricade containing its expansion. And Iran knew how to break it: not by defeating Israel, but by dividing it from its Arab partners. A protracted war in Gaza, for instance, could inflame Arab public opinion, jeopardize normalization, and raise the cost for any Gulf ruler seeking cooperation with Jerusalem. In this sense, policy became an extension of war. The objective was not to conquer a coalition, but to fracture it. By aiding, abetting, and planning the October 7 massacre, that is precisely what Iran did. And it worked.

If the Abraham Accords collapse and the West fails to contain Iran, the shock would reverberate far beyond the Middle East—ushering in a perilous realignment of global power. Iran's grip on energy would reengineer world markets and reorder alliances. The anti-Western bloc led by Russia and China would inherit the muscle of the Middle East's vast resources, dethroning America as the world's singular superpower and replacing it with a coalition of authoritarian regimes.

Tehran had already built the skeleton of that vision—a web of capitals, corridors, and clients stretching unbroken from the Mediterranean to the Gulf. But Iran's fatal mistake was assuming that its network could target Israel and survive. Iran believed Israel would confine its response to Gaza, the site of the massacre, and that its assets in Lebanon, Syria, Iraq, and Yemen would remain untouched. But a tiny, defiant Jewish state had other plans.

Barely eighty years after the Holocaust, the Jewish people manned the front line of civilization—the forward vanguard of the West. Standing alone between the Ayatollah and his demonic dreams, Israel leaned into the fight with clarity and conviction. As in the Valley of Elah, Goliath once again set his sights on David. But this time, David had a different strategy: to sever the arms of the axis before striking at its head.

The Fall of the House of Assad

"Syria is the golden ring in the chain of resistance against Israel." Those were the fateful words of Ali Akbar Velayati, senior adviser to Iran's supreme leader. More than an ally to Tehran, Damascus was the hinge binding Iran to Lebanon, Hezbollah, and the Mediterranean. As Bashar al-Assad fought for his survival amid the chaos of civil war, Saeed Jalili, Head of Iran's Supreme National Security Council, made clear just how far Iran would go to preserve this vital link in the Iranian proxy chain: "Iran will not tolerate, in any form, the breaking of the axis of resistance, of which Syria is an intrinsic part." In the arch of Iranian influence, Syria was a keystone.

Technically, Israel and Syria have been in a state of war since the day Israel was born in 1948. They fought three major wars—in 1948, 1967, and 1973—each leaving the hostility unresolved. A fragile ceasefire established in 1974 along the so-called Purple Line kept their armies apart, but never their enmity. In 1982, the two powers clashed directly in Lebanon's Beqaa Valley, fighting the largest air battle since World War II. Israel downed more than eighty Syrian jets without losing a single plane.

By the early 2000s, Syria had become a crucial conduit for Iranian arms transfers to Hezbollah, providing and protecting supply routes through its territory. Despite this growing logistics network, for years, Israel refused to strike Syria. But when Bashar al-Assad moved to acquire a nuclear weapons capability, Prime Minister Ehud Olmert invoked the 1981 Begin Doctrine—Israel's pledge to preempt any enemy effort to obtain nuclear arms—and ordered a unilateral strike to destroy the facility at al-Kibar. Syria didn't strike back; instead, Assad channeled his vengeance into helping Iran arm its terrorist proxies.

When Syria descended into civil war in 2011, Israel declared strict neutrality. But as Assad clawed back territory lost to the rebels, the Iranian footprint expanded in step. It soon became clear that Tehran was transforming Syria into a forward operating base: a lattice of missile factories, drone hangars, and fortified outposts aimed at the Jewish state.

Already a year after the outbreak of the Syrian Civil War, Israel began to fight back. Though Israel stayed mum on its operations, by late 2017, the Israeli Air Force had struck Iranian and Hezbollah arms convoys in Syria nearly a hundred times. Then, in February 2018, the conflict escalated dramatically. A drone operated directly by Iran breached Israeli airspace before being shot down by an IDF Apache helicopter. Israel retaliated with a wave of airstrikes on Iranian positions in Syria. Amid the exchange, a Syrian missile brought down an Israeli F-16—the first Israeli plane lost in combat since 1986. Both pilots ejected safely, but the incident marked a historic threshold: the first direct confrontation between Israel and Iran since the Islamic Revolution of 1979. Three months later, the shadow war went overt. After Iranian forces launched twenty rockets at Israeli positions in the Golan Heights, Israel responded with Operation House of Cards, a sweeping campaign that struck more than fifty Iranian targets, crippling the bulk of Tehran's military infrastructure in Syria. In the years that followed, precision airstrikes from Deir ez-Zor to Damascus killed Iranian officers, Hezbollah commanders, and Syrian troops alike. The mission remained constant: to block the flow of advanced weapons to Hezbollah and to obstruct Iranian entrenchment on Israel's northern frontier.

When Hamas's October 7 assault ignited war in Gaza, Israel's campaign swiftly widened into a multi-front confrontation, with Syria becoming one of its most active battlegrounds. From late 2023 through 2024, Israeli aircraft and commandos carried out hundreds of precision strikes across Syrian territory, targeting Iranian operatives, Hezbollah infrastructure, weapons convoys, and Syrian air defenses. It became the most sustained Israeli air campaign in Syria's history.

Within days of the Hamas massacre, on October 10, mortars were launched from Syria at northern Israel, to which the IDF responded with artillery shelling. Days later, Israeli jets repeatedly hit Aleppo and Damascus airports, crippling their runways and killing Syrian personnel. According to reports, two inbound flights were forced to divert: one carried Iran's Foreign Minister Hossein Amir-Abdollahian along with senior IRGC officials, and the other carried ten tons of missiles. By late October, after rockets were fired from Syria toward the Golan Heights, Israel retaliated with a series of raids that killed eight Syrian soldiers and destroyed air-defense batteries near Daraa and Aleppo. The campaign escalated in November, when an explosive drone launched from Syria crashed into a school in Israel's southernmost city of Eilat. Forty students were in the basement of the school when it was hit; miraculously, none were physically injured. Later that month, Israel launched at least five more attacks against Hezbollah and IRGC hubs around Damascus, Sayyida Zeinab, and Homs.

Through December 2023, more than a dozen Israeli strikes continued to systematically degrade Iran's command infrastructure. Dozens of Hezbollah operatives, IRGC officers, and local militia commanders were killed—including Brigadier General Sayyed Razi Mousavi, Tehran's chief liaison in Syria. By year's end, the Israeli Air Force had rendered all of Syria's major airports inoperable. Throughout early 2024, Israel continued killing senior Hamas, Hezbollah, and IRGC figures in Mezzeh, Aleppo, and Damascus. One strike, on January 20, flattened an entire building—killing General Sadegh Omidzadeh, Iran's Quds Force intelligence head for Syria. According to the *Washington Post*, he had been involved in targeting US Humvee and Cougar armored vehicles in Syrian territory. Days later, Israel took out the IRGC Syrian headquarters outside Damascus. On March 24, predawn strikes targeted assets belonging to Iran's Unit 4000, the IRGC Intelligence branch's Special Operations Division, and the special operations unit of the IRGC's Quds Force in Syria, known as Unit 18840—units that were involved in a plot to smuggle advanced arms to terrorists in Judea and Samaria. On March 29, an Israeli airstrike rocked a Hezbollah rocket warehouse at the Aleppo International Airport, killing thirty-eight Syrian soldiers, seven Hezbollah fighters, and seven militiamen—the deadliest Israeli strike in Syria in years.

The campaign reached a turning point on April 1, 2024, when Israel obliterated the Iranian consulate in Damascus, killing senior IRGC commanders, including the Quds Force commander for all of Syria and Lebanon, Brigadier General Mohammad Reza Zahedi. He would be the most senior IRGC officer to be killed since the assassination of Qasem Soleimani by the US in January 2020. The unprecedented strike symbolized Israel's rejection of Iranian "immunity zones." IDF spokesperson Rear Adm. Daniel Hagari pointed out, "This is no consulate, and this is no embassy. This is a military building of the Quds Force disguised as a civilian building." On April 13, 2024, the Iranian military launched its Operation True Promise, attacking Israel from its own soil for the first time. It was the largest single drone attack in history—at least 170 aerial UAVs—along with thirty cruise missiles, and 120 ballistic missiles. Israel, with help from American-led coalition forces, destroyed almost all the incoming weapons before they could reach their targets. Israel also fired back, targeting a major Iranian military airbase near Isfahan.

In the months that followed, Israel's campaign inside Syria reached a new level of audacity. Repeated strikes in Baniyas, Furqlus, Aleppo, and Palmyra killed scores of IRGC personnel and Hezbollah fighters. On September8, 2024, in a mission code-named Operation Many Ways, Israeli special forces executed one of the most complex raids of the war—the destruction of an underground precision-guided missile plant hidden beneath the Syrian Scientific Studies and Research Center (SSRC), the same regime body responsible for Syria's chemical weapons.

The site lay hundreds of feet below ground, in one of the most heavily defended zones in Syria, second only to Damascus. After two months of training, commandos from the Shaldag Unit and the 669 Search and Rescue Unit infiltrated Syrian airspace aboard four Sikorsky CH-53 Sea Stallions, escorted by attack helicopters, twenty-one fighter jets, five drones, and fourteen reconnaissance aircraft. Simultaneously, Israeli jets, drones, and Navy missile boats struck multiple SSRC facilities across Syria—a diversion meant to disguise the raid as another routine airstrike and draw regime troops away from the target. Flying low to evade radar, the commandos breached the subterranean complex roughly fifty minutes after insertion. Inside, they commandeered forklifts to open sealed entrances and laid over 300 kilograms of explosives along the production lines. While one team secured the perimeter, the other planted charges and seized intelligence documents detailing Iran's missile supply chain. Within hours, all of the soldiers were safely extracted. Moments later, the Shaldag demolition chief triggered the detonator. The explosion—equal to nearly one ton of TNT—collapsed the entire facility, erasing years of Iranian investment in an instant.

The Israeli campaign in Syria surged through the autumn of 2024. On October 1, Israeli forces carried out a targeted strike near Damascus, killing senior figures from Hezbollah and Hamas, among them Dhu al-Fiqar Hanawi, commander of the Imam Hussein Shia militia. The very next day, Hezbollah's Unit 4400 commander in Syria—responsible for arms transfers from Iran to Lebanon—was also eliminated. In mid-November, Israel expanded its reach. A November 14 strike leveled buildings in Mazzeh and

Qudsaya, destroying Palestinian Islamic Jihad (PIJ) command centers and killing twenty-three terrorists. Then, on November 20, Israeli jets struck a clandestine summit of militia leaders in Palmyra, attended by commanders of the Al-Nujaba Iraqi Movement and Hezbollah: ninety-two Iran-backed fighters, including four senior Hezbollah operatives, were killed.

By late 2024, more than 120 Israeli airstrikes had turned Syria into a graveyard for Iran's proxies and expeditionary forces—decapitating command structures, severing supply lines, and reasserting Israeli dominance across the Levant. It was more than the Assad regime could bear.

For years, Assad's survival had depended on imported lifelines: Iranian militias, Hezbollah brigades, and Russian airpower. But by the year's end, each of those pillars had splintered. Moscow, consumed by its quagmire in Ukraine, quietly scaled back its forces from Latakia and Hmeimim. Tehran's reinforcements were obliterated almost daily by Israeli jets that gutted the IRGC's command network. And Hezbollah, which by late 2024 had its leadership decapitated by Israel, could no longer afford to bleed for Damascus. In November, Hezbollah's forward brigades withdrew from al-Qusayr, evacuating nearly 150 armored vehicles and hundreds of fighters. The connective tissue of Iran's military network in western Syria atrophied into paralysis. By the end of 2024, the Assad regime—the "golden ring" of Iran's Axis of Resistance—began to collapse. The dictator who had outlasted a decade of revolution withered in the face of the relentless Israeli firepower.

Over the course of 2024, rebels backed by Turkey began to put together a two-pronged lightning offensive aimed at Damascus. In late November, the plan sprang into action. In the South, the Southern Operations Room, a coalition of anti-Assad factions including the remnants of the Western-trained opposition, launched a lightning campaign across Daraa and the Golan corridor. In the north, Hay'at Tahrir al-Sham (HTS)—once a splinter of al-Qaeda—surged south from Idlib, coordinated in rare unity with Turkish-supplied units of the Syrian National Army (SNA). Within days, opposition forces had captured key military installations around Damascus. Regime soldiers deserted en masse, peeling off uniforms and abandoning equipment as rebel columns pushed into the capital's outer ring.

Within two weeks, on December 8, 2024, Damascus was overrun. Along the highways leading into the capital, Syrian tanks sat abandoned, their crews long fled. Rebel convoys streamed through the suburbs and into the heart of the city. After thirteen years of war, the people of Damascus—battered, starved, and shelled—poured into the streets, waving the green-white-black flags of the revolution, ransacking palaces, and pulling down statues and symbols of the Assad regime. At Sednaya Prison—the infamous "human slaughterhouse" where some thirty thousand detainees were executed—opposition fighters broke through the gates and freed the surviving inmates, exposing the horror the regime had long denied.

Amid the chaos, Assad fled north by helicopter to a Russian base near Latakia, where he boarded a plane bound for Moscow. He left the last loyalists behind, including his own brother. His flight marked the death of the Ba'athist state his father had forged through purges, massacres, and fear since 1971. After more than half a century of hereditary dictatorship, the Assads were gone. And with them, Iran's most prized satellite was lost. Qassem Soleimani's dream of a continuous "resistance highway" from Tehran to the Mediterranean lay shattered in the ruins of Damascus.

In the days that followed, the Syrian opposition proclaimed a caretaker government, while Turkish advisers and reconstruction teams moved swiftly to stabilize key population centers and transportation corridors. To the south, Israel acted decisively. Fearing that the collapse of Assad's regime would leave advanced weaponry adrift among militias and terrorists, the IDF launched Operation Arrow of Bashan—a sweeping aerial and naval offensive across Syrian territory. Israeli jets and missile boats struck more than 320 strategic targets: chemical weapons sites, air-defense batteries, missile factories, drone hubs, radar stations, and airbases housing helicopters and fighter jets. Syrian naval vessels were sunk in port, tank columns obliterated, and entire weapons depots reduced to ash. By the operation's end, Israeli intelligence estimated that over 70 percent of the Assad regime's remaining military infrastructure had been destroyed. Simultaneously, Israeli ground forces advanced into southern Syria to establish a defensive buffer zone along the Golan frontier—preventing spillover from the chaos and blocking Hezbollah or Iranian remnants from taking root on Israel's border.

Damascus tried a cosmetic pivot. Ahmed a-Shaara—hailed by sympathetic outlets as a "reformer"—appeared in tailored suits while the same warlords and militias manned the checkpoints behind him. But the façade quickly shattered. No makeover could obscure the fact that the bearded former al-Qaeda member was still a terrorist. His followers soon revealed it. By April 28, 2025, militias aligned with Syria's new regime were massacring Druze civilians near Damascus. In response, Israel conducted airstrikes against Syrian government targets on April 30 and again in early May.

Israel had already vowed to "protect the Syrian Druze" and threatened strikes if regime troops entered the three southern governorates Israel had declared demilitarized zones. For Jerusalem, the Druze were not an abstraction. Inside Israel, Druze citizens have served in every branch of the IDF. Their loyalty and sacrifice are woven into the fabric of the state. Protecting their kin across the border was both a moral reflex and strategic logic: deny a-Shaara a foothold on Israel's frontier and prove that terrorizing the mountain would not come cheap.

The warnings went unheeded. On July 13, 2025, clashes erupted between Druze and Bedouin militias in Suwayda, leaving more than two hundred dead. Videos soon circulated on social media, documenting scenes of massacre and humiliation: corpses scattered across hospital corridors; the Druze elder Marhej Shahine, aged eighty, publicly degraded as jihadis shaved his beard; detainees forced onto their hands and knees, ridden like animals. Prime Minister Netanyahu later described the atrocities in searing terms: "They went into the town of Suwayda and butchered the men. They raped the women and nurses, burned babies, and added horrors beyond imagination. You see a Druze civilian wounded, and one of these fanatics—unbelievable savages—knifes him, tears out his heart, and eats it." When the Syrian transitional government sent troops to "restore order," Druze spiritual leader Hikmat al-Hijri called for armed resistance and appealed directly to Israel: "Save Suwayda."

Israel answered. On July 16, the Israeli Air Force launched Operation Mountain Shield—four precision strikes over Damascus that hit the Army General Command, the Defense Ministry, and several buildings near Umayyad Square and the presidential palace. The attacks inflicted extensive damage and forced regime forces to withdraw from Suwayda. "We stopped the savage massacre of the Druze," Netanyahu later declared.

Israel's rescue of the Druze signaled a historic shift in the Middle East's center of gravity. For the first time in modern history, it had not tilted toward an empire or a caliphate, but toward a democracy. Israel had withstood a multi-front war and emerged transformed—a regional power calling the shots from the Red Sea to the Euphrates. With Iran's proxy network being reduced to ruins, one truth had become unmistakable. Israel was now the power broker of the Middle East—the strongest state in a region once sworn to erase it.

The Red Sea Raiders

From the dust of Yemen's northern highlands rose Ansar Allah—"the Helpers of God." The world would come to know them as the Houthis: a radical Shia terror group and one of Iran's most lethal and strategically positioned proxies.

The Houthis come from Yemen's Zaidi sect, an offshoot of Shia Islam that ruled northern Yemen for nearly a thousand years, until a 1962 military coup drove them from power. Many Zaidis—roughly a third of Yemen's population—felt marginalized in the republic that followed. Into that cauldron of resentment stepped Hussein al-Houthi, a fiery cleric who claimed descent from the Prophet Muhammad and turned his tribe into a movement. In the 1990s, the Houthis' founding cadre trained in the Iranian city of Qom, embracing the Ayatollah's model of revolutionary warfare. Upon his return to Yemen, Hussein's message resonated with disaffected youth who despised the Sunni-dominated government in Sana'a—one that had aligned itself with Washington in the war on terror.

Modeling themselves on Hezbollah, the Houthis built a formidable propaganda machine complete with regular televised sermons, twenty-five print and electronic newspapers, and two radio networks. They even formed jihadi boy bands—terrorist church choirs harmonizing about death and martyrdom, rifles in hand, in slickly produced music videos. By 2003, the movement adopted a new motto, lifted almost word for word from Ayatollah Khomeini's revolutionary slogan: "God is great. Death to America. Death to Israel. Curse on the Jews. Victory to Islam."

When Hussein al-Houthi was killed in 2004 after defying arrest, his death ignited a permanent insurgency led by his brother Abdul-Malik al-Houthi, who was then in his twenties. Even then, the Houthis' brutality was unmistakable—reports surfaced of women forced into sexual slavery and children as young as seven conscripted as soldiers. Houthi courts are still known to sentence those accused of homosexuality to death by stoning—and even crucifixion. During the chaos of the Arab Spring, the Houthis established full control of Sa'dah province. By 2014, they seized the capital of Sana'a, toppling Yemen's government and drawing in a Saudi-led coalition.

All the while, Iran was spending hundreds of millions of dollars supporting the Houthis with arms, fuel, cash, and training. Iran would get its money's worth. On September 14, 2019, Houthi drones struck Saudi Arabia's Abqaiq oil facility—the largest crude-processing site on earth—temporarily wiping out 5 percent of global supply. Israeli missile defense expert Uzi Rubin called it "a kind of Pearl Harbor," one of the boldest surprise attacks in modern warfare.

When the Gaza war erupted in 2023, the Houthis controlled around a third of Yemen's territory, along with ports, state companies, and other economic assets that yield the group as much as $2 billion in annual revenue. They were also armed to the teeth by Iran—outfitted with advanced drones, sea mines, speed boats, and fleets of cruise and ballistic missiles. They wasted no time unleashing them on Israel and Western shipping, transforming Yemen's coast into Iran's southern front—the final link in its long-dreamed crescent of fire.

Within days of October 7, the Houthis declared war on the world's trade routes. Drones and missiles began streaking across the sea, targeting civilian merchant vessels and naval patrols alike. Abdul-Malik al-Houthi claimed the attacks were acts of "solidarity" with Hamas. In truth, it was a campaign of maritime terror designed to hold global commerce captive to Tehran's ambitions. Though they professed to strike only "Israeli-linked" ships, the Houthis attacked indiscriminately: Greek tankers, Norwegian freighters, Japanese cargo ships. Many of the ships hit had no connection to Israel at all. They were targeted simply for sailing through a sea the Houthis now claimed as their own.

The world first grasped the scale of the threat on November 19, 2023, when the cargo ship *Galaxy Leader* was boarded by at least ten Houthi terrorists descending from a military helicopter. The footage—shot and edited like an action movie—showed masked Houthis storming the bridge. The ship's twenty-five-member crew was taken hostage and held for over a year. The Houthis turned the vessel into a floating propaganda monument. They hoisted their flag, installed a radar system to track passing ships, and invited influencers to take selfies on the boat as if it were a tourist attraction. They even used the captured freighter as the set for a music video titled "Axis of Jihad," which included the lyrics, "Death to America and hostile Zion / By God, we shall not be defeated."

By February 2024, forty ships had been attacked. By autumn, the number had climbed to 107 vessels, targeted by over six hundred drones and ballistic missiles. The Red Sea—a key corridor of global commerce—had turned into a war zone.

The shockwaves rippled through every economy on earth. Between November and December 2023, global trade contracted by 1.3 percent. By March 2024, more than two thousand ships had diverted around the Cape of Good Hope, adding up to three weeks and over a million dollars in extra costs per voyage. Shipping to Eilat, Israel's southern port, vanished entirely. By summer, traffic had fallen by 85 percent; in July, the port declared bankruptcy and announced mass layoffs. The tremors spread far beyond Israel. Tesla temporarily shut its German factory due to supply chain issues caused by Houthi attacks. Maersk—the world's largest shipping line—reported a 15–20 percent capacity loss across the maritime industry. Shell and COSCO, the world's energy and shipping giants, halted transits through the area altogether. Some vessels began broadcasting "No contact Israel" on their transponders—a maritime white flag. By June, the US Defense Intelligence Agency confirmed the scope: a 90 percent collapse in container shipping through the Red Sea in the first months of 2024. The Houthis had disrupted the bloodstream of global trade.

US officials confirmed that Iranian Quds Force commanders and advisers were embedded inside Yemen, directing Houthi missile launches and drone operations. Intelligence intercepts revealed Iranian trainers stationed in Houthi strongholds, and even an IRGC surveillance ship feeding live targeting data to help identify vessels that tried to go dark. The weapons themselves told the same story. When the Norwegian-flagged *Strinda* was struck in December 2023, investigators recovered fragments of an Iranian-made Tolu-4 turbojet—the same engine used in Tehran's Noor cruise missiles. The evidence was irrefutable: the Houthis were not acting alone. They were Iran's Southern Command, another failed state repurposed for Tehran's pursuit of global leverage. As retired US General Kenneth McKenzie observed, "Iran has the luxury of fighting a hidden-hand operation. They're choking world shipping in the Bab el-Mandab—and they're doing it at a very low price."

Houthi aggression did not stop at the seas; it climbed into the skies. On October 19, the group fired four cruise missiles and fifteen drones toward Israel—all intercepted by the USS *Carney*, an American destroyer stationed in the Red Sea. A week later, two more drones bound for Israel crashed in Egypt's Sinai, wounding civilians. Then, on October 31, the stakes climbed even higher: Houthi ballistic missiles streaked toward Israel, only to be obliterated by the IDF's Arrow system—the world's first missile defense to destroy a hostile target beyond Earth's atmosphere. For the first time in history, combat had reached outer space.

The chaos quickly reached a level that Washington could not ignore. On December 18, the US launched Operation Prosperity Guardian, a multinational naval task force to defend commercial shipping. Two weeks later, US Navy helicopters sank several Houthi boats attempting to board the Maersk Hangzhou. When the attacks continued, the gloves came off. On January 12, 2024, the US and UK launched Operation Poseidon Archer, striking radar sites, missile depots, and launch platforms across Yemen. The coalition's campaign continued through May 31, when US and British forces struck thirteen Houthi targets across Yemen in response to three American MQ-9 Reaper drones being downed in a single month.

But it was Israel's entry into the Yemeni theater that changed the calculus. On July 19, 2024, a Houthi drone slammed into an apartment building near the US consular office in Tel Aviv, killing one and injuring ten. The next day, Israel struck back. Codenamed Operation Outstretched

Arm, the Israeli Air Force unleashed a hail of airstrikes on Hodeida, Yemen's main Red Sea port. The strikes hit oil refineries, port cranes, and weapons depots, turning the horizon into a wall of fire. Israeli jets—refueled midair—had flown nearly 1,800 kilometers, farther than the distance from Israel to Tehran. Prime Minister Benjamin Netanyahu declared, "There is no place the long arm of Israel cannot reach." The message was aimed at Iran.

On September 29, after a Houthi missile narrowly missed Ben Gurion Airport, Israel struck again, flattening Hodeida's power stations and naval facilities in a barrage that lit up the Red Sea coast. In the months that followed, the campaign surged onward: airports, ports, refineries, command centers—all reduced to smoldering ruins. Each wave carried the same unmistakable message: Israel could now project power anywhere in the Middle East, in multiple theaters at once. An Israeli official summed it up: "If they strike us, we strike everywhere. Today we hit Gaza, Lebanon, Syria, and Yemen—all in the same day." Once besieged on every front, Israel was now striking back on every front.

In March 2025, as Houthi missiles kept raining on Red Sea traffic, the United States launched Operation Rough Rider—the most intense bombing campaign in Yemen since the Saudi war. On its first day alone, American aircraft hit dozens of targets across seven provinces. President Donald Trump announced the strikes were designed to "defend US shipping and American interests." Over the following month, hundreds more sorties followed. By the time Washington declared a ceasefire on May 6, the US had hit over one thousand targets, lost seven MQ-9 Reaper drones, and spent $750 million. Three US warplanes had also been lost due to accidents. Though they steered clear of US vessels, the Houthis quickly resumed their campaign against commercial shipping. Shortly after the ceasefire, armed terrorists in small boats attacked two vessels off the Yemeni coast, sinking both and killing several crewmembers in one of their most violent and coordinated assaults.

They also continued launching attacks against Israel. Despite the American offensive, from the collapse of the Gaza ceasefire in March 2025 through early May, the Houthis fired twenty-six missiles toward Israel. On May 4, they escalated dramatically—launching what they claimed was a hypersonic missile at Ben Gurion Airport. It pierced multiple layers of Israeli air defense and exploded near the main terminal, injuring eight and prompting airlines to cancel flights en masse. Israel's retaliation was immediate and devastating. Over the following month, it leveled Sana'a International Airport, destroyed Yemen's entire civilian airline fleet, and crippled oil and power infrastructure along the Red Sea coast. The campaign culminated in June 2025, when the Israeli Navy entered the fight, firing precision missiles from Sa'ar 6 corvettes into Hodeida Port.

During the Iran-Israel War in June 2025, the Houthis were the only one of Tehran's once-vast network of proxies to join the fight. In coordination with Iranian strikes, drones and missiles flew north from Yemen. On June 14, Israel attempted to assassinate Houthi chief of staff Muhammad Abd al-Karim al-Ghamari in Sana'a. He was wounded but survived. At midnight on July 6, Israel launched Operation Black Flag, striking Hodeida, Ras Isa, As-Salif, and Ras Qantib. Among the targets was the *Galaxy Leader*—still moored off the coast and converted into a radar base. The explosion that consumed it erased both a symbol and a sensor of Iran's shadow war. By late August, Israel had conducted fifteen strikes in Yemen. The climax came on August 28, with Operation Lucky Drop. Acting on intercepted intelligence that the Houthi leadership was convening, Israeli fighter jets struck a conference hall in Sana'a, killing at least twelve senior officials, including the prime minister, foreign minister, and the Houthi chief of staff al-Ghamari—who had survived the failed assassination two months earlier. But Israel did not eliminate Abdul-Malik al-Houthi—the last terrorist leader still standing in the Axis of Resistance.

The following month, Houthi drones struck Eilat and Ramon Airport, injuring civilians and testing Israel's air defenses yet again. The Israeli response was overwhelming: multiple rounds of air raids under Operation Ringing Bells targeting the Houthis' propaganda division, military camps, and a fuel storage facility. "Many dozens" of Houthis were killed, Defense Minister Israel Katz said, "and more will follow."

By the end of 2025, even as Trump and much of the Arab world were promoting a new peace plan for Gaza, the Houthis struck a Dutch-flagged vessel with a cruise missile, leaving it in danger of sinking. Yet there was no doubt they had faced a reckoning. Israeli airstrikes had crippled their economic lifelines, US sanctions had tightened, humanitarian aid had collapsed, and an already-impoverished population was buckling under years of heavy taxation. Worse still, their patrons in Tehran and Beirut—both bloodied and overstretched—could no longer provide the support the Houthis had come to expect. After years of exploiting advantages over the Saudi-led coalition, they now faced a far more capable and relentless adversary—one that had delivered the most punishing blows in their history.

The once-fringe terrorist pirates of Yemen had dragged the world's superpowers into the Red Sea. They shattered supply chains and redrew the map of global trade. But in doing so, they also exposed the limits of Iranian power—and the full extent of Israel's reach. The message was unmistakable: a Jewish canopy of firepower now spanned the entire Middle East.

Shadows over Baghdad

Iraq's role as a launchpad for attacks on Israel stretches back decades before drones, missiles, or the Gaza war. From the moment Israel declared itself a state in 1948, Iraq was among those Arab nations that went to war to destroy it. Iraqi forces entered the 1948 conflict, and deployed troops and armor to the Syrian front in both the 1967 Six-Day War and the 1973 Yom Kippur War. Since then, Israel and Iraq technically remained in a state of war, with Baghdad refusing to foster diplomatic relations while openly embracing the goal of Israel's destruction.

The modern flashpoint began on June 7, 1981, when Israel launched Operation Opera—a daring strike by F-16 and F-15 fighter jets on Iraq's Osirak nuclear reactor outside Baghdad. It was the first of three Israeli operations aimed at preventing hostile regimes from acquiring nuclear weapons—a policy that came to be known as the Begin Doctrine, after the prime minister who had ordered the attack, Menachem Begin. Iraq, preoccupied with the Iran-Iraq war, did not initially retaliate. But a decade later, Saddam got his revenge.

During the 1991 Gulf War, Iraq fired more than forty Scud missiles at Israel. In one of the great miracles of Israel's history, only two civilians were killed directly, despite direct hits on Tel Aviv and Haifa. One goal of the strikes was to shatter the US-led coalition by provoking Israel into retaliating, thereby forcing Arab partners to withdraw. But Washington urged restraint, and for the sake of the alliance, Israel held its fire. Though open exchanges of fire ceased throughout the 1990s and early 2000s, Iraq's hostility toward Israel endured. During the Second Intifada, Saddam Hussein financed the families of Arab terrorists in Israel—a foreign extension of the Palestinian Authority's "pay-for-slay" policy.

America's invasion took out Saddam's regime. But it also opened the gates for Iran's silent conquest of Iraq. Across the porous 994-mile border, Tehran poured money, influence, and militias into every organ of the new Iraqi state. The post-2003 *Muhasasa* system—conceived to balance Iraq's factions—quickly decayed into a patronage machine run by Iran's clients. Under the Iran-aligned Prime Minister Nouri al-Maliki, Iraq's foreign policy hardened along sectarian lines, and hostility toward Israel again became dogma. By 2022, that hatred was written into law: death or life imprisonment for anyone who dared call for peace with Israel.

As in Syria and Yemen, Iran's domination came not through invasion, but through infiltration. It cultivated a network of proxies—the Badr Organization, Kata'ib Hezbollah, Asa'ib Ahl al-Haq, and later the Popular Mobilization Forces—that first drew blood fighting American forces in Iraq. According to the US Department of Defense, Iran-backed militias were responsible for the deaths of more than six hundred American troops during the occupation.

After the ISIS blitz of 2014, Tehran doubled down on its investment in Iraq. Its militias metastasized into a shadow state—capturing seats in parliament, seizing ministries, and securing lucrative government contracts. In 2019, mass protests erupted across Iraq, demanding an end to corruption and to Iranian interference. Iranian-backed militias joined government forces in crushing the uprising, using live fire and snipers against demonstrators and killing hundreds. Two years later, in the 2021 elections, pro-Iran parties lost seats in parliament. They responded with renewed violence—and even attempted to assassinate Iraq's new prime minister using explosive-laden drones.

By 2023, Iran's grip on Iraq had tightened—secured through a hostile takeover of the country's digital infrastructure. In 2022, Prime Minister

Mohammed al-Sudani—an Iranian proxy—established the Muhandis General Company, named for a slain IRGC commander and former head of the Popular Mobilization Forces. Controlled by the Ayatollah, the organization's tendrils now reach deep into every branch of the state, functioning as Iraq's own Revolutionary Guard. Though sanctioned by the US Treasury as a terrorist front, the company has been showered with government contracts—from construction projects to fiber-optic control grids and even Iraq's 5G network—granting Iran's proxies the ability to surveil an entire nation. "These guys are still militants," observed Maria Fantappie of the Institute for International Affairs, "but now they wear suits and are embedded within the state."

After October 7, the long and cold standoff between Israel and Iraq gave way to open warfare. From Iraqi soil, Iranian-backed terrorist militias unleashed swarms of drones and missiles toward Israel—a new front in Tehran's regional campaign. They aimed to stretch Israel's defenses to the breaking point, to force it to fight in every direction at once, and to prove that Iran could still set the pace of the conflict.

As early as November 2023, the Iraqi Shia militia coalition known as the Islamic Resistance in Iraq (IRI) began launching drones and missiles toward Tel Aviv, Haifa, Eilat, the Dead Sea coast, and the Golan Heights. Few of the attacks hit their targets, but they served a powerful propaganda purpose—signaling that Iran's Iraqi proxies had entered the war.

Beyond its proxies, Iraq became the arena where Iran struck both Israel and the United States—directly and through intermediaries. In January 2024, Iran launched ballistic missiles at what it called an Israeli "spy headquarters" near Erbil in the Kurdish region, killing at least four people, including Kurdish businessman Peshraw Dizayi. But the strike backfired: Baghdad condemned the attack as a violation of sovereignty, recalled its ambassador from Tehran, and summoned Iran's chargé d'affaires in protest, calling the assault a breach of "the principles of good neighborliness."

Meanwhile, Iran's Iraqi proxies turned their fire on the United States. Militias aligned with Tehran—chief among them Kata'ib Hezbollah—launched rockets and ballistic missiles at American forces across the region. By late January 2024, US troops in Iraq and Syria had come under attack at least 150 times since October 17, 2023—each assault part of a coordinated Iranian campaign to bleed the United States while striking Israel both directly and by proxy. In February, following a wave of US airstrikes in Iraq and Syria, the attacks subsided.

By April 2024, multiple launches of drones and cruise missiles from Iraq toward Israel had been documented, prompting Jerusalem to treat Iraqi territory as part of its operational theater. The surge in attacks was significant: by the summer of 2024, the Islamic Resistance in Iraq coalition claimed responsibility for more than one hundred strikes on Israeli soil since the start of the war. The campaign forced Israel to expend interceptor missiles. Yet it fell far short of its aims. Israel's aerial defense network proved far more resilient than the IRI anticipated. Although the group claimed hundreds of attacks, independent verification tells another story: according to the Alma Research Center, of the 312 attacks claimed by the IRI between November 2023 and November 2024, only 89 reached Israeli airspace—and just four hit confirmed targets. In the end, Iraq's role in the Gaza war—through Iran-backed militias—did not overwhelm Israel's defenses. It proved them.

Meanwhile, Israel had adopted not only a confident defensive posture toward Iraq—but a dominant one. And it had done so without a single major airstrike.

By late 2025, reports surfaced that Iran-backed militias in Iraq were scrambling to relocate or shutter their offices, desperate to avoid potential Israeli strikes. The panic followed reports that US Chargé d'Affaires Joshua Harris had met with former Prime Minister Nouri al-Maliki, warning that Israel might target terrorist command centers inside Iraq if the attacks continued. One Iraqi political analyst summarized the message bluntly: "Spare your country from Israeli targeting." Britain's ambassador reportedly delivered a similar warning to Prime Minister al-Sudani. "Washington now acts as a guarantor against Israeli strikes," observed another analyst based in Geneva—an admission that Israeli deterrence had become a regional fact.

The Iraqi political establishment—long bound to Tehran—began quietly edging out of Iran's orbit. Even a proxy prime minister like Mohammed al-Sudani was forced to show distance. In an interview with *The Wall Street Journal* published that November, al-Sudani declared that

Iraq's relationship with Iran "will not be at the expense of our national decisions and the interests of Iraq and Iraqis." In essence, Israel was redefining the regional balance not through violence, but through fear. From Damascus to Baghdad, Tehran's proxies were learning the new rule of the Middle East: Israeli power now cast a shadow long enough to reach them all.

Tehran had poured money, weapons, and Quds Force advisers into Iraq, turning the country into another springboard for short-range attacks on US forces and long-range strikes on Israel. But the plan was unraveling. Iraqi leaders had seen what happened in Damascus and Sana'a, and they knew what awaited them if they crossed the line. What Iran had intended as a show of strength had become a showcase of Israeli deterrence. As an old Syrian proverb warns, "Kiss the arm you cannot break." And across the region, Israel's enemies were left to accept what decades of war had already proven: the Jewish state does not break.

CHAPTER NINE

THE SERPENT'S SKULL: TWELVE-DAY TURNAROUND IN IRAN

They beset me, they surround me;
by God's name I will surely cut them down.
They have beset me like bees;
They shall be extinguished like burning thorns
by God's name I will surely cut them down.
Psalms 118:11-12

In the blood and rubble of October 7, Iran's fingerprints stained every corner of the crime scene. For years, Tehran had bankrolled, armed, trained, and directed Hamas and Islamic Jihad—the very militias whose death squads carried out the massacre. Yahya Sinwar, chief architect of October 7, admitted as much in 2017: Iran, he told reporters, is "the largest supporter" of Hamas's military wing, providing "both money and arms." By 2018, Tehran was reportedly funneling some $70 million a year into Hamas's war machine. In 2019, it offered to quintuple that sum—$360 million annually—in exchange for deeper operational coordination against Israel. And only months before the slaughter, Ayatollah Khamenei personally welcomed Hamas leader Ismail Haniyeh in Tehran, while Iran's president met the head of Islamic Jihad.

Whatever doubts remained about Iran's role evaporated in the days immediately after the massacre. Rockets and drones began streaking toward Israel not only from Gaza, but from Lebanon, Yemen, Syria, and Iraq—every launch point an Iranian franchise. The entire "Axis of Resistance" moved in unison, like a stitched-together terror conglomerate, the Ayatollah's Frankenstein lurching to life.

The evidence was everywhere. The Islamic Republic's demonic role in the slaughter was beyond the realm of speculation. From the war's first hours, Israelis began to grasp a grim truth: the campaign before them passed through Gaza, but its final destination was in Iran.

Since the fall of the Shah in 1979, Israel and Iran were suspended in a decades-long diplomatic standoff. Eighty years after the Holocaust, the Jewish people once again faced a genocidal tyrant who openly vowed to exterminate them. Confronting—and defeating—a budding Hitler before he could realize his ambitions was Israel's most sacred mandate. But for Benjamin Netanyahu, it was something deeper still: a personal, almost cosmic calling.

From the outset of his leadership in the mid-1990s, Benjamin Netanyahu regarded Iran as the paramount test of Jewish survival in the modern age—and the struggle he had been ordained to wage and win. In 1996, in his first address to a joint session of the US Congress, he warned that an Iranian bomb "could presage catastrophic consequences, not only for my country, and not only for the Middle East, but for all mankind." He left office in 1999, only to return a decade later with the same singular obsession. At the 2012 UN General Assembly, he lifted the now-iconic cartoon bomb and cautioned the world that Iran was approaching weapons-grade enrichment. And when President Barack Obama advanced the nuclear deal, Netanyahu flew to Washington and denounced it from another joint session of Congress—a direct challenge to a sitting American president unprecedented in Israeli-US relations. In the end, Netanyahu could not prevent the deal from being born. But he could make sure it did not live long.

The death of Obama's catastrophic Iran deal came through one of the boldest intelligence coups in a century. In the early hours of January

31, 2018, about two dozen Mossad operatives slipped into a nondescript warehouse in Tehran's Kahrizak district. It was the vault of Iran's most guarded secret: its nuclear archive. The operation had been months in the making. A female Mossad operative, fluent in Farsi and disguised in full Islamic dress, had spent weeks quietly mapping the area, down to every camera and police patrol. At one minute past midnight, the team jammed the alarms, sliced through iron doors, and began cracking open safes. Out of thirty-two vaults, they managed to breach only six. But those six held the mother lode: one hundred thousand files, photos, blueprints, and discs detailing the AMAD Project—Iran's clandestine nuclear weapons program. The archive proved conclusively that Tehran had lied to the world. Its nuclear project was never a peaceful, civilian enterprise. And Iran had never abandoned its pursuit of the bomb. It had simply hidden it, while preserving every capability and component. Iran meticulously maintained the means to resume its mad dash for a nuclear weapon whenever it so chose.

Within hours, the archive was spirited out of Iran in an exfiltration so audacious that its full mechanics remain a mystery to this day. Two months later, Netanyahu unveiled the trove before the world—standing in front of a wall of stolen Iranian binders and a giant slide blaring the simple verdict: "Iran lied." In Washington, President Donald Trump had already been privately briefed. Days later, he pulled the United States out of the Iran Deal, denouncing it as "a terrible, one-sided deal that should never have been made." Sanctions snapped back into place, and the long-simmering confrontation between Israel and Iran burst once again into the open.

Behind the scenes, a shadow war raged. The Mossad's campaign of assassinations and sabotage had long spanned continents—eliminating nuclear scientists, blowing apart enrichment sites, and dismantling Iranian networks from Europe to Africa to the Gulf. The depth of Israel's penetration into the Islamic Republic was staggering. In 2024, former Iranian president Mahmoud Ahmadinejad admitted that the regime's own counterintelligence unit—built specifically to stop Mossad operations—had been run by a Mossad double agent. He further revealed that roughly twenty members of the same team were secretly feeding intelligence to Israel, with some even assisting in the 2018 archive heist itself.

And yet, even those vast Mossad networks could not stop Iran from delivering its most devastating blow. Through its proxies, Tehran had spent years forging a ring of fire around Israel—Hamas in Gaza, Hezbollah in Lebanon, the Houthis in Yemen, and Shiite militias sprawled across Syria and Iraq—a noose that gradually tightened in plain sight. On October 7, that noose snapped shut. The bloodiest assault on the Jewish people since the Holocaust was executed by Iran's most loyal clients. And still, even after that day of horror, both nations clung to the fiction of proxy warfare, as if the war between them had not already begun.

Then, in April 2024, the masks came off. An Israeli airstrike demolished Iran's consulate in Syria, killing two Iranian generals, including Quds Force Commander Mohammad Reza Zahedi—the strategic brain of Tehran's regional war machine. The message was unmistakable: Israel wasn't circling the problem anymore. It was striking the source.

Within days, Tehran launched Operation True Promise I. Swarms of drones, cruise missiles, and ballistic warheads marked Iran's first direct, large-scale strike on Israeli soil. Desperate to avoid a regional inferno of its own making, Iran quietly notified Arab governments hosting US bases seventy-two hours in advance and signaled through back channels that it sought "no wider war." But the barrage was impossible to ignore: 350 projectiles launched from Iran, Iraq, Lebanon, and Yemen, carrying nearly sixty tons of explosives.

In Operation Iron Shield, Israel's response to the Iranian strike, the country's multilayered air defense network performed with astonishing precision. With support from the United States, Britain, Jordan, and reportedly several Gulf states, the incoming barrage was shredded in the sky; 99 percent of the aerial threats were intercepted. Frustrated in its military aims, Tehran reached for a propaganda victory instead. Iranian state media rushed to announce catastrophic Israeli losses. But when analysts examined the "evidence" distributed by Iranian state media—footage that quickly saturated social networks—the narrative collapsed into farce: the images of Israel supposedly burning turned out to be stock video of wildfires in Chile.

Iran's historic assault achieved little more than smoke and noise, but its precedent was seismic. For the first time, the Islamic Republic had fired openly at the Jewish state. Israel answered in kind. Within forty-eight hours, Israeli aircraft pierced Iranian airspace and struck deep inside the country, obliterating radars near Natanz—one of the prized hubs of Iran's nuclear program. The shadow war between the two powers was over; the fiction of "plausible deniability" was gone for good. For Israel and Iran, the duel was now direct.

In July, Israel would reach straight into the heart of the Islamic Republic. Hours after Israel struck down Hezbollah's military mastermind Fuad Shukr in Beirut, Hamas leader Ismail Haniyeh was blown to pieces inside a Revolutionary Guard guesthouse in Tehran. Reports emerged that the explosives were planted in the guesthouse by members of the Ansar al-Mahdi protection corps—the very unit charged with safeguarding Iran's senior dignitaries—who had been quietly turned by the Mossad. Iran's capital, once a sanctuary for Axis chiefs, had been silently drawn into the Jewish state's ever-expanding hunting grounds of retribution.

Then came October. After Israel had systematically decapitated Hezbollah's senior command, Tehran lashed out to salvage its pride. In a massive retaliatory barrage dubbed True Promise II, Iran fired roughly two hundred ballistic missiles in twin waves on October 1. Unlike April, when Tehran offered regional states a seventy-two-hour warning, this time it issued only a token alert just hours before impact. Moments later, trails of fire carved across Israel's skies. Interceptors arced upward like meteors. Shockwaves rippled through the Negev. Around Nevatim Airbase, two to three dozen missiles slammed into the desert floor, damaging a hangar and taxiway. Others struck Tel Nof Airbase, a school in Gedera, and an area north of Tel Aviv near the headquarters of the Mossad and Unit 8200, collapsing homes and a restaurant. The human toll was light but sobering. Two civilians were killed: an Israeli man who suffered a heart attack amid the chaos, and an Arab man struck by falling interceptor debris.

This time, Israel's response took longer to materialize. But when it did, it was categorically stronger. On October 26, 2024, the IDF launched Operation Days of Repentance—three punishing waves of airstrikes across more than twenty sites in Iran, Iraq, and Syria. Over one hundred aircraft took part, many penetrating deep into Iranian airspace. The strikes were surgical and devastating: air defense batteries, radar arrays, missile depots, planetary mixers for rocket propulsion, and nuclear research sites. Iran's state media later conceded that four soldiers had been killed, but satellite imagery told a far more humiliating story: key facilities were gutted, airbases were damaged or rendered inoperable, and wide sections of Iran's air defense network were exposed—if not outright erased. The strikes also enabled Israel to map, probe, and stress-test Iran's air defense network in real time. "Israel can now operate with greater freedom in Iranian skies," one senior Israeli official said flatly. Iran should have taken the hint.

Strike by strike, the fragile equilibrium that had kept Israel and Iran from open war was beginning to fray. Every exchange chipped away at the invisible wall of deterrence that had kept a regional conflagration at bay. The missiles, air raids, and assassinations were each a rehearsal for the inevitable. The storm long foretold was no longer on the horizon—it was gathering overhead.

For decades, Israel had been preparing for full-scale war with Iran. Already in the 1990s, Israeli intelligence identified the embryonic Iranian nuclear weapons program. The Mossad responded by burrowing deep into the Islamic Republic, constructing a clandestine lattice of invisible men—agents, couriers, and dissidents—who could move money, weapons, and information across Iran undetected. Through the years, that network carried out precision acts of sabotage: centrifuges spiraled out of control, systems abruptly crashed, and nuclear scientists suddenly met their ends. To outside observers, these were isolated incidents. But inside Israel's security establishment, they were seen as strokes in a far larger design—a deliberate war of attrition meant to slow Tehran's march toward the bomb until Israel had assembled the strength and capabilities to end the threat outright.

That plan demanded capability on a scale that, even as late as 2024, Israel simply did not possess. The targets that mattered most—Natanz, Fordow, Isfahan, Arak—sat more than a thousand miles from Israeli soil, shielded by some of the densest air defenses on the planet. Reaching them meant coordinating dozens of aircraft across multiple fronts—each refueling multiple times midair, evading radars and surface-to-air missiles, and then hitting fortified bunkers carved into mountains of reinforced concrete. It required not only dauntless courage, but flawless coordination—unified movements, simultaneous detonations, and timing calibrated to the second.

Training for such a feat had been underway since 2008. In what became known as Operation Glorious Spartan, more than a hundred Israeli F-15s and F-16s flew over a thousand miles to Greece, rehearsing the precise distances, flight paths, and refueling patterns they would one day need to reach Iran. Pilots practiced clustering around a single tanker, each jet gliding forward to sip fuel before sliding back into formation. Over the years, these drills became routine—a generation of pilots conditioned for the day Israel would fly farther than ever before.

By late 2024, conditions began to ripen for the strike. Throughout the Fall, the IDF was tearing Hezbollah limb from limb in Lebanon. The state-sized terror group had long been Iran's great deterrent—the Ayatollah's "insurance policy" against an Israeli strike on his nuclear program. Now, they were out of the way. By early December, the Assad regime in Syria collapsed, taking with it the advanced Russian air defense network that had long protected Iran's western flank. For the Israeli Air Force, the sky highway to Iran suddenly lay wide open.

Meanwhile, Israeli intelligence determined that Iran had enough enriched uranium for nine nuclear warheads, and the clock was down to months. Still, the IDF lacked the combat-grade capability for a strike on Iran. "The Air Force did not have the ability," Israel's defense minister later admitted. "We instructed the Air Force to acquire that ability within months."

Deep in an underground facility, 120 of Israel's top officers—from the Air Force, Military Intelligence, and Unit 8200—locked themselves into a ten-hour workshop that would shape the war to come. Their task was to turn decades of data into a battle plan. The mood was electric and grim. "We thought if we put 130 of our best people in one room, we'd get a breakthrough," recalled Maj. Y., commander of the maintenance branch at Squadron 101. "It came slowly, but it came."

With time, the room gradually produced a map overlaid with a matrix of over 250 targets arranged by priority: nuclear sites, command headquarters, missile bases, scientists, industrial choke points, and even elements of Iran's banking and energy grid. The officers also compiled detailed intelligence dossiers on senior military officials and nuclear scientists, enabling precise targeted assassinations. Each target was assigned to a specific team and weapon system. The mission, boiled down, was this: seize aerial dominance, decapitate Iran's military and nuclear leadership, and cripple its ability to retaliate.

The following months turned the blueprint into reality. But progress was jagged and tense. "November and December went by, and we didn't have what we wanted in hand," Maj. Y. admitted. "In January, we started to panic." They kept grinding. By February 2025, the pieces began to click. Analysts fused satellite imagery, cyber intrusions, and human intelligence into a single, actionable picture. Soon, the target bank was finished. Israel would soon arrive at the moment of truth. As a senior planner put it, "When operational readiness meets strategic timing—that's when you strike."

While the air force built its battle plan, the Mossad worked on the ground. The agency knew that victory would require more than jets and munitions—it would need eyes and hands inside Iran. That meant saboteurs planted close enough to kill radars, jam launchers, and disable air defenses before fighter jets lit up the sky. It meant ground teams feeding real-time coordinates and targeting data to aircraft overhead. Airpower had to be married to on-the-ground clandestine work—the quiet, lethal plumbing that makes a long-range raid possible.

Within months, the invisible infrastructure became ruthlessly real. Mossad operatives—many of them women, fluent in Persian and anonymous even inside the agency—had melted into Iranian cities to gather intelligence and seed caches of comms gear and munitions. Parts for hundreds of quadcopters were funneled in piece by piece—stripped, hidden in suitcases and shipping containers, carried by unwitting couriers, then quietly reassembled, armed, and handed off to forward cells. Sleeper teams equipped with precision munitions and vehicle-mounted weapons platforms embedded themselves beside air defense radars, missile depots, and key communications hubs. In one of the most ambitious elements of the operation, an entire secret drone base was constructed inside Iran. Everything was set to ignite at once. Within seconds of the first Israeli jets appearing on the horizon, swarms of UAVs, pre-planted charges, and pinpoint ground strikes would blind radars, destroy launchers, and sever command link. Iran's response would be reduced to chaos.

On June 9, the prime minister and his war cabinet gave the green light: the attack, named Operation Rising Lion, would launch in four days. The day before, President Trump had given tacit approval for Israel to proceed after a critical briefing from Chairman of the Joint Chiefs Gen. Dan Caine. The timing was deliberate. June 12 marked the expiration of Trump's sixty-day window for negotiations over Iran's nuclear program, a deadline Tehran had recklessly allowed to run out. That same day, the International Atomic Energy Agency—backed by the United States, Britain, France, and Germany—passed a historic resolution declaring Iran in violation of its nuclear obligations for the first time in two decades. In retrospect, that resolution was not a reprimand. It was Iran's final warning.

Netanyahu and his generals began the final countdown. Pilots pored over maps and strike packets; Mossad teams slid into their last positions; electronic-warfare suites were recalibrated. But for the operation to succeed, Iran had to remain blind until the moment of impact.

Delivering a masterclass in psychological warfare, Netanyahu publicly announced that he was taking time off for the wedding of his son Avner. The prime minister knew the wedding would be postponed, but even the bride and the groom were kept in the dark. At the same time, controlled leaks were dispersed, suggesting a rift between Jerusalem and Washington. The illusion that Israel would never strike without American authorization was carefully reinforced. Reporters were told that President Trump was urging restraint, demanding diplomacy before war. The US appeared committed to negotiation, and as long as they did, Iran's leaders felt safe. Iranian commanders and scientists were allowed to remain at home, even as Israel moved its aircraft into final formation.

Even when the United States began evacuating nonessential personnel from the region the day before the strike, Tehran still bought Trump's performance. Just hours before Zero Hour, the president told reporters that Washington and Iran were "fairly close to an agreement" and that he didn't want Israel "going in." Hours later, as the first Israeli jets lifted off the tarmac, he posted on Truth Social: "We remain committed to a Diplomatic Resolution to the Iran Nuclear Issue!"

It was all a part of the act. Trump was not about to negotiate. Netanyahu was not going to his son's wedding.

Israel's prime minister had another wedding to attend.

A red wedding.

Plague of the Firstborn

At midnight on June 13, in a bunker beneath IAF headquarters, generals watched as squadrons of Israeli jets streaked toward Tehran. The operation code-named Red Wedding began. Hours later, a thousand miles away, Iran's senior military leadership was gone. The image was gruesomely theatrical—a concentrated strike on concentrated power, decapitating the regime's chain of command in one calibrated blow.

This was not an exception but the rule. The systematic decapitation of enemy leadership had become a defining feature of Israel's way of war—a disciplined, clinical method of breaking an enemy, starting with its brain.

The method was tested in Lebanon and Yemen. In mid-September 2024, Israel targeted anyone in Hezbollah important enough to carry a beeper—a brutal, efficient purge that gutted the group's middle ranks. Days later, Israeli intelligence intercepted a conclave of senior commanders plotting an operation named "Conquer the Galilee." The strike that followed vaporized Ibrahim Aqil and Ahmed Wahbi, senior chiefs of the Radwan Force, along with fourteen other top officers. Then came the death blow: eighty bombs rained down on Hezbollah's central command compound, killing its leader Hassan Nasrallah, senior commander Ali Karaki, the IRGC's Abbas Nilforoushan, and much of the organization's top brass. The same logic played out again in Sanaa. When the Houthi leaders assembled in August 2025 to hear a televised address by their leader, Israel answered with the same cold calculus—a single strike that killed the prime minister, the defense minister, the chief of staff, and half the Houthi cabinet.

By turning powwows into death traps, Israel rewrote the equation of war: stay scattered or die together. Coordination invited annihilation.

The strategy had ancient roots. The Hebrew Bible coined the precedent for concentrated retribution. In Egypt, the plague of the firstborn was a direct strike at the leadership structure of Pharaoh's regime: an instrument designed to break a foe by erasing its symbolic center of authority. Samson's final act in Gaza followed the same logic: bound and blinded, he waited until the Philistine rulers crowded above him, then tore down the pillars and buried them all beneath the ruins of their banquet. Modern Israeli planners borrowed scripture's ancient code—when the enemy huddles, destroy them in one stroke.

For Iran, this tactic would hit especially hard. Unlike the IDF, which refreshes its command structure every few years, Iran's military and security networks depend on entrenched figures who can hold their positions for three or four decades. These individuals don't just command authority—they embody institutional memory, carrying with them the operational know-how, trusted aides, deputies, and secretaries who form the living infrastructure of command. The elimination of such a figure yields systemic effects. "The moment you take them, you cut the decision-making chain in the middle," a security source explained. "No process afterwards looks the same."

But strikes of such ambition also carry the greatest risks. In the tense minutes before Operation Red Wedding began, the entire plan nearly unraveled. Israel's most audacious strike—designed to decapitate Iran's air command—hinged on a single figure: Amir Ali Hajizadeh, the powerful and feared commander of the IRGC Aerospace Force.

Intelligence officers who spent years building Hajizadeh's file described him as "a source of evil, cruelty, and unimaginable brutality—almost Nazi-like." Yet behind that savagery lay a sharp and calculating mind. He was, by every assessment, a cunning strategist—a man who, as one Israeli analyst put it, "understood the Israeli military mind." For months, Israeli intelligence had tracked his every move, preparing to eliminate him and his deputies in their homes. But on the eve of the strike, he seemed to understand something was afoot. The "deception plan" Israel had seeded across Iranian channels to lull the regime into complacency was working almost too well. Hajizadeh began to suspect that calm was camouflage.

Ignoring his schedule and security advice, Hajizadeh abruptly left his residence and drove to the Iranian Air Force's underground command bunker. In Tel Aviv, the move set off alarms. Generals in the Kirya feared the entire strike had been compromised, and there were discussions about aborting the operation. If Hajizadeh scattered his officers, the carefully choreographed opening blow would be lost, and the war could begin with disaster. But others saw an opening. If he could be pinned in place and even coaxed into gathering his senior lieutenants beside him, the blow would fall all the harder.

What began as a potential disaster became an opportunity. Through a classified ruse still buried in secrecy, Israeli cyber and intelligence units fed false signals into Iran's command networks, creating the illusion of an unfolding emergency that required his direct oversight. One by one, his senior lieutenants and aides converged on the underground command center. Iran's entire air command had assembled at one site—a fatal concentration Israel had engineered.

When the Israeli bombs hit, the results were absolute. Hajizadeh—architect of Iran's ballistic-missile empire—was killed alongside his deputy, Brigadier General Amir Pourjoudaki. The strike also eliminated IRGC Air Defense Commander Brig. Gen. Davoud Sheikhian and Drone Commander Brig. Gen. Mohammad Taherpour. Joining them were the IRGC Aerospace Division's deputy intelligence chief, Brig. Gen. Khosro Hassani; Tehran's aerospace commander, Brig. Gen. Mansour Safarpour; and Brig. Gen. Masoud Tayeb and Javad Jarsara—the officers responsible for Iran's radar network, UAV operations, and the capital's air defenses. "In the end," said an Israeli official, "we took more people than we planned." In a single, perfectly timed strike, Israel had cut out the core of Iran's strategic deterrence. The chain of command that could have unleashed hundreds of missiles toward Israel was buried beneath the rubble. It would take Iran nearly a whole day to even begin to counterattack.

Beyond the Aerospace bunker, the devastation was unprecedented. Thirty Iranian generals were killed in a matter of hours. Among them was Maj. Gen. Mohammad Bagheri, the supreme commander of Iran's entire military apparatus, overseeing the army, air force, navy, and air defenses. Hossein Salami, the fire-breathing commander in chief of the IRGC who once vowed to "cleanse the planet" of America and Israel, was killed alongside his chief of staff, Brig. Gen. Masoud Shanei, and his intelligence representative, Maj. Gen. Mohammad Reza Nasir Baghban.

Also eliminated was Gholam Ali Rashid, Iran's foremost strategist and head of the Khatam al-Anbiya Central Headquarters—the center for Iran's wartime command and strategic planning. Israel also wiped out the Iranian armed forces' deputy head for intelligence, Brig. Gen. Gholamreza Mehrabi, and deputy chief of operations, Brig. Gen. Mehdi Rabbani. Brig. Gen. Reza Mozaffarinia, commander of the Special Weapons Center at the Organization of Defensive Innovation and Research, and Brig. Gen. Mohammad Jafar Asadi, deputy inspector general of Central Command, were almost certainly among those killed in the opening strike.

Satellite imagery later confirmed strikes on six major military installations around the capital, including Parchin, the heavily guarded complex long associated with Iran's nuclear and missile research. Fortified residential compounds that had housed the republic's top generals and intelligence chiefs were leveled to dust. The men who built the machinery designed to erase Israel from the map were gone.

If Operation Red Wedding was theatrical, Operation Narnia bordered on myth. For over a decade, Israel had stalked Iran's nuclear scientists one by one—killing six between 2007 and 2020 with the motorbike assassins and computerized machine guns. But in the opening strike of Operation Rising Lion, nine of Iran's top nuclear minds were killed almost simultaneously, their homes erupting across Tehran in a sonata of explosions. It was as if the entire Manhattan Project had been erased in minutes. Iran's nuclear brain trust was swept from the earth.

By dawn, Israel's first act was complete. In about four hours, Israel had flown five waves of sorties—more than two hundred fighter jets dropping over 330 precision munitions on roughly one hundred targets, including dozens of Iranian nuclear facilities, military bases, and infrastructure installations. The psychological impact was as powerful as the kinetic strikes themselves. "No one in Iran's high echelons can now be sure he isn't known to Israeli intelligence," observed former Mossad official Sima Shine. "It's not just the damage caused—it's the nervousness it brings." That nervousness was part of the design: an invisible contagion spreading through Tehran's surviving hierarchy.

Inside the IDF command centers, relief mixed with disbelief. The operation had worked by the narrowest of margins. "When we started to plan this thing in detail, it was very difficult to know that this would work," admitted Maj. Gen. Oded Basiuk, one of the architects of the campaign. Everything could easily have gone the other way. Had a Mossad team been exposed, had the timing slipped by even a minute, had any of the targets scattered or taken shelter, the result could have been disaster: a living Iranian command structure, hundreds of missiles already in flight, and Israel staring into the abyss of uncontrolled escalation. Worse still, Iran's nuclear program could have remained intact. Everything—from Operation Red Wedding's decapitation strike to Operation Narnia's simultaneous assassinations—depended on precision bordering on the supernatural. Thousands of interlocking parts, years of preparation, and a few seconds of flawless execution determined the difference between triumph and catastrophe.

The airstrikes were the spine of the assault, but they were only possible because of the audacious ground teams operating deep inside Iran. For months, Mossad operatives had saturated the country with drones, explosives, and covert beacons. At the onset of the Israeli attack, they crept to within meters of radar stations and anti-aircraft batteries, crippling them seconds before they could lock onto the jets roaring overhead. Other teams coordinated the strikes in real time or ambushed convoys hauling ballistic missiles from subterranean depots to their launchpads. Working in tandem with the air force, they destroyed dozens of missiles and launchers before they could be used. They made sure to prioritize the destruction of the missile transporters. The logic was simple: Iran had four times as many missiles as it did trucks that could transport them. Take out the trucks, and the missiles become useless.

The results of the opening strike were felt by every Israeli. As the first bombs detonated in Tehran, air-raid sirens wailed across Israel. Civilians sprinted into stairwells and fortified shelters, bracing for the inevitable counterblow. In any full-scale war with Iran, Israelis had long expected hundreds—even thousands—of drones and missiles to rain down within minutes. But minutes passed. Then hours. And still nothing came. Thanks to the IAF's opening wave—and the Mossad's sabotage of Iran's aerospace command and launch sites—many of Iran's missiles were effectively stranded on the proverbial tarmac. When the order to retaliate finally came, the regime found its strike apparatus blinded, crippled, or simply unable to move. Almost eighteen hours would pass before Iran managed to fire in return. And when the barrages finally came, they were costly but far from the catastrophe Israel had braced itself for. Israel's multilayered air defenses, combined with the preemptive decapitation of Iran's launch network, had turned what could have been an apocalyptic onslaught into a contained reprisal. "We chose to strike first," Defense Minister Israel Katz said flatly. "They were not prepared."

Following the opening act, Prime Minister Benjamin Netanyahu addressed the nation: "Our voice is now heard. The purpose of this unprecedented attack is to hit Iran's nuclear facilities and its military capabilities until we remove the threat to us. If we do not act now, we will simply not exist." Chief of Staff Eyal Zamir added the final note: "We began this operation because the time has come. We are at the point of no return."

Even amid triumph, the risk loomed. Iran was wounded, not dead. The architects of Rising Lion knew that what they had unleashed was only the beginning—a furious, precise, and deadly commencement whose real measure would come only in what followed.

Twelve Days in June

From the first strike, the firepower did not let up. Explosions rippled across Iran in relentless succession. The Parchin weapons complex, the Fordow enrichment plant, Isfahan's nuclear research center, the airfields at Hamadan and Tabriz—one after another, fire lit up the Iranian landscape. The pilots delivering those blows were taking on greater risks than any airmen in Israel's history. One senior air force officer sought to describe their courage: "the mental capacity to confront fear—to face a professional challenge, at night, alone, 1,500 to 2,000 kilometers from here, deep in enemy territory, with fuel and munitions constraints. It means carrying out a mission where the price of a mistake could be catastrophic and tragic for the State of Israel."

Meanwhile, Iran responded as it knows best: with a boldfaced lie. The regime claimed to have downed an Israeli F-35 and captured a pilot. None of it was true. Then, as night fell, Operation True Promise III began.

Around 9:00 p.m., ten minutes before dozens of missiles hit, Israeli citizens received phone alerts about an incoming attack. Soon, alarms wailed across Israel. Six waves of drones and missiles poured in through the night. A mother of four was killed in Ramat Gan; her seventy-six-year-old partner died soon after. Two more civilians—an elderly man and his caregiver—were killed in Rishon LeZion. Iranian missiles also struck Tel Aviv, one hitting within the vicinity of the IDF headquarters.

By dawn on June 14, Israel struck again—this time in the heart of Tehran. Strikes crashed into the Iranian Defense Ministry, the Organization of Defensive Innovation and Research. Entire neighborhoods of the capital were plunged into darkness as power grids failed. Explosions rattled Mehrabad Airport and ignited fires across the oil fields of Bushehr. In just the first days of the war, Israel had attacked eighteen of the thirty-one provinces of Iran. The IDF announced that it had achieved air superiority from Iran's western edge to Tehran.

Aerial dominance is the dream of any air force. But what stunned even Israel's closest allies was the breathtaking speed with which it was achieved. As the defense minister later recalled, "Even when we presented parts of the plan to the Americans at various levels—including at the very top—they were deeply skeptical of our ability to pull it off. They measured everything according to their capabilities." Washington assumed such an operation would take a month, perhaps six weeks. Israel had estimated three days. In reality, it gained mastery over the skies of Tehran in a mere day and a half. The gap between American expectations and Israeli performance revealed a simple truth: a tiny Jewish state had built arguably the most agile, precise, and capable strike force anywhere on earth.

While Israel rewrote the rules of modern warfare, Iran cooked up unsubstantiated claims—this time claiming to have downed three Israeli F-35 jets, capturing two pilots, and killing a third. But Iran's retaliation also grew steadily wilder. Waves of missiles continued to rain on Israel. In the Israeli-Arab town of Tamra, four members of one family, including a thirteen-year-old girl, were killed. Twenty others were wounded. The toll would continue to rise.

The next day, June 15, became the bloodiest for Israel in the entire campaign. Waves of ballistic missiles tore across the country, killing fifteen and wounding hundreds. Bat Yam, one of the hardest-hit cities of the war, absorbed the worst of it. Nine people were killed there, among them a Ukrainian family of five—including three children—who had come to Israel seeking cancer treatment for their eight-year-old daughter. Sixty buildings were damaged across the city; six were so mangled they later had to be demolished. In Haifa, a missile slammed into the oil refinery complex—a long-coveted target of Israel's enemies—killing three. Another struck Bnei Brak, killing a man in his eighties. In Rehovot, an elderly man and his Filipino caregiver would later succumb to their wounds. In the same city, a missile ripped through laboratories at the Weizmann Institute of Science, badly damaging one of the world's premier research centers. The near misses were also harrowing. In one shattered apartment block, rescuers found a four-day-old baby miraculously shielded amid the ruin. Medics kept the infant inside an ambulance until, an hour later, crews pulled his mother—also alive—from the rubble. Israel's air defense shield was formidable, but it was not impenetrable.

As emergency teams combed the wreckage for survivors, Israeli jets answered with some of the fiercest strikes since the war began. Striking at the Iranian Supreme National Security Council's underground bunker in Tehran, Israeli forces wounded Iranian President Masoud Pezeshkian, who was forced to crawl through a smoke-choked escape tunnel with senior officials. Minutes later, another precision strike leveled the IRGC Intelligence Organization headquarters, killing Iran's leading intelligence chiefs. Among those killed were Maj. Gen. Mohammad Kazemi—the man who oversaw Iran's vast surveillance and repression network—along with his deputy, Gen. Hassan Mohaghegh. The same blast eliminated the senior coordinators of Iran's Axis of Resistance—Mohsen Bakri, chief of the Quds Force intelligence directorate, and his deputy, Abu al-Fadl Nikuei. Hours later, five car bombs detonated across Tehran, reportedly killing several nuclear scientists. Israel denied any role in the exploding automobiles, but the denial seemed irrelevant. Fear was spreading throughout the capital. No one in Tehran felt safe anymore.

Shortly before dawn on June 16, an Iranian missile slammed into Petah Tikvah, killing four—among them a ninety-five-year-old Holocaust survivor and her eighty-five-year-old neighbor, along with a husband and wife living nearby. Though they had taken shelter in their safe rooms, the missile struck the couple's twenty-story apartment building with such force that it overwhelmed even their hardened protection.

In response, the IAF leveled the Quds Force headquarters in Tehran and destroyed centrifuge halls at Fordow and Natanz. According to the head of the IAEA, nearly all of Iran's fifteen thousand centrifuges were "damaged or destroyed." Israel also bombed Iran's state TV station while they were live on air, literally broadcasting its capabilities while inverting the machines of Iranian propaganda. The IDF later announced that it had disabled 120 surface-to-surface rockets before launch and eliminated roughly 30 percent of Iran's missile launchers. Barely five days into the war, Iran's military hierarchy—and much of its offensive and defensive arsenal—lay in ruins.

As the smoke still rose, movement began in the West. Flight trackers recorded dozens of US Air Force refueling aircraft—KC-135s and KC-46s—departing the United States for Europe. The USS *Nimitz* carrier group was said to be en route to the Middle East. Officially, Secretary of Defense Pete Hegseth called the deployments "a defensive measure." But the offensive military options that these movements afforded President Trump were impossible to ignore.

While America positioned itself to possibly partake in the conflict, Iran's barrages seemed to be thinning. On June 17, a handful of missiles struck Bat Yam, Tamra, Herzliya, and Tel Aviv. One impact damaged an apartment building and blew up a bus—but no one was killed. In the meantime, the IDF estimated that 40 percent of Iran's ballistic launchers were now gone. Another evening salvo toward northern Israel was intercepted entirely. Trump, for his part, released several posts hinting that something "much bigger" than a peace deal was coming for Iran. That same day, Trump called on Iran to "unconditionally surrender."

Israel's tempo only grew. Sixty fighter jets hammered Isfahan, obliterating a dozen missile launch sites. Then came a devastating coup de grâce: intelligence tracked Iran's newly appointed Chief of Staff, General Ali Shadmani, fleeing Tehran with senior IRGC officers to a "secret" mountain compound. The IAF waited until they gathered—then erased the site in one strike. Iran's high command had been decapitated twice in five days. Tehran's propaganda grew desperate, boasting absurdly that it had shot down "28 hostile aircraft." No one believed it—not even inside Iran.

Just after midnight on June 18, fifty Israeli jets roared over Tehran, striking twenty key sites, including missile factories and an IRGC-affiliated university. The IAEA independently verified that Israel had crippled centrifuge production facilities at Karaj's TESA Complex and the Tehran Research Center. In addition, seventy missile batteries were wiped out that night alone.

At dawn, new strikes pummeled southern Tehran. Explosions consumed Iran's internal security headquarters, the heart of its domestic surveillance machine. By afternoon, another twenty-five Israeli jets destroyed forty military sites across western Iran, including a primed Emad missile launcher. Brig. Gen. Effie Defrin announced that Israel had hit over eleven hundred targets since the war began, including eight AH-1 attack helicopters and a weapons plant producing anti-tank missiles for Hezbollah.

Iran, cornered and humiliated, fired a single long-range Sejjil missile toward Tel Aviv. It was intercepted midair. By the end of June 18, Tehran had launched some four hundred missiles and one thousand drones. Every missile had been aimed at civilian population centers. Yet only twenty managed to hit them—a staggering 95 percent failure rate for Iran's missile arsenal.

Through the night, Israeli jets pounded missile production and air defense sites. The IR-40 reactor containment building at Arak was struck, along with the distillation towers at the adjacent heavy water production plant. Israeli drones were reported cutting down soldiers repairing launchers. The IDF estimated that up to two-thirds of Iran's missile-launch capacity was gone.

Around dawn on June 19, twenty ballistic missiles were fired at Israel. Four struck populated areas—Tel Aviv, Ramat Gan, Holon, and Beersheba—and one slammed into Soroka Medical Center in Beersheba, exploding in the surgical wing. Eighty were wounded; eight operating rooms and six research labs were destroyed. Miraculously, a massacre had been averted: the day before, hospital director Dr. Hezi Codish had ordered the evacuation of 60 percent of Building 12, the very ward that was hit. "People talk about the miracle," he said. "But we can't rely on miracles."

Elsewhere, an Iranian cluster warhead was used, likely as compensation for Iran's inability to launch large missile salvos and reliably penetrate Israeli defenses. It didn't work. Of the twenty two-and-a-half-kilogram submunitions released by the warhead, only one struck a home in Azor, injuring several civilians. The other nineteen failed to detonate and were safely destroyed by Israeli forces. In Ramat Gan, a missile impacted near a row of high-rises, wounding twenty-two and shattering dozens of apartments. Another wave of at least ten missiles was fired at northern Israel that evening, all of which were intercepted. Three barrages were launched in a single day, causing hundreds of millions of dollars in damage. Miraculously, no one in Israel was killed. For all its bluster and brutality, Iran's war machine was faltering. Israel's message was unmistakable: it could take the blows and keep on flying.

Meanwhile, Iran's Foreign Minister Abbas Araghchi announced talks in Geneva with European powers to discuss "the nuclear issue." He floated "scaling back" enrichment—far short of US demands for zero enrichment—but it was the first real sign of strain. Iran was looking for an exit.

Through the night of June 19 and into the next day, Israel pressed its advantage. Fighter jets struck deep into Tehran, hammering the headquarters of the SPND—Iran's military R&D arm—and a nuclear research center. The Law Enforcement Command (LEC) headquarters and its Special Units base were both destroyed—a targeted blow at the regime's riot-control and repression apparatus, undermining Tehran's ability to crush future protests.

Elsewhere, the IAF hit the Sefid Roud Industrial Complex, home to the Navid Composite Material Company, which had been sanctioned years earlier for producing carbon fiber for Iran's missile program. Thirty-five missile launchers in Tabriz and Kermanshah were destroyed, along with an IRGC battalion commander who oversaw fifteen of them. In Tehran's Gisha neighborhood, a drone strike killed another senior nuclear scientist. By then, Israel had taken out multiple Ghadir radars capable of tracking aircraft over a thousand kilometers away. IDF Chief Eyal Zamir announced that "IAF pilots are operating at the greatest range and intensity in the force's history."

It wasn't only pilots: drones carried out more than five hundred precision strikes, accounted for 60 percent of Israeli Air Force flight hours, and half of all targeted assassinations. In outer space, another unmanned asset was hard at work. At all hours, day and night, Israel's satellite network was photographing tens of millions of square kilometers, producing more than twelve thousand images and enabling rapid target acquisition without putting ground forces at risk.

Iran's counterfire remained feeble. A morning barrage struck Beersheba, injuring seven and damaging the central rail station. Another wave hit Haifa and central Israel, wounding twenty-three. In Haifa, the Al-Jarina Mosque was struck—proof of Iran's collapsing accuracy. By then, Cabinet Secretary Yossi Fox reported, Iran had launched 520 ballistic missiles, of which only twenty-five had hit the ground. Iran was still running at about a 5 percent success rate.

Overnight into June 21, the IAF pounded the Isfahan Nuclear Technology Center, demolishing two centrifuge production facilities and dozens of military installations. New explosions hit Shiraz, Bandar Abbas, and the IRGC Shahroud Missile Facility—the core of Iran's solid fuel missile program. In Tehran, Israel destroyed the headquarters of the Cyber Police (FATA), a key regime surveillance unit.

Then came more assassinations. In western Iran, an airstrike vaporized the car of Behnam Shahriari, commander of the Quds Force's Unit 190—the man who smuggled weapons and funds to every corner of the Axis of Resistance. Hours later, a drone strike in Qom killed Brig. Gen. Mohammad Saeed Izadi, head of the Quds Force's "Palestine Desk." An architect of Hamas's October 7 massacre, Izadi had survived three previous assassination attempts by Israel. Soon after, Israel confirmed the death of Amin Pour Joudaki, commander of the IRGC Aerospace Force's 2nd Drone Regiment, whose predecessor had been killed in Operation Red Wedding.

Inside Iran, the regime was cracking. Sources told *The New York Times* that Supreme Leader Ali Khamenei had fled to a fortified bunker, cut digital communications, and now issued orders only through a single aide. He named three clerics as potential successors—a historic break from precedent—and instructed senior officials to abandon phones and work from underground.

Meanwhile, across the ocean, the United States moved into position. Six US Air Force refueling tankers were redeployed from bases in California and Oklahoma—positioning for long-range support. Soon thereafter, B-2 stealth bombers left Whiteman Air Force Base for Guam, escorted by more refueling aircraft. The deployment followed a call between Netanyahu, Katz, and Trump, discussing what the Israelis called "a limited window of opportunity" to strike Iran's remaining nuclear sites. Washington was preparing to move.

Uncle Sam's Revenge

June 22 began like any other day of Israel's Iran campaign. Throughout the night, Israeli jets continued to fly in their seemingly endless sorties. They struck weapons plants, air defenses, and missile hubs in Kermanshah, Hamadan, and Tehran. In Dezful, two Iranian F-5s sat smoldering on the tarmac beside the wreckage of eight missile launchers. In Isfahan, drone hangars and radar arrays were razed to the ground. Deep in Eastern Iran, the Shahroud solid fuel plant was struck. The IDF also bombed the IRGC division headquarters in Tabriz and the Imam Hussein strategic missile complex in Yazd, from which Iran had launched sixty missiles at Israel earlier in the war. Iran, for its part, fired twenty-seven ballistic missiles toward Israel, hitting eleven sites from the Golan to Haifa. Eighty-six people were wounded, but thankfully, none were killed. Tehran again claimed to have downed an Israeli drone, but the truth was plain: Iran's skies belonged to Israel. And the absolute freedom of movement that Israel had secured for its own aircraft was now about to be shared with those of its foremost ally, who had thus far stood out of the fight.

A few hours after midnight on June 22, Operation Midnight Hammer began. Seven B-2 Spirit bombers of the 509th Bomb Wing departed Whiteman Air Force Base, Missouri, eighteen hours earlier, flying east in radio silence. They refueled mid-air three times over the Atlantic, a ghost armada moving through the night. At 2:10 a.m. local time in Iran, six of the stealth bombers dropped 12 GBU-57 Massive Ordnance Penetrators (MOPs)—thirty-thousand-pound bunker-busters never before used in combat—directly onto the Fordow nuclear complex. Each weapon plunged through the mountain at over one thousand feet per second, detonating deep in the core of the site that had defied decades of sanctions and cyberattacks. The seventh bomber peeled off toward Natanz and released two more MOPs on its enrichment halls. Simultaneously, a US submarine launched thirty Tomahawk missiles at Natanz and Isfahan, finishing the assault within half an hour. In all, 125 aircraft took part—including fifty-two refueling tankers and a constellation of reconnaissance planes. "Our B-2s went in and out and back without the world knowing," Secretary of Defense Pete Hegseth later said.

But it was Israel that made the operation possible. In the words of military historian Mark Bowden, "It's doubtful that the [B-2's] state-of-the-art stealth . . . was even necessary. Iran's airspace, by then, was like a red carpet." He clarified that "the accomplishment was not America's. It was Israel's." While the IDF had cleared the military path, it was Netanyahu himself who had paved the moral road that made such a strike conceivable. In the words of an Israeli official, "If Netanyahu hadn't spoken before Congress, the strike on Iran in 2025 would never have happened . . . He turned it into a political issue in the United States, and without that speech, Trump would not have acted—or spoken—the way he did against the nuclear deal."

But Trump himself deserved immense credit for carrying out the strike. He had overcome major opposition from within his own party. Inside Washington, the possibility of a strike had split his inner circle. Director of National Intelligence Tulsi Gabbard had urged restraint, arguing that Iran was not actively building a bomb. Trump got her to change her mind. When the Israel-hating conservative pundit Tucker Carlson warned against perpetrating "an act of war" against Iran, Trump fired back on Truth Social: "Somebody please explain to kooky Tucker Carlson that IRAN CAN NEVER HAVE A NUCLEAR WEAPON."

And, just as he had at the outset of Rising Lion, Trump again showed his uncanny talent for strategic misdirection. Days before the strike, Trump had publicly said he would "decide within two weeks" whether to act, a deliberate feint meant to lull Tehran's defenses. On June 21, two B-2s had been sent west toward Guam in a decoy maneuver. Only a handful of commanders knew the real plan.

For the first time since a limited naval campaign in 1988, the United States had struck directly inside Iran. And, it had struck hard. In total, four thousand Americans took part in the mission, which had been years in the making. "It felt like the Super Bowl," one airman recalled. "Thousands of scientists, pilots, and maintainers all coming together for one perfect play." Two Defense Threat Reduction Agency scientists had spent fifteen years modeling Fordow's bedrock and tunnels while designing a bomb that could pierce it. "They literally dreamed about this target," said Gen. Dan Caine, chairman of the Joint Chiefs. And Fordow deserved their focus. Embedded hundreds of feet in the earth, the plant was producing enough highly enriched uranium to fuel one new nuclear weapon every single month.

When the American airstrikes were over, Trump posted on Truth Social that the strike was a "spectacular military success" and that the facilities had been "totally obliterated." He later delivered a televised address to the nation. "A full payload of bombs was dropped on the primary site," he related. "We will not allow a regime that chants 'Death to America' to possess the means to make good on that threat." Israel confirmed it had coordinated every phase of the attack with Washington. Prime Minister Netanyahu called it "a historic turning point." President Herzog thanked the United States "for ensuring that liberty triumphed over tyranny." Ron Dermer, Israel's minister of strategic affairs, posted the Hebrew blessing made for miracles and new beginnings. Translated into English, it reads: "Blessed are You, L-rd our G-d, King of the Universe, who has granted us life, sustained us, and enabled us to reach this occasion."

In Tehran, the regime issued no fiery vow of vengeance, only a stiff IRGC communiqué warning of "regrettable responses." The rhetorical restraint—so utterly out of character for Iran—was a message in itself. Iran's leadership—scattered, bunker-bound, and increasingly cut off from one another—was barely able to communicate. Its command networks had been bombed, its missile infrastructure disemboweled, and its nuclear program buried under tons of rock and rubble. Still, the government insisted Fordow had suffered "no serious damage." The satellite imagery appeared to disagree. Entrances were visibly collapsed, access tunnels had been sealed shut, and the mountain bunkers were pockmarked with massive craters where MOPs had gone in. Even Foreign Minister Abbas Araghchi finally conceded the truth: Iran's nuclear enterprise had suffered "severe damage."

The following day, Tehran made a desperate show of defiance. A volley of missiles was launched toward Israel; most were intercepted, though falling shrapnel injured several civilians. The real theater, however, was farther south. Iran announced Operation Annunciation of Victory—a salvo of nineteen missiles fired at the American Al Udeid Air Base in Qatar. The strike was little more than a signal to save face. Minutes before launch, Iranian officials called Doha, warning that missiles would target only the base, not the city. Qatar relayed the message to Washington. By then, most US aircraft and personnel had already been moved, and the embassy had instructed Americans to shelter in place. The missiles were intercepted; no one was hurt. Tehran had thrown a punch it never meant to land.

Israel's reply was less restrained. Even as Washington held its fire, the IDF struck six Iranian airfields across Iran, destroying fifteen fighter jets and helicopters along with missile depots and refueling facilities.

That evening, President Trump posted that "a ceasefire between Israel and Iran will take effect tomorrow." It was in that post that he gave the campaign its name: The Twelve-Day War. His decision to end the war had been made hours earlier. Immediately after the B-2 strikes, Trump had phoned Netanyahu. "We've done what we came to do," he told him. The United States would halt its operations; Israel, he said, should do the same. Behind the scenes, White House envoy Steven Witkoff delivered the same message to Araghchi: return to negotiations, or face something far worse.

Iran publicly denied agreeing to a ceasefire. But it signaled a willingness to stop hostilities if Israel would hold its fire beginning "no later than 4 a.m. Tehran time." Israel had no intention of waiting. Four hours before the deadline, the IAF launched one final wave—perhaps the most punishing of the war. Fifty warplanes roared over Tehran, dropping more than a hundred munitions in two hours. Targets included the Basij headquarters, the IRGC command center, and Evin Prison—the regime's foremost symbol of repression. Even the monumental countdown clock in Palestine Square, forever ticking toward Israel's supposed destruction, was blown apart. Netanyahu later claimed that "hundreds" of Basij paramilitary operatives affiliated with the IRGC had been killed, along with one of Iran's senior nuclear scientists.

As the ceasefire took hold, Iran managed to launch another ballistic missile wave. Beginning shortly before 5:00 a.m.—and with the last missile launched at 7:06 a.m., after the truce had already begun—roughly twenty missiles were fired at Israel. One struck a seven-story apartment building in Be'er Sheva, killing four Israelis in one of the war's deadliest moments on its final day. Twenty-two more were injured. More than three hours after the truce, Iran broke its commitments yet again. Three more missiles were fired from Iran at around 10:30 a.m. in Israel. They caused no damage, but IDF Chief of Staff Eyal Zamir warned, "In light of this violation, we will respond with force." Israeli jets were dispatched, but Trump himself intervened. Stepping out onto the South Lawn before departing for a NATO summit, he fumed to reporters: "Israel, as soon as we made the deal, dropped a load of bombs the likes of which I've never seen before. They've been fighting so long they don't know what the hell they're doing." Minutes later, aboard Marine One, he posted in all caps: "DO NOT DROP THOSE BOMBS. IF YOU DO IT IS A MAJOR VIOLATION. BRING YOUR PILOTS HOME, NOW!" Thirty-eight minutes later, Netanyahu called to confirm that the jets were returning. "Nobody will be hurt," Trump announced. "The ceasefire is in effect."

It was only when the war ended that the full meaning of those twelve days came into view. Gradually, a new era began to emerge.

For decades, Israel had been one of America's strongest allies in the Middle East. After the Twelve-Day War, it emerged as something greater: a full-spectrum strategic partner—the only democracy capable of matching American intelligence, precision, and resolve in the highest tiers of modern warfare. Historian Walter Russell Mead captured the shift clearly. America, he wrote, now confronts "the axis of revisionists—China, Russia, North Korea, and, until quite recently, Iran." Europe has struggled to push Putin back in Ukraine; Taiwan, if attacked, would likely require American boots on the ground. But Israel had reversed the tide almost entirely on its own. The Israeli prime minister, Mead argued, is "the only leader, really, to have been able to throw back the revisionist axis in a very serious way." And further still: "Israel is a fantastic ally—it spends a higher percentage of its GDP on defense than we do. It's an ally America must hold back rather than whip on. It is more eager for the fight than we are."

In 2021, Netanyahu's adviser Ron Dermer openly predicted that Jerusalem would become Washington's most important ally. It was a radical claim for a country the size of New Jersey. But after the Twelve-Day War, the logic of that prediction no longer felt far-fetched.

As much as Operation Rising Lion demonstrated Israel's unmatched power in the region, it also left Iran exposed for the failed state it has become. In the aftermath of the conflict, a kilo of rice—a staple of the Persian table—leapt past 400,000 toman. That's about four US dollars in a country where the minimum monthly wage hovers near 100 dollars a month. Lamb, beef, and even chicken were gradually phased out of the shopping carts of families that could no longer afford them. For many Iranians, trips to the market became a weekly humiliation. At the same time, rolling blackouts swept millions of homes, hospitals, and factory floors—even as Iran sits atop nearly a fifth of the world's oil and gas. Losses mounted across Iranian industries, including steel, cement, petrochemicals, food, and cars. Eighty thousand workers were furloughed without pay. At the same time, Iran staggered through a sixth year of drought. Reservoirs feeding the capital sank to 5 percent of reserve capacity, and dams began to dry up. Officials openly discussed plans to evacuate large parts of Tehran.

For Iranians who already doubted the regime's basic competence, the evidence had become impossible to ignore. The Islamic Republic could not reliably provide food, power, or even water. And everyone understood the cause. Even when Iran earned billions, none of it flowed to ordinary people; it vanished into the sump of corruption or was diverted into missiles, militias, and a genocidal nuclear project that delivered only misery and ruin. Israel's war did not create this crisis—it exposed it. For Iran's leadership, another truth was impossible to escape: a regime incapable of caring for its own people would never be the foremost power in the Middle

East. Israel, on the other hand, seemed to have undeniably claimed that title for itself.

But, for all of Israel's achievements, victory came with caveats. Initial Pentagon estimates suggested the strikes had set Iran's nuclear ambitions back by nearly two years; later assessments were more cautious. Fordow's centrifuges, entombed beneath eighty meters of granite, might one day spin again. "We delayed, not destroyed," one US official admitted.

In September 2013, Netanyahu laid out what he called the only formula capable of truly ending Iran's nuclear ambitions: first, halt all uranium enrichment; second, remove all enriched uranium; third, shut down the Qom facility; and fourth, terminate the plutonium track. "Only the combination of all four steps," he warned, "constitutes a genuine halt to the nuclear program." Yet for all the war's staggering feats, significant stores of highly enriched uranium almost certainly remained inside Iran.

Moreover, though Iran's nuclear sites were reduced to rubble, the regime had still survived. Israel had broken the sword, but not the hand that forged it. Beneath the ruins of Fordow and the smoke drifting over Natanz, the machinery of the Islamic Republic continued to pulse. The question would still linger: Did Israel and the United States terminate the Iranian threat, or simply kick it further down the road?

Israel would be wise not to let time decide. It is a verdict that the Jewish state has no choice but to guarantee.

The massive protests that erupted across Iran in December 2025 and January 2026 brought these themes into stark relief. The largest uprising since the 1979 Islamic Revolution, the unrest swept all thirty-one provinces and drew millions into the streets. President Trump warned Tehran that if it opened fire on its own citizens, the United States would come to their rescue. The regime answered with one of the most brutal crackdowns in its modern history, deploying local Basij militias and imported proxy forces in a campaign that reportedly left tens of thousands dead. Though full details are still emerging, footage already confirms the use of heavy battlefield weaponry against civilians, and armored vehicles deployed to run over demonstrators in the streets—a grim reminder of the car-ramming terror attacks Iran has long sponsored in Israel.

But a regime that survives only through massacre advertises its own fragility. History is unforgiving to governments that rule exclusively by fear. They may endure for a time, but they live on borrowed days. The Ayatollah, who helped topple a Shah sustained by secret police and intimidation, should understand that better than anyone.

At the same time, President Trump's warnings—and the negotiations that followed—underscored the other reality: Iran has no intention of relinquishing its nuclear ambitions. Even after the United States repositioned more airpower and carrier strike groups into the Middle East than at any time since the 2003 invasion of Iraq, the Supreme Leader escalated his rhetoric, boasting that "the strongest military force in the world may at times be struck so hard that it cannot get up again," and warning that weapons exist "more dangerous than that warship . . . capable of sending it to the bottom of the sea." The Ayatollah understood the stakes. Without the shadow of nuclear capability, his regime would have lost its ultimate instrument of intimidation. If he could not project fear abroad, he could not sustain it at home. That is the trap of tyrants: damned if they advance, damned if they retreat. And so, like so many before him, Iran's terrorist-in-chief found himself cornered by the very logic of his rule.

And yet neither the courage of the Iranian people nor the resolve of the President of the United States would have carried the same force had the physically small but spiritually immense Jewish State not shattered the illusion of the Ayatollah's invincibility. For decades, the regime thrived not only on repression, but on perception—on the cultivated aura that it was untouchable, that its reach was endless, that it could plunge the world into war. Israel punctured the myth. It demonstrated to the Iranian people and to the world that the bullies of the global stage are no different from the bullies we once knew in school. They posture, threaten, and roar. But beneath the spectacle lies not strength, but insecurity. They depend less on actual might than on the belief that no one will challenge them. Their dominance is psychological.

And more often than not, their collapse begins with a single act of defiance that exposes the myth for what it is.

CHAPTER TEN

DEALS WITH THE DEVIL: THE LONGEST HOSTAGE RESCUE

Opening eyes deprived of light,
Rescuing prisoners from confinement,
From the dungeon those who sit in darkness.
Isaiah 42:7

With the ceasefire between Israel and Iran secured, President Donald J. Trump turned his attention to the final, unfinished front: Gaza. In Jerusalem, the mood was also shifting. Senior Israeli ministers and top IDF generals were beginning to coalesce around the same conclusion. By crippling Iran's command infrastructure and nuclear program, Israel had neutralized—at least for now—the primary existential threat facing the nation. And with Tehran sidelined, Hamas stood stripped of its most powerful patron and might finally be set to break. For the first time since October 7, an end to the war felt within reach.

Four months after the Twelve-Day War, Trump chose to force the issue. The same president who turned back fighter jets minutes before a parting shot against Tehran would do it again—this time grounding Israeli ground forces halfway through a renewed offensive in Gaza City.

He understood the dynamic behind the war. Destroying Hamas—or at least disarming it—could be managed later, with an international force if necessary. But Israel could not stop fighting so long as its sons and daughters were still buried alive beneath Gaza. Ending the war depended on bringing home the hostages, down to the last one.

Hostage-taking is one of the oldest and most demonic weapons in the terrorists' arsenal, honed over decades by the PLO, Hezbollah, and every self-styled "resistance" faction that discovered how easy it was to snatch a Jew and trade his freedom for the release of mass murderers. Geopolitical specialist Dr. Melanie Garson explained the loathsome rationale: "They know the value Israel has always placed on every single life and the explicit promise between the government and the people that they would never leave anyone behind enemy lines." And so, from its earliest years, Israel lived with the nightmare of its soldiers and civilians being dragged into dungeons beyond its borders.

Over the years, Hamas developed and deployed the tactic of taking captives, whom it used as leverage to pry open the gates of Israeli jails and release hundreds, sometimes thousands, of convicted killers. In 2014, it kidnapped and murdered three Israeli teenagers—Eyal Yifrach, Naftali Fraenkel, and Gilad Shaar—which set off Operation Protective Edge. That war ended as it began, with Hamas abducting the bodies of IDF soldiers Hadar Goldin and Oron Shaul, to be held as bargaining chips for more than a decade. Before October 7, Hamas already held two living Israeli civilians, too: Avera Mengistu and Hisham al-Sayed, both mentally vulnerable and stowed away in Gaza for years. And only weeks before October 7, Israel issued a travel warning that Hamas was actively hunting for new captives ahead of the holiday season. At the time, no one understood how foretelling that warning would be.

Israel had long been familiar with Hamas's brutal brand of human trafficking. But October 7 was something else entirely. It was hostage-taking industrialized, elevated from a terror tactic to a grand strategy. In a single morning, Hamas and its henchmen hauled more than 250 human beings into Gaza: Holocaust survivors, grandparents, infants, teenagers, music-festival revelers, foreign laborers, and soldiers. Whole families were seized together and dragged across the border. Couples were ripped from their homes, still clinging to each other. Babies were wrenched from their parents' arms. And all of it was meticulously planned to forestall the possibility of rescue.

Israel could shatter battalions, level headquarters, and kill field commanders by the dozen. It could dismantle Hamas's rocket arrays and tunnel networks. But it could not raid its way to the freedom of hundreds of hostages held in a subterranean labyrinth built precisely to thwart rescue. They were scattered across dozens of locations, shuttled constantly from one underground cage to the next. The entire "Gaza Metro" had been engineered as an impenetrable supermax prison—a fortress designed so that even one of the world's most formidable armies could not reach its captives. Combat operations could squeeze Hamas. Targeted assassination could add to the pressure and shift the balance of negotiations. But beyond a tiny minority, Israel would not extract the hostages by force. For nearly all of them, negotiations—not operations—were the only path out of hell.

That excruciating truth forced Israel into one of the most agonizing strategic ruptures in its history. For decades, Israel held an iron line: it negotiated for soldiers, but never for civilians. The logic was harsh, but unassailable. Soldiers are armed, trained, and deployed into danger; civilians are unarmed, unprotected, and everywhere. If Israel began trading terrorists for civilians, every bus stop, every kindergarten, every roadside café would become an abduction zone. Civilians were simply too easy to take. Reward that strategy once, even for the noblest reasons, and the kidnapping industry would explode overnight.

This policy was written in blood. In 1972, Black September terrorists affiliated with the Palestine Liberation Organization broke into the Munich Olympic Village, murdering two Israeli athletes and kidnapping nine more. They demanded the release of 234 terrorists, for which West Germany tried to negotiate. But Prime Minister Golda Meir refused to trade innocents for killers. Israel offered to send its most elite commandos, but this time, it was the Germans who said no. The rescue was entrusted to a pathetic and ill-equipped German police force whose so-called "snipers" lacked even basic scopes. The results of the botched operation were catastrophic: every hostage was murdered, in a country that had killed six million Jews less than thirty years before.

Two years later, in Ma'alot, terrorists from the Popular Front for the Liberation of Palestine seized 115 hostages, most of them Israeli teenagers on a field trip. The terrorists demanded that twenty-three terrorists be released from Israeli prisons. Golda Meir weighed negotiations but ultimately sent in elite forces to storm the building. During the thirty-five-second operation, one of the terrorists threw grenades at the students and sprayed them with machine-gun fire. Twenty-five hostages were killed—including twenty-two children—and sixty-eight were wounded.

Two years after that, in Entebbe, terrorists hijacked an Air France jet and took 106 hostages. They demanded the release of fifty-three Arab prisoners. Israel refused to negotiate their release and instead launched one of the most daring operations in the history of warfare. Flying across a continent, the IDF killed the terrorists and rescued 103 of the hostages in what later came to be called "Operation Jonathan," named after Prime Minister Netanyahu's elder brother who led the operation and fell there. Three hostages were lost in the battle, along with the heroic leader of the operation, who is remembered as one of Israel's greatest military heroes.

Through these painful episodes, Israel's refusal to negotiate for civilian hostages held firm because it had to. Trading terrorists for civilians would have turned kidnapping into a profitable business model, an open invitation for every fanatic with a rifle to seize the nearest Israeli and wait for a payout. The cycles would never end; the ransom price would only rise. But on October 7, that doctrine collapsed under the sheer, staggering number of people abducted by Hamas.

Wherever it could, Israel staged astonishingly bold rescue operations. On October 30, 2023, Israel liberated a young IDF private named Ori Megidish in a precision operation that electrified the nation. In February 2024, the IDF launched Operation Golden Hand, a midnight assault deep in Rafah where special units broke into a safehouse holding two Argentine Israeli hostages: seventy-year-old Fernando Marman and his sixty-year-old brother-in-law, Luis Har. The two men hid on a balcony for eight excruciating minutes as Yamam counterterror officers and Hamas terrorists exchanged fire across the narrow courtyard. A missile from an IAF Apache helicopter struck terrorists just fifteen meters from where the hostages were hiding. The miracle of the operation's success was underscored by the fact that, just days earlier, Argentina's President Javier Milei had stood at the Western Wall in tears, praying for their release.

Israel's most dramatic hostage rescue came on June 8, 2024, in Operation Arnon—named for the fearless Yamam officer who fell leading it. Under deep cover, IDF commandos disguised as Arab laborers slipped into the heart of Nuseirat and closed in on two apartment blocks where four hostages—Noa Argamani, Almog Meir Jan, Andrey Kozlov, and Shlomi Ziv—were being held. They reached the doors undetected. Then all hell broke loose. Helmet-camera footage captured the moment the commandos smashed inside, hurling their bodies over the hostages as bullets shredded the plaster around them. "We're here to take you home!" they shouted, shielding the captives with their own flesh. Within moments, they were rushing the hostages down the stairs, shoving bulletproof vests onto their trembling bodies. The team radioed their commanders: "We have the diamonds in our hands." Yamam squad commander Arnon Zamora was struck by Hamas gunfire. Mortally wounded, he continued fighting until the hostages were clear. With the teams exposed and Gaza erupting around them, the Israeli Air Force unleashed a wall of fire—dozens of precision strikes to drown out the rescue and pry Hamas fighters away from the fleeing convoy. Even so, a vehicle carrying hostages and special forces was hit, forced to a grinding halt under fierce fire. An armored personnel carrier barreled in to extract them, only to be disabled moments later. Another team tore through the chaos and finally delivered the hostages to helicopters, which were waiting on the beach. Minutes later, the aircraft lifted off for Israel.

These operations carried a heroism that felt biblical in scale. But they were also the exception that proved the rule. The vast majority of hostages could not be freed through daring raids. Even the exceptional operations that succeeded only managed to liberate the captives being held aboveground. Those kept underground were all but impossible to reach. The rare marvel was Qaid Farhan Alkadi, a Bedouin father of eleven, held for 326 days. When he suddenly heard Hebrew outside the door, he thought he was hallucinating. Moments later, he became the first hostage ever pulled alive from Hamas's tunnels—and the eighth, and last, living hostage Israeli forces would rescue.

Not all operations were successful. In December 2023, Israeli forces launched a clandestine attempt to free hostage Sahar Baruch. Commandos reached the building, quietly placed a charge at the entrance, and blew the door. They were met by a storm of grenades. Several soldiers were wounded, and Hamas fighters immediately executed Baruch and escaped with his body. The operation confirmed what Israel had suspected: if Hamas believed a rescue was underway, it would execute the hostages immediately. For this reason, other operations never left the ground. Early in the war, the IDF prepared a mission to rescue several children and a woman. Special units reached high readiness. At the last minute, the IDF General Staff canceled the plan. These particular hostages, commanders believed, would almost certainly be released in a future deal. But if Hamas sensed a rescue attempt, they would be shot on the spot.

More common were missions undertaken not to rescue the living, but to recover the bodies of hostages who had been killed. But those were also fraught with danger. In December 2023, two Israeli soldiers were killed in an operation to recover two hostage bodies, and more were wounded. Still, Israel pressed on, determined to bring its dead home for burial. In May 2024, four bodies of hostages taken from the Nova festival were recovered. By the end of that month, after a brutal, block-by-block operation in Jabalia, seven more deceased hostages were found. On August 2024, the country would be shocked to its core: in a tunnel complex, the bodies of six hostages were discovered. All six had been executed at close range, just a day or two before the forces arrived. Netanyahu stripped away the euphemisms: speaking to reporters at a press conference, he said Hamas had "shot them in the back of the head." In January 2025, Israel finally recovered the body of Oron Shaul, held by Hamas since 2014. Three separate operations in June 2025 brought home the remains of seven more hostages.

Israel also undertook remarkable operations to recover the bodies of hostages and bring them home for burial. Among the most extraordinary was the effort to retrieve the body of Lt. Hadar Goldin, killed and taken during Operation Protective Edge in 2014. For more than a decade, Hamas held Goldin's remains underground as a bargaining chip, denying his family even the most basic measure of closure. In the summer of

2025, with Israeli forces operating inside the Gaza Strip, new opportunities emerged. Israeli intelligence focused on Dr. Marwan al-Hams, a Hamas-affiliated physician who had declared Goldin's death in 2014 and was "suspected of knowing where he was buried," according to the IDF and Shin Bet. Al-Hams had served in Hamas's military wing as a brigade doctor and managed field hospitals; footage later released showed him participating in Hamas military activity, including carrying a rocket and entering a terror tunnel.

To apprehend him, Israel's security services turned to a classic tool of spycraft: the honeypot. Under the guise of casting him as the star of a documentary titled *Hero of Gaza*, an Israeli agent—posing as a woman named "Charlotte"—made contact and gradually drew him in. The exchange turned flirtatious. Al-Hams boasted, "I don't want to say I am smart, but I am smart." He wrote, "I have only known you for a short time, but I feel that we have known each other for a long time." He promised to host her in Gaza and offered to take her to the beach. As it turned out, al-Hams was not as smart as he believed. Nor would he ever consummate his beachside rendezvous. When he arrived for their first meeting with "Charlotte," Israeli forces closed in and took him into custody. What followed was a broader intelligence effort, incorporating interrogations and on-the-ground verification, to assess and narrow down possible burial locations. During this process, soldiers even strapped al-Hams into a harness and lowered him into a tunnel where Hadar Goldin's remains were believed to be hidden. Finally, after eleven years, Israel brought its fallen soldier home. His family was at last granted the fundamental dignity of mourning.

Yet the most dramatic recovery came in January 2026, when Israel retrieved the remains of the final hostage held in Gaza, demonstrating just how far the state and its soldiers were willing to go to bring every captive home.

Operation Courageous Heart marked the culmination of more than two years of painstaking intelligence work to locate the body of Ran Gvili. Gvili, a police officer in a special forces unit, had gone out to fight on October 7 despite being on leave for a shoulder injury. Shot twice in battle, his arm was shattered. Yet he continued fighting—saving partygoers fleeing the Nova music festival near Re'im, defending Kibbutz Alumim, and killing fourteen Hamas terrorists before falling. After his death, terrorists abducted Gvili's body and moved it repeatedly, shuttling it from site to site before deliberately concealing it beneath the bodies of terrorists in a cemetery in northern Gaza, in an effort to deny Israel the ability to recover its fallen officer. Despite those efforts, a decisive breakthrough came when an Islamic Jihad operative, captured in southern Gaza City, was interrogated by the Shin Bet. He admitted to having personally transferred the body between locations, reinforcing the intelligence assessment that Gvili was buried in a specific cemetery in Gaza City.

In late January 2026, forces from the Alexandroni Brigade, operating alongside the elite Yahalom engineering unit, entered the Shuja'iyya area and began the search. Twenty military dentists deployed to the field with Unit 6017—the Medical Identification and Cause of Death Investigation Unit—conducting rapid forensic screening under combat conditions. Representatives of the Military Rabbinate accompanied the operation, ensuring the body would be treated with dignity. Over several days, more than 700 bodies were disinterred. Of those, 250 were examined. The 250th was Ran Gvili, still clothed in his police uniform and boots. On January 26, 2026, the last hostage body held in Gaza was brought home, and for the first time since 2014, no Israelis remained captive in the enclave. "His return," the Shin Bet said, "is a meaningful and moral closing of a circle." When identification was confirmed, his mother wrote simply: "The first to go out. The last to come back. Our hero."

Each return was a sacred act, reaffirming a long-held covenant between Israel and its citizens: no one is left behind, not even in death. And yet each was also a devastating reminder that those brought home for burial had not been saved and perhaps never could have been.

When the dust finally settled, the numbers told a brutal truth. Of the 251 hostages taken on October 7, only eight were rescued alive. That was the hard limit of what military action alone could achieve. By contrast, negotiations succeeded in returning more than 160 living hostages. Hamas had engineered this reality from the outset: there would be no Entebbe-style rescue. The captives were too numerous, scattered across too many tunnels, guarded by men prepared to kill them the moment a rescue was detected. If Israel was to bring its sons and daughters home, it would require not a single daring raid, but a long and grinding war to pressure Hamas into release.

Hamas had prepared for that too. It had welded its subterranean archipelago of hostage-dungeons directly to every vital organ of its war machine: command rooms, rocket factories, IED workshops, and ambush nests. Hamas consistently placed hostages right beside its most valuable assets and senior commanders to deter Israeli strikes. For years, Hamas had hidden behind Gaza's population. Now, its commanders, engineers, and political elite would hide behind Israelis as well—a barricade built from the very innocents it had dragged into the darkness.

Besides obstructing pinpoint strikes, Hamas also used Israeli hostages strategically to restrict the IDF's freedom of action and manipulate Israeli maneuvers. Time and again, it claimed that hostages had been killed in Israeli airstrikes—nine on one day, sixty on another—each announcement calibrated to pierce Israeli morale and force hesitation at critical moments. As the IDF closed in on Gaza City in the final weeks, Hamas moved Israeli hostages directly into combat zones and threatened to publish photos of any captives who were killed. The terror group even released a chilling video of two hostages being driven through Gaza City in a car, a grotesque propaganda stunt designed to paralyze Israel's military and fracture public opinion at home. In effect, the hostages were both a Kevlar vest shielding Hamas VIPs and a human wall designed to slow, deter, and complicate every Israeli advance.

Hamas also leveraged the hostages to force pauses in the fighting precisely when it most needed to regroup. In November 2023, with its fighters reeling, it agreed to a truce that freed 105 hostages in exchange for 240 terrorists. For seven days, Israel halted all military action—granting Hamas a lifeline. In January 2025, another ceasefire brought home thirty living hostages and eight bodies, in exchange for roughly 2,000 imprisoned terrorists. This time, Hamas gained not days, but two full months to rebuild, rearm, and slip fighters back north by hiding them among civilians returning to the area. In October 2025, the final release of the remaining hostages came as President Trump and Prime Minister Netanyahu unveiled their Gaza peace framework. Hamas immediately used the breathing room not only to regroup, but to crush rival factions and reassert its grip over the Strip. Every pause also brought hundreds of truckloads of aid, allowing Hamas to resupply and recover just as it neared collapse. It was a war unlike any other—a prizefight in which only one side could call a time-out whenever it was on the ropes.

The dilemmas Hamas created for Israel were unprecedented. No democracy had ever been forced to confront such a brutal choice: press forward to destroy a genocidal enemy or restrain the offensive to protect your own. For Israel, the hostages were the face of the war; for Hamas, the means to set the pace of the war.

Ultimately, in kidnapping hundreds of Israelis, Hamas sought not merely to abduct individuals but to take the war itself hostage. Every captive became a psychological, political, and strategic weapon. Hamas starved them to the edge of death, filmed their torment, and forced them at gunpoint to perform for the cameras. It then used their suffering to shield its fighters, manipulate Israeli operations, and extract concessions, intermissions, and, ultimately, a ceasefire to preserve its rule.

And still, under battlefield conditions unprecedented in modern warfare, Israel imposed an entirely new layer of intelligence discipline on every maneuver, every strike, every advance. Entire Hamas redoubts had to be bypassed because a single misstep could endanger the very people Israel was fighting to save. It was tactical gymnastics that no military had ever attempted. But Israel was committed to reuniting every single hostage with their families. It would do whatever had to be done.

Despite the impossible constraints and excruciating dilemmas, Israel pushed deeper and harder into enemy territory than any army had ever done in pursuit of its captured citizens. What unfolded over those two years was more than a war. It was the largest, longest, and most complex hostage-rescue mission in the history of mankind—hundreds of thousands of troops, tens of thousands of targets, and a nation fighting with one hand tied behind its back to bring its people home.

The Pressure Cooker Method

Before Israel could shift its full focus toward bringing home every last hostage, it first had to eliminate the existential threats that had made October 7 possible. In the south, Hamas still had battalions capable of storming border communities and kidnapping civilians all over again. In the north, Hezbollah's Radwan forces were positioned for a mirror-image invasion—one that could have produced thousands of new hostages in a single morning. Israel's first order of business therefore was to secure its frontiers, dismantle the terror armies poised for repeat massacres, and ensure that they would never again have a clear path to Israeli towns. Only after neutralizing those threats—breaking Hamas's brigades in Gaza and shattering Hezbollah's forward units in southern Lebanon—was Israel able to focus fully on the relentless work of retrieving the captives already in enemy hands.

By the fall of 2024, Israel had contained the immediate threats and could finally turn its focus toward rescuing the hostages. As October began, the war in Gaza entered its second year, and Israel shifted into a grinding campaign designed to force Hamas to move on the hostage file.

Traditionally, Israeli counterterror units use the "pressure cooker" tactic to corner a high-value terrorist barricaded inside a house or apartment. It involves encircling the target, cutting off every escape route, and tightening the pressure with escalating firepower until the terrorist is psychologically smashed and compelled to surrender—or, if that fails, eliminated with minimal risk to IDF soldiers and innocent bystanders. But now, for the first time in history, this doctrine would not be applied to a single building. The IDF would execute the pressure cooker method across an entire war zone.

Remarkably, the kickoff for this new phase came not from an elite unit or a precision strike, but from a tank team pushing through the ruins of Rafah. On October 16, 2024, IDF ground forces got into a firefight in the Tal as-Sultan neighborhood. Only later did they discover that, among the dead, was Yahya Sinwar himself—the most powerful Hamas leader in Gaza and the chief architect of October 7. His identity was confirmed the next day through dental records. Incredibly, the biggest kill of the war came at the hands of conscript soldiers doing the same grueling work they had been doing for months. At the time, Israel was cutting Hezbollah to pieces in the north. Sinwar's death signaled that the tide was beginning to turn in the south as well.

Israel renewed its offensive in Gaza with a sweeping campaign through the northern towns of Jabalia, Beit Lahiya, and Beit Hanoun. Twice before, the IDF had fought its way through these notorious strongholds. And twice, after Israel withdrew, the areas rose again from the rubble—reconstituting themselves into a threat to the Israeli population centers just across the northern border. Since Israel's last operation there in mid-2024, Hamas had rebuilt with ruthless efficiency: recruiting thousands of new local fighters and booby-trapping virtually every single building.

This new campaign began by clearing northern Gaza of civilians through evacuation orders, allowing Israel to root out the embedded terrorist networks. By mid-October, Prime Minister Benjamin Netanyahu announced that the IDF had reached "the heart of Jabalia" and was dismantling Hamas's entrenched strongholds. Throughout the fighting, Israeli soldiers faced constant hit-and-run attacks from Hamas operatives firing out of bombed-out buildings. On October 20, Colonel Ehsan Daxa, commander of the IDF's 401st Brigade in Jabalia, was killed in combat—the highest-ranking officer to fall in ground fighting since the start of the Gaza war. By early December, thirty-one Israeli soldiers had been killed in this operation alone. In that same period, Israeli forces eliminated 1,750 Hamas fighters and detained another 1,300.

Of those apprehended, 240 were Hamas and Islamic Jihad terrorists who had entrenched themselves inside Kamal Adwan Hospital, yet another medical facility converted into a terror hub. Hospitals were a preferred refuge for Hamas. Shifa Hospital housed command centers, weapons stockpiles, and explosives. Rantisi Hospital served as a headquarters, weapons conduit, and hideout for senior operatives. Both sat atop tunnel networks and both bore signs that Israeli hostages had been held there. The pattern extended across Gaza. The IDF uncovered a tunnel leading to a major weapons plant beside the Jordanian Hospital, an extensive tunnel system beneath Hamad Hospital, and a vast underground complex beneath the Turkish Hospital in the Netzarim corridor.

The months of suffocating military pressure finally forced Hamas to concede—at least, partially. On January 15, 2025, days before President Trump entered office, Hamas agreed to a hostage deal that Israel code-named Operation Wings of Freedom. In the first phase, Hamas released twenty-five living Israeli hostages—mostly women and men over fifty—and five living Thai hostages. Among those released were the young female IDF lookouts kidnapped from their base, whose captivity had become a national trauma. Hamas also handed over the bodies of eight murdered hostages, including Shiri Bibas and her two red-headed babies, Kfir and Ariel—the toddlers whose faces had come to symbolize the war. But even in surrender, Hamas could not resist cruelty.

Every release was staged as a grotesque public spectacle. Hamas forced the hostages onto a platform in Gaza's Palestine Square, commanded them to wave and smile, and handed them a macabre "diploma" certifying their captivity—as if months of starvation, abuse, and terror were something to celebrate. For the dead, Hamas put on an even darker, more depraved parade: the Bibas family arrived in tiny black coffins, displayed beneath a massive poster of Netanyahu—labeled a "Nazi" and depicted with vampire teeth and blood dripping from his mouth. Shiri's coffin didn't even contain her remains. It was a level of sadism that the devil himself could not conceive. When Eli Sharabi, Ohad Ben Ami, and Or Levy were released in early February, the images shocked the world. They were skeletal—sunken cheeks, hollow eyes, bones visible beneath the skin. They looked like Holocaust survivors, a stomach-churning flashback to the Jewish people's deepest national trauma.

The price Israel was forced to pay was a humiliation in itself. To bring its people home, Israel released 1,900 terrorist prisoners—many with blood on their hands. It allowed hundreds of aid trucks into Gaza every day, fully aware that Hamas would siphon off supplies to feed its operatives and fund its operations. And it permitted a mass civilian return to northern Gaza, a region the IDF had just bled to clear, effectively restoring Hamas's human shield.

After the initial exchanges, Netanyahu endorsed an American plan for a broader truce—one that might free the rest of the hostages. Hamas, sensing leverage, stalled, hedged, and postured. Its leaders chose not only to refuse an extension of the ceasefire, but they also violated its terms by rearming. Hamas believed it could outwait Israel, outmaneuver Washington, and survive the pressure. They were mistaken.

On March 18, Israel launched a surprise wave of airstrikes across Gaza, killing senior figures in the Hamas government and political bureau: Issam al-Da'alis, whose position might be described as prime minister of Gaza; Chief of Internal Security Bahjat Abu Sultan; members of the Hamas politburo Salah al-Bardawil and Ismail Barhoum; Undersecretary of the Interior Ministry of the Gaza Strip Mahmoud Abu Watfa; and PIJ spokesman Abu Hamza. The strike decapitated key elements of Hamas's upper command and demonstrated that Israel had significantly upgraded its intelligence capabilities in the Strip.

Almost immediately, Israel began carving a new east-west axis across southern Gaza, which it called the Morag corridor. It was a revival of the IDF strategy of controlling open terrain between population centers rather than holding the cities themselves. This was followed by a thrust into the Netzarim corridor and the controlled demolition of the Turkish Hospital, which had been exposed as a major Hamas operations center. Days later, protests erupted in Gaza—hundreds, perhaps thousands—taking part. Spurred by growing weariness from the war, protesters openly expressed dissatisfaction with Hamas, specifically their theft of humanitarian aid, suppression of the press, and abuse of civilians. In the first month of Israel's new offensive, Hamas was already showing cracks in its armor.

April brought steady, if limited, clearing operations across the zones the IDF already controlled. By mid-month, Rafah was fully encircled, and Israeli airpower was striking Shijaiyah, Khan Yunis, and Gaza City. At the same time, Israel shifted part of its pressure campaign toward one of Hamas's most vulnerable points: its wallet. By March, salary payments to Gaza's government employees were already drying up, and many senior Hamas fighters and political operatives were receiving barely half their wages. In early April, Israel assassinated Saeed Ahmad Abed Khudari, described by the IDF as "a key terror-financing facilitator within Hamas." On April 15, Israel eliminated Yahya Fathi Abd al-Qader Abu Shaar, Hamas's chief weapons-smuggling officer. At the same time, Israel began restricting the flow of humanitarian goods into Gaza—supplies that Hamas had been seizing and reselling to refill its coffers—and started crafting a new system for distributing aid directly to civilians. Hamas was bleeding leaders, land, and cash. With every strike and terror chief removed from command, the day of the hostages' release moved closer. By late Spring, Israel was ready for its next big move.

On May 16, Israel launched Operation Gideon's Chariots, one of the largest IDF maneuvers of the entire war. The name came from the biblical warrior Gideon—the man who routed an implacable enemy through strength, faith, and courage. The IDF intended to do the same. The offensive was a three-front assault: air, sea, and ground, with up to five divisions driving into northern and southern Gaza simultaneously.

Gideon's Chariots marked Israel's shift toward waging a new kind of war. Throughout 2024, the Biden administration had held back Israel's operations, diverted military bandwidth, and created new political headaches. Biden had forced Israel to divert forces to secure the failed floating pier in central Gaza and held up weapons shipments in an effort to pressure Jerusalem into abandoning its assault on Rafah, where Hamas's main battalions were still entrenched. At the same time, large portions of the IDF had been tied down in the north, facing Hezbollah. With Hezbollah crushed and Trump driving US policy, the gloves could finally come off.

Israel would no longer raid and withdraw. It would no longer be constrained from holding the ground it had taken. Wherever the IDF went now, it intended to stay. This was not a return to the old pattern of dismantling Hamas positions only to leave a vacuum behind. Israel was now aiming for full command over Gaza. Defense Minister Israel Katz put the mission in blunt, military terms: conquer, clear, and hold. Under the leadership of the new Chief of Staff Eyal Zamir, the IDF advanced more slowly, deliberately, and methodically. The goal was twofold: to save lives and to ensure that every area seized was cleared deeply and thoroughly enough to be brought under sustained Israeli control.

Moreover, aid would now be distributed under Israeli and American oversight—not through Hamas's extortion machine. Working with the American Gaza Humanitarian Foundation, the IDF brought in more than ten thousand aid trucks over the course of the operation and established designated distribution sites that provided over 2.2 million food packages a week to families in need. At long last, Israel was cutting Hamas off from the humanitarian supplies it had looted for years to finance its war effort.

The offensive started strong. A week before ground troops advanced, a massive wave of airstrikes pounded Gaza City. Days later, on May 13, the IDF eliminated Mohammed Sinwar—Yahya Sinwar's brother and Hamas's new leader in the Strip—along with senior Hamas commander Muhammad Shabana, head of the Rafah Brigade, and Mahdi Quara, commander of the South Khan Yunis Battalion. All three were hiding in the underground chambers beneath the European Hospital in Khan Yunis. Their deaths exposed the depth of Israel's intelligence penetration into Hamas. And they showed that no tunnel was deep enough to shield Hamas's senior command.

With the launch of the ground campaign, Israel advanced under a canopy of overwhelming airpower, clearing buildings from a distance, rooting out IEDs, collapsing tunnels, and grinding down Hamas strongholds block by block. But it wasn't just bullets and bombs that shaped the battlefield. Humanitarian aid itself became a front in the war. When the new US-Israeli aid system finally rolled out, Hamas immediately recognized it as an existential threat. For years, aid had been its lifeline—a pipeline it looted to feed its fighters, fund its officers, and control Gaza's population. The Gaza Humanitarian Foundation (GHF), backed by both Washington and Jerusalem, severed that artery and drained Hamas's coffers. Hamas responded with pure terror.

In early June, GHF was forced to temporarily suspend its operations after chaos erupted near its Tel al-Sultan distribution sites in Rafah. Though the zones were fully fenced, secured by US contractors, and patrolled by the IDF, large crowds were deliberately pushed toward the aid centers by Hamas, which then opened fire near civilians to scare them away from the new system. The IDF released drone footage showing Hamas terrorists shooting at Gazans near the aid lines before the chaos—directly contradicting media claims that it was Israeli forces who were responsible for the mayhem. At the same time, Hamas began flooding the global media with fantastically inflated casualty figures, desperate to delegitimize the new aid mechanism before it could take root. Of course, the UN, Oxfam, and Human Rights Watch immediately jumped on the opportunity to disempower Israel and keep the UN-sponsored scam alive.

Ultimately, any reduction in Hamas's control over food and water was a blow to its rule—and Hamas fought it with its trademark brutality. On June 11, Hamas terrorists escalated further, ambushing a GHF bus near Khan Yunis, murdering at least eight local staffers. On July 5, GHF announced that two more US aid workers were injured after two Hamas terrorists threw grenades at its aid center in Khan Yunis. Days later, twenty were killed in a stampede at another aid site, with GHF claiming that Hamas affiliates had "deliberately fomented the unrest."

Even as the IDF secured the massive aid network that Hamas kept trying to hijack, it continued to push forward. By early July, Israeli forces had encircled Beit Hanoun. Elsewhere, they began advancing into areas untouched since the start of the war—territory comprising nearly half the Strip, where Hamas had retained uninterrupted control. On July 20, Israel issued new evacuation orders for Deir al-Balah, and the IDF pushed into its outskirts the next day. Israeli forces also established the "Morag" Corridor, severing Hamas's Rafah and Khan Yunis Brigades, and the "Magen Oz" Corridor, bisecting the Khan Yunis Brigade from east to west. With each move, Israel telegraphed a sharp message to Hamas: every delay at the negotiating table would be paid for not only in blood, but in land.

By the end of the first phase of Gideon's Chariots in early August, forty-eight Israeli soldiers had been killed in the operation, almost all from the booby-traps, IEDs, and ambushes. But Israel achieved operational control of approximately 75 percent of the Strip's territory—more than it had at any point in the war. The IDF also killed 2,100 terrorists, dozens of whom had infiltrated Israel during the October 7 attacks, and it had systematically dismantled sixteen thousand terrorist infrastructure targets, including approximately 30 kilometers of underground tunnels. The last Hamas fighters in Beit Hanoun surrendered. Every inch of land that Israel squeezed out of Hamas's hands squeezed its remaining network tighter. But one line remained: the IDF did not push into known hostage zones.

Besides losing terrorists, cash, and land, Hamas was also losing its grip over its own subjects. Within the first weeks of the operation, open opposition began to surface across Gaza. By late May, the Abu Shabab clan announced the formation of a new militia—the "Popular

Forces"—declaring itself openly against Hamas. A population once terrified into silence had begun to sense that Hamas was losing the war. Hamas could no longer enforce its decrees or project authority as it once had. It was shrinking back into the tunnels that had long been its refuge but had now become its cage.

On August 20, Israel initiated the second phase: Gideon's Chariots II. This time, the target was the heart: five IDF divisions would storm Gaza City, Hamas's capital and foremost fortress. The Israeli security cabinet voted to occupy the city outright. Israel called up 60,000 reservists, a figure that would quickly surge to 130,000. That same day, Israel announced it had assassinated Muhammad Abd al-Aziz Abu Zubaida, head of ISIS's Palestine District, who directed the group's strategic activities across Judea and Samaria, Gaza, and the Sinai Peninsula.

Within days, Israel began escalating its threats while dialing up the pressure. Defense Minister Israel Katz warned that Gaza City could "turn into Rafah and Beit Hanoun." He went on, "The gates of hell will soon open on the heads of Hamas's murderers and rapists in Gaza—until they agree to Israel's conditions for ending the war." Airstrikes rolled across Hamas strongpoints throughout the city, and Israeli ground forces pushed into the Zeitoun and Sheikh Radwan neighborhoods—securing roughly 40 percent of Gaza City. Then, on August 31, Israel achieved one of its most significant assassinations of the war. Abu Obeida—the keffiyeh-clad, red-masked spokesman of Hamas's armed wing—was killed in an aerial strike in Gaza City. He was one of the last senior commanders still holding the position he held on October 7, and had become an icon for Hamas supporters across the Middle East. Fittingly, he died in a dental clinic; witnesses described hundreds of thousands of dollars in cash fluttering into the air as the building was hit.

On September 9, Israel ordered the full evacuation of the remaining sectors of Gaza City. To prepare, new humanitarian areas were established in Khan Yunis, with an additional twenty thousand family-sized tents erected and three hundred food trucks entering daily. By September 15, armored and infantry divisions surged inward, seizing key positions around Hamas's last major stronghold. By September 23, the IDF had encircled Gaza City completely. Days later, with Hamas still refusing to agree to terms, the IDF announced that eight hundred thousand civilians had evacuated to designated humanitarian zones and that it was beginning the "decisive phase" of the operation. "Hamas is currently in a state of confusion," a military source said at the time. "It doesn't know where the IDF is striking from and has no clear sense of the scale of forces we're using against them."

Meanwhile, the IDF reinforced its combat forces on land, at sea, and in the air, placing dozens of battalions on high alert throughout the High Holidays. This was the moment of maximum pressure—the point at which Hamas could feel the walls closing in. Its leadership now understood that Israel would not stop: not until the hostages were home, or Hamas was destroyed. For the first time since October 7, Hamas was truly ready for a deal—one that no longer demanded preserving its military grip on Gaza.

Throughout, the Trump administration stood firmly behind Israel's offensive. Even when major Western allies of the United States—France, the UK, and Canada—used the UN General Assembly in September 2025 to announce formal recognition of a "Palestinian State" that, in reality, did not exist in any functional sense, the administration did not budge. While others rushed to score diplomatic points or signal virtue, Trump held the line. He made it clear that Israel had the full backing of the United States to continue its campaign until Hamas broke. He would not cave to calls for premature ceasefires, he would not embrace artificial timelines, and he would not be swayed by the political posturing that would reward October 7 and rescue a terrorist regime. For the first time in decades, Israel had an American administration that matched its resolve, instead of tempering it.

With Washington holding firm and Israel operating at maximum pressure, the IDF began achieving its objectives sooner than expected. On September 29—just over a month into the Gaza City conquest—President Trump unveiled a comprehensive twenty-point peace plan. Its core demands were clear: the release of all hostages, a staged Israeli withdrawal, Hamas's disarmament, and a formal end to the war. On October 4, after Trump publicly called on Israel to cease its attacks, the Israeli government ordered the IDF to halt its campaign to conquer Gaza City and shift into a strictly defensive posture. The battlefield momentum, coupled with American political leverage, had brought Israel and Hamas to the edge of a final deal.

The largest hostage-rescue mission in human history had accomplished its purpose. After two years of unrelenting war, Israel had carved Gaza into isolated compartments, crushed Hamas's brigades, pulverized its command structure, and even ignited open revolt among the very population it claimed to rule. The territory it once ruled with an iron fist had collapsed into pockets of resistance with no air, no cash, no command, and no choice but to let Israel's people go.

The Peacemaker

From the moment Donald Trump was reelected, the atmosphere inside Hamas's bunkers shifted. Confidence gave way to fear; defiance gave way to calculation. Days before he returned to the White House, Hamas agreed to a ceasefire that included the release of dozens of hostages. Months later, on the eve of Trump's arrival in the Middle East, Hamas abruptly and unanimously freed another hostage—Israeli American citizen Eden Alexander—calling it a "gesture of goodwill." It was nothing of the sort. Hamas was trying to get on Trump's good side because it understood exactly what the alternative would be. Whereas President Biden had tried to tame Hamas through diplomacy, President Trump sought to tame it through fear. And with Hamas, fear—not persuasion—was the only language that ever worked.

Over more than a year, Hamas rejected every major deal the Biden administration put forward—even though those proposals were relatively generous to them. Biden's plans would have allowed Hamas to stagger hostage releases in tiny batches, stretching the process out for months. That, in turn, would have given Hamas time to siphon off humanitarian aid, rebuild its military networks, and subject the Israeli public to prolonged psychological torture, all while retaining enough hostages to extract further concessions. Yet Hamas still refused. Its leaders clung to two uncompromising red lines: Israel must fully withdraw from Gaza, and Hamas must be allowed to preserve its military capabilities. In other words, Hamas demanded a return to the status quo of "October 6"—armed to the teeth, dug into the Strip, and positioned to launch the next October 7. No responsible Israeli government could accept terms so reckless, so delusional, and so lethal to its own people.

Hamas also rejected Biden's deals because it grasped the core premise behind his approach: Biden believed the road to ending the war ran through strong-arming Israel rather than breaking Hamas. Seeing that Biden's instinct was to lean on Jerusalem, and not the terrorists who started the war, Hamas calculated it could hold out longer and demand more.

Moreover, the pressure that Biden put on Israel was not confined to negotiations, nor did it emerge only after months of fighting. Immediately after October 7—despite the massacres, the incinerations, the rapes, the executions—Biden urged Israel not to launch a ground invasion of Gaza. He pushed instead for "surgical raids" and a limited counterterrorism campaign, the very formula that had allowed Hamas to metastasize into the monster that butchered Israel's communities. Israel's war cabinet rejected the plan outright. It was a fantasy so dangerously detached from reality that following it would have removed all deterrence to future terror and driven Israel toward national suicide.

And as the war dragged on, Biden began to hold up and delay the very weapons shipments Israel needed to survive. Bulldozers used to clear roads of IEDs, attack helicopters used for infantry support, and bunker-buster bombs used to reach deeply embedded command centers—Washington blocked all of it. Biden's national security advisor, Jake Sullivan, later admitted the reason: the administration wanted to "prevent the war from strengthening Israel's right wing." While Israelis fought for their lives, the White House was embroiled in a domestic political battle against Netanyahu. As Pulitzer Prize–winning commentator Paul Gigot put it, "The U.S. should be putting pressure on Hamas to surrender and release the hostages. The more Hamas thinks it might be saved by U.S. pressure on Israel, the less likely Hamas is to agree to a cease-fire." Ultimately, Hamas concluded exactly what any rational actor would: America and the world were gradually turning against the Jewish state. Time was on their side—all they needed to do was wait out the storm.

Then Trump returned to the scene. The restoration of the Trump administration was, for Hamas, a whiplash moment. Trump's view of diplomacy was never subtle. It was not built on illusions of mutual understanding or international goodwill. To him, diplomacy was made of leverage, intimidation, and credible threats. Treaties didn't hold because countries loved each other. They held because someone feared the consequences of breaking them. In that kind of diplomacy, Hamas would be hopelessly outclassed.

Trump restored the moral clarity that had vanished under Biden. Biden wanted a deal just as much as Trump did—perhaps even more—but he approached it backward: pressuring Israel to make the concessions that should have been demanded of Hamas. Trump understood what Biden seemed to miss: there were not "two sides" in this conflict. Hamas had started the war. Hamas had slaughtered and kidnapped babies and grandmothers. Hamas had built its command centers in schools and hospitals. The democratic and faithful American ally was not the problem. The barbaric terrorist death cult was.

Overnight, American weapons began flowing into Israel again. Jerusalem was given full backing to launch a full-scale offensive in Gaza. Biden's "drip-by-drip" approach to hostage releases was tossed out. Trump made it clear: hostages would be released at once and immediately. The idea of releasing hostages in humiliating, weeks-long cycles was no longer negotiable; human beings would never again be exploited to conduct a slow-bleeding pressure campaign against Israel. Trump also insisted that there would be no degrading "ceremonies," no public parading of hostages on stages, no Hamas propaganda stunts in Palestine Square. Whereas Biden's drip-feed hostage strategy kept Hamas alive, Trump's shock-release doctrine would kill its leverage on day one.

The difference between Trump and Biden was nowhere clearer than in their approach to the mastermind behind the never-ending negotiations: Qatar. Qatar was a state that openly backed terror while posing as a friendly mediator—and it played both sides with masterful cynicism. For years, it bankrolled Hamas, hosted its political bureau, lodged Khaled Mashal and the entire senior leadership in five-star luxury, and broadcast anti-Western propaganda on Al Jazeera, all while pretending to be an indispensable American partner. Early in the war, the Biden administration politely asked Qatar to consider evicting Hamas. Qatar politely declined.

Biden, in turn, rewarded Doha's defiance by renewing a ten-year extension of America's massive airbase on Qatari soil—the very asset that keeps the emirate's regime secure and untouchable. Under Trump, the approach would be different.

On September 9, Israel struck a Hamas stronghold in Doha, the very place where Hamas's senior leadership had taken refuge under Qatari protection. The strike hit the residential compound housing top Hamas officials. It missed the leadership itself, but it landed close enough to send a message: You are not safe—not under Qatari patronage, not beneath the roof of an American ally, not even steps away from the negotiating table. Publicly, Trump denied any knowledge of the strike, criticized it, and later asked Israel to apologize to Qatar for the death of a Qatari official. But it remains overwhelmingly unlikely that Netanyahu would have ordered a strike on Qatari soil without at least some tacit understanding with Washington. Nor would it have been the first time Qatar, however perfidious, was pressed by Washington to "take one for the team," absorbing a calibrated blow in service of a larger American diplomatic objective. Just months earlier, Iranian missiles had struck Qatari territory on the eve of a Trump-brokered ceasefire between Israel and Iran—an episode widely interpreted in regional capitals as a controlled escalation, tolerated if not quietly choreographed, to give Tehran a face-saving outlet while clearing the path for a broader agreement.

But far more important than the plausible intrigue were the irrefutable results. Within a month of the Doha strike, Hamas agreed to a deal to release all the hostages at once—without an Israeli withdrawal from Gaza. As commentator Elliot Kaufman observed, the strike in Doha "seemed to have got the ball rolling." Suddenly, Hamas displayed a level of flexibility in negotiations that had been absent for two years. And for anyone who wondered whether Qatar had always possessed the leverage to pressure Hamas—but simply chose not to—the speed of Hamas's capitulation appeared to answer the question.

In the weeks leading up to the deal, Trump issued blunt warnings that left Hamas with little doubt about its predicament. "They won't give up the last twenty hostages," he said, "because they know that will be the end of Hamas." And if Hamas rejected the deal, Trump vowed that Israel would receive "full backing" to pursue its "rapid annihilation." It was a classic Hobbesian choice: surrender and die slowly, or refuse and die quickly. Either way, for Hamas, the end was closing in.

On September 30, Trump's proposal was formally delivered to Hamas. It had been drafted by former UK Prime Minister Tony Blair, Trump's son-in-law Jared Kushner, and Trump's chief negotiator Steve Witkoff. Hamas was warned it had "three or four days" to respond. On October 3, Trump set a public deadline: October 5 at 6 p.m. Washington time. Accept the deal, he said, or face "all hell." Hours later, Hamas announced it would release all Israeli hostages—the living and the dead—and begin negotiations based on Trump's plan. The war that had consumed the Middle East for two years seemed to be entering its final act.

Netanyahu immediately halted the assault on Gaza City. Delegations from Israel and Hamas flew to Sharm el-Sheikh for indirect talks overseen by Kushner and Witkoff. The mediators—Egyptians, Qataris, Turks, and Americans—sat Hamas down and delivered the final ultimatum: accept Trump's plan or face endless war. By then, IDF divisions had fully surrounded Gaza City. Military analyst Steve Ganyard put it bluntly: "Hamas had no choice."

On October 8, while at a White House gathering of conservative media influencers, Trump received a handwritten note from Secretary of State Marco Rubio instructing him to "approve a Truth Social post soon so you can announce the deal first." Five days later, Hamas released the final twenty living hostages. Their release was timed to coincide with Trump's arrival on the tarmac in Tel Aviv, with news channels broadcasting the two events in split screen. Trump addressed the Knesset for the first time in his presidency.

Meanwhile, Israel released nearly 2,000 terrorist prisoners, including 250 serving life sentences for murder. Of those, 154 were deported to Egypt because they were deemed too dangerous to enter either Judea and Samaria or Gaza. Days later, they were photographed lounging poolside at a five-star resort. Israel redeployed its forces, pulling back from the heart of Gaza City while maintaining control over roughly half the Strip—including every border. US troops began arriving to help enforce the ceasefire. Six hundred aid trucks poured into Gaza with food, medicine, tents, and fuel. But one question hovered above everything: How had Hamas agreed to such a deal—releasing every last hostage while Israel still controlled half the Strip?

There are the obvious explanations: Hamas's key allies—and much of the Arab world—had rallied around the deal, and Israel was poised to deliver the final blow. But the deeper reason is more chilling, and it has less to do with Israel's strength than with the world's weakness. Hamas had learned it could rely on international pressure to restrain Israel more reliably than the hostages could. In Hamas's mind, the hostages had become the reason Israel had been able to wage a full-scale war that the world would otherwise never have tolerated. Once the hostages were returned, Hamas calculated, Israel would lose the legitimacy for any future ground campaign, and international pressure would snap back into place like a steel trap. Any new Israeli operation—no matter how justified—would be crushed by global outrage before it began.

Hamas also felt comfortable entering the new arrangement in which an international hodgepodge of forces would combine with a technocratic governing body to "manage" Gaza. This was precisely the kind of vague, undefined political structure that Hamas knew it could subvert with ease. Whatever postwar stabilization force emerged—so long as it did not include Israel—Hamas understood it would never dare confront them directly. Regardless of who "governed" Gaza on paper, Hamas would rule from the shadows. As Elliot Kaufman noted, this was exactly what Hezbollah had done in Lebanon for decades. A dysfunctional and factionalized Lebanese government existed—but only in a technical sense. Hezbollah fielded the most potent armed force in the country. They were the true "power behind the throne."

The early days of the hostage deal seemed to confirm the fact that Hamas never intended to disarm. The terror group began a wave of internal purges, executions, and crackdowns across Gaza. Far from dissolving its power, Hamas was consolidating it. Still, the ceasefire largely held—despite Hamas violating it within the first few weeks, killing three IDF soldiers. Its psychological warfare continued as well. Hamas delayed returning the bodies of the dead; on one occasion, it handed the Red Cross not a body at all, but fragments of one which Israel had already recovered a year earlier. Israeli drones watched as Hamas fighters reburied remains, staged a "discovery," and presented the spectacle as compliance. Hamas's grotesque theater persisted—but for the most part, the guns fell silent.

And in the silence, something even more troubling emerged: in Gaza, Hamas's popularity rose. A poll by the Palestinian Center for Policy and Survey Research found that 51 percent of Gazans supported Hamas's performance in the war, up from 39 percent the previous year. Fifty-three percent said October 7 had been "the right decision." Khalil Shikaki, the center's director, put it plainly: "Hamas isn't going to disappear tomorrow. We have to live with that." Two years of war gave way to an uneasy quiet. But the enemy did not melt away. Hamas went underground—politically and literally—biding its time, waiting until the next opportunity to strike.

And Israel—triumphant yet forever scarred—stepped into the uncertain dawn of the postwar era with one unshakable truth: the strength that brought the hostages home would forever be the price of survival.

The Good and the Evil

When the hostages were finally released, Israel experienced a wave of joy. But as with every prior hostage deal, that joy collided head-on with the horror of what the hostages had endured.

For those kidnapped into Gaza, the trauma was as immediate as it was merciless. All of those who were abducted had themselves endured the worst of the October 7 massacre. They bore witness to death squads tearing through communities and kibbutzim of Southern Israel. Many were torn away from the corpses of their loved ones. Some were kidnapped with open gunshot wounds, shrapnel injuries, severe burns, or bone fractures. And then came the gauntlet into Gaza, where "ordinary civilians" cheered the Hamas terrorists as they paraded their human spoils in a gruesome spectacle of unprecedented horror. Bound and wounded, captives were spit on, pelted with stones, and struck by the seething crowds. One team of medical debriefers described the entry into Gaza on October 7 as "akin to repeated lynchings occurring throughout the day."

The moment the captives crossed the border, Israel understood that they were locked in something worse than captivity. It was a laboratory of the most demonic cruelty—a satanic system engineered to break a human soul. But it was only after they returned that Israelis came to comprehend the scale of the nightmare. The first stomach-churning reports came from doctors and nurses, and later, in the harrowing testimony of the hostages themselves.

Doctors accustomed to battlefield injuries were shocked to see the returning captives, who looked as though they were walking right off the pages of Jewish history's darkest chapters. Children, the elderly, kidnapped festivalgoers, and young soldiers alike—all arrived severely malnourished and dehydrated. Others were skeletal, their skin dimmed from malnutrition. Some were unable to stand; others were shaking uncontrollably and struggled to breathe. Many had lost 10 to 15 percent of their body weight in weeks. Some—held for longer—had lost up to 40 percent. Several suffered from scurvy-like symptoms: bleeding gums, swollen joints, and muscle tissue bleeding beneath the skin. One man, waiting to embrace his brother, later said that nothing could have prepared him for what he saw: "I didn't see a hostage. I saw a Holocaust survivor."

Hostages received one meal a day, sometimes none. A "meal" was a pita or a handful of rice. It was usually moldy or riddled with worms and insects. Water came from contaminated jugs—often seawater or sewage, always insufficient. By early 2025, Israeli intelligence concluded that Yahya Sinwar himself had ordered the deliberate starvation of male hostages. Their bodies told the story. Emaciated. Lice-infested. Rashes blooming across their limbs. Vitamin levels were so depleted that their bones became brittle.

The Israeli Ministry of Health's report could barely contain its own horror. It spoke of "harrowing patterns of abuse," "subhuman conditions," and "violations constituting torture and grave breaches of international humanitarian law." In other words, evil in its purest form.

Hostages were crammed into tiny, airless spaces, bound so tightly they often could not move for days. Many spent months underground, denied sunlight entirely and forced to endure weeks of searing heat or bitter cold as the seasons changed. They slept on hard floors, without mattresses or blankets, surrounded by insects and pests. The only toilet was a pit latrine that contaminated their very living space. Though they were confined in filth, showers were allowed "every few months," if at all. Underwear was replaced once every half a year.

Recurrent infections were constant—intestinal, respiratory, skin borne—and never treated. Antibiotics were withheld even when fevers climbed to dangerous levels. Chronic illnesses were ignored. Injuries festered untreated. One hostage fainted while attempting to treat his own wound. Another was given a medication so inappropriate for his condition that it nearly killed him. Some drank so little that they entered states of delirium, hallucinating voices and lights inside the pitch-black tunnels.

Transfers between captivity sites echoed the death marches of the Holocaust. Hostages were shoved out of their cells and forced to walk for kilometers at night. Blindfolded and barefoot, they would be marched through tunnels—stumbling in the dark, beaten when they fell behind, and threatened with death at every turn.

If their bodies revealed one form of torture, their minds revealed another. Many hostages had spent weeks in total darkness, a form of sensory deprivation known to induce hallucinations and psychotic breaks. At least two were kept in total solitary confinement for over a year. Meanwhile, captors did all they could to amplify the terror, issuing a hail of threats, statements meant to fuel despair: "No one loves you," "No one is waiting for you," "Your family has forgotten you." Captors also conducted mock executions, with several survivors describing terrorists pulling grenade pins and counting down before stopping at the last second.

The effects were especially devastating for the children taken hostage. Prof. Itai Pessach, head of the Safra Children's Hospital at Sheba Medical Center, oversaw the treatment of many of them. He said the survivors' stories "shook" even his most seasoned staff—professionals with years of experience treating severe trauma. He compared the children's accounts to those of Jews emerging from the ghettos and camps of the Holocaust, noting that "they experienced every kind of abuse you can imagine." His observations were echoed by Dr. Yael Mozer-Glassberg of Schneider Children's Medical Center, where nineteen children and seven women were brought after their release. The patterns were unmistakable: deliberate isolation, engineered sleep deprivation, relentless intimidation, and constant emotional assault—all designed to destroy not only their sense of safety, but their sense of self. Mozer-Glassberg described one of the most chilling symptoms: "A lot of the kids had a distorted sense of time. They didn't know how long they had been in Gaza and when we said they would stay with us in the hospital for four to five days, they confused that with a month." She would add, "We teach our kids that monsters aren't real, but they are."

Even once home, the terror lingered. Children refused to sleep, convinced that if they drifted off, they would wake up back in Gaza. Others suffered dissociative episodes: one moment aware they knew they were in Israel, but the next, certain they were still underground with terrorists standing over them. Many showed classic signs of PTSD: flashbacks, nightmares, intrusive images, avoidance of anything reminiscent of captivity—certain foods, large crowds, solitude, or darkness. Survivors claimed to have difficulty concentrating, memory lapses, confusion, and trouble making simple decisions.

Some survivors said they no longer felt like themselves. They experienced a fracture in their personalities, feeling increased suspicion toward their surroundings and emotional detachment toward relatives and loved ones. Normal sleep patterns became a challenge—insomnia, frequent awakenings, and recurring traumatic dreams. This, in turn, brought chronic fatigue, mood swings, emotional dysregulation, and unpredictable outbursts.

There was also a profound and pervasive sense of survivor's guilt—guilt for having lived while friends and family were murdered, or for being released while others remained in captivity. Many felt shame over the choices they made while in captivity, haunted by the thought that they "could have done more." This anguish was compounded by the fact that many returnees first learned of the deaths of loved ones only after their release. They were forced to confront shattering news at the very moment they were reentering the world.

As if the psychological torment was not enough, Hamas also deployed chemical control. Doctors reported that many hostages—especially children—were forcibly drugged with ketamine or benzodiazepines. In the final days before their release, Hamas increased the dosages to make them appear "calm" and "content" for the cameras. It was propaganda lacquered over torture, a performance coerced through pharmacology.

As the hostages returned home, their testimonies surfaced in layers: first the hunger, then the isolation, the neglect, and the violence. But with time, the most horrifying details emerged—the systematic sexual assault, wielded as a weapon of domination and humiliation.

One female hostage was chained with an iron ankle cuff for three weeks and repeatedly sexually assaulted at gunpoint. Another was forced into a child's bedroom and made to perform sexual acts under threat of execution. A third woman was groped so violently and terrifyingly that she lost consciousness. When she awoke, her shirt had been lifted, her pants pulled down, and seven terrorists were standing over her.

After the first hostage release in November 2023, one doctor assessed that "many" of the freed Israeli female hostages—roughly thirty women and girls between the ages of twelve and forty-eight—had been sexually assaulted while held by Hamas in Gaza. Another report reviewing the testimonies of fifteen former hostages, some as young as twelve, described women being threatened with rape framed as "forced marriage." Nearly all reported verbal sexual harassment, and many described physical sexual assault.

Male hostages were not spared. Several testified to being stripped, tied, taunted, and assaulted. One described being beaten, starved, and violated in ways he struggled to put into words. "They stripped me of all my clothes, my underwear, everything. They tied me up from the . . ." He could not even finish his sentence. "You just pray to God for it to stop," he said later, "And while I was there—every day, every beating—I'd say to myself, 'I survived another day in hell. Tomorrow morning, I'll wake up to another hell. And another hell. And another hell."

Another hostage recounted being tied to a chair, blindfolded, touched, then dragged to the ground while his captor unbuckled his pants. "Are you crazy?" he asked the terrorist. "You're a Muslim—this is forbidden." The captor ignored him. "I didn't know how to deal with that situation," he said. "I felt him rubbing himself on my back . . . I froze."

None of this was incidental depravity. None of it was the chaos of war or the cruelty of a few. This was Hamas's diabolical policy—deliberate, sanctioned, and systematized. The exploitation of the bodies of men, women, and children—and the devastation of their souls—was not a by-product of their terrorist mission. It was the mission.

And yet—amid the hell—the hostages fought to remain human. Some struggled to keep their minds alive. Guy Gilboa-Dalal recalled trying to learn Arabic, recite the Quran, and understand his captors, saying his purpose was simply "to absorb as much information as possible and keep my mind running." Avinatan Or, an engineer, counted steps, mapped tunnel layouts, and fashioned makeshift lamps from broken wires. Others found ways to embrace faith. Omer Shem Tov began to keep the Sabbath in captivity. He found a bottle of grape juice and made the Sabbath sanctification prayer over it every week for six months. Later, a guard brought him a booklet of Jewish teachings left by an IDF soldier. In it, he found a verse that became a lifeline in the darkness: "I am God. I will free you from the oppression of the Egyptians, rescue you from their servitude, and redeem you with an outstretched arm . . ."

The hostages revealed something else, too—something that cut against the national myth that the Jewish people's modern generations were softer than those who survived the furnaces of Europe and the massacres of the Middle East. These young men and women proved the opposite. In the tunnels of Gaza, in the darkness and starvation and terror, they summoned an inner strength few knew still existed. They displayed reserves of courage that matched the bravery of the great Jewish forebears who survived expulsions, pogroms, and the Holocaust. Even in 2025, the Jewish people were still producing men and women worthy of the greatest heroes of their history.

Though it was the hostages themselves who endured the unspeakable evils of captivity, they were never the terrorists' sole targets. Their abduction was designed to break Israel itself. Throughout the war, the hostages became Hamas's cruelest weapon—instruments of propaganda and leverage in a conflict fought as much in the mind as in the streets of Gaza. Hamas and their helpers sought to fracture Israel from within: to corrode trust between its citizens and leaders, and to make Israelis question whether their own government had betrayed its most sacred mandate—the duty to protect its own people.

The hostage videos revealed this intent in its truest and cruelest form. Every frame—each depicting captives starved, wounded, and dragged before a camera—was a surgical strike against Israel's psyche, a psychological projectile aimed at morale, unity, and national resolve.

The earliest footage was already grotesque. Hamas terrorists rocked kidnapped babies as if posing for a family portrait, pushed toddlers in strollers, handed trembling children cups of water—tormenting Israelis with the knowledge that their most defenseless were being manhandled by the most brutal men on earth. Weeks later, Hamas released another video of three young women, one of whom was coerced into accusing Netanyahu of failing to protect Israel on October 7. In April 2024, they forced Hersh Goldberg-Polin—his arm amputated and his face gaunt—to accuse his own country of abandoning him. That same month, two more hostages were filmed asking their families to continue pressuring the Israeli government to cut a deal with Hamas.

By the second hostage release in the spring of 2025, the videos became even more manipulative. In January 2025, shortly before the second hostage release, they released a video of a nineteen-year-old female hostage telling the Israeli public, "The world is starting to forget about us. No one cares about us. We're living in a nightmare." Another video showed brothers Iair and Eitan Horn locked in an embrace. Iair was on the release list; Eitan was not. "This is not logical in any way," Eitan said, choking back tears. "Sign the second and third phase. Enough of war." The script literally weaponized brotherly love. Another clip showed hostages Evyatar David and Guy Gilboa-Dalal being compelled to watch other captives walk toward freedom while they remained in the hands of Hamas.

Throughout 2025, Hamas continued to cross every threshold of depravity. In May 2025, they released a video showing two hostages applying pressure on others who had been freed to speak up more on their behalf. And then, in August 2025, they released the horrific footage of twenty-four-year-old Evyatar David, whose bones were showing through his skin, marking the passage of days onto a tunnel wall and digging his own grave.

"Psychological warfare" is far too tame a description to accurately describe the satanic practices of Hamas. This was evil in its purest, most concentrated form—filmed in high definition and broadcast for global consumption. That so many could watch this and remain silent will forever stain the conscience of the world.

One thing is sure: No one will be able to say they didn't know.

In the end, Israel had fought for its sons and daughters in captivity with a combination of courage, creativity, and restraint unprecedented in the history of warfare. Hamas had constructed a factory of agony—a system engineered not merely to kill Jews, but to shatter their spirit and humiliate them before the world. The hostages bore the full weight of that malice. Their scars—physical, psychological, and spiritual—will mark a generation.

Their stories tear away every illusion, every excuse, every cynical moral equivocation ever laid upon this war. And they stand as the litmus test of the modern age, dividing humanity into those who choose to stand for good—and those who are evil.

In the end, as Israel fought an unprecedented seven-front war against genocidal forces converging from every direction, it demonstrated that "Never Again" was never meant as a consoling slogan for the aftermath of catastrophe. It was a binding oath. An oath that Jewish life would never again be treated as expendable, never again be abandoned to the mercy of murderers, never again be reduced to a footnote in the conscience of the world. "Never Again" meant that the Jewish people would no longer wait helplessly for rescue that never came, or entrust their survival to the goodwill of others. It meant that Jews would defend themselves, pursue their enemies, and impose consequences on those who sought their destruction. It meant that the age in which Jews could be hunted like animals—unseen, unprotected, and unavenged—had ended.

In standing its ground, striking back across borders, and dismantling the machinery of annihilation aimed at its people, Israel affirmed that Jewish history had crossed an irreversible threshold. The promise of "Never Again" was no longer a plea to the world. It was a reality enforced by Jewish power, Jewish resolve, and a sovereign Jewish state prepared to fight—alone if necessary—for the right of its people to live.

AFTERWORD

THE BLESSING OF THE EIGHTH DECADE

There are moments in a nation's life when an entire people feels its past and future collide in a single, blinding instant. A collective near-death experience.

For Israel, that moment came in the aftermath of October 7.

Since its founding in 1948, the State of Israel has endured wars, intifadas, and devastating waves of terror. But what began on October 7 was not another turn of a tragically familiar cycle. It was an existential breach, an assault on the most basic promise of sovereignty: the sanctity of the border and the security of the home. And it posed the deeper, more terrifying question of whether Israel was truly what it claimed to be—a sovereign state, a permanent and everlasting nation. The old taunt resurfaced: that Israel was a historical deviation, a temporary aberration, an ephemeral post-Holocaust construct, a "spider's web" that could be torn apart with sufficient force. For a fleeting but searing moment, even Israelis felt the tremor of that accusation. The attack bore down on something larger than Israel alone. For Jews beyond its borders, it felt as though the clocks of exile had begun to tick again. The ancient entropic force that stalked us across continents and cut us down for centuries seemed suddenly present. The old story of Jewish vulnerability, which sovereignty was meant to end, appeared to be knocking once more at the door.

But with time, Israel proved the opposite was true. As the motto of the Purim holiday declares, *Ve'nahafoch Hu*—the tables were turned. Instead of reliving the darkest chapters of their past, the Jewish State reversed them. Before the eyes of the world, Israel faced its gravest test since its founding. And in passing that test and annihilating its genocidal enemies, it demonstrated that the modern state of Israel is not another painful episode in the long chronicle of Jewish suffering—but the moment Jews closed that chapter for good.

Israel did not pass the test easily or joyfully. It incurred the kind of tragedy and grief that defy healing. But it passed in the only way that ultimately matters in the Middle East: it remained unbroken and standing, unbent and defiant, courageous and eternal. After years of continuous war, Israel emerged as potent, as powerful, and as poised to strike as at any moment in its history. Israel faced conditions unseen by any democracy in modern history—a simultaneous, multi-front assault that even the most sophisticated war games could not have conjured. And still, Israel not only preserved its formidable force posture; it strengthened it. As of this writing, some of those threats still linger—and Israel must finish the task of dismantling them. Yet even the enemies that still draw breath have been reduced to fragments of their former power. Meanwhile, Israel's ability to strike, absorb, adapt, and prevail across every theater has settled the question for good: Israel is here to stay.

In the Holy Land, permanence is more awe-inspiring than perhaps anywhere else on earth. Israel's soil—so fruitful for farmers—has long seemed inhospitable to political longevity. Here, powers wilt almost as quickly as they bloom. Indeed, the story of the Jewish homeland reads like a calendar of empires and an obituary page for kingdoms. This reputation for civilizational turnover stretches back to the Bible itself. When Moses dispatched the spies to scout the Land of Israel, they returned with a fearful report, describing it as "a land that devours its inhabitants." Millennia later, the historian Simon Sebag Montefiore observed that "possession of Jerusalem has time and time again been a poisoned chalice, a piece of imperial hubris that brings the fates . . . down upon the state that possesses it." He compared the city to a praying mantis—luring and then decapitating the mate that seeks to claim it.

There is even a cruel benchmark that appears to signal the onset of decline: eighty years. In the Land of Israel, sovereign societies have often lasted little longer than a human lifetime. The eighth decade becomes the high-water mark, the zenith before the collapse. It is a threshold local polities rarely surpass.

Israel's enemies were counting on this pattern, something they made clear by their constant comparison of Israel to the Crusader states. True to the logic of the "eighth decade," the Crusader Kingdom of Jerusalem began its irreversible decline with the rise of the great Muslim conqueror Salah ad-Din in the eighth decade after its founding. His campaigns culminated in the Battle of Hattin in 1187, the decisive blow that shattered Crusader power and terminated the Jerusalem Crusader kingdom. That single victory made Saladin the enduring standard of leadership in the Middle East, and the ruler who restored Islamic greatness by expelling a foreign kingdom from the heartland of Islamic dominion. For centuries, Muslim political rhetoric has drawn upon his memory. Modern leaders from Gamal Abdel Nasser to Anwar Sadat to Ayatollah Ali Khamenei have each, in their own way, sought to cast themselves as heirs to Saladin's mantle: the man who would dislodge a Western-backed state from the Middle East—this time, Israel—and secure immortal glory.

Indeed, the Eagle of Saladin today serves as the emblem of the Palestinian Authority. Hamas, for its part, staged what it called a military "rehearsal for the liberation of Palestine." The event, held in 2021 in Khan Yunis, featured a figure portraying Saladin, alongside swords and even catapults—deliberate nods to the medieval arsenal of one of Islam's most celebrated rulers. It was an attempt to summon the spirit of Hattin for a modern campaign meant to unfold, once again, in Israel's fateful eighth decade.

It is important to note that Saladin himself was widely regarded as a magnanimous ruler. After his conquest of Jerusalem, he permitted the Jews to return to the city and treated them with relative tolerance. He even counted among his personal physicians the great Jewish sage Moses Maimonides, the towering codifier of Jewish law and philosophy of whom it is written, "from Moses until Moses there arose none like Moses." But the point here is not Saladin the man; it is Saladin the myth. The framing casts Israel as a modern Crusader state. A temporary Western implant destined to be expelled. A colonial anomaly that would wither with time. The assumption was simple: as Israel approached its eighth decade, history itself would finish the job.

For Jews, the curse of the eighth decade is not borrowed mythology. It's a personal warning, a recurring nightmare of the Jewish story. Twice before, sovereign Jewish kingdoms rose in Israel. And twice before, the unraveling began around their eightieth year.

The first united monarchy of Israel, established by King David around 1000 BCE, reshaped Jewish destiny. David forged unity among the tribes and established Jerusalem as the eternal capital. His son Solomon built the First Temple, transforming the city into a spiritual center for billions to this very day. Each king reigned for roughly forty years. For those eight decades, the kingdom held together. But after Solomon's death, ten tribes chose secession, crowning a new king and inaugurating a new temple. The nation was split into the Kingdom of Judah, centered in Jerusalem, and the Kingdom of Israel in the north. Divided, both kingdoms would eventually fall.

The second sovereign Jewish state, the Hasmonean kingdom of the Second Temple era, began with a revolt against the Seleucid Greeks, the political heirs of Alexander the Great. Fighting for religious freedom, the Maccabees achieved independence around 140 BCE. The state they established endured as a united and sovereign Jewish kingdom for roughly seventy-seven years. And then, as it approached the close of its eighth decade, it began to tear itself apart. Rival factions within the Hasmonean dynasty turned against one another. Instead of resolving their disputes internally, competing claimants to the throne appealed to the Roman general Pompey. In 63 BCE, after a three-month siege—sparked by one brother's invitation—Pompey conquered Jerusalem. Sovereignty deteriorated into dependency. Judea became a client state of Rome. Roman dominion in the Land of Israel would endure for centuries, culminating in the destruction of the Second Temple and, on multiple occasions, the mass slaughter and exile of millions of Jews.

October 7 seemed, at first, to mark Israel's relapse into this ancient trap of history. As it approached its eightieth Independence Day, the country was struck by a crisis that placed its very viability in question. Rabbi Shmuley remembers sober, expert political and military commentators on CNN saying in the days after the massacre that it may well be that Israel will completely collapse as a result of the Hamas invasion. Worse still, the civil strife that had once torn apart two Jewish kingdoms appeared to have returned. The internal battle over judicial reform sparked some of the largest protests in Israel's history. Political rhetoric hardened into barefaced contempt. Friends and families found themselves on opposite sides of an increasingly bitter divide. Reservists even threatened publicly not to report for duty. The language of existential threat—once reserved for foreign enemies—was now turned inward. A state founded on the ingathering of exiles began to flirt with something unthinkable: a national divorce.

For Jews, internecine division has long been understood as the prelude to national disaster. It is a lesson seared into Jewish consciousness by one of the greatest catastrophes in Jewish history: the Great Revolt against Rome in 66–70 CE. The Jewish historian Josephus records how the brief years of restored sovereignty during the revolt were undone less by Roman legions than by Jewish infighting. The people, he writes, were "vexed to pieces every day by their civil wars and dissensions." At one point, Josephus describes Roman commanders urging Vespasian to attack Jerusalem immediately. Vespasian refused. An assault, he argued, would only "occasion their enemies to unite together." Far better to wait and watch, he told them, "while their enemies are destroying each other with their own hands . . . They will be consumed in this sedition." This idea was not lost on Israel's enemies in the modern era. Former Tunisian President Habib Bourguiba once said that "Arabs should not fight Israel; the Jews in their internal quarrels will destroy themselves." In the months leading up to October 7, Israel seemed dangerously close to proving him right. Hamas leaders even explicitly referenced Israel's "internal situation" as a central factor compelling them to move toward what they called a "strategic battle."

And yet, in the face of the deadliest single day in Israel's history, the country did what Jewish history demanded of it: it stopped fighting itself. In an instant, the political battles that had consumed Israeli discourse were eclipsed by a single, undeniable truth—the nation was under attack.

What had appeared a society nearing rupture found, at its center, an unbroken core.

In the years that followed, Israel faced a multi-front war of unprecedented scope—seven active theaters, daily rocket bombardments at close range, long-distance drone and missile salvos, low-tech urban terror, and the unceasing psychological torment of hostages holed up in captivity. Layered atop the armed struggle was the excruciating whiplash of hostage negotiations, diplomatic pressure that surged with every headline, a sustained international media onslaught across both social and traditional channels, and recurring air-traffic suspensions that isolated Israel from the world.

For Israel, as for its predecessors, the eighth decade would be the great test of permanence. Miraculously, Israel endured. It secured its survival long into the future, not only as the Jewish national home but as an undisputed regional superpower. It is set to become the longest-lasting united Jewish state this land has ever known.

Israel's enemies were wrong. It is not an implanted colonial Crusader fiefdom that imports foreign armies to survive. It is not a novel Jewish kingdom predisposed to secession. And it is not an intrigue-ridden Hasmonean court that needs empires to resolve its own disputes. With four thousand years of collective memory, Israel in 2026 is quite simply the most historically experienced nation on earth. The exiles and expulsions, the persecutions and pogroms, the Holocaust and the eviction of nearly one million Jews from Arab lands—all have fused into a hardened national resolve to learn from the past and correct it. Israel is a dream come true, the fruition of a hope that will never be surrendered. It is united. It is indefatigable. And it is an immovable fact. Mount Hermon would be more easily pushed into the sea.

Israel's enemies internalized a crucial truth: the Jews will fight forever. Whatever propagandists proclaim and whatever men in pulpits promise, the reality remains: Israel can be hit, but it cannot be uprooted. The seven-front war could just as well have been a seventy-front war; Israel still would have won. Its fighting spirit is simply inexhaustible.

If October 7 and the years that followed proved Israel's military resilience, they also forced a deeper reckoning—one less material, but no less consequential. In the years since the Holocaust, Jews in Israel and across the world came to believe that Jewish survival depended on international compassion: the pity of the Gentile nations for eternal Jewish victimhood. It rested on a desperate hope that, deep down, the world means well. That cultivating its pity could elicit its mercy and insulate Jews from destruction. That the right speech at the United Nations, the right headline in a major newspaper, or the right administration in Washington could slow the threats long enough for life to go on. But since October 7, the world community's indifference—and Israel's sovereign strength—smashed that psychological dependency.

To begin with, it had been exposed as worthless. For decades, the world had comforted itself by repeating the ubiquitous mantra, "Never Again." Jews, in turn, took solace in the belief that world leaders had signed on to its promise. And then, it happened again. In a single morning, 1200 Jews were slaughtered—burned alive, hunted from house to house, raped and dismembered, and hundreds taken hostage. Meanwhile, the world had done nothing to prevent the massacre and would do nothing to avenge it. On the contrary, international pressure had constrained Israel's freedom of action for years, urging ceasefires and political arrangements with a genocidal enemy no less obsessed with killing Jews than the Nazis. Already in the first days after October 7—while Israelis were still counting their dead—pundits and demonstrators in Western capitals sought to frame the slaughter as resistance. Governments demanded Israel "show restraint," and a chorus of world leaders ordered yet another ceasefire. "Never Again" was exposed as an empty shell.

The truth is that "Never Again" carried moral force only so long as memory was raw, when a multitude of survivors still bore witness and images of death camps and mass graves remained vivid in the global conscience. For a time, the world recoiled from the horror. Sympathy and shame functioned as a kind of makeshift deterrent. But time erodes everything—even the memory of the deadliest crime ever committed. Surveys in recent years reveal alarming levels of Holocaust denial and ignorance among younger generations worldwide. More than 65 percent of American millennials and Gen Z have not heard of Auschwitz, and a growing number of America's most followed influencers and podcasters, like antisemites

Tucker Carlson and Candace Owens, deny the Holocaust outright. These are not fringe voices but rather unrepentant Jew-haters with millions of daily listeners. In academic and cultural spaces, anti-Zionism has merged seamlessly with classical antisemitic tropes. As pity loses its potency, it becomes painfully clear that Jews cannot depend on the world's sympathy. In the end, they depend on God—and on themselves.

Rabbi Shmuley offers a case in point. He was invited to speak in Australia shortly after a December 2025 mass shooting at a Hanukkah gathering at Sydney's Bondi Beach left fifteen Jews dead. It was an antisemitic terror attack that shocked the nation. For a brief moment, there was outrage and sympathy. And then Rabbi Shmuley's speech was postponed. The explanation was that Australia did not need an "aggressive" message. This was not the time. Communicating that Jews must fight back against the tide of antisemitism was off-message. The new message was indulging the newfound pity of the Australian government and people. After all, Jews had the nation's mercy—why risk jeopardizing it? Rabbi Shmuley warned them that the world would basically forget about the massacre within three months. Sadly, he was right. By February 2026, when the president of Israel visited Australia, antisemitic protesters forced police to lock down the event hall for nearly an hour as violent demonstrators were cleared from the streets. At one of those protests, former "Australian of the Year" Grace Tame urged the crowd to "globalize the intifada"—a phrase that openly romanticizes the mass killing of Jews on every continent. The sympathy Australian Jews were so careful to preserve proved to be an apparition.

That story lays out an urgent lesson. Jews cannot simply display their wounds and trust that decency will do the rest. When Jews are seen only as victims, they become more—not less—targeted. Vulnerability invites aggression. Medieval Europe's ghettos did not inspire tolerance. The defenselessness of Jews in Nazi-occupied territories did not mitigate genocide. And in the aftermath of October 7, Israel's sudden vulnerability did not soften the hatred against it. Far from affording protection, sympathy simply creates the illusion of safety while hostility reorganizes itself. The Jews of Australia did not need softer messaging. They needed resolve. They needed clarity. They needed to insist—openly and unapologetically—on their right to live securely and proudly as Jews.

Ultimately, the Hamas massacre and the unchecked resurgence of antisemitism made one truth unequivocally clear: "Never Again" was never a plea to the world. It is a promise to ourselves. Never again can Jewish survival depend on the goodwill of others. Never again can Israel court international sympathy while terrorist armies mobilize on its borders. Jews must confront terrorists and antisemites on our own terms and on our own timeline, whatever the outcry.

In the war of redemption that began on October 7, Israelis and Jews worldwide began to abandon the fatal fantasy. They finally understood that the goal is not to be loved, but to be respected by friends and feared by enemies. That the solution is not in the United Nations. It is not in trending hashtags. It is not in the approval of foreign celebrities who will forget you the moment the next fashion wave arrives.

For Israel, the solution lies in Jerusalem, on the battlefield, and in the decision to rely on its own arms and its own political strategy. For Jews worldwide, it lies in confronting antisemites with boldness and resolve—from the halls of power to podcast studios to the campus quad. It lies in internalizing Jewish history's harshest lesson, that Jewish weakness invites violence and Jewish strength deters it. Strength silences the enemy. Strength commands respect. Strength saves lives.

Jews today are beginning to absorb that message. One striking example was the debate that erupted in America over a Super Bowl ad funded by Robert Kraft's Blue Square campaign. The ad showed a Jewish boy with a Post-it note stuck to his backpack reading, "Dirty Jew." He does not confront the bully or remove the hateful label. He stands by his locker, humiliated and silent, until a compassionate non-Jewish classmate places a blue Post-it over the slur. The message was clear: the world should be more like this heroic student who feels sympathy for the bullied Jew.

Robert Kraft has done serious and meaningful work combating antisemitism. But the wave of criticism from within the Jewish community that followed the ad revealed something deeper than a disagreement over creative direction. It exposed a turning point in Jewish self-understanding. Creators and influencers quickly circulated a reimagining of the ad that quickly went viral. In this version, the Jewish boy does not stand motionless waiting for rescue. His eyes narrow with resolve. He grows up, enlists in the IDF, and stands in uniform—no longer an object of pity, but a symbol of Jewish defiance and resilience. The message shifts entirely: Jews do not wait for protection. They assume it. The marketing dispute revealed a burgeoning cultural correction. A generation shaped by one of the greatest wars for Jewish sovereignty instinctively rejected the image of passive humiliation and replaced it with the model set by the warriors of the IDF.

And that is the true Jewish way. Judaism has never been a faith of submission. Moses was not a supplicant but a destroyer of Pharaoh and Egypt. King David was not a victim but a warrior-poet who laid waste to his enemies. The Maccabees did not plead for understanding; they fought an empire. Israel's rebirth was not a petition, and it did not occur because of the United Nations. It happened because Jews built armies that gave the world little choice but to accept the permanence of their presence. It happened because they waged a blistering military campaign that defeated a massive Arab alliance and decisively closed the chapter of Jewish helplessness that had culminated in the Holocaust.

Even as Israel eviscerated its enemies across the region, many insisted it had lost on the battlefield of public relations, the so-called "PR War." This parallel struggle, which Prime Minister Benjamin Netanyahu has called "the eighth front," is important. But it is also misunderstood. Yes, Israel was condemned in international bodies, demonized on campuses, attacked on red carpets, and in editorial pages. Yes, the hatred was loud. But none of that means Israel was defeated. On the contrary, being hated was never the problem. The fear of being hated was.

Many people ask Rabbi Shmuley why he debates the world's sorriest lowlife antisemites on CNN, Fox, and Piers Morgan. "You're never going to convince them or their followers," they tell him, "They hate us. No facts or history will change that." Rabbi Shmuley always responds: "I debate not necessarily to change minds but to show our enemies we never fear them. The facts are with us, the truth is undeniable, and listen or not, we stand tall and defiant."

And that understanding, more than anything, represents the core of Israel's victory—and its immortality.

For years, Israeli leaders sought approval and applause. They treated the Jewish State as though its legitimacy depended on winning popularity contests in foreign capitals or trending favorably in news cycles. This was the rationale behind disastrous concessions where Israel surrendered vital strategic territory, risking its life for a handshake on the White House lawn. This was the logic that empowered men like Arafat and spared monsters like Yahya Sinwar. This was the pretext under which deterrence eroded, and terror gained steam. That failure of conviction—that utter loss of self-esteem—paved the road to October 7. But since that day, Israel has entered a different mindset. Gone are the illusions of Oslo. Gone is the belief that foreign leaders will determine whether we strike Rafah or confront Iran. Gone is the fantasy that external goodwill can substitute for internal strength. Because Israel is the only force that upholds "Never Again." And that phrase does not mean "Never Again Hurt" or "Never Again Hated." It means "Never Again Helpless."

In that sense, strength is the only PR that matters. The greatest messaging is not a slogan, but clear victories—won on the battlefield and upheld in the public arena. Since October 7, Israel has reaffirmed in the minds of its enemies that if you kill Jews, the price will be unbearable. And it has reminded the world that the Jews of the modern age cannot be trodden on and will not be ignored. They are people restored to their homeland—fully indigenous to it, continuously present in it, and resolved there to remain. A nation with a memory older than empires and the ideologies that oppose it. A people strong enough to outfight and outlast any foe. Even if the smiles fade, the smirks of those condemning us cannot conceal their respect.

This mindset—born in Israel and spreading among Jews worldwide—won this war and will win any war to come. It is the mindset of sovereignty over supplication, of responsibility over dependency. And it has given the indestructible people an indestructible state.

The Jewish people are eternal. And in the greatest war in its history, Israel has proven that the Jewish State is, too.

We look forward to the day when Israel's permanence will no longer be secured by the force of arms nor, God forbid, by the sacrifice of its brave soldiers, but by a world transformed—when humanity beats its swords into ploughshares and no man ever again teaches his son the art of war.

May the Messianic Epoch—an era of enduring peace and human brotherhood—dawn upon us all speedily, immediately, NOW!

ACKNOWLEDGMENTS

This book contains much analysis and commentary. But at its heart, it is a chronicle of one of the greatest stories ever told. It records what may well be the single greatest epic in the history of the State of Israel, and one of the paramount chapters in the long and unbroken saga of the Jewish people.

This astonishing narrative was not written by us. It was written by the brave men and women of the State of Israel—by those who gave their lives and by those who set their lives aside, to inscribe with courage and sacrifice a story of Jewish strength and victory that will resound for millennia. In this instance, the pen is not mightier than the sword. We are merely the humble scribes entrusted with telling the epoch-defining story of Israel's greatest generation. Our first and deepest gratitude, therefore, belongs to the heroes of Israel's defense, the Jewish State's courageous men and women, young and old, professional soldiers and "Milu'im" reservists.

To the soldiers and commanders of the Israel Defense Forces—the men and women of the Ground Forces, the Air Force, and the Navy. To the regional commands and the Home Front Command. To the Directorates of Operations, Planning, Military Intelligence, Manpower, Technology and Logistics, and Cyber Defense. To the Israel Police and Border Police. To the Shin Bet, the Mossad, and the Ministry of Defense. You stood watch. You ran toward danger. You bore the heaviest burden of the war.

In particular, we offer special thanks to the brave soldiers of the Reconnaissance Company of the 8th Armored Brigade—"Palsar Shmoneh"—the unit in which Mendy has the great privilege to serve. For more than twelve months of service across two relentless years—and counting—they have fought on the Northern Border, in Gaza, and in Lebanon with courage and distinction. To the lions of Palsar Shmoneh, you are not merely comrades-in-arms; you are family.

Mendy conveys special thanks to Maj. S, who welcomed him into the unit even after a knee injury was expected to end his combat service. You allowed him to prove that he could contribute to the full extent of his ability, as a pair of boots on the ground. Your faith in him was an act of generosity he will never forget. And to all his fellow reconnaissance soldiers: the opportunity you have given him to witness a first-rate military defending the Jewish people in our ancestral homeland is something he will cherish forever. Standing in your ranks is the defining honor of his life.

Rabbi Shmuley, in turn, conveys special thanks to his sons Mendy and Yosef, and his daughter Chana and daughter-in-law Dalia, for making him and Debbie the proudest father and mother on earth: parents to four IDF heroes.

A special note of gratitude belongs to the reservists, to the citizens who became soldiers in an instant, who risked careers, postponed dreams, and scarcely saw their families for months at a time over the course of years. You carried a double weight: the rifle in one hand, the life you left behind in the other. And to the wives and husbands, the parents and children, who bore the brunt of those reservists' absence, this book honors you no less.

We must also acknowledge the extraordinary men and women of Israel's defense industries—IMI Systems (Israel Military Industries), Israel Aerospace Industries, Rafael, Elbit, and the many firms whose names are mentioned in boardrooms and listed on stock exchanges worldwide. These are companies whose truest work is measured not in profits, but in lives saved. Each is a model of Israel's innovation and global reach. Yet in these years of trial, there was no doubt that what their engineers, technicians, programmers, and executives did, they did not do for advantage or advancement. They did it for the survival of their people.

Mendy recalls that men in his unit were pulled directly from the front lines in Gaza and Lebanon and sent across the country to work in defense facilities on critical technologies and hardware components—systems that would shield cities and save thousands. Israel understood that service in a laboratory, at a drafting table, or on a production floor could be as decisive as service in a trench. In a nation fighting for its future, every arena is a front line.

This brings us to the ordinary men and women of Israel—the civilians who carried the weight of a multi-year, multi-front war with dignity and resolve. They sent food, equipment, clothing, and spiritual strength to soldiers they had never met. Families in kibbutzim in the north and south opened their homes so exhausted soldiers could shower, wash their uniforms, or sit quietly for an hour without the dust and din of the barracks. Hundreds of thousands of Shabbat meals were packed into giant boxes and delivered to bases across the country—meals Mendy can attest were awaited all week, not merely for nourishment, but for the reminder of home.

Children wrote tens of thousands of postcards and drew bright, hopeful pictures to lift the spirits of soldiers enduring both the intensity and the strange torpor of wartime deployment. All the while, those same families were running to and from bomb shelters, month after month, rocket sirens interrupting daily life. Yet there was no wavering in their conviction that the war was just—and therefore necessary. The soldiers fought on the battlefield. But in truth, the entire nation answered the call.

It must also be said that the resolve of a people requires the courage of leadership. The bold and consequential decisions of the political echelon unlocked the latent strength of the nation. Our gratitude, therefore, extends to the members of the Knesset and their staffs; to the cabinet ministers and the public servants in their ministries; and to the war cabinet, whose deliberations carried the weight of history. We also thank our friend of more than a decade, Speaker of the Knesset Amir Ohana, for whom Mendy serves as chief English speechwriter, and whose resolute leadership of Israel's legislative body and unwavering defense of the Jewish state have left an everlasting mark on the nation's history.

Above all, these acknowledgments would be largely vacuous without naming two leaders who, in this war, distinguished themselves as historic figures of monumental consequence. The first, of course, is Israel's longest-serving prime minister and Rabbi Shmuley's friend of nearly four decades, Binyamin Netanyahu. No Jew in our time has been more greatly vilified, and no Jew in our time has shown greater leadership and courage. In a thousand years, Netanyahu's name—as a fearless and indefatigable wartime leader—will be spoken alongside Joshua, conqueror of Israel; Samson, destroyer of the Philistines; King David, Israel's timeless shepherd; Judah the Maccabee, "the Hammer" that smashed the Seleucids; Theodore Herzl, prophet of the Jewish State; Mordechai Anielewicz, leader of the Warsaw Ghetto Uprising; and Avigdor Kahalani, who faced down thousands of Syrian troops in the Yom Kippur War and saved the entire North of Israel.

At Netanyahu's side, at all times, stood his most trusted lieutenant and Rabbi Shmuley's friend and student of three decades, Ron Dermer—Israel's former ambassador to the United States and the man who largely ran the war with the prime minister as Israel's minister of strategic affairs. Dermer's mastery of logistics, strategy, and diplomatic engagement was indispensable to the war effort and the return of the hostages. His unparalleled ability to articulate Israel's strategic objectives to a largely antisemitic global press was also crucial in defending Israel and the IDF. His skills allowed Israel's brave soldiers to achieve their military objectives while pressing against the disgusting and fraudulent blood libel of genocide, invented by Israel's enemies to ensure that Jews die without defense.

In the greatest war of its history, Israel did not stand alone. She fought with the steadfast support of her allies. First among them was the United States. President Biden provided Israel with crucial material assistance and moral backing at decisive moments. Even as parts of his party drifted from that support, he remained largely steadfast, notwithstanding a few minor lapses. For that, he deserves significant credit. And to President Trump—by far the greatest friend Israel has ever had in the White House—who demonstrated historic leadership in tackling Iran's nuclear ambitions and securing the return of the hostages: history will record the magnitude of those decisions. Nothing either administration achieved would have been possible without the brave men and women of the United States Armed Forces, whose strength, sacrifice, and global reach have safeguarded freedom and deterred tyranny for generations. Nor would it have been possible without the millions of Americans whose faith in God and heartfelt support for Israel have sustained the US–Israel alliance from its inception. You too are part of this story.

On a personal note, we owe an immeasurable debt to Debbie—the wife of Rabbi Shmuley and the mother of Mendy—who read and reread this manuscript, offering not only sharp insight and invaluable guidance, but something even more essential: unwavering moral support. You are the rock of our lives. Your love and devotion to God, to Judaism, to the Jewish people, and to Israel animate everything we do. This book would not exist without you.

We also wish to thank the children of Rabbi Shmuley, Mendy's eight siblings: Mushki, Chana, Shterny, Shaina, Rochel Leah, Yosef, Dovid Chaim, and Cheftziba. Each of you played a part in bringing this work to fruition, helping in countless ways as we rushed to complete what we felt was an urgent and necessary account. All of you are fierce advocates for the IDF, for Israel, and for the Jewish people. And that shared mission is the heartbeat behind these pages.

Yosef, a "Chayal Boded" lone soldier, served a full IDF term of three years, including more than a year in wartime. He got married while in active duty, just two weeks after October 7, and spent the earliest months of his marriage under the inhuman strain of a military at war. His wife, Dalia, served as a social worker in the IDF at the same time. In the weeks before her wedding, she was planning dozens of funerals for soldiers murdered on that terrible day—a haunting contrast to the celebration she was meant to be preparing for. She carried that burden because she was raised, as Israelis are, to place their people first—always.

Chana deserves special recognition as well. She was the first of Rabbi Shmuley's children to enlist in the IDF, becoming the inspiration for Mendy and Yosef to follow. At nineteen, she made the courageous decision to move to another country and serve in the first Jewish army in two thousand years. She made that decision alone, based entirely on her own moral conviction and sense of Jewish identity. That leap of faith shaped our family's destiny—and, in no small way, made this book possible.

We must offer a very special and unconditional thank you to our friend, confidante, and Rabbi Shmuley's Torah study partner and spiritual inspiration Yoel Goldenberg for his steadfast support of Judaism, the Torah,

Yeshivas the world over, and projects that strengthen Jewish security and faith in God as our protector. Without Yoel, this book might have remained only a dream. Yoel, your nightly study with Rabbi Shmuley, especially in his darker bouts of consternation over Jewish suffering and the deaths of Israeli civilians and IDF soldiers, helped to strengthen him to fight the Jewish people's battles in global media and debate.

We must also thank our dear friend and attorney, Scott Piekarsky—a consummate gentleman and tireless Jewish advocate who has been an integral part of so much of what we do. Scott, your steadiness, counsel, and friendship have meant more than we can adequately express.

Our gratitude extends as well to Skyhorse Publishing Inc., including its president and publisher, Tony Lyons, and our editor, Stephan Zguta. Your professionalism, skill, and integrity have been indispensable. You believed in this project and helped shape it with care and conviction. For that, we are deeply thankful.

We must also express our thanks to Moshe Feiglin, for whom Mendy had the privilege of working as an editor before undertaking this book. Moshe's bold, original, and often prophetic ideas helped shape the intellectual and spiritual framework within which much of this book was conceived. His willingness to challenge convention, to think in civilizational terms, and to articulate a vision rooted in Jewish destiny and sovereignty has inspired countless readers—and inspired much of what these pages seek to convey.

And, of course, last but certainly never least, our immense appreciation to Simon Falic, a steadfast supporter of our work for years, who planted the seed that grew into this entire endeavor. This book, Simon, was largely your idea. You saw the urgency before we did. You insisted that this story of Israel's astonishing and miraculous victory be told. We are eternally grateful for your vision, partnership, and valuable counsel.

This book advances ideas that fuse political sovereignty with Jewish faith and eternal values. Those ideas did not originate with us. They were given to us by the Lubavitcher Rebbe, Rabbi Menachem Mendel Schneerson, whose teachings and example remain the foremost influence on our lives and on our understanding of the world.

The Rebbe's love for the Jewish people was boundless, yet it was inseparable from his love for all humanity. He believed not only in the singular mission of the Jewish people but in mankind's capacity to elevate the world and redeem it for God. His vision was at once uncompromising and compassionate, spiritual and practical. He spoke with rare moral clarity about the security and integrity of the Land of Israel, about the moral obligations that accompany Jewish sovereignty, and about the sacred responsibility that accompanies political power. He taught that strength is not the opposite of holiness, but one of its instruments. That conviction animates every page of this book.

His faith in the Jewish people—and in Israel's ability to defeat any adversary—was resolute and unwavering. When Israel faced the specter of annihilation in the Six-Day War of 1967, the Yom Kippur War of 1973, and the threat of chemical weapons in the Gulf War of 1991, the Rebbe did not succumb to fear or fatalism. He spoke with confidence and conviction, insisting that Israel would endure and prevail. That spirit of optimism, rooted not in naïveté but in profound trust in God, continues to carry the Jewish people through the trials of our own day. And once again, it has been vindicated.

Mendy is named after the Rebbe. That name is not merely an inheritance, but a charge. This book is one small step in our effort to advance the Rebbe's vision—to help build the perfected world he taught us to see, and to summon the courage to believe that it is within reach.

And finally, we offer our ultimate and eternal gratitude to God Almighty, Creator of heaven and earth, and He who consecrated Israel as the Holy Land and made the Jews His Chosen People.

After thousands of years of exile and longing, He kept His promise to the Jewish nation. He returned us to our land and restored us to sovereignty for the first time since antiquity. He endowed us with the courage, the ingenuity, the tools, the leadership, and the brave men and women required to defend ourselves. He strengthened the hands of our soldiers and steadied the hearts of our people. In an age shadowed by genocidal tyrants and ancient hatreds reborn, we have witnessed again what King David declared: that "the Guardian of Israel neither slumbers nor sleeps." We pray that God's justice prevails, and that the evil which has so often sought, and still seeks, to destroy the Jewish people is brought to an end.

More than any human force, God is the hidden yet unmistakable strength behind this extraordinary chapter—the miraculous force behind a miraculous war. To the Master of the Universe, who bends the arc of exile toward redemption and turns peril into renewal, we offer our deepest gratitude.

Writing *Comeback Nation* has been both an inspiration and an honor for us. To all who stood on the front lines, in uniform or out; to all who opened homes, hearts, and hands; and to all those whose kindness, support, and sacrifice made this story possible—this book, and our deepest thanks, belong to you.

Rabbi Shmuley Boteach
New York City, USA

Mendy Boteach
Jerusalem, Israel
I Adar 5786 – 18 February 2026

INDEX

K

L

M

N

Q

R

S